The
DEVIL'S
PLAYBOOK

The
DEVIL'S
PLAYBOOK

BIG TOBACCO, JUUL, AND
THE ADDICTION OF A
NEW GENERATION

LAUREN ETTER

 CROWN
NEW YORK

Copyright © 2021 by Lauren Etter

Published in the United States by Crown, an imprint of Random House, a division of Penguin Random House LLC, New York.

Crown and the Crown colophon are registered trademarks of Penguin Random House LLC.

LIBRARY OF CONGRESS CATALOGING-IN-PUBLICATION DATA
Names: Etter, Lauren, author.
Title: The Devil's playbook / Lauren Etter.
Description: First edition. | New York : Crown, [2021] | Includes index.
Identifiers: LCCN 2021004354 (print) | LCCN 2021004355 (ebook) |
ISBN 9780593237984 (hardcover) | International edition ISBN 9780593240687 |
ISBN 9780593237991 (ebook)
Subjects: LCSH: Vaping. | Substance abuse. | Cigarette industry. | Tobacco industry.
Classification: LCC HV5748 .E57 2021 (print) | LCC HV5748 (ebook) |
DDC 338.7/67973—dc23
LC record available at https://lccn.loc.gov/2021004354
LC ebook record available at https://lccn.loc.gov/2021004355

Printed in the United States of America on acid-free paper

crownpublishing.com

9 8 7 6 5 4 3 2 1

First Edition

Designed by Debbie Glasserman

FOR DAVID AND MY THREE LITTLE STARS

CONTENTS

PROLOGUE

ON THE SIDE OF THE ANGELS

The loveliest trick of the Devil is to
persuade you that they don't exist!
—CHARLES BAUDELAIRE

On Sunday, November 14, 1999, Steven Parrish's airplane touched
down at the Luis Muñoz Marín International Airport in San Juan,
Puerto Rico. It was humid and overcast, and an approaching storm
made for a bumpy final descent. That day, a late-season tropical depression was forming over the Cayman Islands, dumping the heaviest rain-
fall the region had seen in years. Meteorologists had been modeling
the storm for days and were now predicting that it could intensify into
hurricane-force winds as it moved eastward toward Jamaica and Haiti.

Parrish was the senior vice president of corporate affairs at Philip
Morris Companies, Inc., the world-famous cigarette company. More
than four hundred Philip Morris employees who worked under him
were due to arrive that day. Many had come from around the world,
from as far as Switzerland and Romania and Hong Kong, to attend the
company's periodic Corporate Affairs Worldwide Conference. The

event was designed to train the company's global army of "corporate affairs" employees who plied a variety of trades, including talking with the news media, whispering in the ear of congressmen, and generally strategizing about how to feed the company's carefully crafted messaging to the world. While others on the tobacco side of the business were focused on the more mundane elements of selling cigarettes—procuring the tobacco from farmers, running the machinery that spit out thousands of cigarettes per minute, convincing store clerks to display Marlboros more prominently than Camels—corporate affairs employees during this high-stakes era were mercenaries engaged in political knife fights. Their militant posturing, and obsessive focus on containing unsavory facts about the company's products, turned what could have been a relatively transient policy disagreement or temporary misalignment between tobacco companies and the public into a long slog through the trenches of the Tobacco Wars.

For a decade, Parrish had been one of Philip Morris's key generals in waging that war. A son of a railroad worker from Moberly, Missouri, and a former trial attorney, Parrish had defended the tobacco industry in the landmark 1983 case involving the smoking-related illness of fifty-seven-year old housewife Rose Cipollone. The verdict in her favor—delivered posthumously since she succumbed to her disease a year after filing the lawsuit—marked the first time that a tobacco company, despite facing hundreds of lawsuits up to that point, had ever suffered defeat in a product liability lawsuit. Even though the industry eventually won the case on appeal, it still was the canary in the coal mine for cigarette makers—a tsunami of litigation was coming. Philip Morris, which had been a defendant in the case (although just one company, Liggett, was found to be liable), snapped up Parrish and named him corporate counsel. From there he quickly climbed to the highest rungs of the company.

Parrish's slight stature and voice kissed with a southern drawl belied a swagger that he'd acquired as a trial lawyer, as well as his effortless ability—and willingness—to wield power. That combined with his calm, unassuming demeanor made him a wolf in sheep's clothing, exactly the trait that made him the perfect pick to lead corporate affairs through the tumultuous era.

He became the omnipresent face of Philip Morris through the company's darkest days. He was a key negotiator in tugs-of-war with a collection of stakeholders, including the Food and Drug Administration, multiple attorneys general, the White House, and scores of advocacy groups like the Campaign for Tobacco-Free Kids. He spoke at press conferences, strategized behind closed doors, and was a constant fixture in the inner sanctum of Philip Morris executive meetings. He was a master at both Kissinger-style shuttle diplomacy and Machiavellian politics—the two keys that guided Philip Morris through crisis after crisis. If Philip Morris in the latter half of the 1990s was a plane crashing, Parrish was the pilot that helped manage to land it, miraculously with not every passenger on board dying.

By then Philip Morris had grown into a conglomerate, with a menagerie of operating companies like Kraft and General Foods and Miller Brewing Company that sold a dizzying array of household staples: Lunchables, Jello-O, Miracle Whip, Velveeta, Miller Genuine Draft. The entire pantheon of Philip Morris brands, which had been cobbled together by the legendary dealmaker Hamish Maxwell, was lodged firmly in the zeitgeist of America. Not one, though, came close to being quite as indelible as Marlboro.

The advertising wizardry unleashed by the legendary adman Leo Burnett had transformed Marlboro in the 1950s from an underperforming cigarette for women into America's number-one brand. With the help of twenty-five scientists, eight consulting firms, six independent labs, and one polling organization, Marlboro was relaunched in 1955 with a filter tip, a red-and-white "flip top box," and a manly ad campaign featuring a Green Bay Packers player, a tattooed sailor, and of course, the square-jawed, salt-of-the-earth cowboy known as the Marlboro Man. Before long, Marlboro was the most popular cigarette brand around the world. Philip Morris had not only created one of the world's most successful consumer brands of all time, it also birthed a Wall Street money machine that spit out lavish salaries for its executives and princely returns for its shareholders. The company would do whatever it took to protect its prize asset.

Parrish carried out his work in the spirit modeled by Philip Morris's then chief executive, Geoffrey Bible, a gregarious beer-drinking, chain-

smoking Australian, whom a colleague once described as the "Crocodile Dundee of the tobacco industry." Bible had a pit bull's instinct for
a scrap. As product liability lawsuits mounted in the 1990s, Bible assured a group of investors not to get too worked up—"We are not
going to be anybody's punching bag," he told them. "We shall fight,
fight, and fight." To celebrate his leadership, his colleagues once presented him with a painting of a gyrfalcon, a bird of prey and the largest falcon on earth. Bible's bellicosity was enshrined in his trademark
phrase repeated over the years in letters to customers, in speeches to
employees, in presentations to investors: "When you are right and you
fight, you will win."

But in this moment, as the winds gathered over San Juan, it was
sinking in for Parrish, just as it soon would for the hundreds of employees on the island, that Philip Morris had lost.

IN 1953, ERNST WYNDER and Evarts Graham published their landmark
study in the journal *Cancer Research* linking cigarettes and cancer after
they painted cigarette tar on the backs of mice and watched tumors
grow. The findings made national news. *Life* magazine had a splashy
spread with photos of Graham in his lab alongside the tumorigenic
mice. *Time* magazine had a caption that read "For cigarette smokers, a
horrendous prediction."

The study prompted panic among the highest ranks of cigarette
companies. "Salesmen in the industry are frantically alarmed," read
one industry memo. In the days after, a group of executives from the
major tobacco companies and public affairs strategists from Hill &
Knowlton held a secret meeting in Manhattan's Plaza Hotel to discuss
how to develop a unified response to the mounting evidence—and
growing unease among smokers—that was potentially devastating for
their business. They decided to smear the scientists and discredit their
findings both about the addictive nature of their product, and about its
link to what they called "you-know-what" (cancer).

Those hardball tactics became the industry's go-to for the next four
decades. When a 1970s British documentary depicted an emphysema-

stricken "Marlboro Man" on horseback with an oxygen tank, Philip Morris forced the filmmaker to destroy his reels. When European governments began raising concerns about the dangers of secondhand smoke, Philip Morris built a network of paid scientists they called "whitecoats" to inject doubt into the debate. When Victor DeNoble learned in Philip Morris's own labs that rats became so addicted to nicotine that they would choose it over food and water, Philip Morris executives fired him and then ordered him to destroy his lab.

But as the last decade of the century dawned, Philip Morris's ramparts weakened. A growing and powerful coalition began attacking the company on everything from obesity caused by its sugary cereals, to its use of genetically modified foods, to whether its beer brands promoted binge drinking among kids. The anti-smoking movement that took root in San Francisco in the 1970s had grown into a full-fledged global movement. The "antis," as the company often called them, were becoming increasingly radical as they pressured universities and pension funds to divest from so-called sin stocks, boycotted its Maxwell House coffee and Kraft macaroni and cheese, and protested at art exhibits sponsored by Philip Morris.

Philip Morris developed a hard shell and an aggressive disdain for its opponents. It internalized the attacks as cheap shots made by an unfair nanny-state hell-bent on regulating its products out of existence. Rather than engage in dialogue with its opponents, it did everything to destroy them.

"Please don't ever forget," said Craig Fuller, the then senior vice president of corporate affairs, to a group of Philip Morris employees at a 1992 corporate affairs conference. "Our opponents are very different. They don't like what we manufacture. They don't like what we sell. They don't like the fact that we have high profit margins. And they think that way not just about tobacco, but about beer, cheese, red meat and many other PM products. I could list a whole slate of accusations that, taken together, comprise the platform—the ideology, if you will—of the people who do not wish us well."

The regulation issue became a dog whistle for the tobacco companies. And it was used freely as a tactic to scare smokers into believing that the government was coming not only for their cigarettes but for everything else they enjoyed in life. They said smoking was, after all, just as fundamental to Americans' rights as free speech and gun ownership, which is why Philip Morris aligned itself with Alexis de Tocqueville.

After the doctor and lawyer David Kessler took over as commissioner of the Food and Drug Administration in 1990, he launched an investigation into the tobacco industry with the ultimate goal of bringing tobacco under the regulatory authority of his agency—a key moment in the history of tobacco regulation and one that touched off a chain of seismic events that continues to reverberate to this day. Kessler, using undercover agents, informants, and gumshoe sleuthing that stretched from the farm fields of Virginia to dusty customs archives in North Carolina to Brazilian patents, sought to uncover whether the tobacco industry was secretly manipulating the levels of nicotine in cigarettes, which would serve as proof that the companies' products met the statutory definition of a drug or a drug device by displaying an intent to affect the structure or any function of the human body. If he could prove that, it would justify the agency regulating cigarettes just like Tylenol or an inhaler.

Philip Morris rightly feared the logical conclusion of that legal designation: There was no way the FDA could ever find that cigarettes would meet its own standard for drugs that stipulated that they be safe and effective, which would almost certainly lead to an all-out ban on cigarettes. The company launched a "ferocious defense" against Kessler's crusade by painting him as a radical bureaucrat set on taking away Americans' right to smoke. The company made buttons and ball caps with FDA in the middle of a "no circle" with phrases like KEEP FDA OFF THE FARM or FDA ON THE WRONG TRACK. The company distributed them at Kiwanis Club events, state fairs, racetracks, and at Calle Ocho festivals in Miami. One executive boasted how they planned to get a well-respected priest named Father Phil to wear one of the anti-FDA buttons while getting photographed as he received an oversize check from Philip Morris.

But by the mid-1990s, the shingles on the roof were starting to peel off. In 1994 Mississippi attorney general Mike Moore became the first to file a lawsuit against the tobacco industry to recover billions of dollars in costs associated with treating sick smokers. Meanwhile, plaintiffs' attorneys began filing an avalanche of class-action lawsuits. And whistleblowers from inside the tobacco companies, one by one, started breaking a previously impenetrable code of silence that bound the industry. DeNoble testified before Congress that he had been silenced. Jeffrey Wigand, a former Brown & Williamson executive whose gripping story was later depicted in the movie *The Insider*, revealed how his employer covered up the addictive and carcinogenic nature of cigarettes. Meanwhile, investigative reporters from major newspapers were churning out one damning story after the next. The *Wall Street Journal* reporter Alix Freedman, who went on to win a Pulitzer Prize for her coverage of the tobacco industry, co-wrote an article titled "Smoke and Mirrors." It revealed for the first time how the cigarette industry had secretly bankrolled a decades-long PR campaign to cast doubt on the link between smoking and disease, in what the writers described as "the longest-running misinformation campaign in U.S. business history."

If it's possible to identify a breaking point in the multifaceted Tobacco Wars, one certainly came on the morning of April 15, 1994, in Room 2123 of the Rayburn House Office Building on Capitol Hill. That morning, seven CEOs of the major tobacco companies appeared before a congressional committee, raised their right hands, and testified under oath that they believed the nicotine in their product was not addictive.

The then CEO of Philip Morris USA, William Campbell, was as strident as any that day on the witness stand in his defense of the cigarette. "Commissioner Kessler and members of the subcommittee contended that nicotine is an addictive drug and, therefore, smokers are drug addicts," he said, with a dose of disdain. "I strenuously object to that premise. I strenuously object to that conclusion. Cigarettes contain nicotine because it occurs naturally in tobacco. Nicotine contributes to the taste of cigarettes and the pleasure of smoking. The presence of nicotine, however, does not make cigarettes a drug or smoking an addiction. Coffee, Mr. Chairman, contains caffeine, and few people seem to enjoy coffee that does not. Does that make coffee a drug? Are coffee drinkers drug addicts? I think not."

The funny thing was, by then, pretty much everybody—public-health experts, lawyers, parents, scientists, politicians, doctors, schoolteachers—already knew the truth about cigarettes. Even Christopher Columbus and his men knew from observing native people smoking tobacco. "I know of Spaniards who imitate this custom," wrote Bartolomé de Las Casas, the Dominican friar who transcribed Columbus's journals. "And when I reprimanded the savage practice, they answered that it was not in their power to refrain from indulging in the habit." Researchers knew of the physiological effects of nicotine as early as or even before the 1920s. Tobacco companies discussed it as early as the 1960s and conducted decades' worth of internal studies on the topic. In 1988, the then U.S. surgeon general, C. Everett Koop, went so far as to say in his six-hundred-page report that "cigarettes and other forms of tobacco are addicting in the same sense as are drugs such as heroin and cocaine."

Which is why watching the row of suit-and-tie-wearing men on national television deny what was by then an almost universally acknowledged fact, crystallized the absurdity of the tobacco companies' position. They maintained that while the product might be "habituating," it didn't meet the legal and scientific definition of *addicting*. It became one of the most brazen *Alice in Wonderland* moments in the long-suffering saga of the tobacco industry. It was as if the public was holding up a black card, and the tobacco executives insisted over and over again, with a straight face, that it was white. But the industry was backed in a corner, and an embattled Philip Morris was buffeted with attacks that posed an existential threat not only to its identity but to its extraordinarily lucrative business.

For much of the twentieth century, working for a tobacco company, whether as a tobacco farmer or a company executive, had been a badge of honor, especially for businessmen who hailed from the South. But that was when smoking was mainstream and well loved—when everyone from Fred Flintstone to James Dean to Lauren Bacall could be seen puffing away, and when ads showed doctors opting for certain cigarette brands over others. To suddenly be so demonized in society was jarring for these men, a breed whose DNA had not an iota of surrender in it. Rather than hear any criticism, they'd simply tune out the world. Which is why it took well-respected people from outside the company to take them by the collar and look them straight in the eye and say, "Something has got to change."

It didn't hurt that the company's stock had started to underperform. Philip Morris has long been one of the best-performing stocks of all time. It's one of those stalwart blue-chip stocks traded on the New York Stock Exchange that attracts pension funds, institutional investors, and other long-term investors seeking solid, incremental growth and reliable dividends. As one insider put it, Philip Morris investors have always had pretty basic needs: "Just milk the cow, pay the dividend, and shut up." And that's exactly what Philip Morris did. Over fifty years the company's earnings had steadily grown, along with its rich dividend that pleased shareholders year after year, and helped wash away any guilt harbored by those who may have otherwise considered pulling their money out of a company that sold a product that killed people.

But by the mid-'90s it was becoming increasingly evident that the twin problems of litigation and regulatory risk were not temporary blips. Meanwhile, cigarette consumption continued to soften. By 1997 just under a quarter of Americans smoked, down from almost half in 1965, the year after the surgeon general first stated that cigarette smoking caused lung cancer. Philip Morris shareholders had learned to stomach a lot over the years, but one thing they wouldn't tolerate was an underperforming stock.

That coincided with a board already grappling with the increasingly loud noise surrounding the public's perception of smoking. For years cigarette companies had been trying to split hairs—maintaining that although studies showed a statistical link between smoking and cancer, there was no definitive proof, and even if there was, the company had lived up to its duty to warn by gluing warning labels on cigarette packs. If a smoker smoked and died of cancer, well, that was their choice. For a while, juries had bought that argument. But as plaintiffs' lawyers tweaked their legal theories, jurors began turning on that defense and siding with smokers who argued that the company's advertising had been so deceitful that they in fact bore responsibility for the harm caused by their product. Soon the company was facing juries across the U.S. that pondered awarding six- and seven-figure judgments to smokers. And with every passing day it became that much harder for a Philip Morris executive to defend the indefensible.

No matter how prideful and recalcitrant the company's executives had been—"We're Philip Morris. We've got more money than God," an executive boasted once—the company was facing a bitter reckoning. The mounting smoking-and-health litigation and government investigations and public scrutiny had become so crushing that there was a real possibility that the company that had more money than God could go bankrupt. It took staring down the barrel at that dim prospect, not necessarily the harm inflicted on smokers, for the tobacco companies to ultimately admit defeat.

In April 1995, the PM board of directors took the corporate jet to Sea Island, Georgia, for their annual board retreat at the secluded, luxurious Mediterranean-style Cloister Hotel. The meeting started off not all that different than previous years, with a discussion about the company's five-year plan that touched on everything from tobacco excise taxes, to capital expenditures, to European confectionaries and cheese.

Even the ultimately pragmatic Parrish, in that moment, was still fighting. In his prepared remarks to the board, he said the company needed to be cautious of Kessler's ambitions. "The political and economic cost of a new national experiment in Prohibition would be far too great," he said. But "I am pleased to report that this strategy of the antis is not working." People were starting to see Kessler as a "bully" and a "thug," he said, which would help them in their efforts to stave him off.

But a group of outside directors had come to Sea Island with a much different tactic in mind. John Reed had been a member of the Philip Morris board since 1975. A former chairman of the New York

Stock Exchange and chairman and chief executive officer of Citigroup, he was one of the longest-serving members of the board and was immensely well respected inside the company. He was backed by two other outside directors, Robert E. R. Huntley, a prominent Virginia lawyer, and Harold Brown, former secretary of defense under Jimmy Carter and a director at Cummins, a company facing health scrutiny over its own product, the diesel engine.

"We're about to lose permission from society to exist," Reed told the board. Board notes capture the essence of his thinking. "This is a watershed meeting. We end the past, go forward. . . . We need to reposition the company. We care more than anyone else about the facts. If we refute it, the impression is that we would lie, we would suppress the truth. We need to change this. The industry is seen as a denier of truth. We should reposition ourselves to be the seeker of truth. We are not credible and not seen on the right side of this issue."

Another board member, John Nichols, who was chairman of the manufacturing conglomerate Illinois Tool Works, agreed with Reed and put his own, succinct point on it. He said that the company needed to do more to not only be seen as "building perceptions of our goodwill" but also "searching for the facts."

The thing the company needed to do, he implored: "Get on the side of the angels."

STEVE PARRISH WAS GOING to Puerto Rico to tell four hundred corporate affairs employees that they were now on the side of the angels. He was not yet sure how the news would land.

More than four years had passed since John Reed implored Parrish and Bible and others at Philip Morris to change their tune and to face reality. During that time, despite internally acknowledging that the walls were closing in, Parrish had continued to publicly dig in his heels, staging aggressive denials about the company's conduct as he came under increasing attack by journalists, lawmakers, and more. But eventually, as the FDA's Kessler gained traction in his efforts to regulate tobacco, as then President Bill Clinton sided against Big Tobacco, as the state settlements gathered steam, he easily shed his fighting skin and slipped into a new one as Parrish the Peacemaker.

He arrived in Puerto Rico bearing a revolutionary message: The world was different now, and as a new millennium was dawning, so was deep-rooted cultural change at Philip Morris. Uncomfortable changes would need to happen inside the organization. That's why the theme of the San Juan event was PM21, a recently unveiled initiative that Parrish helped create that stood for Philip Morris in the Twenty-first Century. Parrish introduced skeptical employees to buzzwords like "societal alignment" and "constructive engagement" and "truth"—concepts that for years were essentially oxymorons inside Philip Morris.

When the PM employees got off their planes in San Juan that November 1999, they made their way to drivers wearing bright blue polo shirts and holding up signs that said CAWC, for Corporate Affairs Worldwide Conference. They were escorted to rickety vans and packed in like sardines—an annoyance to those who caught a glimpse of some of the top executives, like Parrish, getting whisked off instead in limousines.

However irked they were, that all dissipated when they pulled up to their destination: the Westin Rio Mar, a ritzy golf and casino resort nestled between the El Yunque National Forest and Playa Fortuna, a secluded stretch of white sand lined with palm trees strung with hammocks. Iguanas lounged by swimming pools lined with bougainvillea. At night the song of coqui frogs filled the air. Philip Morris rarely spared a cent on events like these, so as was customary, when they entered their rooms they each had gifts waiting for them: a Marlboro T-shirt, a jacket with an embroidered Philip Morris crest, and, if they were a smoker, a carton of cigarettes of a Philip Morris brand that they had chosen ahead of time on the "Cigarette Request Form." They all had a pad of paper on their nightstand that read "Good Luck at the Casino."

That night, as Parrish stood at his hotel room window and gazed out over the tempestuous ocean, he could see the palm trees bending in the wind as torrential rains raged. He knew what was coming. This did not bode well for the event, which was planned with several outdoor activities in mind, including evening cocktails on the terrace, salsa dancing under the stars, and intermittent beach lounging, golfing, and shopping for trinkets in Old San Juan. And it was looking more likely by the hour that some of the keynote speakers, including CEO Bible, might not be able to even make it to the island to deliver their remarks.

By the next morning, the storm had turned into a full-blown hurricane with winds clocking in at more than eighty miles per hour. Now called Hurricane Lenny, it had passed south of Jamaica, and the National Hurricane Center in Miami was predicting that it could slam right into Puerto Rico in a matter of hours. "There appears to be an eye forming," a weather forecaster said. To say that the news was a distraction would be an understatement. People were glued to the Weather Channel and some couldn't help but wonder what had possessed the company to hold a global conference in the Caribbean in the middle of hurricane season.

But there was no time to waste. It was almost exactly a year since November 16, 1998, when state attorneys general from forty-six states and the major cigarette manufacturers signed an accord that drew to an apparent end the multiyear legal battle that laid bare a generation's worth of scorched earth tactics waged by the tobacco industry to conceal the dangers of its products. The so-called Master Settlement Agreement required tobacco companies to pay billions of dollars annually in perpetuity—an estimated $206 billion by the year 2025—to reimburse the states for costs related to smoking, in exchange for being released from any future smoking-and-health claims brought by those states. The agreement also nailed the companies for their marketing practices toward children, which had resulted in an alarming spike in youth cigarette smoking in the 1990s, peaking at nearly 40 percent of high school students in 1997.

Over the next three days, CEOs of the various Philip Morris operating companies, including Kraft and Miller and the international division of Philip Morris, were going to be talking about how their businesses planned to survive in this new world.

Employees streamed into a ballroom where they were welcomed

by a video featuring key historical figures that had overcome adversity and prevailed—all themes that Parrish was eager to drive home. They were shown photos of Winston Churchill flashing the victory sign, Pablo Picasso in his painting studio, Gandhi with a look of determination on his face, Pelé driving the soccer ball into the net, Mother Teresa. Then the video shifted to a track star jumping over hurdles and Michael Jordan slamming a dunk. "What does it take," the narrator boomed, "to make a difference?"

Parrish made his way to the lectern to deliver opening remarks to the group. His graying hair and thick eyebrows framed his face. He was welcomed as a prominent member of a secret society. Philip Morris's high priest.

"The opening video you just saw sets the theme for this morning, and for our entire three days together," he said. "Making a difference. Changing the world. Being the best you can be. Achieving the goals you have set."

For an outsider, the aspirational theme of the conference might have seemed laughably over the top. *Being the best you can be?* This was a company that had just spent the past four decades slinging mud and obfuscating science and disparaging dissenters. Now they were equating themselves with Mother Teresa.

But for Parrish, that was the whole point. Radical reinvention was needed if the company had any hope of a future. "We have learned a number of lessons from the tobacco wars that many of you have heard me speak about before," he told the crowd. "First, we learned that we must not simply reject or ignore criticisms. We have to see criticisms as opportunities to engage in discussion. Facts are not always the issue, particularly in a media environment. Even the wildest accusations can gain attention and credibility if you don't respond to them. We cannot just sit by when issues are raised; we have to engage in the discussion and debate." If a time-traveling tobacco executive from forty years earlier had dropped in on Parrish's speech, he might have believed he was in an alternate universe.

"If we are silent," Parrish continued, "we will be seen as uncaring, unconcerned, or, worst of all, guilty." Guilty had been the problem for

Philip Morris. Too many guilty verdicts in the courtroom. Too many guilty smokers weaning off a habit so disastrous to their health. And Parrish knew that there was a contingent of employees—those who liked the good old days just the way they were—who thought the new way forward was a result of guilty executives caving under pressure. And there was a sense of betrayal, even. When Parrish first announced a proposed settlement with the attorneys general before a final deal was done, he'd invited colleagues from across the business to speak honestly about the change. While he expected some criticisms, he was surprised when he was excoriated in a private meeting with Philip Morris USA cigarette executives who laid into him and accused him of having developed Stockholm syndrome. One person said to him: "Let's not get carried away with this good-guy stuff."

So he was used to it, and his steel spine was even sturdier now. So in San Juan, even if some of the most hardened corporate affairs folks might have been startled by such a whiplash-inducing about-face, Parrish reassured them with ease that sentiments that the company they loved was somehow rolling over, or growing weak, couldn't be further from the truth. The approach of "constructive engagement" and "societal alignment" and holding up the company's end of the social contract was "not a rollover strategy," Parrish assured any doubters. It was one of renewal and strategic repositioning so the brands could all live for another day. It was one of not viewing every critic as a "zealot and extremist." It was coming to the table to listen to concerns. It was building trust.

But by no means, Parrish reassured the ranks, did it mean full, unconditional surrender. "We all remember, 'When you are right, and you fight, you win,'" said Parrish, alluding to Bible's famous remarks. "It is still true. But it always starts with being right in the first place. Which means that we must pick our fights carefully."

BY TUESDAY THE OUTER reach of Hurricane Lenny began battering Puerto Rico with torrential rain. The inside of the Rio Mar was turning into a real-life scene from Humphrey Bogart's *Key Largo*. Hotel staff furiously prepared for the arrival of the storm and everybody hunkered inside. Anxiety levels were rising as people wondered whether Philip Morris, to err on the side of caution, should simply cancel the entire conference and send everybody home. "Like everyone, I am sure, I felt trapped in that hotel," described one person who attended. But it was too late. The storm was upon them.

Planned outdoor events were brought inside. Recreational events were canceled. No deep-sea fishing. No shopping in Old San Juan. No eighteen holes of golf, like the schedule had promised. Instead they were stuck inside a poorly ventilated ballroom that was filling up with smoke. Despite a nonsmoking section in the back, many Philip Morris employees, perhaps unsurprisingly, smoked inside ad libitum.

Inside that ballroom, the employees needed to learn not only to hear but to truly internalize Parrish's new philosophy and figure out how to integrate it into their operating businesses. Getting employee buy-in was crucial. So they camped out for hours at a time and acquired the new "tools" to interact with society. They participated in small brainstorming sessions called Creative Cafes, where discussions took place around small round tables covered in red-and-white checkered tablecloths that were set up throughout the ballroom. They talked about the new responsibility that came along with working for a tobacco company in the twenty-first century, including the importance of being not antagonists but bridge-builders. They analyzed how employees should know when to "fight" (when "fighting would be consistent with company policies [or when] we clearly have the better factual/legal argument") and when to compromise ("when there is long-term advantage in compromise").

They learned how Philip Morris USA had recently launched a $100 million program designed to prevent youth smoking, and how the company was expanding advertising about its initiatives on television and distributing its new message to rotary clubs and PTAs. Employees were trained to share the good-news "story" of Philip Morris with family and friends; that it was a proud company that made not just cigarettes but family-friendly brands like breakfast cereal and baloney, chocolate and coffee. They were instructed to listen to critics and, instead of being defensive, to respond in a nonconfrontational manner rooted in the idea of constructive engagement.

There was some level of irony to the fact that the employees were literally barricaded inside as Parrish exhorted his employees to do away with the bunker mentality. "We have learned that it's a mistake to climb into a bunker when under attack," he said. "Nothing to me is more exciting than the fact that we are starting to open up after far too many years in the bunker." The old "fortress Philip Morris," as Parrish once described his company, was history.

Geoffrey Bible ultimately had to cancel his trip to Puerto Rico because of the severe weather. Instead, he gave a speech over video. "Someday," he said, "we will look back at this conference and say, 'That's when we finally got it right.'"

By Wednesday morning, the storm was due to finally make landfall on Puerto Rico. Already, several homes had been destroyed on the island, and nearly 150,000 Puerto Ricans were left without water or electricity. But at the last minute, Hurricane Lenny took a sudden turn eastward, turning its 150-mile-per-hour winds instead on St. Croix.

By evening, it was clear that Puerto Rico had been spared the worst. As Parrish gave his closing remarks at a cocktail party inside the Rio Mar, employees toasted with glasses of champagne and joked about having survived the "wettest" corporate affairs conference in the company's history. He wove in serious notes with the levity, warning employees, "We can never fall out of step with society anywhere, anytime."

As the winds in San Juan retreated and the sun glinted over the ocean, Parrish also left his people with a message of hope. After all, everyone was relieved that the ordeal was over. Both ordeals: the hurricane and the Tobacco Wars.

"I knew," Parrish said, "that no hurricane would stop us."

The
DEVIL'S
PLAYBOOK

1

THE QUEST

Long before the dream of a perfect e-cigarette was a gleam in the eye of Howard A. Willard III—and before, as Altria's CEO, he would make a $12.8 billion investment in an e-cigarette start-up that addicted millions of American children to nicotine—the lifelong tobacco executive held one of the most paradoxical jobs a tobacco executive could have: He was head of Philip Morris's Youth Smoking Prevention program. On its face the job was a study in cognitive dissonance. Willard was supposed to help convince the very same people that Philip Morris once viewed as future customers that, in fact, buying his company's product was a bad idea.

It was a testament to the awkward position in which the tobacco industry found itself, in the early 2000s, that the company was running a program to discourage youth smoking. And yet the program was a crucial down payment on the price of staying in business. De-normalizing smoking, particularly among youth, was the driving heart of the Master Settlement Agreement, which not only banned tobacco companies from sticking their products in movies and on billboards but forbade them from advertising cigarettes to children in any way. No more Joe Camel backpacks, or Marlboro Man T-shirts. By foreclosing tobacco companies' ability to deploy its bottomless ad budgets, slick marketing, and iconic imagery to reach adolescents, the core demographic once referred to by tobacco executives as "replacement customers," the legal settlement ushered in a new era for the tobacco industry that proved to be nothing less than tectonic.

Philip Morris didn't start the youth prevention program out of pure altruism. The tobacco settlement required the signatory companies to "promulgate or reaffirm" a set of "corporate culture commitments" related to youth smoking, and also to "designate" an executive devoted to reducing the consumption of youth tobacco use. Moreover, the company's Youth Smoking Prevention program was a good look in a moment when the company's legal issues were far from fully resolved. In the spring of 2000, as a jury in a Florida class-action lawsuit weighed whether to award plaintiffs billions of dollars in damages, the then Philip Morris USA chief executive, Michael Szymanczyk, took the witness stand and testified about the company's new youth prevention efforts in a bid to persuade the jury to go easy on his company. It was critical for Philip Morris to demonstrate to regulators and courts and lawmakers that it was committed to being in "alignment" with society writ large, and willing to sacrifice the pipeline of future smokers for the greater good, not an easy feat for a company that sold Marlboro, the most popular brand among high schoolers.

Serving as the company's face in this effort was a job that required a particular kind of company man—equal parts aggression and ambition, with an iron-fisted devotion to his maligned employer. Howard Willard was that kind of company man.

The son of a restorer of historic homes and grandson of an antiques salesman, Willard was raised in the quaint town of Wethersfield, Connecticut, an old Puritan settlement and seaport for local farmers and merchants who sent their flaxseed and red onions to the West Indies. With a tousled head of curls and studious glasses, Willard fit in among the clubby circles of the Northeast. He graduated from Colgate University, the preppy liberal arts school nestled in the rolling hills of upstate New York's dairy country, where he studied computer science and economics. He received an MBA from the University of Chicago, one of the top business schools in the country.

Willard learned early on what it took to be a Master of the Universe. In 1985 he got a job as an analyst working mergers and acquisitions at Salomon Brothers, the storied, now-defunct Wall Street investment bank that fell from grace during a bond-trading scandal and became the basis of Tom Wolfe's novel *Bonfire of the Vanities* and Michael Lewis's insider account in *Liar's Poker*. He then moved to Bain & Company, the consulting firm, where in 1991 one of the accounts given to him was Philip Morris USA. Willard was impressed with the talent of the management at the cigarette company. The following year, in November 1992, when Philip Morris's CFO, Harry Steele, offered him a job, he took it.

With his gangly six-foot-six frame and goofy smile, Willard stood out at Philip Morris. One former executive described the younger Willard as a spitting image of the actor Judge Reinhold from when he starred in *Fast Times at Ridgemont High*. Even though he had an affable salesman's personality, he wasn't a natural extrovert. His loud guffaws and jokes sometimes seemed strained, almost deliberately designed to fit into the backslapping, good-old-boy culture at the rough-and-tumble cigarette company. Another colleague described him as a little like Eddie Haskell from *Leave It to Beaver*. "That's the vibe that pops into my head. Like, 'You look lovely today, Mrs. Cleaver,'" remembered the former executive, adopting the television character's ingratiating voice. "He was always nice. And well liked. But I would not say dynamic in any way. And not assertive. He would speak when spoken to."

It was perhaps Willard's willingness to please, combined with his technical acumen, that allowed him to thrive among the ranks of Philip Morris's rigid, hierarchical culture that prized people who fell in line and respected authority. In April 1995, an internal career planning document extolled Willard's accomplishments, noting that he "demonstrated comprehensive strategic planning skills" and "leads by personal demonstration."

In his Midwest VP sales position, Willard emerged as a loyal company soldier, personally writing letters to clients urging them to donate to the company's political action committee and to contact their lawmakers to express displeasure with pieces of legislation that might be detrimental to the cigarette business. "Once the FDA gets its foot in the door," Willard wrote in one letter, "there is little doubt it will quickly move in the direction of banning tobacco products." That public-policy role served as a natural segue into a job as vice president of information services, before he was eventually put in charge of the company's new e-commerce division.

Working at a tobacco company has never been for the faint of heart, and it's long had a way of toughening people up. Michael Szymanczyk, chief executive of Philip Morris USA through the turn of the century, once recalled when anti-tobacco activists showed up at his home in Connecticut just before Christmas and hung a wreath laced with cigarette butts on his front door while singing crude Christmas carols. Even though his wife's feelings were hurt, he was unmoved: "I can't be distracted by people like that," he said.

WILLARD ULTIMATELY NEVER GOT distracted, and as a result of finding his rhythm early on at Philip Morris he powered through promotions faster than others. Ultimately he was named a member of the Philip Morris senior leadership team, and, starting in September 2000, he began reporting directly to Szymanczyk. That meant Willard was learning from the best. Szymanczyk was a well loved, preternaturally gifted executive whose towering physique at six feet eight inches was only outmatched by his booming voice, which seemed to overpower anybody in his orbit. Szymanczyk had a successful career at Procter & Gamble before going to Kraft and ultimately landing at Philip Morris as a seasoned executive in 1990. He was named CEO of the domestic cigarette company in 1997 just as the Tobacco Wars were getting under way. Like his boss Geoffrey Bible, Szymanczyk had the fight of a bull elk in him and was imbued with more than a fair share of confidence. He was always the first to speak up in a meeting, leading some people to call it for what it was: arrogance. But his business acumen largely forgave any conceit.

Szymanczyk took Willard under his wing. The up-and-coming executive so revered his mentor that people at the company jokingly took to calling him "Little Mike." But Willard, who retained the Judge Reinhold aura, never quite matched his boss's je ne sais quoi. While Willard also was a member of the tall club, he was still at least a couple of inches shorter than Szymanczyk. And while Willard also was always the first to speak in a meeting, he often came across as a brash know-it-all rather than an enlightened manager. But he had promise, and ambition; that much was evident early on.

Willard's rise coincided with Philip Morris's compulsory reawakening that Parrish had engineered and Szymanczyk drove home. In October 1999 the company launched its first website, which as vice president of information services Willard had helped oversee. On it, Philip Morris for the first time publicly acknowledged that cigarettes not only caused lung cancer but were also addictive, stunning public-health advocates who'd been screaming that exact truth into the void for years. "Integrity, trust, passion, creativity, quality and sharing," the website said. "They're the values that guide us as a business and as individuals."

The PM21 project that Parrish was unfolding in Puerto Rico was just the tip of the iceberg in the company's plan to reorient its culture. Like other executives at the time, Willard participated in mandatory Master Settlement Agreement "training sessions" and town halls at various venues across the country. Back then the headquarters of Philip Morris was still based in midtown Manhattan at the 120 Park Avenue building, where conference rooms kept wooden boxes filled with cigarettes, and ashtrays hung in elevator banks and above urinals. The company brought in the top thought leaders of the era to help impart to employees the new normal. Employees were asked to read books like *Faces of the Enemy*, by Sam Keen, in order to better understand why the company had been so villainized. Themes like "healing and reconciliation" and lessons from "truth commissions" were topics at Corporate Social Responsibility meetings hosted by Harvard Law negotiation experts, where questions like "What *is* 'Big Tobacco'?" and "What would take away the anger?" were discussed. One hand-scribbled note from such a meeting mentioned, "People outside of PM really do think we are individually bad. (I'm not Medusa!)."

At one event, Philip Morris hired a consulting company for more than $200,000 to write a script and stage a play about Ernest Shackleton, the famous twentieth-century British explorer who became stranded with his crew on the *Endurance* during an expedition to Antarctica. The play, whose production included four actors, a scriptwriter, an executive producer, and a theatrical director, depicted the harrowing journey that ended with the devastating sinking of the ship and Shackleton's crew being stranded on a drifting iceberg for months before finally being rescued by a Chilean Navy boat with the entire crew, miraculously, alive. Afterward, facilitators from the consulting company led employees through discussions about lessons learned from the heroic event and what metaphors could be drawn. It was lost on none of those employees what the metaphor was. Philip Morris had crashed and was now fighting for its life.

Though the tobacco settlement was behind the company, Philip Morris was still getting flagellated. In 1999, the U.S. Department of Justice sued the company under the Racketeer Influenced and Corrupt Organizations Act, the law more often used to prosecute the Mafia. After all the dirt that had come out during the FDA's investigation, the probes by the attorneys general, and the hundreds of class-action lawsuits, federal prosecutors ended up bringing their own case against several tobacco companies, alleging that they had engaged in a decades-long conspiracy to mislead the public about its products. Ultimately, the federal judge ruled against the companies, and in a nearly seventeen-hundred-page opinion, excoriated Big Tobacco for its conduct.

"Defendants have marketed and sold their lethal products with zeal, with deception, with a single-minded focus on their financial success, and without regard for the human tragedy or social costs that success exacted," it read. "Over the course of more than 50 years, Defendants lied, misrepresented and deceived the American public, including smokers and the young people they avidly sought as 'replacement' smokers about the devastating health effects of smoking."

Amid the DOJ's multiyear case, Philip Morris decided it needed to make a clean break with its increasingly controversial tobacco past. It set about choosing a new name for the parent company. While Philip Morris USA would still be the name of the tobacco operating company, executives were eager to change the narrative.

"Our goal is to be seen—as much as possible—as a normal corporation, one with legal, regulatory and public opinion challenges to be sure, but with challenges that are manageable and do not threaten the legitimacy or the survival of the company," Parrish told the Philip Morris board of directors in August 2001. The company anticipated critics but wanted to roll out the new name in a way that prevented others from characterizing the name change as "Big Tobacco putting on a new dress," according to an external communications plan.

They hired a branding firm that had worked with FedEx and Lucent Technologies. The firm did hundreds of hours of research and surveys and ultimately came up with a thousand potential new names for Philip Morris. From those they narrowed it down to one hundred. And then ten. Among the runners-up for Philip Morris's new name: Marcade and Consumarc. Ultimately, in November 2001 the company announced that it would ask shareholders at the next annual meeting, in April 2002, to approve the proposed new name: Altria. The name was derived from the Latin word for high, "altus." Then the company added "ria" "to balance the word" with "a softer suffix" to create a "phonetic balance," according to an internal email discussing the name change. The new name went off largely without a hitch, and before long employees began referring to each other as Altrians.

About a year later, the tobacco arm of Altria, Philip Morris USA, announced that it was relocating its headquarters from New York City to Richmond, Virginia. The company desperately needed to cut costs, and the move outside the city would save the company $60 million a year. Even though the parent company, Altria, would remain in New York for the time being, the move marked a retreat from the marketing lairs on Madison Avenue to a prototypical tobacco town steeped in the folksier traditions of the crop.

Despite the new name, controversy kept coming. And in all of it, there was one constant: youth smoking. The issue had emerged in the latter half of the 1990s as one of the most contentious and nettlesome issues facing the company. It turned out that aligning with society started with fixing the youth tobacco epidemic. Even though hiding the truth about smoking was seen as a moral transgression, it was the intentional marketing toward kids that was seen as nothing less than sinful. Adults had the ability to come to a rational decision whether they wanted to take up a deadly habit, but kids often had neither the sense nor the facts to do the same. If Philip Morris expected to come clean with society, it had to start there. In early 2002, when Willard was put in charge of the Youth Smoking Prevention program, he was thrust right into the middle of that not indelicate assignment.

> *This taboo is for you*
> *Playing with fire*
> *Forbidden fruit*
> *U.B.U*
> *Badge of Honor*
> *It hurts so good*
> *Dare to be me*
> *The rite to be me*

The lines weren't a poorly written poem but rather the handwritten notes taken by a Philip Morris executive named Carolyn Levy in 1991 as part of the company's inquiry into the psychology of children. Snagging ever younger customers had long been an intense focus for the tobacco industry, largely because that demographic was seen, simply, as their future customers. As smokers quit or died, it became critical for cigarette companies to find and cultivate the newest, and youngest, customers. Tobacco companies had long known, based on research they conducted, that the earlier a company hooked a smoker on their brand, the longer they'd keep them as customers. Terms like "brand loyalty" essentially translated into "How can we addict customers on *our* product and not *theirs*?" Over more than half a century that race for younger and younger customers became its own long and surprisingly crass (even for tobacco companies) battle royal.

In the 1940s Philip Morris paid college students to hand out free cigarettes to friends, and in the 1960s the company ran newspaper ads touting Marlboro as a "campus favorite in all 50 states" and "a top seller at colleges from U.S.C. to Yale." By the 1970s, Philip Morris executives were nervous that Marlboro was losing cachet among teens, and the company began targeting kids as young as twelve years old. In 1974 the company proposed conducting a long-term study of a cohort of third graders in Richmond public schools that displayed "hyperactive" behavior to test a hypothesis that such children would grow into smokers. Rival R. J. Reynolds referred to its young customers as its "replacement smokers."

In 1981, an internal Philip Morris report titled *Young Smokers* cautioned how important it was to understand that demographic. "Today's teenager is tomorrow's potential regular customer," said the report. "At least a part of the success of Marlboro Red during its most rapid growth period was because it became the brand of choice among teenagers."

Later that decade, in 1988, Philip Morris's director of consumer research, David Dangoor, asked Carolyn Levy, the youth research expert, to undertake a more formal study of this key demographic. "Can we gain a better understanding of young smokers?" the director asked. The question touched off a yearslong, cross-departmental project to "determine the American archetype of smoking." The project, which was conducted with the help of Clotaire Rapaille, a renowned branding consultant and "cultural shrink" steeped in Freud and Jung, was designed to unearth the "personality traits, beliefs, values, lifestyles" and overall motivations of young smokers to better ensure that they flocked to Marlboro as their "starter" brand instead of Philip Morris's rivals.

By 1994, CEO Geoffrey Bible boasted to analysts at a conference in Scottsdale, Arizona, that Marlboro was competing so well against its competitors that it "remains the brand of choice among young adults" with the median age of its smokers trending "younger than its closest competitor." Even then, it was clear to company officials that it wasn't a great idea to boast about such things. In handwritten notes in the margins somebody scribbled "You may wish to take this out" next to an exclamation point and two question marks.

The following year, the FDA's David Kessler gave a speech at Columbia University School of Law in which he characterized the tobacco problem as a "pediatric disease." "The tobacco industry has argued that the decision to smoke and continue to smoke is a free choice made by an adult," Kessler said. "But ask a smoker when he or she began to smoke. Chances are you will hear the tale of a child." Throughout the 1990s, as adult smoking declined, the number of underage smokers was on the rise, not least because of the $5 billion a year the tobacco industry spent on advertising to them—the second-most heavily advertised commodity after automobiles at the time. Between 1991 and 1997 the number of high school students who reported smoking grew by an alarming 32 percent. Public-health officials panicked, and as Kessler hurried to bring the industry under his agency's jurisdiction, he zeroed in on that fact as a way to turn the public's tide against tobacco.

"If we could affect the smoking habits of just one generation, we could radically reduce the incidence of smoking-related death and disease," Kessler said in the speech. "And a second unaddicted generation could see nicotine addiction go the way of smallpox and polio."

A year later, in August 1996, President Bill Clinton announced that he was authorizing the FDA to regulate nicotine in cigarettes and smokeless tobacco as an addictive drug, delivering a sweeping victory to Kessler and anti-tobacco opponents who'd fought for years to gain the wide regulatory latitude over the tobacco industry. "This epidemic is no accident," Clinton said, in a speech in the Rose Garden to a group of teenagers wearing red T shirts emblazoned with the phrase TOBACCO-FREE KIDS. "Children are bombarded daily by massive marketing campaigns that play on their vulnerabilities, their insecurities, their longings to be something in the world." He promised that "with this historic action . . . the Marlboro Man will be out of our children's reach forever."

That victory was short-lived. Despite Philip Morris's public change of heart, the company and three other cigarette manufacturers waged legal warfare against Clinton and the FDA. The case made it all the way up to the U.S. Supreme Court, which in March 2000 struck down the federal authority, holding that Congress had never delegated authority to the FDA to regulate tobacco products.

Meanwhile, Philip Morris launched its new youth smoking prevention department, which was designed to demonstrate its stated commitments to youth smoking reduction. As they looked for somebody to head it, they settled on Levy, putting the former youth marketing expert in charge of making sure the company didn't market to youth.

Almost immediately, the YSP thrust Philip Morris deeper into controversy rather than lift it out. It was armed with a massive annual $100 million budget to spend. Part of the funds went to create a massive psychometric study designed to discover more information about tween and teen smokers' attitudes and behaviors. Using a telephone survey firm, the company reached tens of thousands of adolescents in their homes and asked a series of questions—what they do with their personal time after school, their personality characteristics, the quality of their relationship with their parents, their smoking habits. The results were ostensibly designed to better inform the company so it could tailor its youth smoking prevention programs, yet the survey had the tinge not of a sincere study in anti-smoking but of bare market research.

Nobody asked Philip Morris to do it, but the company thought it would be a good idea to blast its new youth prevention message to the widest possible audience. One of the company's first major ads aired as part of the "Think. Don't Smoke" campaign was unveiled during the Super Bowl in January 2000, just before halftime. The ad was aimed at kids ages ten to fourteen and was designed "to communicate to children that they do not need to smoke to be 'cool' or to redefine themselves," said Levy in a press release. "There will be an estimated 6.2 million children in the target age group watching the Super Bowl, more than double the number who watch other popular teen shows such as 'Dawson's Creek,' 'Sabrina, The Teenage Witch,' and 'Buffy the Vampire Slayer.'"

But Philip Morris wasn't alone in running anti-smoking ads. One of the requirements of the Master Settlement had been for the tobacco industry to provide funding for an independent foundation to create awareness campaigns targeted at kids to educate them about the dangers of smoking. That resulted in the creation of a group called the American Legacy Foundation, which rolled out a series of controversial "truth" ad campaigns. During the 2000 Summer Olympics, the foundation aired a parody Marlboro Man ad that showed galloping horses on a range carrying body bags with the Marlboro logo. The tagline was "What if tobacco ads told the truth?" Another ad showed three kids bungee jumping. When the third kid took his turn, he exploded midair. The tagline was "Only one product actually kills a third of the people who use it. Tobacco."

Not surprisingly, the people behind the two dueling ad campaigns—those by Philip Morris and the others by the independent Legacy Foundation—ended up clashing. When Philip Morris distributed millions of free textbook jackets to schools across the United States, immediately the Legacy Foundation pounced. One of the images on the jackets displayed a brightly colored snowboarder jumping into a cloud of snow beneath the words "Don't Wipe Out." Legacy and other critics alleged that the covers were a shameless violation of the Master Settlement Agreement's ban on youth advertising since they were printed with the company's name. They also pointed out that the snowboard looked suspiciously like a cigarette, and the snow like smoke. An uproar ensued, with students, parents, principals, and school districts complaining that Philip Morris was using subliminal messaging to deceptively market to kids. "This is a marketing ploy by Philip Morris, plain and simple," John Garrison, the CEO of the American Lung Association told Katie Couric and Matt Lauer on the *Today* show about the book covers.

In damage control mode, Levy wrote letters to school principals across the country. "I can assure you that our intention with that book cover and with all of our efforts is to help reduce youth smoking," she said in one of the letters.

But critics at the American Legacy Foundation were furious. They not only felt that the Philip Morris youth smoking prevention program wasn't working, they were gathering evidence that they believed showed the company was using the prevention program to secretly continue advertising to youth.

In October 2001, the National Association of Attorneys General convened its first triennial conference as required by the Master Settlement Agreement, which stipulated that a "major conference" needed to be held every three years with the state attorneys general, the American Legacy Foundation, and the tobacco companies. The idea was that all the stakeholders would evaluate the success of the agreement and coordinate efforts to continue reducing youth smoking. That year, the event was held in Overland Park, Kansas, at a DoubleTree hotel. Several people gave presentations, including Levy and executives from other major tobacco companies. During lunchtime, a group of teens performed *Tobacco: The Musical*.

Later, Lyndon Haviland, executive vice president of the American Legacy Foundation, appeared on a panel dedicated to youth smoking prevention programs. She discussed research the foundation had conducted, and would be soon publishing, that showed that Philip Morris's youth prevention ads were actually attracting kids to smoking, the opposite of what the company promised. The "Think. Don't Smoke" ads are "prolonging the period during which teens are at risk of smoking," Haviland said, according to notes of the event. And they appeared to be "associated with openness to smoking in the future."

Haviland's comments touched off a bomb at Philip Morris. The following week, Levy fired off a letter to Haviland. "I was disturbed by some of the results you reported," she wrote. "I am eager to hold a follow-up meeting with you. . . . In the meantime, please note that the two ads you tested are no longer running."

Four months later, Haviland sent some of the data that the Legacy

Foundation used and said that she expected "that the data will be available on our website by mid-May," which stood to put Philip Morris on blast in a highly uncomfortable way.

About a week later, Haviland received a letter back. This time it wasn't from Levy. It was from Howard Willard, the Marlboro salesman.

LEVY HAD JUST ANNOUNCED that after thirty years at Philip Morris she was leaving the company. Willard and Levy had gotten to know each other over the years in part because their offices for a time had been next to each other. When trying to find a new head for the YSP, Szymanczyk asked Levy whether she thought Willard might be a good fit for the job. "I thought it was a great idea," she told him. "He was very smart and had a lot of energy and I thought he would be terrific. . . . Howard is one of the up-and-coming younger senior vice presidents. . . . He's smart, high energy, he's a good leader, he's well regarded."

It was an unlikely career move for Willard but one that almost instantly raised his profile at the company, both internally and externally. In truth he was being thrust into a quagmire. In a March 2002 letter back to Haviland at the American Legacy Foundation he came out swinging at the notion that anything Philip Morris had done was enticing children.

"We believe that the data you collected on our youth smoking advertising is seriously flawed," Willard wrote. Three days later, Haviland retorted to Willard: "Since you have not been part of any prior discussions with Legacy, you may not be fully aware of what actually transpired in our December meeting," she wrote. "I am confident that the data that we have collected, analyzed and shared is accurate." More letters were exchanged between Willard and Haviland over the next few days, each one more heated than the last.

A few months later, in June 2002, Legacy published its study in the *American Journal of Public Health*. "We found that exposure to 'Think. Don't Smoke' engendered more favorable feelings toward the tobacco industry than we found among those not exposed" to the ads, the study found. The study made headlines across the country. Within three months, Philip Morris caved. Willard's youth smoking prevention group pulled the company's "Think. Don't Smoke" ad campaign.

The American Legacy Foundation considered it a coup. "We never asked them to get involved in making teen prevention ads," said Cheryl Healton, dean of New York University's School of Global Public Health and the founding director of the American Legacy Foundation. "It's like asking the fox to watch the chicken coop." Their campaign, she said, "was absolutely working to encourage kids to smoke. It was working so well it was almost impossible not to view it not designed for that purpose."

Even though the campaign got sidelined, Willard didn't back down and doggedly defended his company's position on the topic of youth smoking. For every perceived slight that was printed in a newspaper, Willard penned a retort. In March 2004, he wrote in a Letter to the Editor in the *Orlando Sentinel* that Philip Morris demanded that Florida stop running some of the "truth" ads because they had "several inaccuracies . . . regarding the companies' business practices and their employees." The next month, he wrote in to the Reader Letters section of the *Alameda Times-Star,* in response to the columnist The Movie Guy who made an offhand mention in a column about the Oscars that tobacco companies paid to have their brands displayed in movies. In July 2004 he wrote an editorial in *Florida Today,* responding to an earlier editorial titled "Big Tobacco's Poison" that suggested companies like Philip Morris still market to kids using "slick ads." "Since 1998, we have decreased our spending on cigarette advertising in newspapers and magazines," he wrote. In 2005, Willard wrote a My View column in the *Tallahassee Democrat* titled, "Philip Morris Is Doing Its Part to Discourage Kids from Smoking."

Yet even as the youth smoking issue had become a third rail, a wave of newly enacted youth smoking prevention efforts in schools and communities across the country were starting to show signs of success. By 2007, the number of high school students who smoked had dropped to about 20 percent, almost half the rate from a decade earlier. Public-health officials and anti-smoking advocates were elated. Their efforts *were working*.

Even though Philip Morris publicly celebrated the declining youth numbers, it was undeniably another ominous sign for the tobacco business. The writing was on the wall. Philip Morris was losing adult smokers. Philip Morris was losing teen smokers. It was looking like the United States might see its first generation of kids who largely went through high school without ever lighting up. While the company was able to hike prices to offset the financial impact of declining consumption, it was nonetheless faced with an inauspicious math equation. Philip Morris needed a plan. If only the company could once and for all come up with a product that didn't *kill* people.

2

THE GOOD GUYS

Silicon Valley. . . . It's a place where
the future is dreamed up, prototyped,
packaged, and ultimately sold.
—ADAM FISHER, *VALLEY OF GENIUS*

The Rational Future of Smoking. A slide flashed up on a projector screen in front of a chalkboard, as the lights were switched off and the classroom darkened. Those words were juxtaposed next to a picture of a guy sucking on what looked like a slender black straw. He sat in front of a universal NO SMOKING sign—a cigarette with a red circle and slash through it.

"The name *was* Solace," said James Monsees, the shaggy student presenter, standing in front of a podium with his MacBook open in front of him. "But it's now Ploom, at least temporarily."

It was the end of the spring semester in 2005. Monsees and his co-presenter, Adam Bowen, were giving a thesis presentation to complete their graduate degrees in product design at Stanford University. The two had met in the one place that every product design student knew best, called the Loft. It was a big building squished between a machine workshop and a campus fire station, nestled in the heart of the idyllic, palm tree–lined campus.

Product design students could be found in the Loft night and day, tinkering away in a rambling space of Rube Goldberg's dreams, cluttered with spools of wire, disassembled electronics, woodworking benches stacked with raw wood, scraps of metal, and boxes that said FLAMMABLE. The space was a designer's utopia where students could access tools and birth their latest invention. Early on Monsees churned out products worthy of the idealized space—a tea-making contraption, a bicycle, a novel kind of furniture that could form into any shape. He learned how to weld. Bowen had worked on business-oriented designs—an idea that used figurines, or "totems," containing RFID identifiers that could be exchanged instead of business cards; a desk that could be folded up with the clutter still left on it. Naturally, with both spending so much time in the Loft, they crossed paths, though their bond was formed just outside the building during shared smoke breaks in a small courtyard area with a basketball hoop, a barbecue, and a hammock hanging from an oak tree.

Monsees had taken up smoking, but he knew better than most how stupid the habit was since he'd lost his grandfather, a bomber pilot in World War II, to lung cancer before he was born. Smoking had always been a contentious issue in his family, and so he felt conflicted every time he lit up. Bowen was an occasional smoker who enjoyed the ritual of it most. Given their line of studies, they eventually began thinking deeper about the burning stick hanging from their lips. Cigarettes were idiotically primitive, they concluded, not to mention disgraceful, especially here, in the heart of California's elite society where smoking wasn't only frowned upon but loathed in a profound way. The Stanford campus had maintained a strict Smoke-Free Environment policy for more than a decade. To smoke on the Stanford campus was to accept skulking in alleyways and to inure oneself to stigma, sideways glances, and upturned noses.

"Adam and I were interested in working on design for social change," Monsees said in front of the classroom. "And we acknowledged right away that smoking was probably an easy target. There's a lot of people who smoke who are really at odds with themselves. They really enjoy the process of smoking, but at the same time every cigarette is really self-destructive."

They flashed up a slide with a picture of a cigarette, as he talked about all the reasons people smoked. *Oral fixation. Ritual. The allure. Fun. Helps me think. Helps me relax.*

Then Monsees flashed up a slide showing the cigarette ripped open, broken down into its constituent parts—a piece of paper, a filter, shreds of tobacco—next to the words *The Anatomy of a Cigarette.* "This is the current solution," Monsees said. "It satisfies all these basic human needs." Laughter filled the room. Monsees had a dry, sarcastic sense of humor, and his jokes sometimes fell flat. But this one was obvious. *What a primeval product! A relic of the Industrial Era!*

They'd zeroed in on the central problem of smoking—combustion. Even though a cigarette is a simple product, when you light it on fire, it produces more than seven thousand chemicals, many of them carcinogens. The toxins form microscopic tar particles in the tobacco smoke that when inhaled over many years, build up and degrade the lining of the lungs, contributing to lung cancer. There are other adverse health consequences of smoking, including heart disease and stroke. Taken together, the ailments caused by smoking cigarettes result in 480,000 deaths in the United States every year, making it the leading preventable cause of death.

Then Monsees cut to the chase: "In reality, a cigarette is for nicotine delivery," he said. Yes, people loved the allure of smoking, the James Dean–Marilyn Monroe aesthetic. But what Bowen and Monsees quickly learned—what *everybody* now knew—was that people largely kept up the habit for one reason: nicotine. Which went a long way to explain why there were still thirty-eight million smokers in America even though it's well-known that the habit would kill up to half its users.

Nicotine is extremely addictive—as addictive as heroin—and in children it can have profound negative effects on the developing brain. But contrary to popular belief, the chemical compound that is the chief active ingredient in the tobacco leaf isn't the main deadly agent in a cigarette. While nicotine has been linked to heart disease, and while in high concentrations it can be a lethal poison (which is why it's been used as both an insecticide and a murder weapon), it has been shown to have benefits, including improving concentration and treating a variety of neurological disorders like Parkinson's disease. Not to mention simple pleasure.

Bowen and Monsees wondered: If the world wanted nicotine so badly, why not just give the people what they want, without all the stuff that kills them? It seemed so obvious. There were one billion smokers in the world. Yet, the cigarette hadn't been redesigned in more than a century, since 1880 when the Bonsack machine introduced the world to the machine-rolled cigarette. Surely somebody must have thought of this before?

Being at the world's premier design school, in the middle of Silicon Valley, where everything from the automobile to the toaster had been disrupted, Bowen and Monsees had a hunch that they'd landed on something special. So in the shadow of Stanford's iconic Hoover Tower, amid the palm trees and the sandstone archways, one that once was inscribed with the words THE PROGRESS OF CIVILIZATION IN AMERICA, Bowen and Monsees set out to disrupt the thing that hadn't been disrupted in a century: the cigarette.

MONSEES WAS RAISED IN an upper-middle-class home in St. Louis by his physician mother and electrical engineer father who imparted a tinkering, entrepreneurial spirit to his son and taught him how to work on computers. He eschewed toys in favor of taking apart computers and other household items, like vacuum cleaners, in a workshop at home. He attended the Whitfield School, an upscale St. Louis prep school, and got his undergraduate degree in art and physics from the private liberal arts school, Kenyon College, in Ohio. Even as he gained fluency in thermodynamics, he nurtured his love of art, spending months shaping materials like hardwood and copper into oversize, pearlescent sculptures.

Monsees had a mop of brown hair, a sometimes-scruffy beard, and the demeanor of a Midwest skater-kid prone to pranks, baggy jeans, and sarcasm. He had a little of the arrogant tech-bro attitude in him, in that he didn't hesitate to suffer fools gladly but he retained an intellectual curiosity that largely kept him from embodying the worst of the Valley's hubris. One of Monsees's first jobs after graduating was in a bike shop, before taking a position at a product design studio in St. Louis. While at the company Metaphase Design Group, he was exposed to a bustling environment filled with engineers making knee-replacement kits for companies like Medtronic and disposable razors for Gillette. The owner of the company, Bryce Rutter, recalled Monsees being an "exceptionally bright young man" but one who needed to be reined in some because of his freewheeling imagination and ambition. "People with that gift, it's challenging for others to keep pace," he said. "It was almost like 'James, you've got to slow down a bit and let everyone catch up to what you're thinking.'" When he learned Monsees was leaving St. Louis to seek fortune and adventure in Silicon Valley, he wasn't surprised. "James needed to be where the action was." Monsees packed up his car and drove out west. When he landed at Stanford he was twenty-three years old.

Bowen, who was just a few years older, was born in Ontario, Canada, but his family moved to Arizona when he was a child. He was a tall, lanky blond who retained the build of a road biker. He spoke in decisive measured sentences with a hint of a Canadian accent, but often wore a saturnine look on his angular face. Bowen was a deeply private individual, the kind of guy content introducing himself to people as just "Adam," never letting on who he was or who he would become. He was an artist at heart early on, drawing and making paper airplanes and designing detailed pencil-sketched contraptions, like the "purpose-simple, home-built invention towed by a car for liftoff" or his rendition of a nuclear-powered hovercraft. He began his studies at the University of Arizona before transferring to Pomona College, where he studied poetry, architecture, and philosophy before settling on a subject he loved and knew well, physics. Bowen possessed the mind of a true scientist—somebody who wanted not only to dream up good ideas but also to indulge in experiential learning. When given the chance to conduct microgravity research at Pomona, he donned an olive-green jumpsuit and boarded a NASA experimental zero-gravity airplane dubbed the "vomit comet" that ascended 34,000 feet into the air before nose-diving 10,000 feet, and then up and down again in a series of parabolic curves that induced weightlessness. Bowen also had a deep technical acumen that led him to undertake a graduate course of study at Stanford University's School of Engineering in mechatronics, the multidisciplinary field combining mechanical, electrical, and software engineering. It wasn't a field for lightweights.

To disrupt the cigarette, Bowen and Monsees realized it might help to know something more about it other than how to light up. One of the first questions they had was why hadn't anybody developed a new tobacco product like this before? Surely, if anyone would benefit from making cigarettes that didn't kill people, it would be the tobacco industry, right?

As they started doing research for their thesis, they stumbled upon an unlikely treasure trove. The Master Settlement Agreement, along with other tobacco litigation, had ordered tobacco companies to make available to the public documents that were produced in the course of their multiyear litigation. The University of California, San Francisco, had put them all online in a database. Together, the companies ended up releasing more than *ninety million* pages of documents, all of which could now be searched by anyone with an internet connection.

The archives contained internal emails and handwritten letters, scientific studies and business plans, patents and product research, all of which opened an incredible window into a secretive industry that had spent billions of dollars over nearly half a century trying to develop a new, noncombustible cigarette. For Bowen and Monsees it was a eureka moment. Somebody *had* tried to disrupt the cigarette before: the tobacco companies themselves! The tobacco companies had simply failed miserably in their years' worth of attempts.

Bowen and Monsees dove into the archives with gusto and found themselves getting lost for hours at a time as they burned through the search engine and combed through one more explosive document after the next. They discovered R. J. Reynolds's carbon-tipped cigarette called Premier that heated up flavor beads instead of tobacco to produce an aerosol instead of smoke. They found a device made by Philip Morris called Accord that used a kazoo-looking device to heat up a cigarette instead of lighting it on fire. They discovered Liggett's "Project XA" that used palladium in its tobacco in an attempt to make combustion more efficient and reduce harmful constituents in the smoke. They found intricate chemistry research that shed light on how to create a smoother cigarette, or one that gave smokers more of a kick. The cigarette industry was ripe for innovation after all.

With a formidable blueprint in hand, Bowen and Monsees set out to create a new, smoking-like experience. It would give users all the things they loved about smoking—the ritual, the social aspect—while getting rid of the combustion to make it healthier and more socially acceptable. They studied cigarette alternatives, like hookahs and table-top vaporizers used primarily by medical marijuana users, and decided they wanted to make something that was sleeker and much more portable.

Ultimately, they created a heated-tobacco gadget that mimicked the round, slender profile of a cigarette but stood out with a different shape and form factor. Powered by butane, it vaporized little tufts of loose-leaf tobacco wrapped in paper. They used the device on campus and in public to gauge how people would respond and were thrilled to discover that not only did people not hate it, as they did secondhand cigarette smoke, but they were intrigued and often commented on how they enjoyed the smell of the lightly scented tobacco vapor it produced. When the two met with their thesis advisers and faculty, "they were thrilled with the idea," Bowen said.

During their final thesis presentation, Bowen and Monsees flashed on the screen a 1986 document marked "Secret" that explained the technology behind one of the tobacco companies' most advanced products at the time, called Project Spa—a code name for Reynolds's early reduced-harm cigarette that was marketed under the name Premier. "This is a Top Secret tobacco document that was really fun for us when we first got started," Monsees said, with a wry smile. "This is a

one-billion-dollar investment project by RJR in 1980s dollars. An unbe-
lievably huge project that barely saw the light of day and it's free, it's
open, it's free domain. At this point you can learn all about it. And
what that taught us, that in combination with a ton of reading a ton of
patents and spending a ton of time with consumers, was that vaporization is awesome."

It was a remarkable moment. Here was Monsees explaining how
he and Bowen had picked up the thread of history where Big Tobacco
had so epically left off. The daisy chain of innovation, in all its seren-
dipitous splendor, had skipped a generation of tobacco executives—
just like Kodak early on had missed out on the digital camera—and
been picked up like a diamond in a junkyard by two Stanford students.

After Bowen and Monsees graduated, Monsees was invited to stay
at Stanford for a stint to help on an ambitious endeavor. Stanford's
School of Engineering had recently received a $35 million gift from
Hasso Plattner, the billionaire founder of German software maker
SAP, to create a multidisciplinary design lab for people from all corners
of Stanford—engineering, medicine, business, the humanities. Monsees was asked to help set up the new institute, which became known
simply as the d.school, and participate as a fellow.

The d.school was the brainchild of the renowned design engineer
David Kelley, who'd also been a longtime Stanford professor. In the
1980s when Steve Jobs had needed a new way for people to navigate
the personal computer, he called Kelley, who together with his engineers fished out the little roller ball from a stick of deodorant and a
butter dish cover and cobbled together the prototype of what became
Apple's first mouse. The contraption made him one of the most
sought-after product design gurus in all of Silicon Valley. *60 Minutes*
called him "one of the most innovative thinkers of our time." Kelley's design firm, IDEO, went on to do work for major corporations
from The North Face to Fender, Samsung to Mattel, and churned
out everything from the squishy handles on toothbrushes to Eli Lilly
auto-injectors.

Kelley was like a rock star on the Stanford campus; students clam-
ored for the opportunity to be under the mustachioed professor's tutelage. Kelley taught his own theory of design, called "design thinking,"

a methodology fusing art and industrial design with a radical human-centered approach. At its heart the theory of design thinking was about more than developing a technology or designing a fancy piece of hardware or coming up with a business plan. It pulled from Ludwig Mies van der Rohe—"less is more"—and Jobs—"make a dent in the universe." It was, Kelley explained, "about deeply understanding human needs." Through the power of empathy and creativity, students could do much more than simply design a widget. Kelley urged them to think bigger. *They could change the world.*

Kelley's students also learned the importance of rapid prototyping, of being able to churn out designs not in weeks or days but in hours, and then getting them in the hands of beta testers as soon as possible. After internalizing feedback and rapidly incorporating any necessary changes, they'd churn out another prototype and begin the cycle anew, doing that over and over again until the product was just right. The Kelley disciples that emerged from the d.school or IDEO often went on to have an outsized impact in Silicon Valley—they're the creators of Apple products and Teslas and Bird scooters and drones and wearables and, well, the future.

As Monsees helped get the d.school off the ground, he and Bowen continued working on their thesis project. Kelley urged them that their idea had potential. So they took up the work on the side, retreating to Bowen's shared, rickety five-bedroom house, which sat on the edge of an old apple orchard just off campus. The house, which friends informally called the Orchard, was well kept for what was essentially a bachelor pad filled with PhD and graduate students, and that had corn growing in the backyard and chickens wandering around. Bowen and Monsees moved a lathe into the house and set up in a tiny closet-size room that was so small there was no room for chairs. From there, the two took the crude prototypes they'd made for their thesis and started breathing life into what they hoped would become a commercial product. Just like Steve Jobs and Steve Wozniak, Bill Hewlett and David Packard, and other famous tech founders had mythologized garages that served as temples of innovation, Bowen and Monsees had the Orchard.

It's not uncommon to be swept up by the romanticism of Stanford—by the siren song that induces its students into believing they're the chosen genius destined to create the next big thing; by the intoxicating allure of the professors and advisers plugged into a moneyed network of VCs on Sand Hill Road; by the simple triumph of an idea born from a ramshackle garage; by the audacity of believing that life can be designed "in the same way that Jonathan Ive designed the iPhone." It's all there, success and ego and power and Palo Alto gold-rush riches, just dangling from the redwood trees, waiting to be plucked.

So perhaps Bowen and Monsees could be forgiven, in that frozen moment of time inside the Stanford bubble, for not fully grasping the weight of their creation. At the design school, a giant black-and-white sign hung from a wire strung across the ceiling. It said: NOTHING IS A MISTAKE. THERE'S NO WIN. AND NO FAIL. THERE'S ONLY MAKE.

CALLING SILICON VALLEY, AND the surrounding Bay Area, anti-tobacco doesn't quite capture the psyche of the place and the significance of the matter. A deep, reflexive disdain for the tobacco industry was as much baked into its DNA as semiconductors, the *Whole Earth Catalog,* and Ram Dass. Starting in the 1960s and over the next three decades, a scrappy but then powerful anti-smoking movement took root in San Francisco. A network of grassroots activists that operated under the name Group Against Smoking Pollution, or GASP, and later Californians for Nonsmokers' Rights, had begun agitating to elevate the topic of smoking alongside the most hot-button issues of the day. The anti-smoking activists teed up victories, including the passage of an anti-smoking ordinance in Berkeley in 1977, followed by a series of pitched battles against the tobacco industry throughout the '80s and '90s that resulted in ever-stricter laws designed to curb smoking in public and in workplaces.

At one point, one of the most prominent anti-smoking activists, Stanton Glantz, an assistant professor of medicine at the University of California, San Francisco, touched off a firestorm when he gained access to a pirated documentary called *Death in the West.* The 1976 film juxtaposed interviews with Philip Morris executives denying that smoking was deadly, alongside Marlboro Man–looking cowboys across the West who'd developed lung disease after a lifetime of smoking. The scenes of the men riding horseback on the range—one with an oxygen tank slung over his saddle—and sitting fireside speaking of impending smoking-related death were unlike anything the world had seen before.

But after a single airing in the United Kingdom, Philip Morris took the filmmaker to court and won assurances that the documentary would never be aired again. Five years later, in 1981, Glantz secretly received a copy of the controversial film, stashing a master copy in the UCSF Library to keep Philip Morris's aggressive lawyers from seizing it. Ultimately, Glantz released *Death in the West* out into the world, where it was aired on television stations and in school classrooms across the country.

A little more than a decade later, Glantz and the UCSF Library became the center of attention again when on May 12, 1994, Glantz received a box at his UCSF office filled with thousands of pages of internal tobacco documents, many marked "Confidential," from an anonymous source who put the name "Mr. Butts" (after the *Doonesbury* cartoon character) as the sender. As Glantz read through the cache, he saw documents covering decades dating back to the 1950s. The papers had originated from the tobacco company Brown & Williamson and its multinational parent British American Tobacco and contained internal company memoranda and documents that detailed legal strategy, scientific research, public relations plans, and more. In their totality they illuminated what the industry had known for decades (and tried to cover up) about the deadly effects of smoking and the addictive nature of nicotine, and how the companies had designed their products to capitalize on nicotine's addictive properties.

Around the same time, the same set of documents had been obtained by the offices of Congressman Henry Waxman and the *New York Times* reporter Philip Hilts, who'd reported on their contents five days earlier in an article titled "Tobacco Company Was Silent on Hazards." David Kessler, the commissioner of the FDA, had recently begun his investigation into the tobacco industry and was also in hot pursuit of the documents.

Knowing he was sitting on a bombshell, Glantz furiously began photocopying the documents before stashing the cache in the UCSF Library archives to keep them safe. The documents became a sensation, and the archivists at the library, located in a building on the school's six-block Parnassus Heights campus next to Golden Gate Park and the San Francisco Botanical Garden, could barely keep up with the stream of visitors.

Lawyers for Brown & Williamson sued the university to get the documents back, claiming they were stolen material. The tobacco lawyers were so furious that they also demanded the UCSF librarians hand over the names of individuals who'd accessed the material. But the university backed Glantz and successfully asserted that the university had a right to make the documents public.

Glantz didn't know it at the time, but the Mr. Butts documents were only the start of a budding collection at the UCSF Library. Working with the librarians he scanned the original B&W collection and had it copied to CDs. As the internet arrived, they began uploading the material to an online database, which grew as more documents became available from the tobacco settlement and other litigation. In 2001, Glantz received a $15 million grant from the American Legacy Foundation (the tobacco-prevention entity created with money from the 1998 Master Settlement Agreement) to speed the process of creating a permanent digital archive of the tobacco documents. The money from the Legacy Foundation also endowed the creation of the Center for Tobacco Control Research and Education at UCSF, of which Glantz served as the longtime director. Eventually, the UCSF archive swelled to more than fourteen million documents, comprising more than ninety million pages.

UCSF had long been home to a prestigious medical school and a research and teaching hospital. Now, as the tobacco industry's misdeeds came to light, the school had become one of the largest repositories of internal tobacco documents in the world. It was an invaluable go-to resource for tobacco-control researchers, lawyers, and any other member of the public who wanted to learn all about Big Tobacco's darkest secrets. "They are the equivalent of the human genome for tobacco," Glantz once said about the documents.

Glantz was used to people coming by his office on the UCSF campus and paying a visit to the library that housed the original Mr. Butts tobacco documents. So it wasn't too surprising one day around 2006 when two Stanford students paid him a visit with a funny-looking heated-tobacco contraption. The young men told Glantz that they admired the work that he'd done and said how useful the archives had been in coming up with their idea that was going to revolutionize smoking. Glantz was happy to chat with them and agreed that, yes, their idea seemed intriguing. It wasn't inconceivable that it could potentially be safer than smoking since there was no combustion. But he told them they had to be extremely cautious of one thing in particular: "It's almost certainly going to be attractive to kids," he said.

FOR THE PAST YEAR Bowen and Monsees had been cranking out prototypes of their heated-tobacco device. Now, in 2006, they'd landed some office space in the Dogpatch, one of San Francisco's most bootstrapping, industrious neighborhoods, a place where massive warehouses and shipyards and factories once churned out staples from another era—gunpowder, rope, ships—amid fields of wild fennel and packs of feral dogs. In the past decade, the Dogpatch had been gradually transformed by an influx of tech wealth, melting the jagged aura of the blight into a slick-but-not-too-slick Instagrammable utopia. A new light rail track had just been completed here, stitching the Dogpatch back onto the rest of the city and hastening the flow of it all. Any glass in the gutters or rusted-out boatyards didn't serve as a detraction but an allure for the flock of artists, makers, and dreamers with cash who opened *fromageries* with cave-aged Gruyère, artisan butchers with hand-cut short ribs, and boutiques hewing leather and wood into $300 bespoke clogs.

Bowen and Monsees landed in the middle of it all. A friend and fellow "Loftee" from Stanford offered them a desk in the massive American Industrial Center building, a hulking old factory that once churned out tin cans and had been transformed into a WeWork-style hive of workshops and offices and storefronts. They spent their time in that ad hoc office overlooking the Bay creating renderings of their latest ideas and drawing up business plans. When they weren't in the office, they were knocking on doors of venture capitalists, trying to get in the game. A start-up in the Valley is nothing without the investors that anoint them. As they made their rounds, the founders came across as smart enough. But smart wasn't in short supply in Silicon Valley.

"It wasn't like walking in the room with Elon, where it's like Thomas Edison and Buzz Aldridge in one room, and the hair on the back of your neck goes up and you say 'holy shit,'" said one investor who was pitched early on by them. "It seemed like they had a pathway to be financially viable. Companies at that stage, the most you can say is the plan is not insane."

Their plan wasn't insane, but it also wasn't an immediate crowd-pleaser. While their Stanford bona fides otherwise would have been a surefire icebreaker on Sand Hill Road, investors were less than thrilled with their whiz-bang cigarette. The yoga-and-kale streak running through the culture was largely inhospitable. A number of investment firms had long turned their backs on companies with ties to tobacco, just as they had with land mines, apartheid, and alcohol.

Dozens of venture capital firms and angel investors said no to Ploom. It didn't take Bowen and Monsees long to figure out that hawking a tobacco product on the same earth that birthed the anti-tobacco movement put them behind enemy lines.

WHEN RALPH ESCHENBACH HEARD about Bowen and Monsees through a friend of a friend, he was intrigued. The seasoned venture capitalist had been in the Valley forever, earning a graduate electrical engineering degree from Stanford in 1970 before going on to work at HP Labs in Palo Alto, where he invented the first commercial Global Positioning System receiver after using military satellite technology to map stretches of California freeways. After a successful career helping run navigation technology start-ups, he joined Sand Hill Angels, a group of high-net-worth individuals and Silicon Valley angel investors that made a name giving seed money to chipmakers and life sciences firms and IT companies. The group had since branched out into companies that more generally made "disruptive, scalable technologies."

Eschenbach had never smoked a cigarette in his life. In fact, he hated them. His mother was a smoker and died of lung cancer. When he first heard about Ploom, he was immediately intrigued by the idea that this might be a novel way to derive the benefits of cigarettes without the carcinogenic side effects. So on a typical sunny day in Palo Alto in early 2007, he gathered with some of his partners in a conference room at a local law firm to hear the pitch.

Bowen and Monsees set up their laptops in front of the room and opened a slide deck they'd meticulously prepared. They'd done this dozens of times before to little end, but this time they had a good feeling. Eschenbach had an old-soul vibe to him with his shock of white hair and deep-set lines in his face that hinted he possessed all the lore of Silicon Valley in him, like an old tree. And he just seemed to get it. By now, after giving their presentation so many times, Bowen and Monsees had crafted a polished and convincing narrative about themselves, their company, and their product.

Their story was undeniably compelling. As they flipped through the slides projected on a screen, they explained that they weren't a traditional tobacco company. In fact they hated Big Tobacco as much as the next person. Their product, Ploom, represented a threat to that very industry and if they could only get their company off the ground, they'd be able to go head-to-head with the industry that had for too long gotten away with murder. The opportunity was enormous from a public-health standpoint, they explained, but since the industry had been stigmatized whole cloth there hadn't been any good, smart outsiders who'd been willing to seize on it. They reiterated that smoking was the world's leading cause of preventable death and, just like condoms, seat belts, or air bags, there were potential public health solutions to save lives. Beyond that, the total addressable market (the key phrase in the Valley) was mind-bogglingly enormous. If they could convince even a fraction of the world's one billion smokers to use their product, they'd be swimming in money and saving lives along the way. They had some design prototypes of Ploom with them, which they passed around for the angel investors to hold. It wasn't finished, and it wasn't perfect, but the basic concept was there.

Eschenbach was sold. The two Stanford grads came across as smart and professional, and they clearly had done their research. While they didn't present much in the way of scientific backing for their claim that the product was safer than cigarettes, it seemed obvious if only through intuition that since most of the burning products were carcinogenic, if you took away the burning you'd take away the carcinogens. Not all of his colleagues were in immediate agreement—there were some who were uneasy about being in the tobacco space at all. But Eschenbach personally felt that the potential health benefits outweighed any downside. Like so much of the investing world that's often rooted in intuition as much as data, Eschenbach had a gut feeling. Ploom had some promise.

Bowen and Monsees had already cobbled together some funds from family and friends, but it wasn't much. They were looking for at least $500,000. Eschenbach said Sand Hill would kick in only a portion of that, but they'd draft a term sheet that they could use to continue looking for other investors.

As luck would have it, not long after the meeting with Sand Hill, they did find another investor. A Stanford professor suggested that Bowen and Monsees post an email on the listserv for the Stanford Graduate School of Business. It wasn't unusual for students and alumni to use the forum for getting advice on starting a company or for fundraising activities. So they wrote up an email that outlined how they were trying to end death and disease with a new noncombustible tobacco product. There were a few responses here and there. But one in particular seemed promising. It came from a man who wasn't a Stanford business school alum but who'd had the message forwarded to him. His name was Riaz Valani.

Valani, a venture capitalist who'd started an investment firm called Global Asset Capital in San Francisco, wasn't a mainstay in the usual Silicon Valley circles, and his name didn't ring bells like Marc Andreessen or John Doerr. It was instead met with "Riaz who?" A short, stocky man of Indian descent with jet-black hair had made his way to the edges of Silicon Valley in an unfamiliar fashion. He didn't arrive via

Stanford or with an engineering degree in hand. Valani started his career in the scrappy world of New York investment banking in the 1990s at Gruntal & Co., one of the oldest brokerage firms in the country, before it got driven into the ground. Ultimately the Securities and Exchange Commission and then federal prosecutors caught up with an embezzlement scheme inside Gruntal involving dummy accounts and stolen customer funds that landed one of the firm's executives in prison. "Gruntal was an oasis for people who 'weren't presentable enough' to work for the big houses," said a March 2003 *Fortune* magazine article. "Gruntal was the Island of the Misfit Toys."

That was one of Valani's first jobs out of college. As part of the small asset securitization group, Valani had been exposed to a colleague working on a bizarre but promising deal involving David Bowie. During the 1990s, Bowie needed extra cash flow, and by a series of chance circumstances he wound up finding it with the help of David Pullman, a grandiloquent penny-loafer-wearing Gruntal banker. Valani had a front-row seat as Pullman concocted a deal that resulted in the issuance of $55 million in bonds backed by future publishing and copyright royalties generated from Bowie's catalog. Before the deal was completed, and just as Gruntal was sinking, Pullman jumped ship and took Valani with him to another investment firm, Fahnestock & Co. From there, the bankers executed the "Bowie Bonds" transaction, which became legendary on Wall Street.

With some cash in his pocket and still a long career ahead of him, Valani headed out west. He believed that the Bowie bond deal had the potential for replication in Silicon Valley with software firms in particular, which he believed had a similar stream from royalties and licensing fees that could be securitized. He also eyed major league sports arenas. "There's no reason why the Giants and the 49ers couldn't finance any stadiums using asset-backed bonds," Valani told the *San Francisco Examiner* in 1997. The following year he became general partner at a San Francisco firm called Global Asset Capital, LLC, and struck a securitized bond deal for the heavy metal group Iron Maiden. Then he broadened his sights to include the tech industry and zeroed in on the emerging world of mp3 music files, with the creator of a revolutionary audio player application for Microsoft Windows called Sonique.

The Sonique deal ended up generating a rich payday for Valani, but also a trail of bad blood with the app's creators and others involved. Introduced to the two founders of Sonique through an investor friend, Valani ended up investing in the firm and taking aggressive control of the company. He named himself a cofounder even though he didn't do anything other than write a check. It was only when the company had taken off and after signing the paperwork for a $70 million deal with Lycos in 1999 that the founders and others realized, in a scene right out of *The Social Network,* that their shares had been diluted while Valani's and a constellation of Valani's friends and investment vehicles had been bumped up substantially. That left multiple people involved in the deal feeling outmaneuvered and wishing they'd read the fine print of the deal more closely. "We got screwed," one of the founders told a colleague, not long after the deal had been inked.

A few years later, Sonique was long gone and Lycos left in tatters amid the internet bubble bursting in the 1990s, but Valani emerged unscathed. As Silicon Valley fortunes were wiped out, Valani kept powering through one investment after the next. In 2003 his firm battled for and ultimately wrested control of the venture capital arm of the French entertainment conglomerate Vivendi Universal. He invested in GoFish Corporation—a digital video aggregator and advertising platform—that featured "made for internet" content, like *America's Dream Date* and *Hidden Celebrity Webcam.* He invested in a company that built "advergames" targeted to "parents of children under the age of six."

By the spring of 2007 Bowen and Monsees were elated and relieved to have finally closed their first round of funding. Valani had kicked in the rest of the seed money they'd wanted, around $400,000, which was enough gas to get started.

WITH VC FUNDS IN their account, the Ploom duo upgraded their digs in the old tin can factory, ultimately landing in a raw space with exposed beams and soaring thirty-foot ceilings that lent an air of theatricality. They shared the space with some other Stanford grads, including

John Pelochino, a mechanical engineer who was working to reinvent the vibrator with his product Ola, described as an "intelligent pleasure product." The whole place oozed raw authenticity and grit. It was the embodiment of San Francisco's futuristic, cyberpunk capitalism. Turning fire into vapor next to a man hacking the orgasm. Monsees quipped early on that he was creating "the dystopian future of tobacco." He didn't realize just how true that would be.

They also hired their first employee, Kurt Sonderegger, a marketing manager at Red Bull they'd found with the help of a recruiter. When Sonderegger got the call, he'd never considered working for a tobacco company. But he was intrigued enough to entertain the idea.

He thought Bowen and Monsees articulated the vision for their product clearly and with passion, even though they had little more than the seed money and some design prototypes. The selling point for him was that Bowen and Monsees agreed to write into Sonderegger's employment contract a "Burning Man Clause" that allowed him to take his annual trip to the Nevada desert festival. Sonderegger quit his job at Red Bull, took a short surfing trip to Bali, and then, in early September 2007, reported to the Dogpatch.

The day he showed up at the office, he was there for just a few minutes before Bowen and Monsees asked him to jump in a van and ride with them to Home Depot. They had to go pick up some doors that they could fashion into desks. Sonderegger was wowed—this must *really* be a start-up.

Not only were there no desks, but Ploom was still in the prototype phase and had a barely conceived logo. Sonderegger spent the early days helping flesh out the ethos of the brand and how people might interface with it. They asked questions like "How would people who are Plooming interact with people in the bar?" While Sonderegger was building out the basics, Bowen and Monsees were furiously working on prototypes to put in the hands of users so they could quickly start iterating and refining their design.

Although Bowen and Monsees were cigarette smokers, they still were learning as much as they could about tobacco. Tobacco is like fine wine—it can have different blends and terroir. Bowen in particular grew obsessed with the art and science of tobacco blends. He went around to the top tobacconists and bought different varieties—Virginia, Kentucky, Burley, pipe tobacco, cigar tobacco. They even sent out requests for samples to tobacco purveyors, thinking they'd get perhaps a little baggie in return. Instead, when the first sample arrived, it was a giant box stuffed with what seemed like an entire bale of tobacco. When they sliced it open, shredded tobacco came spilling out everywhere.

Bowen would mix the tobacco in big metal kitchen bowls and soak it in a rainbow of flavors—*peach, coffee, mint*—that he'd obtained from various specialty flavor companies. He'd create test batches with different strengths and flavors and arrange them numbered one through ten, for people to taste and rate. The tobacco vapor wafting through the workshop produced an aroma that was part grandpa's pipe and part sweet perfume.

That December of 2007, Valani invited the small Ploom team to a holiday party at his downtown San Francisco penthouse, and suggested that they use the opportunity to demo Ploom. When they arrived at his apartment, he showed them to a corner where they set up a little table to serve as the "tasting station." All night long, Valani's guests, including business associates from GoFish and Sonique, tried the tobacco contraption, and Valani bragged about the wunderkinds behind the product. Valani had a somewhat odd, instinctual belief in Bowen and Monsees, and from the beginning he was a happy warrior for the men behind his modest investment. Valani handled Bowen and Monsees's start-up with a level of nurturing care that a mother bird might handle an egg. He didn't know then that he was in possession of a Fabergé.

Having the backing and support of Valani gave Bowen and Monsees the momentum they needed to forge ahead. He bought into Bowen and Monsees's mission—that this was a company that could change the world and save lives. There was a shared sense that together they could unite around a common enemy: Big Tobacco. "That's what made it so exciting," recalled one early Ploom employee. "We were the good guys."

3

THE CIGARETTE MAKER'S DILEMMA

The world is moving, and a company
that contents itself with present
accomplishments soon falls behind.
—GEORGE EASTMAN, FOUNDER OF
THE EASTMAN KODAK COMPANY

What the hell is this shit?" asked a Philip Morris executive one day
in 2004 as he threw the hunk of metal to the side of his desk. The
people around him in the Richmond offices of the company were just
as perplexed.

Rumors of this nicotine-dispensing gadget had been swirling
around for weeks now. In May of that year, an employee circulated
an article from the Chinese government's *Science and Technology Daily*
newspaper about a stainless steel "cigarette" that didn't burn any tobacco but instead relied on a lithium battery to heat and vaporize a
nicotine-containing liquid. The device was called the Ruyan Atomizing
Electronic Cigarette. Ruyan, which translated into "like smoke," was
developed by a Chinese pharmacist and herbalist named Hon Lik,
who'd smoked since he was a teenager, after being sent to a tobacco

farm to work the fields during Mao Zedong's Cultural Revolution, and was desperate to quit.

Lik bought a humidifier and poured liquid nicotine into it, using a straw to inhale the vapor it produced. After about twenty minutes, he realized he was on to something. He took it to a lab at Golden Dragon Pharmaceutical in the city of Shenyang to perfect the nicotine formulation to the best of his abilities. In a workshop, he assembled a crude device out of a battery, heating wire, and quartz fiber. Eventually, when Lik's device hit the market in the early 2000s, it came in different designs shaped like a pipe or a cigarette with names like "Love of Angel" and "Viscount," and was offered with cartridges of varying nicotine strengths and flavors like jasmine tea.

Philip Morris's research and development team began scrambling to procure one of the devices. It had long been customary at Philip Morris, like at any tobacco company worth its salt, to scour the market for new innovations, gather intelligence, and run tests on competitors' products. The intent was to glean secrets or ascertain whether they might want to simply write a check to snap something off the market. So when R&D heard about this Chinese contraption, which had already sold out in stores in Beijing, they were eager to get their hands on it and tear it apart.

By the end of June, the U.S.-based team had purchased five kits and the "New Product Focus Team" had begun testing the Ruyan. By September an operational analysis had been done on the device—dissecting it down to its bare components and evaluating everything from the flow sensor, to the circuit board, to the aerosol chamber, to the glowing LED tip that illuminated when the user sucked on it.

Yet within months, despite the Chinese device having formally landed on the company's radar and been circulated within the Richmond offices, the company got bored and moved on. Internal teams were so focused on developing their own products that it never rose much above a curiosity. Multiple top Philip Morris executives brushed it off.

"Nobody's going to want this," said another Philip Morris executive. "There's no tobacco in it."

PHILIP MORRIS, LIKE NEARLY every other tobacco company, worked constantly on developing products designed to innovate on every aspect of the cigarette. Starting in the 1970s, they did so largely to respond to the growing apprehension of smokers and the public-health community about the dangers of smoking. But the companies were still in denial mode, so early research took place in secret, inside American tobacco company labs with darkened windows and in clandestine research centers in far-flung places like Brussels, Cologne, and Neuchâtel. The projects went by code names like Libra, Conqueror, Gypsy, and Truth. Scientists toted jars of cat lungs to and fro for their research. They tracheostomized beagles so they'd involuntarily inhale cigarette smoke. They trained baboons to smoke. The studies confirmed again and again that smoking was carcinogenic and addictive. Yet the more the evidence mounted, the more vociferously the tobacco companies doubled down on their denials. And the more fervently they worked on a Cigarette 2.0 that could minimize or eliminate the inherent danger.

By the early 1980s, Philip Morris scientists had started tinkering around with cigarettes of the future—an electric one made from metal coils, small photoflash bulbs, and the same batteries used in a Polaroid camera; a device modeled after a Panasonic microcassette recorder that featured a tiny "tape" made of a pliable reel of tobacco that could be wound through the device, heated, and smoked. A cigarette called Ambrosia gave off a vanilla scent to placate nonsmokers increasingly upset about secondhand smoke. The company even tried making a cigarette with no nicotine, drawing from the same supercritical extraction process used to make decaffeinated coffee at its Maxwell House coffee brand.

In 1987, R. J. Reynolds announced that it would soon be releasing what it called a "revolutionary" smokeless cigarette—an aluminum cylinder filled with tiny green pellets coated with nicotine and glycerin and finished with a carbon tip that when lit would heat the pellets and produce a vapor. The product, Premier, was launched in test markets with an advertising campaign promoting it as "The Cleaner Smoke." But despite spending as much as $325 million to develop it, Premier was a flop. In the book *Barbarians at the Gate,* which famously chronicled the rough-and-tumble leveraged buyout era on Wall Street that engulfed RJR Nabisco, the authors described how early users of the product said it tasted like shit. Others said it smelled oddly like a raspberry or tasted like a tennis shoe.

Despite Premier's failure, Reynolds had been first to market with an entirely new kind of cigarette, and it served as a shot across the bow. The intensely competitive nature of the cigarette business meant that Philip Morris was suddenly thrown into crisis, as it worked around the clock to respond with its own reduced-harm product. An internal Philip Morris white paper from the early 1990s titled "Products of the Future" captured the mood of the moment: "Premier probably changed the cigarette business forever."

Throughout the 1990s it was becoming abundantly clear that the tobacco companies no longer had the luxury of depending on the same smoldering cash cow that had reliably fueled their business for decades. Despite the tobacco industry's attempts to keep the truth about the harms of smoking from getting out, there was ever-mounting evidence in the public-health community about just how deadly cigarette smoking was. On top of that, Philip Morris was worried about competition bubbling up in the pharmaceutical industry, which was beginning to cut into the cigarette market with cessation products like nicotine gum and patches, which by the 1990s represented an industry of more than $1 billion. Even more troubling was a flurry of patents being filed for pharmaceutical-grade nicotine inhalers, which, according to an internal company memo, "could evolve into replacements for cigarettes rather than cessation devices."

Almost immediately after Premier was announced, Philip Morris began scrambling to come up with a competing reduced-harm product, even as it was wary about introducing a product that could cannibalize its own, lucrative cigarette market. The company knew long before Bowen and Monsees that combustion was a problem. They ramped up work on products collectively known as The Greeks, for their names Beta, Delta, and Sigma. Each technology relied on a different heating source, like carbon or iron nitride, and new materials like graphite to contain tobacco pellets that could be heated up. They accelerated work on Project Leap (as in a potential "leap in paradigm"), a nicotine vaporizer that was designed to deliver an "ideal smoke" in the form of a fine aqueous mist via an inhaler called a "capillary aerosol generator."

Developing the electrical heated-tobacco cigarette, called Beta, while also continuing research on vaporization became the two parallel paths that Philip Morris pursued with the most gusto. With Beta in particular, there were early stumbling blocks. Philip Morris, a company rooted in the agrarian discipline of tobacco farming, knew next to nothing about the emerging semiconductor industry and miniaturization of battery technology. And because Beta entailed specialty materials, like battery technology, sensors, electronics, and miniature circuits—mostly made in Asia—it had to cobble together a network of unfamiliar manufacturers and contractors, some of whom started to have second thoughts about the public price of working with a smoking product.

With all the half-baked technologies floating around inside the company, there was a lack of focus and top executives were growing impatient, as every quarter they seemed to be bleeding money on a suite of technologies that didn't show promising commercial appeal. The trick was creating something smokers actually thought tasted good and that delivered them the nicotine in a way that was deemed to be "satisfying"—the all-important buzzword in the industry. But nobody could agree on what exactly that would look like. The company did sophisticated research on the human senses, including studies to shed light on the trigeminal nerve, which had been shown to be linked to the sensory satisfaction of cigarettes. They dropped nicotine on human tongues and measured the response. They hooked gold-plated electrodes to humans' scalps to monitor how the body responded to smoking cigarettes of varying nicotine levels. Philip Morris scientists disagreed over how to proceed and whether the company was dumping money into an abyss.

"The kinds of things we have heard today sort of makes me wonder what the hell we are actually doing here," said a Philip Morris R&D
vice president at an internal research conference in 1990 that discussed
the sensory research. "Should we be isolating receptors, sticking electrodes into cells, looking at fluorescent blips go up in neurons? That's
so far away from somebody puffing on a cigarette and saying, 'I like
this.' You're telling me that something that's happening on the receptor end is going to be useful to some guy down at Stockton Street puffing a cigarette out on the corner?"

Around 1995, the company formed a panel to review their own
nonconventional tobacco products. Steve Parrish was appointed to
help lead the group, which was given the name Project Table (yes, after
a table), comprising employees from various Philip Morris departments, including marketing, legal, behavioral research, and R&D.

Parrish's group delved deeply into the history of tobacco as a
mechanism to determine the next best strategic move for the company. They reviewed literature on smoking behavior and habits. They
read *Cigarettes Are Sublime,* a book that was as much a repudiation of
the growing cultural disdain for smoking as an "ode and an elegy to
cigarettes" that drew on a wide range of thinkers, including Nietzsche,
Kant, Erasmus, and Bizet. And they discussed the need for a separate
Skunk Works company inside Philip Morris that would eschew its rigid
hierarchy in favor of "FLEXIBILITY, CREATIVITY and INNOVA-
TION." The internal start-up would be modeled after "the computer
industry" in "Silicon Valley" and also (perhaps forebodingly so) after
"industrial firms like Eastman Kodak" that "have made major changes
in the way they are organized and in the way they operate."

In the end the members of Project Table produced a report that
described their findings. The report listed dozens of patents and various "nicotine delivery devices" that were deemed competitive products, including other brands of cigarettes, cigars, pipes, snuff, nicotine
gum and patches, and even an injectable form of nicotine.

The report might have not generated a stir, except for one thing.
Just as they were dreaming up the next advance in cigarette technology, David Kessler, the then chairman of the FDA, was embarking on

his investigation of the tobacco industry. And it just so happened that his primary line of inquiry rested on proving that cigarette manufacturers had been intentionally manipulating the levels of nicotine in cigarettes for optimal delivery into the human body to promote and sustain addiction. If that were true, then wouldn't that make the mere cigarette a drug delivery device? And if they were drug delivery devices, then why wouldn't the FDA be regulating them?

The Table report became somewhat of a damning sensation primarily for what at the time was considered a stunning admission: "Different people smoke cigarettes for different reasons. But the primary reason is to deliver nicotine into their bodies," said the report, noting that nicotine was like other organic chemicals, including cocaine. Suddenly, all of the newfangled cigarettes that Philip Morris had been dreaming up in its laboratories appeared to be the exact evidence Kessler was in search of to support the theory that the company was in fact a drug company that sold nicotine-delivery devices.

In 1997, Philip Morris quietly released a commercial version of its heated-tobacco product, which it called Accord, but only on a limited basis in retail stores in Richmond, and for test marketing purposes in Japan, where the product was sold under the brand name Oasis. The product, which the company had spent huge sums to develop, was an entirely new way to smoke. Instead of lighting a cigarette on fire, the user would partially insert a specially designed Accord cigarette into a "lighter" about the size of a small cellphone and then bring the contraption up to the mouth and puff. Each puff would activate a battery, which in turn would gently heat the tobacco rather than burn it, resulting in no ash, less odor, and in theory fewer harmful compounds. Accord was eventually withdrawn from the market due to poor sales and a lack of consumer appeal.

Meanwhile, development of the Leap aerosol device was largely shelved, although a patent was filed and internal research on it continued. Just as Philip Morris had come *this* close to shaking up the cigarette market, the company's innovations largely sputtered out. All its grand ambitions of tapping into the Silicon Valley zeitgeist were engulfed by the weight of the moment—the attorneys general, the whistleblowers, the litigation, the FDA. As the end of the century dawned, so did Philip Morris's grandest ambitions.

ON MARCH 21, 2000, the U.S. Supreme Court delivered a stunning decision, one that gave the tobacco companies reason for hope. In the case, *FDA v. Brown & Williamson*, the court struck down the FDA's 1996 regulations that put tobacco products under its authority by declaring them drugs and drug-delivery devices. In a 5–4 decision, the justices held that Congress never delegated authority to the FDA to regulate tobacco products "as customarily marketed" and therefore found the agency's assertion of jurisdiction overstepped its bounds.

Writing for the majority, Sandra Day O'Connor recognized that the case involved "one of the most troubling public health problems facing our Nation today." But she wrote that since the FDA's mandate in essence required only the sale of products that were considered safe and effective, the agency would be forced to remove cigarettes from the market, "a result the court found clearly contrary to congressional intent." Given everything known about the dangers of smoking, "it would be impossible to prove they were safe for their intended use," wrote O'Connor. "The inescapable conclusion is that there is no room for tobacco products within the [agency's] regulatory scheme. If they cannot be used safely for any therapeutic purpose, and yet they cannot be banned, they simply do not fit," O'Connor wrote.

The court decision was a resounding, albeit temporary, win for the tobacco industry. The day the decision came down, tobacco companies cheered, with a Philip Morris statement praising the court for a decision that otherwise "could have led to Prohibition." However, the court left the door open for Congress to create a brand-new regulatory scheme for tobacco that could once and for all solve "the tobacco problem." That left the ball squarely in the hands of Congress.

The decision came at a moment when new thinking was emerging around smoking, not about the health risks of smoke and combustion but about the cigarette's raison d'être: nicotine. The persistence of smoking despite nearly four decades of the truth about cigarettes coming into public view left health advocates stuck facing an unsettling truth: Nicotine's spell had a powerful hold on America that would not be easily shrugged off. That realization touched off a simmering worry that as cigarettes had become such a contentious issue, largely centered on the scourge of youth smoking, adult smokers themselves had been demonized and left to cope with this deadly addiction, alone and in shame. The former surgeon general, Koop, who'd authored the seminal 1988 report stating the addictiveness of nicotine, wrote an op-ed in *The Washington Post* titled "Don't Forget the Smokers" in which he encouraged a regulatory scheme that would allow the FDA to "combine tobacco prevention initiatives with efforts to ensure that those who are hooked can obtain effective treatments" such as nicotine replacement therapies, like the patch or gum.

Then, in 2001, the Institute of Medicine of the National Academies released a much-anticipated report, commissioned by the FDA, that signaled a profound shift in thinking about nicotine among America's top public-health experts. The Institute had in recent years endorsed a concept that had been floating around for more than a decade, which was rooted in the idea that there were some public-health problems that could be solved not by eradicating an unhealthy behavior but by mitigating the harm caused by it, such as encouraging safe needle exchanges and bleach distribution for intravenous drug users to reduce the spread of HIV. Could a similar philosophy be applied to the tobacco epidemic?

The question was hotly debated. There were some in the public-health community who believed nothing less than complete abstinence from cigarettes, or at the most short-term use of cessation products strictly regulated by the FDA, such as nicotine gum and the patch, was in the public's interest. They argued that it simply wasn't a worthy goal to get behind a host of new products marketed by tobacco companies, even if they might be quote-unquote safer than a traditional cigarette. Others, including those in the tobacco industry, argued that if less deadly nicotine products existed, then regulators and policy experts would be remiss *not* to jump at the chance to make them available to the public even if their relative harm wasn't reduced to zero.

In its 2001 report, titled *Clearing the Smoke: Assessing the Science Base for Tobacco Harm Reduction,* the panel tried to strike a middle ground. "Harm reduction is a feasible and justifiable public health policy," wrote the committee, which comprised the nation's top experts in smoking-related health issues and nicotine dependency. "But only if it is implemented carefully." The committee cautioned that such products could be attractive to youth, and could prolong nicotine addiction among former smokers. Also, they said that not enough research had been done to draw any categorical conclusions about the health or safety of the new breed of products. Nevertheless, the committee urged lawmakers to develop a framework for the FDA to evaluate the safety and efficacy of "potential reduced exposure products" that could give smokers a less harmful way to get their nicotine fix.

Suddenly, in the wake of the Tobacco Wars nonetheless, there was a new national conversation about nicotine and its role in society. The field of nicotine research exploded. Health experts, including top officials at the FDA, began talking about "clean" ways for people to get their nicotine fix rather than the "dirty" route through a cigarette. More and more people were embracing this idea that smokers who wanted to quit shouldn't have to quit nicotine altogether. Like coffee drinkers or beer drinkers, they argued, there were people who enjoyed having nicotine in their life and as adults should have the right to do so.

That shifting conversation had a profound impact on the cigarette companies themselves. For the first time in years, they weren't apparently on death row. Instead, as amazing as it seemed, it was looking like they could very well be given an entirely new lease on life. Yes, it was a foregone conclusion that in one way or another there was going to be government regulation. But by now Philip Morris had announced that as part of its "realignment" with society it would support FDA regulation rather than thwart it at every turn. This wasn't simply an act of goodwill. Under Parrish's tutelage, Philip Morris was masterfully positioning itself so that instead of locking horns with government regulators, it could work in concert with them to shape the details of any bill that would inevitably emerge from Congress, however distant in the future that may be.

The company had warmed up to the idea of FDA regulation so long as the agency treated cigarettes as a complex product that, no matter how deadly, still could be accessed by smoking adults for continued legal use. Importantly, Philip Morris was pushing for regulations that would establish standards for determining what constituted a "reduced-risk" tobacco product. That would allow for a more predictable business environment, so its engineers could rekindle work on reduced-harm products without getting pegged as a drug company.

Like an apparition, Philip Morris was beginning to shape-shift. Instead of people talking about how the FDA might put the cigarette companies out of business, the dialogue moved with a sleight of hand to how the tobacco companies might be bearers of a solution to the problem that they created in the first place.

IN APRIL 2005, JOHN R. "Jack" Nelson, Philip Morris's then president of operations and technology, stood next to the then governor of Virginia, Mark Warner, near a patch of land in downtown Richmond. Two years earlier, Altria had moved its Philip Morris USA headquarters just south of this historic tobacco town. Now, the cigarette company was staking out its future in an increasingly post-cigarette world.

Nelson was a distinguished-looking gentleman, with a shock of white hair. A brilliant tobacco businessman and loyal foot soldier for Philip Morris, Nelson also had a chip on his shoulder. He'd obtained his doctorate in economic history from Northern Illinois University in 1979 and easily could have been an elite in academia. Instead, he chose a career in tobacco and had been with Philip Morris since 1982, long enough to see the company slog through the depths of skulduggery, past an era filled with the pangs of unrealized promise, into stuffy lawyers' offices to sit for grueling depositions as the company was buried in litigation.

Nelson managed to stay the course over those years, working in public and corporate affairs on topics like cigarette taxation, smoking restrictions, advertising bans, even working with Parrish on Project Table, as he climbed through the ranks. Ultimately, as president of operations and technology, he oversaw eight thousand employees and worked closely with the company's research and development initiatives. That role is what had brought him to this spot in downtown Richmond, on this day, to the site of what in two years' time would be the Philip Morris USA Research & Development Center, a 450,000-square-foot structure that ultimately would cost $350 million to build—its largest capital project in decades. It would employ five hundred scientists, researchers, and engineers, many with PhDs, recruited from around the world, who specialized in everything from nanotechnology to plant genomics.

"Innovation will carry us into the future," said Nelson, at the ceremonial event. Every day at Philip Morris, the future was becoming a matter of increased importance. Just because the Supreme Court and the shifting conversation had granted the company license to live didn't mean that the public thought their product was any more respectable. By 2005 the number of cigarettes sold in the United States had dropped to under 352 billion, down nearly 25 percent from 1998. Every year, the company increased the price of cigarettes to offset the money it had to pay to the states to adhere to the terms of the tobacco settlement. That had the effect of pricing out more current or future consumers.

"Over the past decade," Nelson continued, "Philip Morris USA has dedicated significant resources toward scientific research, new product development and commercialization, which might help address the harm caused by smoking. This center is another step in that effort."

There was a sort of gravitas, and perhaps paradox, to the moment: a cigarette company developing products that could kill the cigarette, in the heart of Virginia where tobacco farms, curing barns, and leaf-trading companies still stood. Nevertheless, the physical manifestation of this attempted rebirth was in the concrete that would soon be poured, the steel that would be erected, and the building that was destined to reshape the footprint of downtown Richmond.

Philip Morris envisioned the center containing not only buzzing research laboratories but also an inspiring incubator where the best and the brightest in tobacco could dream up new cigarette concepts over coffee or brainstorm new tobacco blends inside Innovation Alley, an area with a library and a "cybercafe." From the research center, board presentations suggested they might work on developing a more advanced cigarette filter. Or create more flavorful tobacco in little pouches called snus. They might make harm-reduction breakthroughs derived from the recently sequenced genome of the tobacco plant.

Philip Morris had long fancied itself an innovator, not least because it innovated its way to the top of the cigarette market, where it remained for more than a generation. When it introduced the "flip-top" cigarette box in the 1950s, that was a bona fide product design revolution for its time. The company invented the Marlboro Man. If that's not innovative, what is? But when it came down to it, the basics of the cigarette hadn't changed all that much since the Industrial Revolution, and most of the company innovations, if they could be characterized as such, had been in marketing and packaging rather than transforming the essence of the industry.

The pressure to do so was clearly felt throughout the company. "Need to be an ENGINE for Creativity and Innovation," wrote Richard Solana, the company's head of research and technology, in a presentation given at a planning meeting in June 2004 outlining steps needed to ramp up innovation. "What CAN the future be?"

Solana's division had recently articulated a new mandate to design products that "offer adults the enjoyable smoking experience of a Marlboro with a significantly lower health risk than conventional cigarette smoking." In 2004, a colleague outlined a series of "Product Visions" that included a spectrum, with a healthier "great tasting" cigarette on one end, new tobacco products that offered a similar smoking experience to cigarettes in the middle, and on the other end non-tobacco products that looked and tasted nothing like a cigarette but still provided smokers nicotine satisfaction. The ideas that fell into those three buckets ran the gamut, and even included the development of a "virtual cigarette" that would connect to a virtual-reality headset and allow users to "smoke" a device with a "puff detector" and a "flavor cylinder" that could be used in "an interactive-computer generated scene."

Some of the ideas that emerged from the brainstorming sessions were like creations from a tobacco-themed Willy Wonka factory: A "pill which partially dissolves in your mouth releasing pleasant taste—

once you swallow the rest dissolves in your stomach and gives you feeling that you had a meal"; "tobacco flavored popcorn"; "cigarette with exotic aroma such as roses, or herbs, which masks the smell of burning tobacco"; "tobacco extracts used for aerosol delivery device whereby consumer can enhance sensorial experience by attaching a cartridge or something . . . that contains a specific flavor such as 'brandy, margarita, white Russian, chocolate, licorice, candy bar, cognac, etc.' Consumer selects specific cartridge depending on mood or desire."; "Green tobacco tea"; "What about combining beer with nicotine?"

In 2005, Philip Morris executives were sent to attend a weeklong custom-made "strategic innovation" course at the Wharton School of the University of Pennsylvania that covered everything from idea generation to project selection to product commercialization. The same year, Philip Morris formed the Corporate Innovation Board, which was designed to bring together various silos across the company to help the most promising technologies get the funding they needed to see the light of day. The board comprised top-tier executives including the then CEO of Philip Morris USA, Mike Szymanczyk, who earlier in his career had been an executive at Procter & Gamble.

Szymanczyk's protégé, Howard Willard, attended the meetings. Willard had recently acquired a new "Corporate Responsibility" title, which built on his Youth Smoking Prevention work and included a broad range of controversial issues related to smoking. He'd also helped take charge of a new Responsibility Leadership Team, which was designed to ensure the company was pursuing opportunities and products that aligned with the company's role as a responsible member of society.

In 2004, Willard had overseen the introduction of a new Philip Morris smoking cessation website called QuitAssist, which—like the controversial "Think. Don't Smoke" ads that Philip Morris created—was shown in some research to have actually discouraged quitting by exposing attempted quitters to so many "repeated visual and auditory references to smoking and cigarettes" that they actually experienced "decreased confidence in quitting and lower likelihood of a quit attempt."

The same year, Willard struck a deal with Duke University, awarding the school of medicine $15 million to establish a new "Center for Nicotine and Smoking Cessation Research," which would be led by the renowned nicotine researcher Jed Rose. Rose had become a sought-after expert in the growing field of nicotine replacement and part of a coterie of eminent scientists suddenly in high demand who studied the complex universe of nicotine, from the pharmacokinetics of the drug, to its abuse liability, to the efficacy of administering it via alternate routes, such as in chewing gums or transdermally. In the 1980s Rose co-invented the nicotine patch, and in 1989 he moved his Nicotine Research Program from the University of California, Los Angeles to Duke University, a learning institution with deep ties to the tobacco industry from its historic endowment by tobacco industrialist, James "Buck" Duke, the father of modern American cigarette manufacturing. The new Philip Morris–funded Duke center was designed to conduct research on adult cessation in the furtherance of Philip Morris's efforts to "help smokers who have decided to quit smoking be more successful at quitting."

Meanwhile, Philip Morris struggled with knowing what to do with its earlier "capillary aerosol generator" invention, arguably a sophisticated precursor to the electronic cigarette. In 2000 the company had established a subsidiary called Chrysalis Technologies to commercialize the nicotine aerosol technology instead as a pharmaceutical pulmonary inhaler that it called Aria. In 2005 Chrysalis licensed its technology to a biotechnology company that sought to use the inhaler as a platform to deliver its proprietary drug into the lungs of breathing-impaired infants in neonatal intensive care units.

Philip Morris was in the throes of metamorphosis. The future was staring the company in its face. Howard Willard was helping reshape the transformation, however halting it was.

THE WINDOW OF INNOVATION at Philip Morris USA was short and the force that pushed it shut was the splitting of its parent company. In August 2007, Altria announced that the Philip Morris International division of the company was being spun off into an independent entity, a hallmark moment in the company's history that had long been in the works. The globe-spanning food-beer-cigarette conglomerate built over two decades was coming apart at the seams as the tobacco company sought to reduce costs, shed assets, and reinvent itself. Just a few months earlier, Kraft had been spun off as an independent company. Before that, the Miller beer brand had been sold to a South African brewing company. The company had recently announced that it was shuttering a once-important cigarette manufacturing plant in North Carolina, citing shrinking demand and a desire to cut costs amounting to $335 million a year.

Over the past several years, tensions had been brewing between Philip Morris USA and the company's international division, in part over the strategic long-term futures of each. In Lausanne, Switzerland, where PMI was based, the company's executives had grown tired of having to deal with the stifling legal woes of an American arm that they believed had become, more or less, uninspired. The split freed PMI from the shackles of the U.S. litigation and protected overseas markets from getting dragged into the morass. It also allowed PMI to go after the global cigarette market with gusto. In many places around the world, in particular in developing economies like Indonesia, China, and Brazil, cigarette consumption was still growing. And, critically, it was unencumbered by the same strict advertising restrictions, settlement costs, and to an extent, die-hard anti-tobacco foes.

But the newly independent international company also made a decision that set it on a radically different path from its counterpart in Richmond. Executives at PMI possessed a deeply held belief that ultimately the nicotine business had to embrace next-generation reduced-harm products, and as a result would start looking less like a consumer-goods industry and more like that of the pharmaceutical or medical device industry. So, the company set out to focus on a new strategy, one that was based almost entirely on developing a reduced-harm, noncombustible tobacco product, to deliver on the promise of creating "a smoke-free future," even as it still heavily marketed Marlboro Reds the world over. The company built a new $100 million R&D center in Neuchâtel that was made almost entirely of glass and built on the banks of a glittering lake aside gardens and terraces and views of the Swiss Alps. The center, known as The Cube, looked more like it belonged to a high tech pharmaceutical company than a dirty cigarette company, which was exactly the point.

In the division of assets between PMI and Altria, the new international company had inherited the rights to various technologies. Among those was the intellectual property associated with the Accord heated cigarette device, which Altria had taken off the market before the companies split, after languishing for years in test markets with lackluster sales. While the U.S. leadership had decided that the product didn't have a future in the United States, PMI took the old technology and ran with it. Using Accord as a basis, they developed a better battery system and improved on the old heat-not-burn technology, ultimately launching a version of the heated cigarette product called IQOS. PMI also began work on nontobacco based nicotine aerosols. At every turn, PMI seemed eager to leverage products for the future.

Meanwhile, Mike Szymanczyk was named chief executive officer of the newly independent Altria, which announced that its new corporate headquarters would be based just outside Richmond, in the same offices that Philip Morris USA had been using for the past few years inside a historic building once home to Reynolds Metals, the aluminum giant. When the split happened, Philip Morris executives were exuberant about their newly won freedom, so much so that they toasted champagne in the grassy inner courtyard of the offices to celebrate. Many of the Richmond-based Philip Morris managers had grown irritated with their Manhattan masters when Altria was still headquartered there. "Finally we don't have to kowtow to Altria anymore" was the attitude of executives who behaved like their ancestors from the Revolutionary War, winning independence from a colonizing king. Some executives even pushed (ultimately in vain) to have the company's name changed back to Philip Morris. After all, now that there was nothing other than good-old tobacco under the hood, why hide behind a corporate façade any longer? That created an air of arrogance. "That group in Richmond, they think the world started when they came around," said one insider.

The attitude was partly a function of the corporate culture created by Szymanczyk. Even before the split Philip Morris had always been somewhat rigid, hierarchical, and insular. But under the consolidated reign of Szymanczyk, it became even more intense. Even as the towering figure had deftly shepherded Philip Morris through its darkest days, he engendered fear throughout the organization, with some people likening him to a Darth Vader who would cause people to shrink in their chairs and a room to fall silent upon his entrance. To the uninitiated, doing something like correcting Szymanczyk in a meeting, or speaking out of turn, would be tantamount to slitting your own throat. He reserved the front parking spots at the Richmond headquarters for the executive leadership team, including the most primo spot for himself and his Ferrari. One former Altria executive described how the parking strategy was deliberately designed to engender a healthy dose of envy so lower-level employees would be incentivized to scramble up the cutthroat corporate ladder.

"Mike ran everything," said another insider. "Everyone was scared shitless. Mike would say something and it was like the Emperor had no clothes—they'd say 'you're exactly right, Mike.'"

Another former executive said that working at the new Altria was like working for the CIA. The dark wood-paneled boardroom that was the onsite location for executive meetings had one wall made of glass. With a flip of a switch, a screen would draw down so nobody could see inside as executives sat around a big mahogany table, leaning back in their leather chairs. Its soundproofed walls kept prying ears away, as did the security team—often retired Secret Service or FBI—who would sweep the room for bugs ahead of important meetings. "It was very tobacco," one former executive described. "There was a high level of paranoia."

That bred a very clubby environment where people who had worked there for decades, long enough to live through the Tobacco Wars, saw one another as allies who fought the entire world together and came out the other side. Outsiders were looked on with suspicion. Rarely would a newer hire make it to the C-suite. People openly talked about the secret to success there: "You've got to be an asshole," said one former executive. "Everybody was Machiavellian."

Szymanczyk had his favorites, and one of them clearly was Howard Willard. Willard thrived, in part out of his eagerness to please Szymanczyk. He moved swiftly up the ranks, mystifying some people around him who wondered what quality, exactly, was contributing to his success. Multiple people, when asked what propelled Willard upward in the company, responded with a similar refrain that seemed to have evolved into lore: He was "Mini Mike." Willard had been diligently following in the footsteps of Szymanczyk and by mimicking his tone and tenor earned the nickname that followed him ever since. "If Mike says whatever, it was Howard who would be the first one to say 'absolutely we should go and make that happen,'" said one former Altria executive.

"Howard, he was Mike's boy," said another.

Upon taking over, Szymanczyk named Willard a member of his new management team, and promoted him to executive vice president for strategy and business development, where he was tasked with, among other things, handling mergers and acquisitions for the company. In that capacity Willard became a high-powered dealmaker atop the company when such transactions were seen as increasingly instrumental to the company's future—and survival.

NOW WITH THE INTERNATIONAL division detached, Szymanczyk was left to steer the storied American cigarette company into the future. Even as the U.S.-based company had been talking about pouring billions into innovation, and recently saw the completion of the massive research center in downtown Richmond, it was facing a tough truth. Despite all the decades of tinkering and testing and sinking billions of dollars into projects like The Greeks and Table and Ambrosia and Accord, and other futuristic imaginings of what tobacco and nicotine could be, essentially all that was left in the new Richmond-based Altria's innovation pipeline was unimaginative variations on the same shredded tobacco sticks it had been hawking for a century.

Yet Szymanczyk was strongly convinced that instead of shooting for the stars with futuristic contraptions or tobacco tea or licorice-flavored aerosols, the company's reduced-risk future lay much closer to home. In particular, he believed that smokeless tobacco products, such as Swedish-like snus and moist smokeless tobacco, could be the company's strategic way forward. Unlike Accord, which had been a sales disaster in the U.S. markets, smokeless tobacco was already widely accepted across wide swaths of the U.S. market, including in the South and among professional athletes. That meant they wouldn't have an uphill battle convincing consumers. It was a known quantity. At the same time, Szymanczyk believed that there was the added benefit of being able to ride on the back of decades of health outcome evidence from Scandinavian countries that showed that snus actually did present a potential reduced-risk option for people—aside, of course, from oral cancer. That would save the company precious time and money on complicated clinical trials. Above all else, the strategy required precious little imagination.

So, as other companies were readying new products to bring to market, Szymanczyk doubled down on good old-fashioned *tobacco* tobacco. Executives began developing what it called an "adjacency" strategy, which entailed expanding its core tobacco business into more tobacco products and capitalizing on existing brands for product-line extensions. In November 2007 Altria paid $2.9 billion to acquire cigar maker John Middleton Inc., maker of the Black & Mild brand that sold the popular "little cigars" that came in flavors like cherry and vanilla, which coincidentally or not had recently become popular among youth. It expanded the distribution of a new Marlboro-branded "spit free" tobacco pouch product, called snus.

Yet, Altria's new smokeless products never gained meaningful traction against the dominant smokeless brands at the time, Skoal and Copenhagen. Those were owned by the smokeless behemoth, UST Inc., a company that Philip Morris USA had long eyed, viewing it as a ripe acquisition target. In 2006, their competitor Reynolds paid $3.5 billion to acquire Conwood, the second-largest smokeless tobacco maker in the United States, which had been owned since the 1980s by the ultra-wealthy Pritzker family in Chicago. From that standpoint, an acquisition made even more sense. On at least one occasion before the split,

Szymanczyk's guys in Richmond had floated the idea of buying UST to the Altria management in New York. They were shot down. The reason? The price tag was too high.

But now, there was nobody to hold them back, and the potential conquest was as tempting as ever. Szymanczyk had put a lot of faith into Willard. And Willard had a lot of reasons to want to please his mentor. So, with his newly empowered M&A role, Willard was eager to flex that muscle. And in a decision that would become the company's—and Willard's—go-to template for growth, Altria executives decided, to hell with launching and branding new products from the ground up. Rather than go head-to-head with the smokeless giant, why not deploy the biggest weapon it had in its arsenal: cash.

In September 2008, just about six months after the PMI split, Willard helped structure a deal that at the time was a blockbuster. Altria paid $10.4 billion to buy UST, which gave the company not only the premium moist-snuff brands but also UST's premium wine brand, Ste. Michelle Wine Estates Ltd.

The UST acquisition was Altria's first major transaction since it spun off Kraft and PMI, and investors were watching the company closely to divine the management ethos at the newly unburdened entity. There was surprise among analysts who questioned whether the company overpaid. "At about $68 a share, Altria would be paying roughly 18 times UST's earnings," wrote *The Wall Street Journal*. "That is 50% more than Altria's own valuation multiple. It also is $2 billion more than UST's market value at Thursday's close."

Willard's first big deal in his new role was getting middling reviews, and though he may not have known it when Altria inked it, the timing couldn't have been worse. The Great Recession was bearing down on the U.S. economy and markets were on the brink of collapse. The UST deal was announced in September 2008, just a week before Lehman Brothers filed for bankruptcy. Not only was the deal price tag eye-popping, but it left no escape hatch or force majeure. That meant when the financial crisis hit, the company had no way of backing out.

Then, only a month after the deal was announced, Altria said that it was being postponed at the request of its lenders. Ultimately to finance the deal, Altria was forced to issue debt at higher-than-usual rates, which ultimately inflated the cost of the transaction. One person inside the company at the time was astounded that Altria had made such a rookie move by signing off on something that left no room for contingencies. But given the tone that had been set from the top, there was little room for second-guessing. "Mike bet the farm on smokeless tobacco so that's the way we're going to go," said another former Altria executive.

What wasn't apparent then was that Willard had only gotten a taste of being a gung-ho dealmaker. He was only getting started.

4

ON THE HUNT

Art is what you can get away with.
—ANDY WARHOL

Steve Parrish listened intently as Bowen and Monsees regaled him with the story of their tobacco creation, Ploom, sitting in their Dogpatch workshop in the middle of 2009. For a tobacco executive, Parrish maintained a surprisingly gentle and open air about him. He'd received a call from Valani and agreed to make the trip. Having recently retired from Philip Morris, after a long, extraordinarily momentous career, he'd already launched his own public relations and crisis management consulting firm. The Ploom team wanted to know if Parrish would consider joining the company as a chief executive officer or as a consultant.

It wasn't hard to see why they'd want Parrish. Despite all the years helping cover for the tobacco company, he'd done a 180, turning himself from the face of one of America's most vilified companies into a paragon of corporate responsibility. Despite the skeptics, Parrish seemed to truly have had a change of heart. He no longer smoked, and his lean physique indicated that he'd had the time to prioritize his health. Now, instead of wearing his usual soul-sucking suit and noose-like tie, he preferred jeans and a T-shirt and a silver chain around his neck. He'd put in his time—and seemed absolved of sin.

His deep insider experience at Altria made him a sought-after sage to major corporations, where he'd school management teams on his trademark buzzwords gleaned from the Tobacco Wars, like "societal alignment" and "permission to exist" and repackage them for executives wanting to learn about business ethics, boardroom strategies, and corporate responsibility. He'd publicly made amends with his former archnemesis, the FDA's David Kessler, appearing at a high-profile addiction and substance abuse conference aside him. He gave speeches to the Rotary Club decrying the tobacco industry's "silence and inaction" over the years.

"What's your endgame here?" Parrish finally asked the two entrepreneurs. "Do you want to grow this into a business or license your technology?"

"We're not sure quite yet," Monsees replied, puffing on his Ploom. "But I can tell you this: It's going to rock the tobacco industry."

Ultimately, Parrish wasn't interested in joining Ploom. "Look, guys," he said. "I'm impressed. But I just retired." He already had a full plate and didn't want to commit to anything else. But he was gracious with his Rolodex and passed along names of former tobacco executives like himself who might consider joining the cause.

Bowen and Monsees had their backs up against a wall. They'd been diligently pouring their heart into Ploom, but it still wasn't much more than a school experiment. They'd hired some additional employees, and they'd started making some of the Ploom devices at a factory in Taiwan that also made butane-powered curling irons. Monsees had been working around the clock, traveling back and forth between San Francisco and Taiwan as he worked to build relationships and expertise with contract manufacturers on the ground. He'd work all day in Taiwan, and then stay up all night making phone calls to California from his cheap motel, concerning those close to him who worried he was burning the candle at both ends. Bowen, meanwhile, was the company's CEO and was trying to keep the company afloat. But months passed and the product still wasn't ready for commercial launch.

Valani, Ploom's single largest shareholder, was getting nervous. The start-up was edging toward running out of money and he wasn't eager to squander his bet, especially before the product even got off the ground. He watched the two cofounders struggle with basic day-to-day managerial tasks. While Bowen, the CEO, was a gifted engineer, he wasn't a bean counter. The books were being kept largely by hand, and the financial data being reported to him and the board of directors was sometimes confusing, leaving an incomplete picture of the company's state of affairs.

Valani had launched an informal search for an outsider to come in and take on a leadership role at the company, which was why Parrish had been summoned to San Francisco. But recruiting somebody to lead the shoestring start-up wasn't going to be easy. One night, while Monsees was in Taiwan, he received an angry phone call from Valani. Bowen was also on the line. "Something has got to change," Valani told the two, according to a person who was told about the call. Bowen and Monsees might've had the purest mission in the world, but Valani was a sharp-eyed venture capitalist, not a philanthropist.

Bowen and Monsees pleaded with Valani to give them some more time. They'd gone to the ends of the earth and back to get as far as they had, and they couldn't fathom giving up now. Ultimately Valani agreed, but on certain conditions. Bowen and Monsees had to switch roles. Bowen would be put into a more inner-facing role as a chief technology officer. And Monsees would become CEO. Not only that, but as CEO Monsees would have to promise that he'd make it his mission to drum up new investors. Valani didn't want to be so overexposed. They agreed, and as it turned out: "James turned out to be a better manager and a better financial guy," said a person familiar with the arrangement.

Valani became an intensely involved investor as he tried to tighten the reins on the young entrepreneurs. He insisted that he get daily updates—about new fundraising prospects; about strategy; about the daily minutiae of the business—to ensure things wouldn't go off the rails.

Finally, by the spring of 2009, the Ploom Model One was finally ready to be rolled out to the world. Unlike their original Stanford design that vaporized tufts of tobacco wrapped in paper, the Model One used butane to heat up little aluminum Keurig-like pods filled with tobacco. A piezoelectric igniter would kick on the heater and vaporize the shredded leaf inside the pods that came in various flavors, including Rocket, Café Noir, and Kick-Ass Mint. The shiny, colorful pods were neatly packaged in a sleek white box that resembled the packaging of an iPhone. To celebrate, Bowen and Monsees turned their Dogpatch office into a party spot for a night and invited friends over to have beers and listen to music. They set up a table in one corner to serve as a tasting area so people could try the device and test out different flavors.

But the celebrating didn't last long. Bowen and Monsees were under the gun. To live up to his end of the bargain with Valani, Monsees became a fundraising machine. As he juggled the launch of the product, he was furiously trying to drum up investor interest, calling everybody he knew, from Stanford to the venture capital world and beyond. The exercise prompted some uncomfortable soul-searching. It became obvious almost immediately that a potentially plentiful source of money was dwelling in a place they'd always treated as taboo: in the coffers of Big Tobacco. No matter how much Bowen and Monsees had demonized the cigarette industry, in their own minds, and as the bedrock of their origin story, they recognized that there was potentially a lot of upside in walking right up to the doorstep of the devil.

BY THE SPRING OF 2009, Monsees, through the grapevine, made a connection with Chris Skillin, a well-connected tobacco executive who'd recently left Altria after a nearly twenty-year career at the company. He'd worked in the Swiss offices of Philip Morris International and also in Richmond, where his last job had been director of corporate business development. He'd recently received a call from some investment bankers with ties to the tobacco industry. The bankers told him they'd heard of these two guys in San Francisco who were working on some crazy project and looking for somebody with financial acumen in the tobacco industry.

Skillin flew out to San Francisco, where he met with Bowen, Monsees, and Valani. Sitting around a conference table at their offices in the Dogpatch, he was amazed at the depth of knowledge the two founders seemed to have about the industry. When they showed him the Ploom, he was impressed by the unique shape and the slick pods. Afterward, he immediately called up some old colleagues at Philip Morris International, thinking they'd have some interest. They did.

Since the split with Philip Morris USA in 2007, PMI had been eager to strike gold in a market that they believed held the promise of the future. Unlike the Richmond guys at Philip Morris USA who'd doubled down on smokeless tobacco as their harm-reduction bet, the group in Switzerland was morphing into a high-end research company. Soon, Lausanne was stacked with heavy hitters from pharmaceutical companies like Novartis, and experts familiar with how to run clinical trials and amass safety data structured in a way to meet regulatory guidelines. All of this was in the service of coming up with a new product that could replace the combustible cigarette.

PMI management was eager to accelerate development of its pipeline of next-generation products and began scouring the globe for novel technologies. Throughout the mid–late 2000s, they hosted a revolving cast of technologists in their impressive Lausanne Rhodanie operations center, including the makers of Hon Lik's Ruyan e-cigarette, a propellant-driven room-temperature inhaler company, and Jed Rose, the world-renowned nicotine expert who'd entered into a research agreement with Philip Morris USA at Duke University a few years earlier. Rose had been conducting groundbreaking research on a type of nicotine "salt" formulation that held out the promise of delivering a more satisfying nicotine hit to smokers unsatisfied with current cessation products.

In May 2009, Bowen, Valani, and Skillin flew to Lausanne, where they met with two top executives at the Philip Morris International offices, Simon Langelier, the president of Next Generation Products, and Doug Dean, the senior vice president of R&D. As Skillin suspected, the PMI people seemed to be impressed. They liked the Stanford smarts behind the product and thought it had a slick look to it with the little Nespresso-like pods. But the Ploom team came off as clueless about the potential regulatory implications of claiming their product was somehow safer than cigarettes. More than anything, they were taken aback by some of the obvious design flaws. At one point, as the seasoned and sophisticated PMI executives passed around a prototype of Ploom, Langelier got a shock from the electric igniter as he tried to fire it up. It seemed unfathomable that anybody in their right mind would want to put this thing, with a burning-hot butane tank, anywhere near their face, let alone in between their lips.

Also, while Bowen came across as smart and engaging, the two Philip Morris International executives wondered what, exactly, Valani brought to the table. He appeared to lack any technical knowledge whatsoever about the product and had nothing substantive to add to the conversation other than talking about money. At one point Valani was abruptly cut off by Langelier, after the investor uncouthly asked what PMI might be willing to pay for Ploom. It was a wholly inappropriate question to be asking on a first meeting.

Nonetheless, the PMI executives didn't give the Ploom team a hard "no." Instead, they signed nondisclosure agreements and asked Bowen to send over some of the devices to R&D for a detailed technical evaluation. But after three months of internal review, PMI decided the technology simply wasn't what they were looking for and they declined the opportunity to invest in the company.

ONE MIGHT CONSIDER AT this juncture whether their new direction perhaps made Bowen and Monsees hypocrites—or whether they had any cognitive dissonance as they set out to build a business ostensibly designed to destroy the cigarette by plugging into a network of people who sold them. But the two had no qualms whatsoever. What better way to unseat the enemy than to turn the enemy's own weapons against them. That was a tried-and-true tactic of war. As Sun Tzu said, "If you know the enemy and know yourself, you need not fear the result of a hundred battles."

Whether it was a matter of fate, or just the simple march of time, there happened to be a veritable sea of tobacco executives nearing retirement after a long career doing the industry's bidding. All somebody had to do was pick up the phone and call them.

Monsees lived up to his end of the bargain—he built an impressive Rolodex filled with tobacco executives who agreed to help, some as paid consultants. For early legal and regulatory advice they recruited Charles Blixt, a combative Reynolds executive and longtime general counsel for the company. To help them better understand the science of smoke, they recruited Christopher Coggins, another retired Reynolds executive who was one of the world's foremost inhalation toxicologists and who, notably, was widely credited for driving the development of the Premier cigarette. They enlisted Bradley Ingebrethsen, a renowned Reynolds expert in tobacco aerosol particles who also invented an early version of a nicotine aerosol inhaler in the early 1990s. And they had on speed dial Thomas Perfetti, a former Reynolds scientist and nicotine salt expert.

Many in the industry had in fact already heard of Bowen and Monsees before they'd even received a call from the "Stanford kids," as they were sometimes called. Tobacco executives are not unlike spies. They pride themselves on having a deep network of contacts that stretched from the corporate boardrooms of Richmond to the research labs of Neuchâtel to the Wall Street investment banks, which had already spent a generation getting fat off a fee-larded trail of tobacco mergers and acquisitions and spin-offs and debt capital.

Meanwhile, beyond Ploom, e-cigarettes and vaping were only just beginning to turn into a fad. Even as tobacco shops had shuttered over the decades, vape shops were starting to pop up around the country, on street corners, in mall kiosks and on informercials. People started experimenting with vaporizing everything they could get their hands on, from tobacco and pot, to vitamin C and Viagra. Giant tabletop

vaporizers with names like "The Volcano" had a cult following. Hobby-
ists used devices that went by names like "mods"—modified vaporizers with variable temperature and wattage measured in joules. And
they engaged in activities with wonky terms like "dripping"—heating
e-liquid on a coil rather than in a tank—or "sub-ohming"—cranking
up the heat and adjusting copper coils to get monster billows of vapor.
Competitions pitted the often tattooed and pierced "cloud chasers"
against one another to see who could generate the biggest vapor
clouds, while spectators called "cloud gazers" cheered them on. Suddenly, it seemed, a new breed of human–turned–fire-breathing dragon
was walking the earth.

Independently owned shops mixed up vape "juice" or "e-liquid"
out of their homes or in commercial kitchens, cooking up crude nicotine potions made with propylene glycol, vegetable glycerin, and flavors, like cola, croissant, Turkish tobacco, gummy bear, or hibiscus.
Vaping began attracting die-hard evangelicals who swore by its power
to get them off cigarettes once and for all. It spread across the country
as it became its own blossoming subculture and cottage industry.

Unlike earlier smokeless cigarettes made by the big tobacco companies, like Premier or Accord, consumers were taking to this latest innovation. The culture around smoking had shifted so radically, with
people frowning on dirty cigarettes more and more, that by 2009
smokers were warming up to new alternatives like e-cigarettes that
delivered a decent nicotine fix and allowed them to use it in the growing number of establishments that had banned stinky cigarettes.

As the exotic mods and vape contraptions were gaining currency in
America, Hon Lik's e-cigarette creation was starting to catch on, and
copycat companies began pumping them out to fulfill a growing demand. Chinese battery and microelectronics technology had improved
so dramatically that the devices could now function with miniaturized
components that could squeeze into slim, cylindrical designs that ap-
proximated a cigarette. Hundreds of companies, some with little more
than a webpage and a relationship with a factory in China, began
sprouting up. E-cigarettes began arriving on American shores by the
boatload. It was the beginning of a new nicotine gold rush.

Rather suddenly, the old tobacco companies were confronted with a potentially viable outsider threat to their business, perhaps the biggest they'd seen since the invention of the nicotine patch. Old-timers at the top of legacy tobacco companies began sizing up the new industry, like Goliath watching out of one eye as David gathered stones. That entailed sending delegations to China to vet key players, to broker relations with manufacturers, and to scout potential talent. "It was like pandemonium in the tobacco industry," recalled one banker who'd done a fair share of sizeable tobacco deals. "Every company was scrambling to find a technology and a bet."

So when Bowen and Monsees rang, many tobacco executives were intrigued, if not slightly amused, upon learning of the plucky whiz kids trying to take on Big Tobacco. *As if,* many of them thought. If nothing else, they'd accept an invitation Bowen and Monsees extended to them and enjoy a jaunt to San Francisco—and maybe derive some schadenfreude watching some scrappy anti-smoking liberals falling on their faces trying to tangle with the beast.

Some tobacco executives had no compunction taking their corporate jets to see the founders in San Francisco, if not out of graciousness or a desire to leave their cozy southern tobacco lairs, at least to get a look under the hood and kick the tires on Ploom. But not Jack Nelson.

By the time Bowen and Monsees came around, Nelson had been named Altria's chief technology officer, reporting directly to Szymanczyk. It might have seemed kind of weird for there to be a "technology" officer at a tobacco company, but the newly independent Altria was almost desperate to see itself an innovator, and innovators needed to have a CTO to signal to the world that the company had big thinkers tackling big challenges.

When Bowen and Monsees requested a meeting with him, the tall, bombastic executive had no intention of budging from his shiny tower firmly ensconced in the ancestral homeland of Big Tobacco. Inside Philip Morris there was no shortage of big personalities, but Nelson had one in spades. Perhaps no one more than he felt that the sun rose and set on Marlboro, every single day. Hell would freeze over before he'd fly out west to meet with Ploom. His mentality was: *I'm the one with the checkbook. If you two kids want something from me, you can drag your asses to the Old Dominion.* Bowen and Monsees weren't beneath schlepping at this point. They were in pursuit of a paycheck.

Bowen, Monsees, and Valani flew to Richmond and made their way to Nelson's office at the company's fancy new innovation center, which sat just a few blocks away from the old Tobacco Row, an industrial neighborhood along the banks of the James River once lined with smoke-belching cigarette factories and fragrant tobacco warehouses that had since been turned into upscale lofts and shops imbued with all the telltale signs of gentrification. Nelson was eager to show off the new digs—and signal that it wasn't only Silicon Valley techies who could innovate.

Bowen and Monsees had been briefed ahead of time. Nelson was a well-respected Philip Morris lifer who had a swashbuckling attitude that could come off as arrogance. He was such a domineering driver of the company's innovation initiatives that some people in the company referred to him simply as Captain Jack.

When the three visitors walked into Captain Jack's domain, the first thing he did after shaking their hands was lean back in his chair and swing his feet up. He explained that they were sitting at the center of Philip Morris's innovation efforts. "What you guys are doing is cute," he said. "But here at Philip Morris, we've got decades of experience in the science of tobacco. If anyone's going to innovate in this space, it's going to be us."

Neither Bowen nor Monsees was the groveling type, and Captain Jack was rubbing them the wrong way. As the two camps sized each other up, a person who was told about the meeting summed it up thusly: On the Altria side, "These guys are like, 'Who the hell are you?'" to Bowen and Monsees. And Bowen and Monsees, in return, "They're like 'Who the hell are *you*, we're going to eat you for lunch.'"

The California founders brought the Ploom kit with them—the little butane canisters, the colorful Keurig-like tobacco pods, and their cherished tobacco vaporizing device that they'd birthed at Stanford and poured their hearts and souls into ever since. Nelson wasn't enthralled. After almost thirty years at the company, he'd seen it all—the

Beta and the Sigma, the VR cigarette and the rose-scented smoke, and the Kodak flashbulbs—practically before Bowen and Monsees were even born. He was accustomed to hearing outsiders claim that they alone possessed the silver bullet to fix the cigarette business.

Nelson practically rolled his eyes when Bowen and Monsees explained that the reason they were so confident in their product was in part because they'd taken it to bars and parties in California and had people come up to them to say how cool it was. For a guy accustomed to digesting piles of studies and reams of data in his sleep, this type of anecdotal research seemed immature at best. *Of course girls would have nice things to say about Ploom,* Nelson told others later, *when it was being pitched by two young, good-looking guys from Stanford.*

Beyond that, and more importantly, Nelson thought that Ploom sucked. This thing that Bowen and Monsees were showing to him was child's play. It barely gave a decent nicotine hit, and the hit it did give was so unrefined that it caused the user to spontaneously cough. It was obvious they hadn't bothered to perfect the science of smoke chemistry. And when it was turned on the damn thing would get so hot that it was nearly impossible to hold. They were clearly amateurs.

It really wasn't much of a stretch at all for Nelson and others at Altria to arrive at a fairly confident conclusion that they weren't going to waste their time with Ploom. They had bigger budgets than the GDP of some small nations, and at that very moment they had an army of scientists and PhDs toiling away. Bowen and Monsees came home not only empty-handed but feeling burned.

KURT SONDEREGGER, THE FIRST Ploom employee, had begun taking the Model One around San Francisco to get it into as many hands as possible. He took it to smoke shops on Haight Street, liquor stores, and upscale convenience stores. He arranged tasting events at bars, using custom-made illuminated trays that held two of the devices and the pods so people could enjoy using the product in darkened nightclubs or bars. Bartenders were left with tiny canisters of butane to distribute to customers.

Over nine days in September 2009, in what came to be called Project Ploomonaut, Bowen and Monsees sent a few of the Ploom devices to Burning Man, the Nevada festival that Silicon Valley start-ups have long used to beta test products, including a Tesla prototype and an early version of Google Maps. They wanted to see how the product would withstand the extreme conditions of the Black Rock Desert.

One beta tester who set up camp at Opulent Temple, the techno-glow-robotic-fire camp, kept a journal about the experience. Day One: "The reality of playa Plooming was quickly realized. It would be more difficult than I thought," read one of the journal entries. "I made the mistake of not finding a proper carrying case for the Ploom before I left. Therefore, I was left with only my jacket or pant pockets to carry the Ploom itself. This didn't work well. The tip fell off every time I removed it from a pocket. Sort of annoying."

Day Two: "I was about to share a Ploom with a camp member. I quickly realized I was out of fuel and forgot to bring the butane with me. Another annoying inconvenience realized."

At the end, the beta tester had successfully shared Ploom with fellow Burners who'd enjoyed the flavor and the concept. But there was a stark takeaway: "The harsh playa conditions and labor intensive camp maintenance work did not mix well with Plooming. Why? Less is more. It takes much more effort to get the Ploom experience up and running than it does to light up a ciggerate [sic]. There are too many working pieces and too many steps in the Plooming process (butane, ploom, ploom tip, pack of pods with sliding tray design, old pod, new pod). Ciggies are simple . . . a pack, ciggie, lighter . . . puff puff smoke smoke."

The Burning Man flop only echoed the feedback that had been coming in, not just from potential investors but from the smoke shops and bars and convenience stores where the product was being sold. Sales were lackluster at best. Those who tried the product routinely said the device was either too cumbersome or simply didn't deliver nicotine nearly as well as a cigarette. Or both. And there wasn't much hope of it improving. To fix the very problematic heat issue, the Ploom team resorted to slapping a sticker that said "Hot" on the device. Even Sonderegger, the sales guy and a smoker, would complain that Ploom didn't deliver enough nicotine. He sometimes taped together two Plooms to get the jolt he craved, pissing off Monsees, who'd flash him an angry look. "He'd take that as a hint that he failed as an engineer," Sonderegger said.

It was becoming clearer by the day that the product might be a flop. That was a tough pill to swallow for the founders. They'd spent so much time babying Ploom, from the feathered Stanford nest to here, that they struggled to come to terms with the prospect of failure. When negative feedback came in from retailers, Monsees was quick to dismiss it and would pin blame on the person selling the device. At one point, Sonderegger grew so frustrated that he implored Bowen to come with him on a sales tour to see firsthand some problems. On one visit to a shop, somebody got shocked. On another, a person burned their lips. Bowen was mortified. It was an eye-opener.

By the end of the year, Bowen and Monsees had struck out enough times and began realizing they might need to pivot. They started conceptualizing the idea for a battery-operated Ploom device, to get rid of the butane. They also pondered whether there was more money to be made in the cannabis space. There was a growing number of people who wanted newer, cleaner ways to consume their favorite weed or cannabis oil as more states began allowing the use of medical and recreational marijuana. Interestingly, that idea gained traction among investors who hadn't wanted to touch tobacco with a ten-foot pole.

In the fall of 2009 Bowen and Monsees were able to bring in more funding. This time they raised nearly $850,000, some from Valani and Sand Hill Angels, and more from other venture capital firms, including Quantum Technology and Originate, valuing Ploom at $10 million. The cash infusion allowed the company to keep growing.

AS ANYBODY WHO HAS ever lusted over the latest version of the Apple iPhone knows, modern consumer technology—and really the entire beating heart of Silicon Valley—was built on design. For everything from Bird scooters and VR glasses to self-driving cars and connected doorbells, the aesthetic of the latest gadgets ranked as high as, and sometimes higher than, the functionality of the device itself.

The elevation of design took on a religiosity in Silicon Valley so much so that design laureates like Jony Ive and Tony Fadell were elevated to avatars of gods. No business in Silicon Valley stood a chance if it lacked the familiar design je ne sais quoi or an appropriately striving gestalt that could potentially land a product in the San Francisco Museum of Modern Art.

Still, it took a little bit of pill swallowing for Bowen and Monsees to pick up the phone and call Yves Béhar. Yes, they'd gone to Stanford design school, and yes, they were supremely confident in their abilities, but the truth was, neither of them had ever made a hit product before. But there certainly were people in San Francisco who had. And Béhar was one of them.

The high-energy Swiss designer with a head of wild blond curls had already made an indelible mark on Silicon Valley from his studio called fuseproject. Known for his sleek high-art designs, like the Herman Miller Sayl chair, or a SodaStream bottle, or the Jawbone, Béhar was a giant in San Francisco. He was named "Most Influential Industrial Designer in the World" by *Forbes* magazine. During a TED Talk, Béhar recounted in his sultry Swiss accent his simple design principle: "Take out all the techie stuff"—he smiled—"and try to make it as beautiful as we can." He'd had a few dicey design moments, including the $400 Juicero, which turned out to be a master class in Silicon Valley narcissism after it was discovered that the highly engineered device was in fact wholly unnecessary to perform the basic task—juicing—for which people paid stupid sums of money. And then his firm's early work helping design the Edison, the scandal-plagued blood testing machine invented by disgraced Stanford dropout Elizabeth Holmes at Theranos.

But in 2009, Béhar was willing to help and that's what mattered. In particular the founders of Ploom wanted to pivot from their tobacco device to one that could vaporize weed. They were attracted to Béhar's star power but also to his ability to turn out stunning products that incorporated miniaturized electronics. The rising awareness surrounding legalized cannabis made it a ripe opportunity for somebody like Béhar, who had a knack for landing in the middle of projects with a high-profile, environmental, or socially conscious sheen.

By the beginning of 2010, not long after getting their second round of funding, Bowen and Monsees struck a deal with Béhar to have him help design a new cannabis vaporizer.

ACROSS TOWN, AS BOWEN and Monsees were scrambling to get their start-up off the ground, another sort of start-up had posted up in an old Victorian-era storefront in the heart of San Francisco's Noe Valley neighborhood. It was called Neon Monster. Oddly shaped stuffed doughnuts and a severed foot festooned the interior window of the sun-dappled store that had the vibe of a hipster's paradise art gallery. Old comics like *Battlestar Galactica* and *Captain America* lined the blond-wood shelves, alongside books like Philip K. Dick's *Do Androids Dream of Electric Sheep* and stacks of old vinyl records from artists like Deep Purple and the Beastie Boys. The feature of the store, though, was the oddly shaped and brightly colored stock of rare designer toys and curios, like Joe Ledbetter's Candy Smash, Tokidoki's Soccer Ball, and Frank Kozik's Smorkin' Labbit.

Neon Monster's founders, and the cocreators of the plush-filled bestiary, were not unlike Bowen and Monsees in that they were just some young hipster-type dudes trying to blaze a path in the creative soup of San Francisco. But unlike the Ploom founders, their venture was extremely well funded. That's because the owners, Jacob and Isaac Pritzker, were the sons of the Hyatt hotels heir and billionaire Nicholas "Nick" Pritzker.

Nick was a cousin of the late Jay Pritzker, the Hyatt hotel magnate who'd also built a sprawling industrial conglomerate with holdings in railcars and tanks and wires and cranes and pipes and other sinews of the global economy's underbelly. Jay Pritzker's wealth grew over the decades and made him and his siblings, and their multigenerational heirs, one of the richest families in the world. The Pritzkers also built wealth on the fringes of the tobacco industry. In 1985 the family paid $400 million to acquire Conwood Corp., a Memphis-based smokeless tobacco company that also sold popcorn.

In 1988 when RJR Nabisco's then CEO, F. Ross Johnson, hatched a plan to take the food-tobacco company private in a leveraged buyout, it sparked a fierce bidding war on Wall Street that drew in titans of finance. The winner, of course, was the famed corporate raider Henry Kravis and his firm, Kohlberg Kravis Roberts & Co. There were several losers, including Jay Pritzker, who wound up in the fight only after an executive at the Wall Street investment bank, First Boston, convinced him to pony up esoteric financing to make a surprise competing bid at the eleventh hour. In 2006, the Pritzkers sold their chewing tobacco company, Conwood, to the cigarette company Reynolds American for $3.5 billion. Flush(er) from that transaction, the Pritzkers were on the prowl for new, promising investments.

Although the Pritzker family was well-known for its strong ties to Chicago and Washington (their relative, J. B. Pritzker, was elected the forty-third governor of the state of Illinois in November 2018, and Penny Pritzker was President Obama's commerce secretary), Nick and his family had grown into a prominent San Francisco clan. He and his wife, Susan, formed the nonprofit Libra Foundation in 2002, which donated to a host of typical San Francisco progressive causes, including Planned Parenthood, the ACLU, and the Drug Policy Alliance. They were one of a handful of wealthy families in the Bay Area to fund the rise of Democratic California governor Gavin Newsom. Nick, through his San Francisco family office called Tao Capital Partners, made early investments in some of Silicon Valley's hottest start-ups, including Tesla, SpaceX, Warby Parker, and Google's DeepMind. In a nod to the hipster San Francisco world, the firm did a deal with United Record Pressing, a manufacturer of vinyl records.

Pritzker's other son, Joseph, who went by the name Joby, was a mainstay in the legalize cannabis world in California and beyond. As a board member of the Marijuana Policy Project, he often was up to speed on any new technological developments in the space. In recent years, he'd kept busy running an organization called Star Sapphire Conscious Events, which threw the annual "Cosmic Love Ball" in San Francisco. When Joby and his father heard about a new high-end vaporizer being made by a start-up in San Francisco, they were intrigued. Also, the elder Pritzker's wife had been a smoker, and so naturally he was interested in the tobacco harm-reduction world that Bowen and Monsees inhabited.

In May 2011, Nick led a new round of funding for Ploom in the amount of $3 million, and the company named Thomas Dykstra, one of the Pritzkers' longtime family advisers, as the fourth Ploom board member, along with Bowen, Monsees, and Valani (Pritzker himself soon sat on the board).

It wasn't long before Joby and Isaac began showing up at the Dogpatch with their dad. As they strolled through the old factory's lofty interior, they were laid-back and inconspicuous. In particular, Nick, a graying but still tall and commanding man, showed up regularly and had as much of an avuncular vibe to him as one of a hard-nosed businessman. He gave tips and business advice on strategic thinking. Some found the Pritzkers to be a little condescending. "They looked at the company as a bunch of kids who don't know what the fuck is going on," a former employee said.

Yet with Pritzker now on board, there was an unmistakable sense that for the first time Ploom had an adult in the room. "Most people didn't know who he was or how many billions of dollars he was worth," recalled one individual. "He was very under the radar. I looked him up and I was like 'Oh, there's serious money behind this, we might be successful after all.'"

MEANWHILE ANOTHER TOBACCO COMPANY, Japan Tobacco Inc., was going through its own convulsions born of regulatory changes, declining cigarette demand, and changing consumer tastes. The Tokyo-based company that was partly owned by the Japanese government was aggressively implementing a new growth template that entailed developing new product categories and unearthing new brands that would help bolster revenue while aligning with the company's corporate motto to deliver "irreplaceable delight" to shareholders and customers. The company's executives running the international arm of the company, which was based in Geneva, Switzerland, had been monitoring the fledgling e-cigarette industry like everyone else, trying to ascertain whether it was gaining meaningful traction or if there were signs that it was a fad.

Like every other tobacco company, they'd by now heard of Ploom. For Japan Tobacco, the executives appreciated the unique design of the San Francisco designer's product, in part because, unlike other e-cigarette companies, it was more than just a website selling a Chinese product. And the fact that Bowen and Monsees owned their own intellectual property set them apart. At the time many of the early e-cigarette companies were selling knockoffs of Hon Lik's Ruyan or other brands without any intellectual property rights. For JT, that was an immediate deal-breaker.

Eventually, members of the Japan Tobacco executive team made a scouting trip to San Francisco. Bowen and Monsees arranged to have the representatives come to their Dogpatch workshop. Upon arrival, one person walked in and cringed. There were vibrators lying around on workbenches, next to all the other stuff cluttering the space. What would the buttoned-up Japanese delegation think of such a setup?

Nonetheless, meetings with representatives of the Japanese company were held with Bowen, Monsees, Valani, and Nick Pritzker. Charles Blixt, the formidable tobacco lawyer, helped Ploom with the negotiations. They discussed what type of deal structure might make sense, the potential ownership stake, and whether international rights to the product might be on the table. Things were looking up. Several weeks later, the Japanese came to do a final layer of due diligence. The start-up founders made a good impression; they came across as smart, relaxed, and eager to finally see their product take flight—and to land their first real paycheck. And there were no sex toys in sight.

Ultimately, in December 2011, Ploom and Japan Tobacco inked a deal worth tens of millions of dollars. Bowen and Monsees gave the company the rights to commercialize Ploom outside the United States, along with a minority stake in Ploom. It was not only a steal, it was a huge sigh of relief. While Japan Tobacco wasn't Marlboro, partnering with a global tobacco company selling billions of cigarettes around the world was nothing to sniff at. Between the Pritzker fortune, an alliance with a global tobacco company, and a secret weapon product designer, Bowen and Monsees were finally starting to see sparks of true momentum.

PLOOM'S ENGINEERS THREW THEMSELVES into the two projects. Day and night, they worked on the Ploom Model Two. The product design evolved. They ditched the butane tank in favor of a lithium battery and perfected the tobacco blends with the help of Japan Tobacco. Instead of the scrappy Pod Squad producing the little tobacco cartridges by hand, now Bowen and Monsees had the heft of a global manufacturing infrastructure behind them along with scientists inside Japan Tobacco to help churn out the devices.

Meanwhile, the new funding allowed the Ploom staff to begin work building the marijuana vaporizer. Béhar brought to bear a completely distinctive vision to the task at hand. In his characteristic style, he aimed for a sensibility and functionality that achieved simplicity and elegance. Bowen and Monsees shuttled back and forth to the designer's fuseproject studios, located just north of the Dogpatch in an industrial building in the Design District.

Monsees and Béhar both had monster egos, and they wound up clashing over everything, from the type of battery to use, to the size of the device, to who came up with which idea. "They were always trying to one-up each other," said an insider. "It was like 'I did this,' 'no, I did this.'"

Nonetheless the work got done. And in June 2012, the new vaporizer was launched. It was called Pax. The design was unmistakably revolutionary, not only for Bowen and Monsees but for the entire vaporizer space. The device looked more like something cut from the Big Silicon Valley mold rather than a rinky-dink student workshop. Pax easily could have been a product birthed from Apple's design studios. And with a retail sticker of $250 when it launched, it had a price to match. Gizmodo hailed it as "stunning." *TechCrunch* called it "ultra-cool." The rave reviews were a welcome change to the heaping critiques they'd received about Model One.

Made of stainless steel with a brushed cobalt-blue exterior, it was marked by a simple, arresting floral-looking cross that illuminated as the battery-operated device fired up. Its simplicity belied its futuristic innards, which included an accelerometer that allowed the user to shake the device to ascertain how much battery was left, or to put it in "party mode" where purple and orange and blue lights would flash out of the cross. Instead of being a "closed" Keurig-like system that relied on pods, Pax was built with a little chamber, or "oven," at the bottom that could be stuffed with whatever struck someone's fancy—tobacco leaves? Sure. Dried chamomile flowers? Why not. A nice nugget of Hindu Kush? *Absolutely!*

Initially Bowen and Monsees didn't market Pax as being for pot, even though it was designed to satisfy exactly that niche, and even though people were clearly buying it for that purpose. Laws surrounding cannabis use were still spotty across the United States, and they didn't want to step on any legal land mines. Also, their Japanese investors, coming from a country where marijuana was culturally shunned, were less than thrilled with the idea of being even tangentially associated with peddling such a product. Nevertheless, it was sold with a wink-wink. After all, Bowen and Monsees finally had a hit on their hands. They were going to milk it for all it was worth.

To spread the word, Ploom hired a well-known San Francisco brand marketing firm and began releasing Pax into the world. In 2013 the company landed a coveted marketing sponsorship spot at the Sundance Film Festival. Ploom, in conjunction with Singha beer, created the "Pax Cabin," an invite-only party house on the festival circuit. A fleet of Lincoln navigators with an X on them ferried a select crowd of people to the "secret" house. Guests were treated to an open bar with Tito's vodka and Tyku sake. Food was cooked by *Top Chef* winner Ilan Hall. And of course, Pax vaporizers were handed out.

The buzz was working: Pax began selling like hotcakes. But it was a double-edged sword. The more successful Pax became, the more irritated the Japanese became. "Japan Tobacco didn't want anything to do with cannabis," said one person familiar with the arrangement. The relationship became a ticking time bomb.

———

BY THE BEGINNING OF 2013 the finishing touches were also being put on the Model Two. The design was much sleeker than the Model One, and it was much more functional. Also the little tobacco pods tasted better. Still high from the success of the Pax marketing campaign, Ploom's marketing team began designing something similarly edgy for its tobacco products. Notably, they began enlisting influencers to showcase the device.

One of them was a young New Yorker named Liam McMullan, an up-and-coming socialite and the son of Patrick McMullan, a famous society photographer who'd been a longtime friend of Andy Warhol and took pictures of celebrities for his famous glossy magazine, *Interview*. Liam was an occasional columnist at the celebrity gossip publication *Page Six* magazine, and a fixture at buzzy soirees and art benefits, seemingly always trailed by leggy, ethereal-looking models. In May 2013, he was asked by an *Observer* reporter at a star-studded party in the West Village how he became a brand ambassador for Ploom. His reply, as he stood next to Kanye West's producer and his model girlfriend, all three using Ploom: "I went to Wonderland and met Alice, and we went to a tea party with the Mad Hatter!"

McMullan's antics aside, he was an early player in the increasingly social-marketing-driven world that Ploom was building. In August 2013, the Model Two was officially launched at a huge bash at a bar called The Chapel, which was housed in a converted church with soaring forty-foot ceilings in the Mission District in San Francisco. The band Stone Foxes played live music while Bowen and Monsees hit Ploom all night long as they snapped pictures with the upper crust of the city, including Bruce Gibney, an early investor in PayPal, and Joby Pritzker. They hired brand ambassadors and models from a modeling agency to facilitate tastings and to ensure the cavernous event space was packed.

Not long after, photos of the event popped up on the websites of *San Francisco* magazine and *Modern Luxury*. In September, Ploom hit Fashion Week in New York City, cosponsoring an album release party for Robin Thicke, along with the erotica magazine *Treats!* The event, held at a club in Chelsea, featured pictures of half-nude women, and fashion plates like Nicole Williams. In what was a promotional coup, the event was covered by *The New York Times*:

The e-cigarette lady was working hard. It was Wednesday night at a party given by Treats!, a newish fashion magazine that mostly eschews clothing in favor of showcasing top models in a state of near-total undress.

"We have mint, mild, bold," she said, as a young man held up a tray of a variety of different colors and cartridges.

What's the brand, someone asked?

"Ploom," she said. "P-L-O-O-M. They're very popular, very international."

A strange scent emanated. "They smell like cookies," she said, as if this were an extra selling point.

The rough template of using social media and influencers and high-end parties was looking like it could be a surefire formula. The event was also covered in *SOCIAL: The Lifestyle Magazine*, in which the writer nailed it:

The event is a hit, with celebrities weaving in and out, gingerly puffing from Ploom products, and taking pictures. Robin Thicke performs, and the crowd goes wild. Forget dusty garages, dull boardrooms, and immature dorm rooms. This is how a start-up parties, and this is a how a brand is cemented.

5

A NEW MARK

What's past is prologue.

—WILLIAM SHAKESPEARE, *THE TEMPEST*

I t was the spring of 2009 and brothers Mark and Craig Weiss, who'd launched an e-cigarette company called NJOY, were furious at the FDA. The brothers were patent and IP attorneys who worked at a family law firm with their dad and two other attorney brothers in Scottsdale, Arizona. As a routine course of their practice, they often met with entrepreneurs and inventors, and in 2005 Mark had a meeting with a client at a trade show in China and saw a crude version of what looked like a big electronic cigar. He was looking at one of the vaporizing devices that had spread like wildfire across China and was similar to the technology developed by Hon Lik.

Mark was immediately drawn to the device. At the time there was virtually nothing like it in the United States. He acquired one of the devices and decided that the thing had legs, and could potentially be a business, if only he could shrink the product size down to something more closely approximating a cigarette. The following year Mark founded NJOY as a side venture of the family firm and started working with a contract manufacturer in China who was happy to send shipments of the novel contraptions to the United States.

While Philip Morris had turned up its nose at Hon Lik's creation, NJOY became one of the earliest American companies to take the technology and run with it, getting the product into mainstream convenience stores like Sheetz and Circle K. The device became one of the United States' most popular "cigalikes," the early version of e-cigarettes that were designed to look like a traditional cigarette, including a cylindrical shape, a paper-looking enamel coating, and a glowing LED tip that looked like a cigarette's lit ember.

But then, just as sales were starting to pick up, twin disasters struck NJOY. In April 2008 the Weiss brothers' beloved patent attorney father, who'd long been the beating heart of the family firm and also its rainmaker, passed away, leaving the family firm in jeopardy of folding. And then, one year later, almost to the day of their father's death, the brothers learned that the FDA had directed U.S. Customs officials to seize shipments of NJOY's e-cigarettes at the U.S. border. The agency declared them to be unapproved drug-device products and therefore illegal to market and sell.

From the get-go, the FDA was blindsided by a sudden flurry of new nicotine devices that were quickly becoming popular as start-ups attracted cash from venture capital firms and tobacco companies. In particular the liquid nicotine vapes stumped regulators. As the craze took off, it took on a dangerous edge, with reports of nicotine poisonings and exploding vape batteries, some so powerful that they'd more than once blown someone's jaw off. But in particular, regulators grew concerned that the products posed a dangerous abuse liability, especially for kids. "Nicotine addiction is one of the hardest addictions to break," said Jonathan Winickoff, chair of the American Academy of Pediatrics Tobacco Consortium, during a call with reporters in 2009 about the product seizures. "An expanding pool of unregulated nicotine products that appeal to youth might increase the overall number of individuals who become nicotine dependent for life and later use regular cigarettes."

Meanwhile, the same public-health groups that had presided over a historic decline in cigarette use in the wake of the Master Settlement Agreement were now gathering reports about these new nicotine devices and starting to agitate. There were no legal-age restrictions on these new products, which were being sold in enticing flavors that might pose a unique appeal to young people. The agency was also concerned the products were so new that there had been no clinical studies done to evaluate the safety of this new genre of tobacco product. The FDA's own laboratory had sampled some of the products on the market and found traces, they noted in a report that summer, of "ingredients that are known to be toxic to humans," including "diethylene glycol, a toxic chemical used in antifreeze. Several other samples were found to contain carcinogens, including nitrosamines."

By 2009, the Food and Drug Administration was still unsure how to treat the new products from a legal standpoint, but they decided they could no longer put off action. So they started directing customs agents to seize them at the border. Among those first in line for seizure were the shipments stuffed with the Weisses' NJOY devices.

As the agency began to refuse entry to the China made devices, regulators believed they were on solid legal ground when they argued that the products should be treated as drug-delivery devices. They reasoned that the products delivered nicotine in a way that was intended to affect the structure and function of the human body and were designed to therapeutically treat the withdrawal symptoms of nicotine addiction.

But that legal position became clouded when on June 22, 2009, President Obama signed into law the Family Smoking Prevention and Tobacco Control Act. It had been thirteen years since Clinton's Rose Garden ceremony and almost a decade since the Supreme Court punted the issue to lawmakers. This time, it was Obama standing in the Rose Garden for a signing ceremony to squash the scourge of smoking. It was a major moment for tobacco-control advocates. Once and for all, the FDA was given proper legal authority to protect the public health by regulating the tobacco industry.

The law created a new Center for Tobacco Products inside the FDA to carry out the agency's new authorities, including the prevention of youth initiation of tobacco use. The law restricted the advertising of tobacco products on billboards, banned sponsorships of music festivals and other entertainment events, and made it illegal for companies to hand out free samples of their products. It also required premarket review of new tobacco products before they could be sold.

The sweeping legislation was designed to help the agency monitor tobacco products already on the market and keep them away from youth, while also serving as a gatekeeper for any new products that sought entry to the tobacco category. But, despite what Kessler and others had hoped for so many years ago, the new law was not a hands-down triumph for public health. Instead, it was a compromise between the demands of public-health authorities and tobacco companies, which had lobbied heavily to shape the bill to their liking. For example, while the FDA was given new powers to control levels of nicotine in cigarettes, the agency was expressly forbidden from executing an outright ban on cigarettes or requiring the total elimination of nicotine in them, something the companies had long feared.

Also, tobacco companies under the new law were restricted from making reduced-harm claims, like "light" or "low tar" or "safe," unless they first sought approval from the FDA to make such "modified risk" or "reduced harm" claims. In order to do so they had to demonstrate that they met a series of agency standards by submitting an application that the agency could subject to a rigorous scientific evidence-based review. That meant that for the first time, cigarette companies had a pathway to winning an imprimatur of sorts from the world's premier health-and-safety regulatory body, which could potentially lend any company a huge competitive advantage.

Despite the FDA's new tobacco framework, e-cigarettes appeared to be in a legal gray zone. They weren't clearly enumerated in the new tobacco control act, and it wasn't evident they could be regulated under the agency's separate drug authority. Being lawyers, and inhabiting a particularly desperate moment, the Weiss brothers decided to make a risky gambit and take the FDA to court. Lawyers for the company, along with another e-cigarette manufacturer caught in the agency's crosshairs, sought an injunction to prevent the agency from blocking its imports, arguing that the FDA was illegally misclassifying its products. They maintained that the products were not, as the agency alleged, designed for therapeutic purposes to treat nicotine withdrawal symptoms. Rather, they were simply designed to deliver nicotine for recreational purposes—the enjoyment of nicotine.

A federal district court in Washington granted a preliminary injunction in January 2010, and then an appeals court upheld the decision eleven months later. The judge agreed with the lower court that the FDA couldn't regulate electronic cigarettes as drug devices unless they were being marketed for therapeutic cessation purposes. The court also pointed out that regardless, the newly signed Tobacco Control Act gave the FDA inherent authority to regulate nontherapeutic, "customarily used" tobacco products and, that e-cigarettes fell under that framework.

The problem was, however, that Congress, in its drive to pass the years-in-the-making legislation, didn't expressly include e-cigarettes in the law. Instead, the law applied only to traditional cigarettes, smokeless tobacco, and roll-your-own tobacco. While it gave the FDA the authority to later extend its jurisdiction to "other tobacco products," such as e-cigarettes, that entailed issuing a rule that would "deem" e-cigarettes to be included under their regulatory authority. That simple word, *deem,* belied the reality of agency rule-making, a grueling, technical, and bureaucratic byzantine process that could span years.

For the tobacco and e-cigarette industries, that meant that time was of the essence. If they wanted to introduce e-cigarettes or other novel nicotine products to the market, they needed to do it fast, before the federal government intervened.

Recognizing this loophole, and sensing a looming problem, the FDA in April 2011 outlined its intent to issue a deeming regulation that would bring e-cigarettes and other novel tobacco products under its watch.

But it would be several years before the rule would be finalized. So, for the time being, the Weiss brothers, along with the entire tobacco industry, relished the win the court had delivered, along with the massive opportunity handed to them by Congress on a silver platter:

Whereas the e-cigarette industry until now had been operating in murky legal territory, now it was suddenly crystal clear. No government agency had authority to regulate e-cigarettes.

IMAGINE WALKING UP TO what appeared to be a locked gate with piles of gold behind it. And then imagine the surprise when upon pushing on the gate, it swung open. That's what happened with e-cigarettes. And when it did, people just started running through the gate and stuffing their pockets with gold, as fast as they could before they got kicked out.

Just as combustible cigarettes had become one of the most highly regulated consumer products in America, e-cigarettes had virtually no shackles. While tobacco companies were banned from selling candy-flavored cigarettes, e-cigarette companies were free to hawk their wares in any flavor they wanted, from rocket pop to SweeTarts, Atomic FireBall to orange soda. And while federal law prevented cigarette companies from advertising their products toward youth, e-cigarette companies could pitch their product to whomever they liked. And the most surprising: While the federal law prohibited sales of tobacco products to anyone under the age of eighteen, e-cigarettes had no such federal restriction. Suddenly, e-cigarette ads began appearing everywhere—on billboards, in *Rolling Stone,* on social media, and, perhaps most surprisingly, on television. The last time a tobacco ad aired on television was on January 1, 1971, before the federal government's ban on the practice went into effect (it was a Philip Morris spot for Virginia Slims on Johnny Carson's *Tonight Show* that the company aired "at exactly one minute before the midnight deadline").

Between the new tobacco law and the NJOY court decision, the series of recent events was all-around good news for the tobacco industry. For Altria, all its lobbying was starting to pay off; the 2009 law was as good as they could ever have hoped for. In particular, the statutory recognition of a regulatory pathway for "reduced risk" products was promising. Not only were tobacco products no longer on the verge of regulatory extinction, but the new law all but assured the tobacco industry would be in business potentially for generations to come. Congress had apparently granted Big Tobacco absolution.

Yet, Altria CEO Mike Szymanczyk, in particular, remained dubious. He simply couldn't fathom that regulators and tobacco control advocates would stand for these new types of recreational nicotine products being marketed for long. "The idea that they were going to allow another tobacco-based inhalation product to go off and not want to take it down was just not likely to happen," a former Altria executive said.

For a time, Szymanczyk "wouldn't even entertain the conversation" about e-cigarettes, another former insider said. During an April 2012 investor call, a stock analyst asked Szymanczyk whether Altria was considering getting into the e-cigarette market. "Well, look," he responded. "We're mindful of it, paying attention to it. That's about all I can say about it."

But behind the scenes, the company's R&D department was ecstatic. Now that it had been made abundantly clear by the courts that these products could not be construed as drug devices, Altria's lawyers had enough tacit assurance to feel confident that the company wouldn't wind up getting sued into oblivion for developing a nicotine product that some FDA bureaucrat would later argue was a medical device.

The company's innovation efforts, which were still being overseen by CTO Jack Nelson, were kicked into high gear and Altria's labs were fired up. Suddenly there were toxicologists and chemists and flavorists and engineers and physicists all working on researching and developing an aerosolized tobacco product that could potentially compete in this crazy new market. The irony of Altria, post–tobacco settlement, was that the company was extremely cautious about introducing new products given its fear of litigation risk. So it treaded more carefully than others into the e-cigarette space and embarked on rigorous safety studies before launching a product.

As part of that, in 2011 Altria scientists at the company's Richmond research center launched a study to evaluate the safety of regularly inhaling aerosolized propylene glycol, a primary solvent used in nicotine aerosol delivery devices. A group of scientists acquired more than two dozen beagle puppies from a New York farm and brought them to a lab. Over twenty-eight days, the puppies were fitted with a face mask that was connected via a tube to a chamber that dosed them daily with different amounts of propylene glycol. The scientists used a variation of its "Capillary Aerosol Generator" technology that Philip Morris scientists had developed so many years ago under the Leap aerosol program to deliver the solvent in a fine aerosol form so that it could be easily inhaled and deposited deeply into the animals' lungs. At the end of the study period, the scientists euthanized the puppies and evaluated their cadavers. While they found "no apparent tissue toxicity of the lung, liver and kidney" in the animals, they did see a negative reaction in their red blood cell count. They also reported "sporadic findings" of inflammation, congestion, and hemorrhaging in the lungs, which the study authors deemed not to be "biologically significant."

Meanwhile, the Richmond group started coming up with other "innovations" for the more traditional smokeless market. Around 2011, Altria began unveiling all kinds of smokeless products, like "Marlboro Tobacco Sticks" and "Skoal Tobacco Sticks" that looked just like that Japanese chocolate cookie stick, Pocky. The two-and-a-half-inch sticks were made of birchwood and coated on the top with a finely milled tobacco and designed for a person to swirl it around in their mouth to get their fix, before throwing it in the trash. They rolled out Marlboro NXT, a cigarette with a "crushable capsule" in the filter that released a minty flavoring.

None of the products took off. Yet the market was only growing more competitive by the day. In addition to the myriad e-cigarette brands, there was a veritable wonderland of new nicotine-laced creations that had been freely unleashed onto the world in the absence of express regulations. Camel offered "Orbs" and "Strips" that melted on the user's tongue, and various brands were now selling tiny tea bags filled with finely ground tobacco leaves that could be tucked in the cheek. Even the so-called little cigars, like Swisher Sweets and Black & Milds, hadn't been covered under the law because the tobacco inside the filtered cigarillos was wrapped in tobacco leaves and not paper. So now, despite the ban on flavored cigarettes, these cherry and orange and vanilla products, and their flavored kretek and bidi brethren, were being sold freely in 7-Elevens everywhere.

But more than anything, the e-cigarette market was on a tear. An analyst at the investment bank UBS said that sales of e-cigarettes would double from 2011 to 2012. A well-known Wells Fargo tobacco industry analyst named Bonnie Herzog said in 2013 that e-cigarette sales by the end of the year would surpass $1 billion in retail sales. Even more startling, she predicted that over the next decade some major tobacco companies could see e-cigarette revenue surpass traditional cigarettes.

NJOY took out a Super Bowl ad in 2012, airing its product to forty million viewers with its trademark tagline, "Cigarettes, you've met your match." The company also distributed samples of its e-cigarettes at music festivals, including Coachella, and to models at New York Fashion Week. It circulated Twitter ads featuring Courtney Love and Bruno Mars.

The company's main rival at the time, a brand called blu (for its blue glowing tip), flashed sexually provocative images on social media, on television, and through a network of influencers that helped the brand gain traction among young adults at nightclubs and music festivals. The company enlisted the smoldering Playboy model Jenny McCarthy, who purred in ads that kissing no longer had to taste "like an ashtray." The hunky actor Stephen Dorff was hired as a brand ambassador to urge customers in print and TV spots to try blu, exhaling the sultry vapor aside the company's motto, "Rise from the ashes." Reynolds began running its own series of ads touting its Vuse product as "the perfect puff." Between 2012 and 2013, spending on television ads for e-cigarette companies soared, with NJOY and blu each spending tens of millions of dollars to air them.

IN JANUARY 2012, SZYMANCZYK announced his retirement, after nearly a quarter century at the company. A few months later, at the annual Altria shareholder meeting, Marty Barrington, a polished lawyer and nearly two-decade-long veteran at the company, took the reins as Altria's new CEO. Barrington had such an integral role in the company's history that during the Master Settlement Agreement negotiations years earlier his signature was on the actual settlement documents.

Losing Szymanczyk left Altria somewhat unmoored at a time of extreme dynamics. The towering figure had shepherded Altria through its darkest days, seeing it through its cathartic split from the larger business, and setting it on its newly sovereign path. While Barrington was a highly respected and competent leader, he struck a much different tone and tenor than his predecessor. Unlike Szymanczyk's "Darth Vader" vibe, Barrington was an affable lawyer whose personality had more in common with a Little League coach. He earned the deep appreciation of Altria employees when he got rid of the executive parking spots and instead reserved them for those who were disabled or pregnant. He was viewed as a man of the people.

Inside the cutthroat halls of Altria, that character trait immediately frustrated others on the management team who'd grown used to a more hard-charging, fast-paced environment. Barrington, with his careful, deliberate personality, had ascended to the top of Altria just as the world of tobacco was getting ready to be turned upside down. Outsiders were flooding into the hyper-insular world of tobacco executives, launching products left and right. The industry was moving at a pace that Altria hadn't seen in decades, if ever. That was intimidating for a group of aged leaders who were used to carefully plotting and plodding, and being content spending money on R&D, with almost no expectation of a product actually ever seeing the light of day.

One industry lifer described the moment at Altria, but also across the normally staid tobacco industry, like this: "There were a lot of gray-haired men who stood to lose their jobs. For the gray-haired men to do nothing, versus taking a risk to go down a new path, they often took the former." Historically, big tobacco companies, like many other legacy industries, often only acted when they realized a new product was starting to steal customers or starting to move in a direction that made action imperative. Once they made the decision to move, they could crush everything in their path. But it was often the choice of whether to move or not that was the harder one for those companies to make.

It was that choice—to move or not to move—that Barrington grappled with, and that at the moment was paralyzing Altria. In one meeting, as senior executives discussed how to move ahead with the company's "adjacency" strategy—finding new products that could sit adjacent to the cigarette business—one person challenged everybody in the room, including Barrington and Willard. "Who was here when we created Marlboro?" this person asked, according to someone in the room. Everybody looked around at one another, silent for a moment. "The last thing we created was Marlboro and that was in 1954."

Even though Altria had spent billions of dollars on R&D over the past several decades, the company hadn't launched a successful new product, from the ground up, since then. Other than Marlboro, almost every product in the company's portfolio had been purchased, not innovated. That bruising fact, now more than ever, weighed on everybody as cigarette sales continued to slide.

By then, Howard Willard had been named chief financial officer. Even though his mentor Szymanczyk was gone, he was becoming increasingly powerful at the highest rungs of the company. Yet his new boss, Barrington, couldn't have been more different from his former boss, whose swing-for-the-fences instincts Willard had inherited. "You have somebody being very thoughtful, and someone wanting to make quick decisions," one person said about Barrington and Willard, respectively. They served as "a yin and a yang in the C-suite," for better or for worse.

FOR ANY CIGARETTE EXECUTIVE, the math of the business had long retained a distressing simplicity: Grow market share through sales trench warfare, while increasing cigarette prices just enough every year to offset declines and increased taxes, but not enough to spook customers. It wasn't rocket science. But now, there were signs that e-cigarettes were beginning to disrupt that simple calculus. It was one thing to have people leave the cigarette category altogether, say by dying or quitting; that was already baked into long-term projections. But to lose them to a new category altogether where Philip Morris had not a single competing product—that was sacrilege.

Then in April 2012, Lorillard, one of the nation's top cigarette manufacturers, became the first major tobacco company to jump into the e-cigarette business, when it acquired the wildly popular brand blu for $135 million. With a big player now in the game, it was clear this market was gathering steam, and it sent a wave of anxiety across Altria. A month later, in May 2012, Altria announced that it had formed Nu Mark, a new branded subsidiary devoted to next-generation tobacco products. Barrington named Jose "Joe" Murillo as its first president and general manager. Upon taking the new job, Murillo hung a sign above his office in the Richmond Altria headquarters that said RELENTLESS INNOVATION. It was an apropos shingle to hang, given that Nu Mark was designed to be a new-products incubator for the tobacco company.

Murillo made for a curious choice. He was not a scientist or an engineer but a longtime Philip Morris regulatory lawyer. For Murillo, "innovation" had typically taken on the form of innovating Altria through the courtroom and through the fine print of legal documents. At first blush, it seemed like the punch line of a bad joke to appoint a regulatory lawyer to the company's top innovation job. But others made the case that Barrington had in fact made a shrewd decision by moving him there. The newly emerging harm-reduction category was in such uncharted waters, legally, that who better than a lawyer to lead the charge?

It was a classic Altria move. More than ever, the company was suffering from a long-lasting hangover from the Tobacco Wars. The disdainful colleagues at PMI were not wrong: Altria had populated its executive ranks with so many lawyers that it had essentially turned into a white-shoe law firm that happened to sell tobacco products. The industry had become so risk averse, largely because its survival depended on containing existing litigation and preventing future lawsuits, that it struggled to eke out a strategy disambiguated from the legal morass that hung over the company like a cloud.

Even in normal times, every endeavor at Altria, it seemed, was just a phrase or a sentence or an utterance away from a crippling lawsuit. It didn't matter if you were a secretary or a vice president, people at the company could barely walk to the bathroom without signing an NDA or write an email that wasn't vetted by a Star Chamber of attorneys.

Many of the company's top executives had lived through the Tobacco Wars and remained so haunted by memories of the hot-lamped depositions, the cold-blooded lawsuits, the tar-and-feather congressional hearings, the beleaguering media stories that they lived with a Pavlovian fear of stepping on a land mine buried in the tobacco settlement that might land the company in court, yet again.

Now, here were these same executives, facing a sweat-inducing environment that showed early signs of shaping up to potentially be Tobacco Wars, Part Deux. That's because the entire premise of e-cigarettes was built on the idea that if smokers were to be successful in switching to e-cigarettes, they'd need to get the same "fix" or "satisfaction" or "satiation" as from a combustible cigarette, which was essentially code for *people need nicotine*. That was a sore subject for a company that had for years tried to cover up and deny pretty much that exact thing. In the 1990s, if tobacco companies had acknowledged that they were manipulating the levels of nicotine in cigarettes, they would have all but committed suicide by admitting to FDA regulators that their product was delivering an addictive drug. Now not only were they expected to be speaking openly about the pharmacologic role of nicotine, but people were literally calling e-cigarettes exactly what everyone knew they were—electronic nicotine delivery systems. That's always what cigarettes were: nicotine delivery systems. Everybody knew it then and they knew it now.

"Altria spent years debating 'can we even design a product that we publicly state is to deliver nicotine?'" recalled one former Altria executive. "Then if you'd said that the product was designed to really get a lot of nicotine in your body—that was like, well we just didn't think like that."

"We were hung up on nicotine and lawsuits and addiction," said another former Altria executive. "Its heritage and scars were really an impediment. It took us a long time to recover. Suddenly you have to be able to talk about satiation and satisfaction, otherwise you'll never get cigarette smokers. It took us a long time to be able to talk frankly."

All in all, it turned out that morphing from Big Tobacco into Big Nicotine was exceedingly uncomfortable for Altria.

———

NEVERTHELESS, IN MAY 2012, Nu Mark announced its first product, a mint-flavored nicotine disc called Verve. The product couldn't have been any more different from e-cigarettes. For starters, there was nothing cool about it. The company touted Verve as a "spitless" product, but apropos to the light-bending semantics of the tobacco industry, the "disc" was actually made of a fibrous material that didn't dissolve, so the user would either chew or suck on it and then, like a wad of gum, spit it out. If that was Altria's idea of innovation, it didn't seem like much of a leap from the product Columbus encountered in the 1500s when he found native peoples chewing on tobacco leaves and crushed-up mussel shells. Instead of moving forward in a brave new world, Altria appeared to be moving backward.

"I don't think anyone's found the magic smoke-free product," Jack Nelson acknowledged in an interview with *The Wall Street Journal* when the product was launched.

All of this was frustrating for Howard Willard, who as CFO was the person in charge of the company's financials. Investors and analysts would have no qualms taking him to task if he failed to deliver adequate share growth or maintain a "pipeline" of products that could meet the rapidly shifting consumer needs. Unlike Barrington, Willard was not known for being a methodical guy. To some, it seemed like Willard often looked for facts to justify positions he wanted to take. It was clear to people around him that it drove him crazy to watch on the sidelines as a legion of newcomers snatched the company's market share.

"This e-cigarette space was booming around us. It was a clear adjacency and we weren't in the space," said a former Altria executive. "It was like all of a sudden holy cow this category is a big threat to my core business where I make 75 percent of my income, and I'm not competing in this space. And I don't have the ability to capture these consumers when they leave."

Willard didn't just fret as the category erupted around Altria. People at the company who worked with him described him as being almost in a state of panic. So, he attempted to do the thing he knew how to do best—take out the checkbook, find an already well-developed brand, and buy them. Then maybe slap the Marlboro name on it and call it good.

In the fall of 2012, no company had more buzz about it than the Weiss brothers' NJOY. The company had just done its big Super Bowl ad, and it had grown to become the biggest e-cigarette brand in the U.S. market, with sales in twenty thousand stores across the country. In April that year the start-up had landed a $20 million investment from Catterton Partners, a Greenwich, Connecticut, private-equity firm that had invested in several consumer products companies, including Sweet Leaf Tea and Kettle Chips. NJOY had recently released an improved product, and it seemed like it was on an unstoppable growth trajectory. NJOY had the *it factor* and it made Willard salivate. He wanted to buy it.

One day, in the late summer of 2012, Craig Weiss's phone rang. He was now the CEO of NJOY. It was an investment banker on the line. "Altria wants to talk to you," the banker said. By now, Weiss was used to being courted. He'd gotten "the call" from several other large tobacco companies. He'd been surprised, actually, that Altria hadn't called sooner.

Weiss was preternaturally opposed to selling to the big tobacco companies. He'd fully embraced the harm-reduction element of his product, telling anybody who would listen that e-cigarettes had the ability to save lives, and hiring top-notch experts, even appointing the former surgeon general, Richard Carmona, to the company's board. He'd entertained discussions with top pharmaceutical companies, including those that made nicotine gum and patches, but the idea of doing a deal with a tobacco company made his stomach turn. The investment banker reassured him, convincingly, that Altria wasn't the same Big Tobacco from twenty years ago, and that the company was genuinely committed to moving toward less deadly products. Ultimately, Weiss felt he at least had a fiduciary duty to his board, so he took the meeting.

In early September, he arrived at the investment bank offices in midtown Manhattan, where he was met by a coterie of bankers and Altria executives, including Sal Mancuso and Jody Begley—two Philip Morris lifers—along with an Altria vice president of engineering and also a company lawyer. Weiss told them his story. Of how he'd been on a mission to make cigarettes obsolete, and how twenty years from now people wouldn't be lighting shit on fire and putting it in their mouths. He clicked through slides as he talked about how so many other industries that came before them—the horse and buggy, the combustion engine, the film camera—had all been out-innovated by disrupters. He was a disrupter.

The Altria executives listened intently. Weiss waited for them to jump in with questions, or give some indication that what the banker had promised about them having new spots was true. "I wanted them to look me in the eye and say 'we don't want to kill people for money anymore,'" Weiss said. Instead, the executives barely asked a single question and maintained poker faces all throughout. Weiss left the meeting, neither excited about the encounter, nor sure a deal would emerge.

About three months passed before he received another call from the same investment banker. Altria wanted to buy NJOY for $200 million. Around the same time, now in early 2013, Weiss was in early discussions about a new funding round that would have valued the company at more than double what Altria was offering. Weiss turned down the Marlboro Man. In June, NJOY raised $75 million from a group of investors, including Napster founder Sean Parker and PayPal cofounder Peter Thiel, that valued the company at more than $400 million. The following year, NJOY received another capital infusion that valued the company at a stunning for its time figure: $1 billion. In the moment it looked like Altria had wildly undervalued the company.

Not long after achieving unicorn status, Weiss departed the company he'd helped build. Then, two years and four CEOs later, NJOY filed for bankruptcy, succumbing to rapidly changing trends and newer, more innovative entrants in the market (NJOY is now sold under a restructured legal entity). The swift rise and fall of the company became a cautionary tale that would reverberate through the halls of the tobacco behemoth.

IN JUNE 2013, AT a swanky event hall in Manhattan, Reynolds announced that it was launching Vuse, its own version of an e-cigarette. A reporter for *The News & Observer* in Raleigh captured the pivotal moment for the home-state company. "Company president Daan Delen, tieless and in a sports jacket, roamed a stage at Pier 59 in New York, channeling the late Apple founder Steve Jobs as he unveiled Vuse," wrote Jay Price. "In interviews, Reynolds executives frequently use words such as 'transformative' and 'game-changing' for their new venture."

Inside Altria, one fact became inescapable: The company had no choice but to offer its own e-cigarette. But since the cigarette giant didn't have any silver bullet lying around inside its massive R&D center, and since the obvious big-name e-cigarette companies had already been sewed up by other players, Altria was running out of time to build. It would take years to try to devise something from scratch, given all the testing that the company's lawyers would insist on, and the bureaucratic molasses that would need to be waded through before anything could take flight.

So, a team of Altria executives began scouring the globe to gain a better understanding of the industry, from the Philippines to Switzerland to Israel. It was immediately clear that the quickest way to market would be to go to the same place as almost every other e-cigarette company: China.

By the time Altria started doing business there, an e-cigarette manufacturing boom was well under way just north of Hong Kong, outside the town of Shenzhen. The same massive factories that had long produced the bulk of the world's electronics, from the iPhone to the PlayStation, were now churning out e-cigarettes. It was the home of Hon Lik's e-cigarette creation, not the rural tobacco fields of North Carolina and Virginia, that had become the new center of the world for the tobacco industry. Armies of workers, primarily women, formed massive assembly lines where they hand-built circuit boards, batteries, and all the other hardware of an e-cigarette. Despite earlier forays into Japanese electronics territory so many years ago, all of this was foreign

territory for Altria. The company knew how to roast and blend tobacco leaves, not solder together capacitors.

Altria ended up doing business with a Chinese manufacturing services company that in turn contracted with a major Chinese e-cigarette
manufacturer called Kimree Inc., which had become a go-to contract
manufacturer for many e-cigarette companies. Suddenly, Richmond
was working on Chinese time.

And on June 11, 2013, Altria unveiled its first electronic cigarette, a
white paper-wrapped metal cylinder, with an LED tip that illuminated
a fiery gold with each draw, named MarkTen.

6

A JUUL IS BORN

In magnis voluisse sat est. (In great endeavors, the will is enough.)
—CHRISTIAN WILHELM POSSELT AND KARL LUDWIG REIMANN,
GERMAN SCIENTISTS WHO FIRST ISOLATED NICOTINE IN 1828

You've got to get the magic molecule . . . to the magic receptor.
—PHILIP MORRIS SCIENTIST, CHEMICAL SENSES SYMPOSIUM, 1990

In the spring of 2013, Chenyue Xing received an unexpected call from a recruiter. The man explained that a company called Ploom was looking for a chemist to help with the development of a new e-cigarette.

Xing was perplexed. Why would they call her? Sure, she was a chemist, but she'd spent most of her career working in biotech and pharmaceuticals. Xing wasn't a smoker. In fact, she loathed cigarettes.

So do my clients! the recruiter replied. He explained that the two founders of this start-up were actually working on a new technology that could *rid* the world of smoking.

Xing started warming up some. The daughter of English and history professors, Xing had grown up in Shanghai and studied chemistry at the city's Fudan University before heading to the University of California, Davis, to get her doctorate in chemical engineering. During her childhood, smoking was rampant in China, and she still had searing memories of being engulfed by secondhand smoke in restaurants and practically anywhere else in public. The idea of helping rid the world of not only a stinky nuisance but also a major public-health threat appealed to her. As did working at a flashy new Silicon Valley start-up. Before she hung up with the recruiter, she agreed to an interview.

Bowen and Monsees had hit a wall with Ploom. They understood all too well the single biggest pain point in both the Model One and Model Two: Neither delivered nicotine in a sufficient quantity and in a sufficient sensorial manner. Prying people from their cigarettes was turning out to be trickier than they could have imagined. They needed to go back to the drawing board. When they did, it was impossible to ignore the booming electronic cigarette market blowing up around them.

By now, there were a good dozen companies selling some variation of Hon Lik's cigalike products, including blu, NJOY, Vuse, and Mark-Ten. Even though Japan Tobacco had gotten the international rights to Ploom, it was clear that the product in the United States was going nowhere. The market had moved so fast and it became abundantly clear that Bowen and Monsees needed to pivot if they were going to survive. Plus, the regulatory environment was such that there were no big roadblocks in their way. Practically all anybody had to do was find one of the dime-a-dozen contract manufacturers in China to make the hardware, call up a flavorist to mix up some nicotine potions, and slap up a website. But they all appeared to share the same design flaw—they didn't deliver enough nicotine, so smokers largely found the products sorely lacking.

Given everything Bowen and Monsees had already learned over the years, and given the revenue pouring in from their successful Pax vaporizer, they concluded that they were not only well positioned to enter this segment of the market, but they could make a product highly superior to the competition. Bowen had already embarked on learning about nicotine chemistry, but since Ploom was largely made up of product designers and mechanical engineers, they needed a chemist—a chemist like Chenyue Xing.

When the recruiter reached her, Xing had been working at MAP Pharmaceuticals, an Irvine, California, company that developed oral inhalation drugs for migraines and pediatric asthma. For almost two years, Xing worked on pressurized metered dose inhalers that delivered drugs deep into the lungs of patients. She was an expert in the field of particle engineering, and knew how to concoct drug formulations that were dissolvable and suited for delivery in a fine mist.

Not long after the phone call, Xing arrived at the old tin can factory in the Dogpatch. She was struck by the ambiance inside this hive of creativity, so different from the sterile halls of a biotech company. Bowen and Monsees were waiting for her in a conference room attached to Ploom's workspace. Sitting with them was a man named Gal Cohen, a consultant with a PhD in molecular and cellular physiology from Stanford who'd also been an early investor in the company via Sand Hill Angels. Cohen had spent the better part of the past decade helping pharmaceutical and biotech and medical device companies develop strategic marketing and corporate development plans. That included conducting exhaustive business analyses of product opportunities, identifying patient populations for a potential new drug, determining which clinical trials the company would need to run, locating where the company could procure ingredients for a drug, and figuring out how much it would all cost. One of the companies he'd recently worked at was a San Francisco–based biotech company called Nektar Therapeutics. If Xing was there to bring Ploom's nicotine vaping device across the finish line, Cohen offered a window into his old employer, where legendary biochemists had already begun trying to unlock the secrets of how the race might be won.

JOHN PATTON WASN'T ANYONE'S idea of the kind of scientist who might one day lead a key breakthrough in the newly emergent field of nicotine absorption. A Vietnam veteran who'd taken up smoking, Patton went on to study marine biology, obtaining a PhD in biochemistry and two postdocs in biomedicine, one at Harvard Medical School. He landed in an obscure field of study researching how fish and clams digested fat and absorbed environmental toxins. He later applied his work to fat digestion in humans and how drugs were absorbed through the digestive tract.

In 1985 he was recruited by the South San Francisco–based pharmaceutical giant, Genentech, to lead a small drug-delivery group and developed work on an inhalable growth hormone used to treat, among other things, dwarfism. Eventually the company pulled the plug on the product over unmaterialized concerns about long-term damage to the lung tissue. Patton believed strongly that inhalation therapies, as opposed to needles, were the holy grail in drug delivery, so he struck out on his own. In 1990 he cofounded his own company in San Carlos, California, named Inhale Therapeutics, with the aerosol specialist Bob Platz from the Stanford Research Institute, and they began work on developing their own pulmonary-delivered drugs.

The lungs are by far the most efficient and fastest route of delivery for a drug to get into the body and quickly to the brain. That's because the absorbent and surprisingly large surface area of the lung, comprising a network of tiny airways and alveoli and capillaries, delivers an inhaled small molecule drug almost instantly to the bloodstream and then to the brain. In contrast, a drug that enters across the skin or through the digestive system takes much longer to get to the brain and can be metabolized and broken down before it arrives. That's the reason why cigarettes are so addictive—the nicotine is absorbed through the lungs and rapidly delivered to the brain, providing the hit or rush of nicotine's psychoactive effects.

In 1995 Patton's company partnered with Pfizer to develop an inhalable version of insulin, and in 2003 the company changed its name to Nektar Therapeutics. In 2006 the drug was approved by the FDA and commercialized under the brand name Exubera, becoming the first inhaled insulin product to market. Although patients loved the product, which delivered an insulin aerosol through a device resembling a bong, it was met with fervent pushback, in particular from entrenched interests among traditional insulin manufacturers. After spending nearly $3 billion, Pfizer cited weak sales and pulled the product from the market, "making it one of the most expensive failures in the history of the pharmaceutical industry."

Patton was crestfallen, but even in defeat he had changed the game. Despite the failure of Exubera, the promise of Patton's work had sparked an explosion of new inhalation companies and a race among drugmakers who realized almost every drug, from those used to treat diabetes to migraines, had the potential of being reformulated for inhalation. Any inhalable analogue of one of their patented drugs offered the potential to expand drug companies' markets beyond the (not small number of) people with chronic fears of hypodermic needles. They also saw value in creating new delivery platforms to administer their patented drugs, thereby extending the life of their patents.

After the Exubera disappointment, Patton and his Nektar colleagues began brainstorming any and every molecule that had the potential of being inhaled, including antibiotics, caffeine, or cannabinoids to treat a variety of ailments, from migraines to anxiety to infections. Then, around 2005, a lightbulb went off. Why not develop inhalable nicotine? The idea was as simple as it was genius.

Patton had long since kicked his smoking habit, but he was well aware of the devastating toll of smoking. There'd been a buzz recently about the field of nicotine, and in particular the principle of harm reduction. People had started unveiling new nicotine delivery devices, like nicotine-laced dental floss or nicotine lollipops, even nicotine water (all of which the FDA clamped down on), along with various nicotine inhalers for smoking cessation. Yet the products had limited success, for a critical reason: They largely didn't deliver nicotine fast enough to the brain, so users never got the satisfying feeling that truly eased their cravings. The relapse rate of smokers using the products was high.

The speed of nicotine absorption and subsequent delivery to the brain was a key factor in determining how "satisfying" users perceived any tobacco product to be. The whole point of lighting up a cigarette was to feel its effects instantly—for the inhale of the smoke to elicit a reflexive leaning back in a chair, and the exhale a satisfying *ahhhhh*.

Patton and his researchers figured out that a main reason why many nicotine inhalers hadn't been able to deliver that relief was in part because the aerosol droplets were too big. As a result they were being slowly absorbed in the lining of the mouth and the upper respiratory tract instead of being delivered rapidly to the cigarette's known sweet spot—the deepest recesses of the lung.

Nektar's board was less than crazy about the idea of getting entangled with tobacco, but Patton nevertheless unleashed a small team of scientists to see if the project had legs. One of his researchers stumbled upon the cache of tobacco documents that had been made public in the wake of the Tobacco Wars, and he started digging in. Over several weeks of plundering through the byzantine archive, the researcher wound up on a crash course in the chemistry of nicotine and the pharmacologic features of the tobacco plant. What he found was enlightening and exciting. The archives contained a massive body of research accumulated over decades by chemists inside the labs of tobacco companies, who'd figured out that the sensory characteristics of tobacco smoke, and thereby the enjoyment factor, could be manipulated by adjusting its pH—an expression of the degree to which something is acidic (like vinegar or lemon, on the low end of the pH scale) or alkaline (like drain cleaner or lye, on the high end of the scale).

The science of tobacco smoke is surprisingly complex, which is why tobacco companies have long maintained stables of elite chemists in their laboratories to tinker away with tobacco blends and the size of smoke particles and smoke chemistry. One of their goals was to design a cigarette that could make smoking tastier and give it a more satisfying punch. When a smoker takes a drag on a cigarette, the nicotine is deposited into the lungs via minuscule smoke particles and onto the lung surface where it is then transferred into the bloodstream. It then passes through the blood-brain barrier, and binds to acetylcholine receptors that, in turn, release neurotransmitters, including dopamine. With smoking, all of that occurs in under fifteen seconds. As time passes, the concentration of nicotine dissipates from the blood, and the brain craves another neurotransmitter spike, which produces an urge in the smoker to light up another cigarette. Again. And again.

The nicotine molecule is alkaline, which means in its purest, "free" form it has a high pH and leaves a sharp, burning sensation in the mouth and throat. But in the green tobacco leaf, as it grows out of the ground, nicotine is found in a crystallized "salt" form as a result of its having reacted with the naturally occurring organic acids in the leaf, which moderates the pH of tobacco smoke.

Cigars and other types of old-world European "air-cured" cigarettes have a relatively high pH because the weeks-long drying allows the leaf's natural metabolic processes to continue for many days, degrading the sugars and organic acids, and resulting in more of the "free" nicotine. That's why people who smoke those products typically swirl the smoke in their mouths rather than inhale them, which means the nicotine is absorbed more slowly through the lining of the cheeks rather than near-instantaneously through the lungs. Inhaling a cigar or a Gauloises can elicit strong coughing. That's because they're delivering a larger amount of the volatile, higher pH, "free" nicotine.

Modern cigarettes, in contrast, have a relatively low pH. That's because the type of flue-cured tobacco (dried in barns via rapid, high temperatures) used in them largely retains its naturally occurring sugars and acids that facilitate nicotine salt formation. The low pH results in a smooth smoke that allows for easier, more comfortable inhalation into the lungs.

In the 1960s, tobacco companies were flush with massive research budgets, and locked in a highly competitive race against one another. As a result they began conducting all kinds of research on the flavor profile of their respective "flue-cured" cigarette brands, experimenting with subtle hints of flavors like maple, tangerine, or licorice in an attempt to zero in on which tobacco "blends" smokers seemed to desire most. That was related to a groundbreaking, and potentially accidental, discovery by Philip Morris in the 1950s when the company began infusing the tobacco in its Marlboro brand with diammonium phosphate. The intention was to allow for a more mechanized processing of the leaves and stems, but it resulted in giving the tobacco a "chocolatey" flavor that consumers appeared to love. Adding the alkaline chemical ammonia also had the incidental effect of increasing the pH of the tobacco smoke, and delivering a higher percentage of "free" nicotine to smokers. Research showed that the higher percentage of free-base nicotine in the smoke gave smokers a bigger "kick" by providing smokers with a little harsher "throat hit" that smokers appeared to enjoy, and potentially allowing for the nicotine to be absorbed more quickly into the blood.

This new ammoniated tobacco recipe has been described as the "secret" and "soul" of the Marlboro brand and seemed to have the effect of getting smokers more powerfully addicted to their product, helping underpin Marlboro's stunning rise to become the world's most popular cigarette. One prominent expert witness testified in 1998 that Marlboro was essentially "crack nicotine"—an apt metaphor since the science of freebasing crack cocaine worked similarly.

Ever in pursuit of more cigarette sales, tobacco companies soon became one of the largest consumers of ammonia as they started adding the chemical to their cigarettes to achieve the same wildly popular freebase Marlboro kick. By 1975, Marlboro overtook all the other cigarette brands on the market and became the number one selling brand in the United States.

Meanwhile, even as smokers were attracted to the friskier freebase cigarettes, there was a parallel research track inside tobacco companies that centered on creating a "youth-appeal" cigarette that could better reach the "pre-smokers" or "learner" smokers who might be turned off by the harshness of the Marlboro-style cigarette. Instead of razzing tobacco with ammonia to induce a more abrasive throat hit, scientists realized they could also soften the blow by treating tobacco with weak organic acids that would lower the pH of tobacco smoke and produce a smoother, lighter hit. This would allow new, younger customers to be more easily initiated since the first inhale didn't obliterate their lungs.

Tobacco companies soon realized they could modulate smoke pH like a dial. Add a weak organic acid like citrate or benzoate to the tobacco to lower the pH, and make a "smoother" cigarette that was easy on the lungs. Add a dash of alkaline chemicals, like ammonia, to increase the pH to design a cigarette that packed a bigger punch. Finding that perfect "Goldilocks" blend turned into a constant and ever-evolving goal of the tobacco industry.

While Philip Morris pioneered nicotine freebasing, Reynolds scientists were ahead of the curve when it came to the science of using "top dressings" of weak organic acids and other chemicals to craft a more enticing youth cigarette. "Realistically, if our company is to survive and prosper, over the long term, we must get our share of the youth market. In my opinion this will require new brands tailored to the youth market," read a now-famous 1973 memo by Claude Teague, a Reynolds research director. He explained that irritancy and harshness of cigarettes for the "pre-smoker" or "learner" smoker needed to be dialed back. "The rate of absorption of nicotine should be kept low by holding pH down," he wrote. "The beginner smoker and inhaler has a low tolerance for smoke irritation, hence the smoke should be as bland as possible." He also noted that tobacco blends in a youth-oriented cigarette should be free from "strong" flavors. "One cultivates a taste for smoke much as one learns to like olives," he wrote.

When e-cigarettes hit the market, almost none of this deep science came into play. Most of the manufacturers simply took nicotine in its pure, freebase form, mixed it in a solution, and put it in a bottle or cartridge. There was little to no application of the sophisticated smoke chemistry and carefully calibrated nicotine delivery mechanisms developed over decades by the tobacco companies.

John Patton's research team was on to something. Carefully guided by the tobacco industry archives, they realized that pH regulation could be applied to a pharmaceutical aerosol preparation of nicotine, just like a smoke. But the starting point was different. The nicotine that came in bottles was largely just oily liquid of distilled nicotine freebase, which meant that it was more alkaline, and hence harsher. To create a solution suitable for inhalation, the nicotine had to be mixed with an excipient or inert carrier system, such as propylene glycol. The resulting solution, to be tolerable to the lungs, wound up being relatively weak in nicotine, and therefore unsatisfying to smokers.

Patton's researchers realized that by adding a weak organic acid to freebase nicotine, it would, in theory, allow for a higher (and more satisfying) nicotine content that could be more comfortably inhaled. They planned to deliver the drug formulation via a metered dose inhaler—the kind used to treat asthma—and in June 2005 filed a patent for an "Aerosolizable formulation comprising nicotine."

But there were two big problems. First, when the research team floated the idea by former FDA officials, they were warned. The agency would likely be extremely wary of the type of product proposed by Patton's team since its highly effective mode of nicotine delivery could pose a high abuse liability. Second, up until the end, the scientists working on the nicotine formulation hadn't subjected it to any human trials. When Patton was finally given a sample puff, he got his throat burned so badly that it took him two weeks to recover. The formulation wasn't right. Patton killed the program right then and there.

But Gal Cohen, the consultant sitting in the room with Bowen and Monsees and Xing, had a lot of that knowledge under his belt from his five-year stint at Nektar. Ploom was effectively morphing into a kind of hybrid tobacco-biotech company. They just needed their own Patton to press forward and zero in on the right formulation.

AS XING SAT DOWN in Ploom's conference room, Monsees asked her if she'd mind if they fired up their strange tobacco devices, which were unlike anything she'd ever seen before. "Not at all," said Xing, a petite woman with jet-black hair and a dainty face. As the two young men puffed away, exhaling clouds of vapor, Xing was struck by how non-offensive the by-product was, compared to nauseating cigarette smoke wafting in your face.

The men peppered her with questions and seemed impressed by her mastery of the topic at hand, the lungs. Xing was in turn struck by how knowledgeable the two entrepreneurs were, in particular Bowen, who seemed to have a firm grasp on the underlying science. It didn't seem to matter to either Bowen or Monsees that Xing had no interest in using the product. She'd already told the recruiter that she had no intention of using a tobacco product and never would.

The Ploom guys explained that the device they were using at the table wasn't actually the product she'd be working on. Instead, they were in the early stages of developing a new product that required somebody with a deep expertise in not only chemistry but also in inhalation drug development. *Interesting,* Xing thought. She was a uniquely perfect candidate.

At Genentech she mostly worked in small-molecule formulation, before transferring to MAP Pharmaceuticals, a company that had most of its pipeline in inhalation products. At MAP, she worked on an inhalable migraine drug, which later became commercialized under the brand name Semprana. Xing had gained an expertise in how drugs are metabolized in the body and how the lungs are an extremely efficient site for drug absorption. She knew everything there was to know about powder inhalers, aerosol inhalers, and nebulizers.

Xing left the interview convinced. She got a good feeling from Bowen and Monsees. And despite her initial trepidation, she liked the idea of trying something new at a fast-moving start-up. In biotech, it takes eons to ever see a product get commercialized; in all her experience, Xing had never seen a full life cycle of a drug, from start to finish. Ploom might offer her an opportunity to do just that. Plus, any queasiness she initially had about working with a tobacco company was laid to rest when she told herself that working in a pharmaceutical company that treats sickness wasn't all that different from what Ploom was trying to achieve. After all, smoking, and all its effects, was a sort of sickness. She viewed this as a potential cure.

Her first day was in July 2013. She was almost instantaneously struck by the caliber of the people working on the yet-unnamed product. They hailed from Apple and Tesla and high-end Silicon Valley design shops. They were all young and brilliant, and everybody seemed excited about working at a cool start-up that had grand ambitions. Since most of the people at Ploom were engineers, she found herself teaching basic chemistry and dropping science to others in the office. While she came across as somewhat quiet at the office, her work was anything but. She experimented with various nicotine liquids with an artist's flair, mixing flavors and testing various chemical formulations in a makeshift lab that was set up in a ventilated corner of the high-ceilinged room that was partially blocked off from view.

Bowen and Monsees gave Xing a simple, specific task: Work on developing a nicotine formulation better than all the rest. More specifically, the founders were searching for a perfect blend that would give the user just the right "kick" in the throat without it being so irritating as to induce coughing, while also delivering a hearty amount of nicotine to impart a "buzz," as they called it. Solving for those two problems—buzz and throat hit—became the guiding principle at Ploom.

Xing had never studied nicotine before, but thankfully Bowen and Monsees and Gal Cohen had. They pointed her to the tobacco archives, and in particular to some of the studies the companies had done on nicotine salts and organic acids. She began an exhaustive literature search, poring over documents that taught her the basics of smoking and smoke chemistry, and about the chemicals and natural substances that smokers are inhaling when they light up. She studied the chemical makeup of nicotine and learned how to deconstruct tobacco leaves to find the constituents suitable for inhalation.

As Xing was researching the thousands of chemicals contained in a natural tobacco plant, she tapped the expertise of the various tobacco-industry consultants Ploom had retained. Their expertise came in handy as she attempted to sort through the millions of pages of documents in the archives and winnow them down to find the most promising and consequential findings that needed to be prioritized. They shared the research they and others had done in the past, and the direction their course of study had taken, and whether it might be possible to move forward now with it. She was amazed at the caliber of research, dating back three decades or more, and found it inspiring that there were so many nuggets of wisdom that could be plucked out. "It was a lot of experience sharing," said Xing of the tobacco industry helpers. "They were great chemists themselves."

Armed with the archives and the tobacco researchers, Xing and Bowen and others were breathing life into long-dormant tobacco science, resurrecting aged wisdom from the dead. Xing began screening dozens of organic acids that were naturally occurring in tobacco leaves and that might play a role in neutralizing the freebase nicotine, by lowering its pH, so more of it could be added to an e-cigarette without being unduly harsh. She studied the physical chemical properties of each, trying to ascertain which would be a good fit for a nicotine e-liquid.

Xing put together a short list of organic acids—pyruvic acid, acetic acid, benzoic acid, levulinic acid—and began mixing up various nicotine concoctions to test on volunteers. They were looking for the recipe that would make their heart rate increase and their body tingle.

Among the first volunteers was Bowen himself. Just like he had boarded the "vomit comet" back in college to study microgravity, he was eager to test Xing's creations. Another beta tester was Ari Atkins, a product designer with a Stanford degree in mechanical engineering who'd invented an electric guitar that could interface with an iPhone and who designed a high-end precision coffee brewer. Gal Cohen was also a beta tester, or guinea pig, as they called themselves.

The volunteers came into a conference room in the Dogpatch offices and were given an e-cigarette device, sometimes fashioned by one of the Ploom engineers, that delivered the various aerosol formulations. Some were asked to do layman's observational research, where they were instructed, for example, to take ten puffs over two minutes, and keep notes along the way to record how they were feeling as the nicotine started kicking in. Anxious? Satiated? Alert? Nauseous? They rated the various formulations based on how or if they eased their nicotine cravings, and whether it was harsh or smooth to inhale. "I was eager to participate," said one of the guinea pigs. "I understood that we were inhaling mystery chemicals to some extent." On one occasion a volunteer took a hit off one of the nicotine formulations and immediately the room started spinning and the person almost lost consciousness. After coming back to the table, and reality, the volunteer high-fived Xing and exclaimed, "I'll never smoke another cigarette again!"

Since nicotine is a stimulant, and its effects can be measured by the rate of the heart, the beta testers had their heart rates monitored to see which nicotine formula was having the desired buzz effect. One graph showed that Bowen's heart rate increased by 70 percent in under two minutes after vaping a solution containing nicotine and benzoic acid. Compared with the other solutions, it was a good indicator that nicotine benzoate solution might be a good candidate for delivering the "buzz" they were looking for. Soon, volunteers were reporting back that the product wasn't just good. They were reaching for it rather than their pack of cigarettes.

Now they needed to run a clinical trial to prove their results. The gold standard among nicotine researchers was drawing somebody's blood to determine how much nicotine was in it after smoking a cigarette. That, they couldn't do at the Dogpatch.

IT'S ABOUT A THIRTY-HOUR flight from San Francisco to Christchurch, an off-the-beaten-path Maori settlement turned European whaling station, and now the largest city on New Zealand's South Island. Not long after the Ploom team landed there in early 2014, they made their way through a city that was still digging out of rubble left in the wake of a devastating earthquake that hit the city three years earlier.

In the city's center, just a few blocks from the historic cathedral that was irreparably damaged by the quake, stood a gleaming, glass-encased building located across the street from the Christchurch Hospital, and squished between a hospital parking garage and a Porsche dealership. Outside, a big sign read CHRISTCHURCH CLINICAL STUDIES TRUST.

In recent years, New Zealand had become a popular locale for biotech and drug companies from around the world seeking to run early-stage clinical trials, in part because its comparatively streamlined regulatory requirements allowed for faster approvals needed to conduct human trials, and because of a more attractive cost. The Christchurch clinic was started in 2000 by a pair of doctors, a nephrologist named Richard Robson and an oncologist named Chris Wynne. For the past decade or so, it had hosted early-stage pharmacokinetic trials, at which paid volunteers gave samples of their blood after receiving varying doses of a drug so that researchers could better understand how the body processed it.

Drug companies would typically run trials here after an active ingredient had already been tested in a petri dish, or in monkeys or rats, and was ready to be given to humans. The facility was equipped with dozens of hospital beds, onsite pathologists and nurses, a suite of diagnostic equipment, and catered meals. Wynne and Robson would recruit patients and pay them to participate in a study, which could last anywhere between twenty-four hours and four weeks.

When Bowen, Xing, Cohen, and Atkins arrived at the clinic, they took an elevator up to the fourth floor that opened into a cheery reception room with art on the walls and a receptionist sitting behind a desk topped with a purple orchid. Sun poured in from across the nearby Pegasus Bay. Behind a set of doors was the ward, where the Ploom volunteers would come for the duration of the study, along with a group of volunteer subjects.

Bowen and Xing brought with them a variety of e-cigarettes, including a Chinese-made cigalike and various nicotine formulations. They also purchased several cartons of Pall Mall cigarettes, which they'd planned to use for the reference cigarette. The volunteers were all men and had been selected based on their age—not younger than eighteen and not older than forty-five. They had to be smokers who smoked at least five cigarettes per day.

The study was set up to have the volunteers use e-cigarette devices to inhale nicotine blends of varying concentrations and formulations. They'd also be asked to smoke a traditional combustible cigarette to evaluate how the e-liquids stacked up.

Given how critical blood studies had been with cigarettes over the decades, as a way to measure nicotine concentrations in the blood, it was somewhat surprising that there hadn't been many, if any, similar blood studies for e-cigarettes. The relative newness of the field meant there were basic questions that Xing and Bowen were seeking to answer: How much nicotine would get into the blood with a traditional cigarette versus an e-cigarette? How quickly would the nicotine reach maximum levels in the blood with each product? And how much carbon dioxide would be in the breath after using each product?

Participants were given an indwelling catheter since blood would need to be frequently extracted. Each subject was to smoke a Pall Mall, and then the e-cigarettes, in randomized order, ninety minutes apart. Blood samples and carbon dioxide samples would be taken before and after using the various formulations, and at various time points over thirty minutes, to measure the concentration of nicotine in their blood.

Xing was on hand to help ensure the study went smoothly. For a typical study like this at Christchurch Clinical Studies Trust, volunteers would arrive at the study area in the morning, starting at around five-thirty, smoke a baseline cigarette, and then be fed breakfast. Shortly after that, the study day would begin. Xing observed as the volunteers lined up and received their blind samples of the e-cigarette formulations—some with higher levels of freebase nicotine, others with varying organic acids. A clinician was on hand to record heart-rate measurements and to take a blood sample before and after the e-cigarette was used. The study participants were also given surveys that asked them questions to gauge the level of satisfaction they got from each product and to record any comments they had after inhaling the various formulations.

As the analysis was conducted, the takeaway was becoming clear. The nicotine salt formulations with the fastest rate of nicotine uptake in the blood were the favorites in the satisfaction surveys. They were also rated as more equivalent to the satisfaction derived from the Pall Malls. One nicotine salt formulation in particular, which contained a mixture of benzoic acid, stood out. They were getting closer to zeroing in on the secret sauce: quick, cigarette-like blood absorption.

Within a few weeks after the Ploom team flew back to San Francisco, they had filed patent number 9,215,895: "Nicotine Salt Formulations for Aerosol Devices and Methods Thereof." The named inventors were Bowen and Xing. Among the patents cited was Nektar's.

"It has been unexpectedly discovered herein that certain nicotine salt formulations provide satisfaction in an individual superior to that of free base nicotine, and more comparable to the satisfaction in an individual smoking a traditional cigarette. The satisfaction effect is consistent with an efficient transfer of nicotine to the lungs of an individual and a rapid rise of nicotine absorption in the plasma."

Studies later showed the level of perfection Xing helped achieve. The preferred formulation that was ultimately commercialized delivered a walloping amount of nicotine, higher than any e-cigarette on the market, but the organic acids had the effect of lowering the pH and tempering the harshness—like a spoonful of sugar helping the medicine go down. A study later described the formulation that was ulti-mately commercialized as the "e-cigarette analogue of Marlboro." Bowen and Monsees, with Xing's help, had caught lightning in a bottle.

MEANWHILE, MONSEES AND HIS team of engineers had started to design the hardware for the new product. Yves Béhar had largely faded from the picture after finishing work on the Pax. His personal-ity clash with Monsees had reached epic and bitter levels. One person described Béhar and Monsees as both having such big personalities that when they interacted they were like "two atoms smashing to-gether." Ultimately their clashes escalated into a dispute over royal-ties and intellectual property rights related to Pax, and their ties were effectively cut.

Bowen and Monsees turned to a pair of Béhar's former business associates for help. Josh Morenstein was a partner at fuseproject and had served as its creative director for more than seven years. Now he was launching his own design firm with another well-known fuse-project designer named Nick Cronan.

Monsees told Morenstein and Cronan that he wanted a type of e-cigarette that looked nothing like the sea of cheap Chinese products on the market already. The market was crowded with e-cigarettes that were largely skeuomorphs of combustible cigarettes. On top of that, they were unrefined and unimaginative. Morenstein asked how much they'd get paid to do it, and Monsees replied that they didn't have a big budget. The two designers, just launching on their own and eager for revenue, agreed to do it for what in hindsight was a paltry sum: $20,000.

They retreated into their little studio near Chinatown, which was nestled in an alley alongside a French restaurant and a strip club, and stood before their whiteboard. As they sketched ideas in dry-erase marker, they asked each other a simple question: What would it be like to smoke in the future? Morenstein reached in his pocket. Inside hap-pened to be a small, rectangular computer flash drive. He held it up to his lips and remarked, "It should be like this."

———

ONE DAY IN LATE 2013, Monsees called everybody to gather in the little conference room. More than a dozen people squished in. Monsees clutched a small napkin in his hand and held it up. There was a small rectangle scribbled on it. It looked like a flash drive.

"This is the future," he said.

The device would contain a tiny disposable liquid-nicotine cartridge that would glow when it was turned on. And it would be made of a type of metal, perhaps copper, that would tarnish, beautifully, like a penny.

Suddenly, all the company's efforts were retrained on this new product. Cole Hatton, an electrical engineer who'd been with the company for more than two years, was tasked with working on the electronics. Steven Christensen, who'd been there almost as long, did the mechanical engineering. Monsees would help perfect the industrial design.

It wasn't an easy task to turn the napkin sketch into a working prototype. Fitting the little cartridges and the battery inside the tiny thing was a daunting challenge for the engineers, like trying to fit an elephant in a shoebox. But they churned out rapid-fire prototypes, one after another. "There were all these things we had to squeeze in. It was impossible," recalled one person involved in the project. "It was just invention after invention. And it was just so much stress—like we're not going to make it."

Then came the marrying of Bowen and Xing's salts and the industrial design, what one former employee called the "golden ticket." Bowen and Monsees insisted that the little cartridges contain the same amount of nicotine contained in a pack of cigarettes, so the device could compete directly in that space. And they wanted it to be approximately as long as a cigarette so it was familiar for smokers to handle. Everything else about it was intended to be a radical rebuke to the burning sticks, announcing appropriately the departure from the cigarette.

It was a group effort all the way down to the minutiae, including meetings to discuss what color the final design would be. They eventually settled on slate. They held votes to name the device. They argued over names. One person suggested "Gem." Another suggested "Joule"—a nod to the unit measurement of heat. At first that was shot down as being "lame and geeky and nobody would get it." But others actually liked the sound of it, since it evoked something precious. Somebody suggested simply changing the spelling. That was it. They settled on the name Juul.

7

A CALGARY STAMPEDE

We're not trying to sell cigarettes, we're selling a way of life,
an exclusive club which has its own song, its own passwords,
and a membership of millions.

—CONGRESSIONAL RECORD, 1966, QUOTING A TOBACCO ADMAN

Around 2014, a Nu Mark marketing executive named Jon Moore
was in a meeting with Barrington, Willard, Murillo, and other top Altria executives to give a pitch about MarkTen, the company's new
e-cigarette. "I'm standing here before you today," he said, "to talk
about two things that I thought I would never speak of at Altria. One
is television ads. The other one is nicotine."

Even though MarkTen had been announced the year before, it had
only been sold in test markets before launching nationwide in the
spring of 2014. By then, the company was effectively the last of the big
tobacco companies to jump with both feet into the hypercompetitive
e-cigarette market.

Companies had also started releasing advertisements in big venues
like the Super Bowl and at SXSW that seemed like reruns of the old

tobacco ads of the 1960s—glamorous models, fun-loving couples, rugged and handsome young men, all imbibing the latest nicotine concoction. Ever since the federal appeals court decision repudiated the FDA's attempts to classify e-cigarettes as drug-delivery devices, and in the absence of any subsequent regulations by the FDA, the manufacturers of those devices had been free to firehose the media market.

Moore was imploring his colleagues to wake up to the new reality. If Altria wanted to compete, it would have to stop being so gun-shy and get comfortable conversing in topics that might have made them squirm in another era. In particular, early consumer feedback showed that the company's product, which contained just 1.5 percent nicotine, was getting negative feedback for its relatively weak nicotine kick. "Why would I switch to something else if I can't derive any satisfaction from it?" Moore asked. "Let's be clear: Nicotine satisfies. We're going to have to replicate that in something other than a cigarette. We've got to talk about nicotine, folks."

Altria's executives listened. Just a few months later, MarkTen began offering a version of its e-cigarette with 2.5 percent nicotine, and then a few months later the company launched MarkTen XL, which had "a larger format" that delivered twice the amount of nicotine liquid. But it was still just the old cigalike that had none of Juul's innovations or nicotine salts.

Its advertising also needed more of a kick, Moore said, and the company shouldn't shy away from TV ads—*everybody else in the industry was doing them!* In June 2014, after the brand launched, the company spent less than $3 million on ads that month.

Moore's pep talk got the dollars moving. By the end of 2014, Altria was spending more than $7 million a month on ads and had spent more than $35 million in total advertising MarkTen, more than any other company. MarkTen ads were in print magazines like *Elle*, *Maxim*, and *Sports Illustrated*. And then, Altria joined its competitors and launched a television ad featuring MarkTen, the company's first in decades. MarkTen's main ad campaign featured the sleek device with models smiling while using it. The tagline was "Let It Glow," which had a suspiciously familiar ring to it, like the hit song from Disney's *Frozen*.

THE INCREASINGLY RISQUÉ E-CIGARETTE marketing landscape had public-health experts alarmed. All the work that had gone into defanging Big Tobacco over nearly two decades—teen smoking rates were at a two-decade low—suddenly seemed in jeopardy of slipping away.

In September 2013, the Centers for Disease Control and Prevention had released a short report titled *Notes from the Field: Electronic Cigarette Use Among Middle and High School Students—United States, 2011–2012*, which said that current e-cigarette use among high school students doubled from 2011 to 2012, reaching 10 percent. In a press release, the then director of the CDC, Tom Frieden, said, "The increased use of e-cigarettes by teens is deeply troubling. Nicotine is a highly addictive drug. Many teens who start with e-cigarettes may be condemned to struggling with a lifelong addiction to nicotine and conventional cigarettes."

Ten days later, a group of lawmakers, including the longtime California Democratic congressman Henry Waxman—the lawmaker who'd grilled tobacco CEOs in that now-infamous hearing in 1994 where they said cigarettes were not addictive—wrote to the then FDA commissioner, Margaret Hamburg, begging for help. "We are writing to urge the Food and Drug Administration to act quickly to appropriately regulate these products," he wrote, along with three other Democratic lawmakers. "E-cigarettes are currently completely unregulated. Manufacturers of e-cigarettes are taking advantage of this regulatory loophole to target children. Manufacturers of traditional cigarettes are banned from introducing flavoring into their products to attract children, but this prohibition does not apply to e-cigarettes. As a result, some e-cigarette makers are producing products with kid-friendly flavors such as 'Cherry Crush' and 'Cookies & Cream Milkshake.'"

At the same time, a group of forty attorneys general wrote a letter to the FDA, practically begging the agency to do something to rein in the freewheeling industry. "State Attorneys General have long fought to protect their States' citizens, particularly youth, from the dangers of tobacco products," the letter read. "Every State Attorney General sued the major cigarette companies for the harm their products caused. With the protection of our States' citizens again in mind, the undersigned Attorneys General write to highlight the need for immediate regulatory oversight of e-cigarettes, an increasingly widespread, addictive product."

The 2009 law that narrowly defined what constituted a "tobacco product" also gave the agency the authority to "deem" other tobacco products to be covered under that statutory definition. But months and then years passed, as the FDA worked to prepare the deeming rule. By November 2013, the Office of Management and Budget began holding meetings about the FDA's imminent deeming regulation, a process that lasted for months as it got sucked into the Washington quicksand. Dozens of lobbyists from all sides, anti-smoking advocates, e-cigarette makers, and tobacco companies packed the calendars of White House officials in an effort to shape the rule. In April 2014, the agency released its proposed rule for public comment. Under the proposed rule, the FDA would make e-cigarettes a "tobacco product" under the law and subject to the same FDA regulations as regular cigarettes. The proposed rule drew in a flood of more than 100,000 comments.

All the time it was taking for the FDA to issue regulations for e-cigarettes translated into a bacchanalia for e-cigarette manufacturers. By January 2014 there were nearly five hundred e-cigarette brands and nearly eight thousand flavors being sold online. The same year the surgeon general released a five-decade review of the health consequences of smoking. In it, e-cigarettes were flagged as a growing concern, largely because of an uptick in youth use. "The tobacco industry continues to introduce and market new products that establish and maintain nicotine addiction," wrote Frieden in a forward to the surgeon general's report.

Between 2013 and 2014 as Altria and others were saturating media with ads, the number of middle and high school students using e-cigarettes *tripled* to nearly 2.4 million, and marked the first time that e-cigarette use became the most popular form of tobacco use, eclipsing traditional cigarettes.

Meanwhile, the no-rules regulatory environment was exactly the kind that Silicon Valley start-ups lived for.

WHEN CHRIS KNEELAND'S CALGARY-BASED marketing firm Cult Collective started talking with James Monsees around the summer of 2014, his first thought was *A tobacco company?* Kneeland had never picked up a cigarette and knew next to nothing about smoking culture. So naturally he questioned the potential collaboration—the same way he'd question whether he'd want his company to work with a pornography company, or an alcohol brand, or any other vice for that matter. But when Monsees talked about his company, and the product he was getting ready to launch, he made it clear this wasn't just any tobacco company. This was a tech start-up that, he told Kneeland, was on the verge of releasing the iPhone of cigarettes. The product would help millions of smokers quit smoking, which in turn would save lives. *He's got a bit of a savior complex,* Kneeland thought as he listened to Monsees wax about his grand vision. But he liked the man's confidence, which was exuded in spades. Monsees wasn't just a salesperson. He was a true believer in his company and his product.

That resonated with Kneeland. As a so-called audience engagement firm, his company wasn't a regular transactional ad agency that slung commercials and billboards. It was a strategy firm that specialized in breathing life into brands, old and new, and turning customers into people who didn't just buy their products but who bought into the brands' ethos and aspirations. Harley-Davidson was one of Kneeland's clients, and he often liked to say that the difference between a customer buying a Honda motorcycle and a customer buying a Harley was that "Honda's just trying to sell you a bike and Harley's trying to sell you a lifestyle." "Only the best businesses," Kneeland told Monsees, "the best *brands,* can get cultlike followers."

That was music to Monsees's ears. He desperately needed followers, let alone *cultlike* followers. While the Pax vaporizer was starting to generate some buzz, it was still a highly niche product since the activity people mostly used it for—smoking marijuana—was illegal in most places. The two tobacco products, the Ploom Model One and Model Two, simply weren't catching on. As a result, a lot was riding on their new product, Juul, which was scheduled to be launched in the spring of 2015.

Not only was it a pressure cooker inside the company, but the chaotic atmosphere left little room for strategic thinking about the vision for the brand. There was no chief marketing officer, and Sonderegger, Ploom's first marketing employee, had left the start-up more than a year earlier. Bowen and Monsees were far from marketing guys. Neither was anybody on the board. Monsees was desperate for help and eager to outsource it to somebody who could do it well.

By the time Kneeland flew to San Francisco to meet with Monsees, Ploom had outgrown its original Dogpatch office and moved into a much bigger space just down the street in the Mission, in the same building that housed the administrative offices of Burning Man.

Over lunch at a nearby restaurant, Monsees went on about his mission and his newest product, Juul. About how barbaric it was that nearly forty million Americans were still committing suicide by burning leaves and inhaling smoke. About the stiff competition in the industry, with a dizzying array of e-cigarettes on the market, like blu and Vuse and MarkTen. About how instead of bending over backward to look like cigarettes, complete with cylindrical designs and glowing tips, Monsees wanted to be the *un-cigarette*. And about how confident he was that Juul would blow them all out of the water with its unique ability to deliver something none of the other brands could: a hefty zap of nicotine into the lungs that would satisfy even the heaviest of smokers, who would be left wondering, "Why would I ever go back to a cigarette?"

As he and Kneeland bounced ideas back and forth, early seeds of a marketing vision emerged right then and there. What Monsees was articulating, really, was how his product was catalyzing an evolution in smoking. Soon after, Kneeland inked a seven-figure deal with Ploom, and back in Calgary, he and his Cult Collective team immediately got to work implementing the ideas from his meeting with Monsees. They drafted a "Manifesto" that outlined what made Juul special and the ethos behind it. "After two centuries, despite being viewed by most as unhealthy, antisocial, dangerous, expensive and environmentally irresponsible, leaf burning remains the planet's number one way to get the stimulation of nicotine," the manifesto read. "Ploom is a technology company, not a tobacco company. So we were able to look at the issue from a very different perspective. Forgetting about cigarettes, e-cigarettes, other vaporizers and even tobacco, we concentrated on the end game. Nicotine. Armed with our proprietary technological advances in both physics and chemistry, we were determined to invent a cleaner, simpler, more effective nicotine delivery mechanism." The manifesto underpinned the first iteration of the marketing plan.

But Kneeland didn't know then that there were things happening behind the scenes that would muck up his vision and pull Juul in a very different and consequential direction. Soon after Cult was hired, the Ploom board realized that they were potentially foolhardy to not have their own internal marketing executive. So, in the fall of 2014, they recruited Richard Mumby, who ultimately became chief marketing officer. A former Bain consultant, Mumby had risen through the marketing ranks at fashion companies like Gilt Groupe—a luxury, invitation-only fashion website—and Bonobos, a trendy online men's apparel brand started in 2007 by two Stanford grads, one of whom had started off selling a line of hand-tailored, pastel-hued chinos from the trunk of his car. With Mumby's help, Bonobos had grown sales by adopting aggressive social media and mobile marketing techniques at a time when Facebook and Twitter were still newer platforms.

Mumby had a pedigree and demeanor that suited Bowen and Monsees. A University of Michigan economics grad with an MBA from Dartmouth, he was articulate, patrician, and handsome, with a thick head of flowing hair and an impeccable sartorial sense. He could wax about European fabrics and Italian buttons just as easily as he could about customer acquisition and impressions and EBITDA.

Kneeland was leery when he learned that Mumby had been hired.

Nobody consulted him ahead of time, as a company normally might have when bringing in a new team. He just got a phone call one day and the speaker on the line basically said, "Hi, I'm Richard. I'm the new marketing guy." Kneeland instantly felt threatened by Mumby. They just didn't seem cut from the same cloth. And while he already had a contract with Ploom, he worried about now having a new face to answer to.

In mid-December 2014, Mumby and Monsees flew to Calgary to meet with Kneeland. He and his Cult Creative team had planned to present mock-ups of their ideas designed to form the basis of a Juul marketing campaign. Mumby and Monsees made their way to the downtown neighborhood of Inglewood, a historic area lined with indie art galleries, pubs, bookshops, and coffee roasters on the banks of the Bow River. Cult Creative was nestled inside a historic redbrick building with a bronze statue of a knight on a horse out front, and two white stone lions flanking its arched glass door.

They all gathered in a conference room, and Kneeland's creative team flashed through a slide deck. "Know Thyself," read one of the opening slides of Cult's presentation. The firm had done a deep-dive analysis of the start-up and its product and had concluded that while the company was driven by a "noble cause," it had some work to do—the early beta devices were performing inconsistently and the company's core principles needed to be articulated more clearly in marketing communications. But there was promise. Juul stood out in the crowded landscape and with Cult's help the brand could shine.

The Cult team explained that their vision was to position Juul as a representation of the evolution from an analog cigarette to a digital one. The best way to do that, they said, was by juxtaposing the flashy-looking Juul with anachronistic technologies: an ad with a picture of a bearded Charles Darwin holding a Juul; a billboard with an Atari joystick next to a Juul; a boombox next to a steaming Juul. They flashed a mock commercial that was to play a remix of the 1978 Blondie song "Heart of Glass" as "a cigarette outline morphs into an actual picture of the Juul product." A mock radio ad urged, "It's time to evolve from burning leaves and sucking on empty vapor promises, to something that doesn't suck. Everything changes, eventually." They all had the tagline "The Evoluution of Smoking" with the play on the double *u* like in the Juul brand.

Kneeland was proud of his team's proposal. He thought it appropriately threaded the needle of an ostensibly controversial product in a catchy, tasteful, and responsible way. But it was clear that the presentation did not have the intended landing. In the days after, Mumby started giving the same refrain almost every time Kneeland or his team tried to follow up on Cult's original idea, or pitch something new.

Kneeland started hearing from his creative team that Mumby thought the campaign lacked sex appeal. It made Kneeland furious.

MUMBY WAS SO UNDERWHELMED by Cult's work that he almost immediately told Monsees that Juul needed a new vision. The problem was, Ploom already had a contract with Cult, which was too expensive to simply forgo. Monsees told Mumby to work with the Cult team, and use them to help execute whatever vision Mumby came up with. In other words, Mumby was stuck with Kneeland, and much to Kneeland's chagrin, Kneeland was stuck with Mumby.

It didn't take long for Kneeland to realize that his entire plan was essentially dead in the water. About three weeks after Cult's pitch, Mumby enlisted a well-known Manhattan-based creative director named Steven Baillie, who'd been the executive creative director at Bonobos. Baillie had helped the Bonobos brand move away from its corny, sophomoric, bro-y humor, with content filled with floral corduroy pants and bad puns—"the pants make your putt look good"—into one with a refined, gentlemanly dirty-martini aesthetic, but still with an irreverent, click-worthy flair.

Baillie had an impeccable eye for high-gloss fashion. After growing up on the Jersey shore and attending art school, Baillie had gone on to make a name for himself as a fast and flashy art director and photographer, shooting covers for *The New York Times Magazine*, *Playboy*, and *GQ*, where he did racy celebrity shoots. Baillie, with a black-leather-jacket sensibility and piercing hazel Scottish eyes, took his talent to high-end advertising agencies where he worked as an art director for retailers, helping to polish and relaunch brands like Target and The Gap.

In January 2015, Baillie flew out to San Francisco, where he met with Mumby and his colleagues Lauryn Livengood and Chelsea Kania at Mumby's swanky home. Over dinner and wine, they all got to know one another and then the next day, Baillie went to Ploom's offices where he was introduced to Bowen and Monsees. That day, Baillie learned about plans for both the Pax vaporizer and for Juul. Mumby briefed him on Cult Collective, and the work the firm had already done on Juul, and how the relationship might take some finessing. Egos might have been bruised, he warned. Baillie didn't give a fuck about egos—he was eager to work his magic on this cool new start-up brand.

By enlisting Baillie, Mumby made abundantly clear the direction in which he wanted to take Juul. Baillie had next to zero interest in touchy-feely talks about mission and saving lives and Charles Darwin. The once self-proclaimed "troublemaker" lived and breathed hard-charging lifestyle brands and rollicking fun, whether it was Gap or the gritty Hypebeast streetwear brand, punk rock, lingerie-clad women holding chain saws, or partying with friends like the legendary, but now #MeToo-fallen, fashion photographer Terry Richardson.

With Baillie on the team, this wasn't going to be a minimalistic Silicon Valley affair. Baillie knew how to deploy the lens of a camera like a weapon. And he had down to a science the formula for launching a lifestyle brand: sex, pop, and awe. Together with Mumby, he would lead the geeky West Coast innocents at Ploom straight into the savage maws of the Manhattan fashion machine.

AS BAILLIE SET TO work crafting his vision, both for Pax and for Juul, Mumby asked him if he'd mind occasionally traveling to Calgary to work out of the office there. Monsees didn't want the Cult contract to go to waste, and so he asked Mumby to try to keep Cult engaged in the process and draw from their deep bench of production design experts. The times Baillie was in Calgary, he got along well with some of Cult's people and worked collegially with them. But it didn't take long for a power struggle to emerge between Baillie and Kneeland.

To Kneeland, Baillie came across as a typical egotistical New Yorker who wasn't interested in collaborating. To Baillie, Kneeland's creative sense was just off; he thought Kneeland's "this isn't your father's ciga-rette" vibe missed the boat entirely on Juul, and otherwise lacked mo-dernity and spice. When Kneeland's team would offer up ideas, Baillie or Mumby would almost instantly shoot them down.

Soon, Kneeland's employees were being used by Baillie and Mumby as little more than junior-level order-takers in a production-design sweatshop, cranking out hundreds upon hundreds of banner ads and email templates and mock websites and in-store displays. It drove Kneeland crazy to have to answer to the pair, whom he'd refer to as the "Steven and Richard Show." And he was annoyed that his sophisticated, accomplished firm had essentially been neutered. But more than any-thing, Kneeland fundamentally disagreed with Baillie's ideas, some of which to him seemed batshit crazy.

Baillie originally zeroed in on the Pax for inspiration—in particular the glowing cross-like emblem on the Pax. In that, Baillie saw an al-most religious mysticism, evocative of Stanley Kubrick's black mono-lith in *2001: A Space Odyssey*, which depicted a black obelisk as an alien object worshipped by a group of apes. Baillie explained how he wanted to create eight-foot-tall replicas of the Pax out of glass or another translucent material to take around the world for promotional photo shoots—to the favelas of Rio de Janeiro or to Savandurga in India. He applied some of that same aesthetic and inspiration to Juul, which he saw as a stunning Apple-like piece of industrial design with its glowing diamond window that he thought deserved to be elevated with the same "godlike global force" he envisioned for Pax. Juul, Baillie be-lieved, should be worshipped by revelers everywhere, from music festi-vals to fashion shows. Even Kneeland, who preached the importance of building cultlike brands, thought Baillie was taking it all a step too far.

At the time, Baillie had been listening to a British space rock band called Spiritualized, which inspired him to create the tagline that eventually got adopted for the Juul ad campaign: "Vaporized." He envisioned using gritty but striking models, and when it came time to cast faces, he drew on the very specific aesthetic of his friend Terry Richardson. The iconic fashion photographer had long taken raw, unstylized, harshly lit, lo-fi portraits of famous people, including Lady Gaga, Liza Minnelli, Ben Stiller, and Rhianna, and had over the years built a collection of images of regular people or models (often topless or naked) for what he called Terry's Diary. As Baillie was building a mood board to cast the "Vaporized" campaign, he included some of Richardson's images and titled it "Come As You Are" after the Nirvana song.

While in New York, Baillie worked out of the famous Starrett-Lehigh Building in West Chelsea, a massive old freight terminal that housed famous designers like Tommy Hilfiger, Ralph Lauren, and Martha Stewart. He'd managed to rent a closet-size space inside, in Jack Studios, an eye-popping all-white 50,000-square-foot photography studio with sweeping views of Manhattan. And he'd convinced the owner to let him bring in his own clients and rent out the larger space as if it were his own so it could be a one-stop shop for his creative endeavors.

For the Juul photo shoot, Baillie enlisted the well-known casting director Douglas Perrett, who was known for scouting models who'd go on to walk the runway for Victoria's Secret or land on the cover of Bazaar. Perrett was tasked with helping find real people who had that cool "Terry's Diary" vibe to them and inviting them in to try out for the ad campaign. On casting day in early February, Baillie, Mumby, and Kania watched as more than a hundred people filed into Jack Studios and had their pictures snapped. Later, they spread out all of the Polaroids on a table and sorted through their favorites, with an eye toward diversity and freshness. They weren't looking for perfection; they wanted real people who inhabited the streets of New York.

Soon, Mumby and Baillie whittled down their cast for the Juul campaign, and a few days later the chosen models were brought back for the official photo shoot at Jack Studios. They hired a photographer who went by the name Marley Kate, who specialized in shooting young, hip women for brands like Bongo and for publications like *Seventeen* magazine. The models, including the model and soccer player Florencia Galarza, held Juuls in crimson-lipsticked lips; they wore Sonic Youth and Jim Morrison T-shirts; they sported black leather jackets; they held a Juul while playing an electric guitar. The photos were offset by a pop-art backdrop saturated with vivid colors, angular designs, and a repetitive pattern of luminating diamonds. The entire aesthetic of the campaign couldn't have been any more different than Kneeland's original "Evoluution of Smoking" mock-ups, with their muted reds and blues and grays. Baillie and Mumby's "Vaporized" campaign channeled next to nothing of Bowen and Monsees's earnest mission to provide a better smoking alternative. Instead, it had a singular focus on conveying pure, unadulterated consumeristic cool—Baillie's métier—with a flashy palette of neon pinks and turquoise blues. It captured perfectly the zeitgeist of the millennial moment.

While the two marketing camps butted heads, it was clear who had the upper hand. Mumby had essentially been given carte blanche to execute the new Juul ad campaign. Nobody, not Monsees, not Bowen, nobody inside Ploom really seemed to pull back the reins on anything. While Mumby and Baillie were careful to not recruit underage models, and even tried to ensure their models were over the age of twenty-five, there wasn't much pushback on whether their youthful appearance might inadvertently appeal to minors, a key blind spot. When the Ploom board of directors met in March, they were presented with the images from the "Vaporized" campaign. There was discussion of how the models looked "youthful" but in the end there was agreement that the ads seemed like they'd be effective. The board gave its stamp of approval. The Juul launch was just a few weeks away.

What went unspoken was that despite Bowen and Monsees's longtime mission to use their products to get smokers off combustible cigarettes, the way they were marketing it didn't seem like it lined up with that vision. Because smoking had fallen out of fashion over the past decade, that meant the smoker demographic wouldn't likely be attending warehouse parties in Chelsea. So it seemed incongruous. If they weren't targeting smokers, who *were* they targeting?

With Monsees and Bowen preoccupied with the rapidly approaching launch, and Mumby and Baillie obsessed with hitting the right fashion-factor notes, there was little time or space to step back and ask, "Is this the right thing to do?" It was all about getting a product to market and making the brand pop, not unlike a limited-edition pair of sneakers, or the latest model of a gadget, or a celebrity's new branded perfume. Everything was moving so fast.

BY THE SPRING, PLOOM was undergoing big changes. The company's deal with Japan Tobacco had started to sour. The Japanese company had grown increasingly prickly about the start-up's cannabis business and didn't want to be tied to that anymore; meanwhile Ploom had felt let down when some promises to back the business didn't fully materialize. The two companies came to an arrangement, and in February they announced that Ploom would buy back Japan Tobacco's minority stake, and Japan Tobacco would keep Ploom's trademark and intellectual property related to the Model Two. That meant that Bowen and Monsees needed a new name for their company, which they changed to Pax Labs. Being cut free from Ploom, rather than serving as a setback, allowed Bowen and Monsees to focus on the future.

Meanwhile Pax Labs started growing its corporate board beyond the core group—Bowen, Monsees, Pritzker, and Valani. They brought on Hoyoung Huh, a medical doctor and biotech investor in Silicon Valley who'd worked with Gal Cohen at Nektar Therapeutics, the pharmaceutical inhalation company. They named Alexander Asseily, the cofounder of Jawbone (which Yves Béhar designed), as a director. They brought on as a director and chief operating officer Scott Dunlap, also a Stanford grad who'd worked at PayPal and branding firms, specializing in using social media and mobile apps to take start-ups into hypergrowth mode, and to make their marketing campaigns go viral. After starting at Pax Labs, Dunlap was interviewed by JackThreads, a men's clothing company, and said this about the company's design philosophy: "We obsess about design here at Pax Labs. We strive to build products that people covet and brag about, and can sit on your coffee table right next to your iPhone and Gucci handbag."

Amidst those atmospherics, Pax 2 was ready to launch. Mumby and Baillie arranged an "exclusive" launch party at Odin, a high-end menswear boutique in Soho, which described itself as "New York's discerning curators of style." The invite-only party featured Pax 2 giveaways, personalized engravings on the devices, free cocktails, music by DJs (whom Baillie considered "the Frank Sinatras of our time"), and guests from New York's fashion elite. A photographer who trained under Patrick McMullan snapped pictures of Mumby and others alongside fashion bloggers and elite designers.

Over that spring, Mumby and Baillie kept aggressively rolling out Pax 2 to the influencer set. They recruited the elite fashion designer Richard Chai, who handed out Pax 2 vaporizers to front-row attendees at his show during Men's New York Fashion Week. "It kind of goes hand in hand with this youthful suburbia in a way," Chai said about the Pax marijuana vaporizer in a *New York* magazine article. Mumby had the product sold at a pop-up trunk show at Tenet, a trendy lifestyle boutique in the Hamptons, and offered free engravings on the device. Pax even launched a limited-edition $325 version of its vaporizer in partnership with the Grammy-winning artist The Weeknd that played the singer's hit song "The Hills" when turned on.

Just as they'd hoped, the buzz started. "Chic gadget alert! RICHARD MUMBY ON THE ALLURE OF THE PAX 2," read an article in *Daily Front Row* magazine. "Pax Has Brilliantly Positioned Itself As Fashion's Vaporizer," read another in *Racked,* a style publication. *The New York Observer* quoted Mumby saying his goal with Pax was "to make a strong connection within fashion and art, similar to what Beats by Dre has done. . . . People in fashion clearly care about products that are designed well, thoughtfully and beautifully. They're passionate about design and premium functionality."

Meanwhile, Baillie was finalizing details of the big Juul launch party that he'd decided to throw at his Jack Studios space on June 4. He sent out invitations. To help ensure that the affair would be packed, Juul enlisted an influencer studio called Grit Creative Group. For $10,000,

Grit provided "influencer seeding" ahead of the launch party, which included the promise to get the product into the hands of influencers or celebrities, and ensure buzz-worthy people would show up to the party.

Finally, on June 4, some four hundred people packed into Baillie's rented space in Jack Studios to celebrate the launch of Juul. Partygoers sipped cocktails and mingled with young women wearing cropped T-shirts and muscular men wearing no T-shirts at all. They danced under glowing blue lights to beats by DJ Phantogram alongside bright-colored posters bearing the words "Juul" and "Vaporized." The idea was to re-create the photo shoot that Baillie had arranged, but in real time. Photographers snapped photos and displayed them on an over-size television screen. White clouds filled the room, the source of which were the Juuls being handed out to the partygoers from the "full vape bar."

The party was a hit, with one small reservation. Some people in attendance were nervous at the younger-looking demographic and wondered why nobody appeared to be carding people walking in the door. The punk-looking skateboarders milling outside Jack Studios didn't bode well. Dunlap, the new chief operating officer, said the crowd for one of the early Juul launch events clearly didn't appear to be in the twenty-five-to-forty-five demo. *Oh, God, look how young they all are,* he thought.

Nonetheless, the mandate for this Silicon Valley firm, just like any other before and after it, was singular in its focus: Get Juul into as many hands as possible. As thousands of young people were gifted Juuls at these parties, often by attractive young women, Juul washed over America's cultural hot spots, from New York to Chicago to Miami to Los Angeles, like a nicotine tidal wave. And Juul was just getting started.

Baillie and Mumby insisted on plastering Juul in as many places as possible. "Let's get this thing up in front of people's faces, like a big, sumptuous Revlon lipstick," Baillie would say. Or "Let's have that thing up there big, like a hero product worship shot." He didn't want medium-size photos of Juul. He wanted something big. *Really* big.

Ultimately, in the summer of 2015, the "Vaporized" campaign was splashed up on billboards in Times Square, the most famous advertising spot in the entire world. Soon, a massive Juul, standing several stories high, in all its glory, was the object of millions of worshipping eyes staring up at it every day. Baillie finally got his *Space Odyssey* monolith.

8

A COURTSHIP

> If it were not for the nicotine in tobacco
> smoke, people would be little more
> inclined to smoke than they are to blow
> bubbles or light sparklers.
>
> —MICHAEL RUSSELL

As Bowen and Monsees rolled out Juul in the summer of 2015, the reaction inside Altria was a mixture of indifference and indignation. Here were the same punks who had once come to Richmond and boasted to Jack Nelson about their crappy butane-fired contraption. Now they were flashing this futuristic space-age creation on billboards in Times Square.

These Silicon Valley guys just didn't seem to get it, thought the Altrians. They didn't seem to get that selling nicotine wasn't like selling smartphones. Or that they were stepping into a market that lived on the third rail of American politics and culture. Everything about Juul annoyed people inside Altria. Their arrogance. Their Silicon Valley bubble. But the way they were marketing Juul seemed plain reckless, and that pissed people off. Sure, Altria was advertising MarkTen, but not like *this*. MarkTen didn't have an Instagram page, let alone a bill-board in Times Square!

How dare these Juul salesmen! *They* hadn't lived through the Tobacco Wars. *They* hadn't been pushed to the brink of ruin. *They* hadn't clawed their way back, through fire and hell, to at least the edges of polite society. Veterans of the Tobacco Wars talked about those days like they'd survived Vietnam. They'd come this far—salvaging a multibillion-dollar business—by being methodical about every strategic move. They'd repented and had plans for a brighter future still, selling harm-reduced products. The last thing they needed was for somebody to come and ruin it all again.

For decades, the number of youth tobacco users had been steadily declining, which won the tobacco companies if not goodwill, at least breathing room to keep tobacco control advocates at bay. "We were highly focused on reduction in underage users," said a company insider. "We knew that was a lightning rod for tobacco control. As long as that number kept coming down they would allow us to continue operating."

At the same time, it wasn't immediately clear that Juul posed an immediate threat, which is why there was also some indifference inside Altria. Yes, the ad campaign looked flashy, with its kaleidoscopic array of diamonds flashing next to young models in ripped jeans and punk-rock T-shirts. But the e-cigarette market was changing so quickly that every few months, it seemed, a new company would be on top, before being overtaken by a new brand. Juul could flame out.

But then again, maybe it wouldn't. Which was why eleven days after Juul's June launch, lawyers for Philip Morris USA sent Pax Labs a cease and desist letter, claiming that Juul was ripping off Marlboro. The cigarette company alleged that Juul's logo and design—with the diamond shape on the ads and on the actual device that formed when the pod snapped into it—looked too similar to the Marlboro logo.

Every one of the billions of packs of Marlboros sold around the world featured the stark but simple "Red Roof" design. The company has long fiercely guarded this design, ever since it was created in the 1950s by the famous packaging designer Frank Gianninoto, with the

assistance of a renowned marketing psychologist named Louis Cheskin, who helped choose the color red after devising a battery of consumer tests, including tobacco executives posing as cashiers and hidden
cameras that tracked eye movements. Ultimately, Philip Morris settled
on a "flip-top box" with a white background that tapered up to a lip
that hinged open, climaxing with a sharp point and a "red roof" that
covered the Marlboro logo and typography.

Marlboro had been consistently recognized as not only the single
most valuable tobacco brand in the world but also as one of the most
valuable consumer brands of all time, ranking in the pantheon alongside Apple, Coca-Cola, Disney, McDonald's, and Nike. Marlboro generated nearly $20 billion in sales every year, accounting for more than
three-quarters of all the company's revenue. At Altria, Marlboro was
like the sun in the solar system. Everything revolved around it.

As a result, the company would deploy an army of lawyers anytime
there was even a hint that somebody might be treading too close to the
likeness of its prized Marlboro logo. Philip Morris threatened or sued
countless companies over the years, including Atari for displaying the
likeness of the Red Roof design in its auto racing arcade game *Final
Lap,* makers of squirt guns, and manufacturers of candy cigarettes.

So when Juul's advertising blitz crashed across the United States,
Altria was more than ready for an ambush after the company's lawyers
saw in Juul's diamond design something of a Rorschach approximation
of Marlboro's famous red diamond design. On June 16, 2015—less
than two weeks after Juul's launch—lawyers for Philip Morris sent a
terse letter to Juul demanding that the company immediately stop
using its logo and design. The lawyers demanded that Pax Labs cease
all use of the diamonds, including scrapping any promotional materials with images of the Juul products. That essentially meant that everything would have to come down—the Times Square billboards, the
magazine ads, the in-store displays. If Pax Labs didn't do it, the lawyers
argued, they "could be subject to an injunction and damages award,
consisting of profits, costs, and attorneys' fees." For full effect, the lawyers took photos of the entire suite of Marlboro products neatly
arranged—its various packs of Marlboro cigarettes, Marlboro Snus,

and a Juul device slotted in next to them, as if to show that it appeared to complete the brand family.

Bowen and Monsees and the Pax Labs board were furious. To do what Altria was demanding would entail completely redesigning the device and the pods, an overwhelming undertaking for a start-up. Lawyers for Pax filed a lawsuit in return, asking a judge in the Northern District of California to prevent Altria "from attempting to monopolize an ornamental design on a package and permit Pax Labs to continue using the diamond window." Philip Morris's infringement claims, they argued, "have created a cloud over" the company's ability to market its product. It was clear, they continued, that the competitor "wishes to stop Pax Labs in its tracks."

It appeared to be exactly Philip Morris's intention. Better to take an easy swipe at Juul now before it became more than a nuisance later. Even though Altria lawyers said that they were simply defending their brand, it seemed as obvious as it was infuriating to people inside Juul what was going on: Altria was playing dirty.

Nevertheless, by the end of the year, Bowen, Monsees, and the board decided against going to the mat with Altria. It would have been a death wish to take on the company that retained some of the world's shrewdest and cutthroat legal strategists. The legal fees alone could ruin any start-up. Bowen and Monsees quietly capitulated. By November 2015, the case was settled. Ultimately Juul had to phase out its diamond cutout shape on the device, and get rid of the characteristic diamond shapes in its marketing that had once formed the heart of the "Vaporized" campaign. It was a low, wounding blow. "They were trying to make us bleed," was how it felt to one Juul employee who described it.

MEANWHILE, ALTRIA WAS WORRIED about its own bleeding. In January 2016, CEO Marty Barrington announced that the company's 2015 fourth-quarter revenue had fallen short of Wall Street expectations, and that Altria's cigarette sales had slipped, with the company shipping 3 percent fewer sticks of Marlboro compared to the same time a year earlier. That day, Barrington announced that the company was laying off nearly five hundred employees, or about 5 percent of its work-force, in order to free up $300 million to reinvest in areas such as "brand building" and "reduced harm products" like its own e-cigarette, MarkTen.

There was no denying it—Altria's cigarette business was shrinking. The company had already closed its only other U.S. cigarette plant, the one outside Charlotte, North Carolina, laying off workers there and leaving Richmond as Philip Morris's sole American cigarette factory. At the same time, new entrants into the e-cigarette market, like Juul, were posing new threats to the company's core products.

But Altria under Barrington was struggling to find its footing. Bar-rington had become CEO following his previous role as vice chairman, where he'd been tasked with various efforts, including innovation. When he first assumed the CEO job, he saw the e-cigarette industry exploding and was initially eager for the company to jump in as quickly as possible, a change compared to Szymanczyk, who'd seen the indus-try as a fad.

Barrington had a very specific strategy prescription. To gain ground, he argued, Altria should foster its own organic innovation efforts, while making smaller strategic bets rather than big mergers or acquisi-tions—a pace of business that was anathema to Willard's inclination toward his wielding-a-checkbook style of growth. To further that goal Barrington helped oversee the establishment of a corporate venture fund inside Altria, similar to one at Procter & Gamble and PepsiCo, to back promising technologies that could serve as natural adjacencies to the tobacco business.

The fund, called Altria Ventures, was run out of the strategy and business development group that historically had assembled some of Altria's biggest deals, including the Willard-led UST acquisition that brought the Copenhagen and Skoal chewing tobacco brands into the company's fold. Those types of deals, though, were so large that they often took mammoth amounts of time and due diligence to see them through. A venture fund would be nimbler and could move faster in part because it would focus on doing smaller transactions. The fund gave the strategy team a vehicle to execute smaller, strategic bets that would afford wide latitude to think creatively about how to grow the business beyond the traditional confines of the tobacco leaf.

The offices of the strategy and business development group were in the lower level of the Altria headquarters in a suite of offices centered between the gym and a cafeteria that employees called "Reds" that served up hamburgers and salads. The group's rooms were behind frosted glass, leaving people to wander by and wonder what was happening inside, lending an air of mystery surrounding the work done by the group. "Everybody would joke that our deepest darkest secrets were hidden in the basement," said one insider. More than a dozen employees worked down there on everything from corporate mergers and acquisitions strategies, to research and consulting for executives running Altria's various operating companies. The group often worked as the eyes and ears on the ground, unearthing trends and identifying competitive intelligence.

One of the first investments made by Altria Ventures was in the amount of $2 million in a company called Sharklet Technologies, which made "bacteria-inhibiting micro-texture surface technology" modeled after the texture of a shark's skin. In theory, that technology could help improve the shelf life of cigarette tobacco. Around 2012, a longtime Altria executive named Kevin Carlyle Crosthwaite, who went by his initials, K.C., was sent to Switzerland on behalf of Altria Ventures to launch a brand of tobacco chewing gum called Tju. The idea was to develop a more palatable nicotine-containing gum that was designed not to be a quitting product but instead simply another way for nicotine users to enjoy nicotine. Crosthwaite established a joint venture called Richmark GmbH with the wealthy Danish Bagger-Sørensen family, who'd been in the chewing gum business for more than a century. Tju was sold in Denmark and was later expanded to Spain and Italy.

By the end of 2015, Altria Ventures was intensively scouting for investments and expanded its scope beyond just tobacco and nicotine, to companies and products that more broadly fell under the umbrella of what Altria executives called "adult sensorial products." That would potentially serve the purpose of getting the company out from behind convenience-store counters where cigarettes and chew were typically stashed.

Since the company already had a stake in the wine business through the Chateau Ste. Michelle brand that it acquired as part of the UST deal, executives began thinking of ways to expand into the spirits category, including eyeing whiskey makers. Dozens of Altria employees spanning multiple departments worked on developing a proprietary pod-based cocktail system that was like a Keurig for alcoholic beverages. The pods would contain various nonalcoholic, concentrated flavors, including Margarita, Scotch, Rum and Coke, and Cosmopolitan. The user would pop in the pod, and instead of filling a reservoir with water like in a Keurig, they could fill it with liquor. The idea was that these contraptions could be sold as a personal bar concept for homes, or for hotel chains like Holiday Inn that lacked bars. Executives were so serious about the project that they flew to Germany to meet with executives at Bosch, the makers of high-end kitchen appliances, to float a potential partnership. Altria received a patent on the device, but it was never commercialized.

The group scouted other nontobacco products that fell into the adult stimulant or sensorial category. One of those products was energy drinks. Altria executives considered investing in 5-hour Energy, which made those little energy-drink shots sold in gas stations, and Hiball Inc., the maker of sparkling energy drinks that contained ingredients like caffeine and guarana and ginseng. That industry had become hot ever since Coca-Cola bought a stake in Monster Beverage Corporation for just over $2 billion. In 2017, the beer giant Anheuser-Busch InBev ended up buying Hiball.

The strategy group also began investigating cannabis, sending employees on scouting missions to states that had legalized the drug, like Colorado and California, before cannabis had gone mainstream. Altria employees visited head shops and talked to industry experts. Because marijuana was still technically illegal under federal law, top Altria executives, including Barrington, remained uneasy about the category and required employees to conduct related work on laptops unconnected to the company network that were kept in locked safes.

The world was changing and Altria knew it. Still, all the attention on these noncore businesses was somewhat befuddling to some executives and employees who watched e-cigarettes become more than a blip on the screen. Altria, in the pursuit of innovation, was starting to veer far away from its core tobacco business. Meanwhile, its own e-cigarette business was at risk of falling behind just as the new category was getting ready to explode.

By 2016, Juul had gone from being a mere wisp in the e-vapor market to a gathering storm cloud. And nobody was more cognizant of it—and more impatient—than Howard Willard.

ALTRIA'S HEADQUARTERS JUST OUTSIDE Richmond sat behind tall black fences, rows of crape myrtles, and yaupon holly hedges, obstructing the view for passersby along a traffic-clogged intersection off Broad Street. Inside the glass-enclosed walls, a succession battle for the top job at the company was heating up.

Marty Barrington was just about three years shy of sixty-five, the age that Altria executives typically would be expected to retire. Altria had a long-standing, informal practice of fostering a competition among a handful of top executives in the years leading up to a CEO's retirement. The three or four chosen ones would know who they were, and they would jockey until the group eventually got whittled down to a two-person horse race. Then, as the time neared, only one would be left triumphant, holding the keys to the Altria kingdom.

Barrington himself had been the one. In 2012, he'd beat out another executive, Dave Beran, who was the then chief operating officer. Three years after Barrington became CEO, Beran stepped down, freeing up a spot for Willard to take his job. That chain of events in turn propelled Willard into the next race for the top spot himself.

If Willard had any competition at all, it was with William "Billy" Gifford, a dyed-in-the-wool Virginian who'd studied at Virginia Commonwealth University and worked at a prominent accounting firm before joining Philip Morris in 1994, just two years after Willard. Gifford was the kind of guy who'd pull out a tin of Copenhagen long cut and, instead of taking a pinch, would "bear claw" it by dipping his cupped hand inside the tin and pulling out a massive plug of the stuff, which he'd stick in his bulging bottom lip.

Gifford had worked his way up at Altria, eventually becoming CEO of Philip Morris USA in 2010 and then taking a role in the strategy and business development department, before becoming chief financial officer in 2015 when Willard left that role to become COO. But while Gifford had a reputation for being a solid numbers guy who knew how to turn the dials of a business, he wasn't known for possessing charisma. The problem was, neither was Willard. The bench of natural talent—the kind that had blessed the cigarette company for decades before with larger-than-life CEOs—wasn't particularly deep at the moment at Altria since many up-and-comers had fled to Lausanne. Also, one by-product of having once been labeled America's Most Reviled Company was the inherent difficulty in attracting top talent, an unending source of frustration for tobacco executives who thought highly of themselves. And the rigid, good-old-boys culture didn't foster turnover, which made it hard for young talent to rise to the top.

In 2016, K.C. Crosthwaite was named vice president of the strategy and business development group. After returning from Switzerland, he'd worked for a stint as vice president of Marlboro before taking on the role overseeing corporate development. A graduate from Marquette University, the private Jesuit school in Wisconsin, Crosthwaite joined Altria right out of college in the late 1990s. He and Willard were considered such close colleagues and friends that one former executive referred to them as "Batman and Robin." Crosthwaite had a reputation for being shy, sometimes painfully so, to the point where he would grow red in the face if he was taken off guard with a question or conversation. "He's the type of guy that if you had to go to a business event and everyone's walking around with drinks in their hands, he would be standing more on the side where the food is," said one former Altria executive.

Yet when he did speak up, his answers were often insightful, and his delivery crisp. Importantly, he was a faithful Altrian to the core. Upper management grew to like him in part because he readily followed orders and was eminently coachable. It's not that he was gullible or a pushover, more that he wasn't the kind of guy who would ever be defiant or rebellious or speak out against management in a way that would spark conflict. That served him well amid the hierarchical Altria. Since the day he stepped foot out of college and into the company, he thrived at every opportunity that was thrown at him, in part because he had a knack for knowing exactly what to say, when, and to whom. With a face resembling Peter Pan's, and the quiet mannerism of a choirboy, Crosthwaite surprised his peers with his guile as he rose through the ranks like a comet, soon landing in the inner sanctum of Altria's executive offices.

By the time Crosthwaite made it to the strategy group in the spring of 2016, he was among friends. Both Willard and Gifford had a keen interest in what was coming out of the group's lower-level lair.

Ever since the NJOY deal had fallen through, Willard had been itching to make a strategic acquisition that could quickly give the company a bigger footprint in the rapidly changing e-cigarette market. In 2014, when he was still CFO, he led the push to acquire an Israeli e-cigarette company called Green Smoke Inc. for $110 million. Green Smoke had a sophisticated network of relationships in China that gave the company a firmer footing on the ground there. Plus, its robust online business offered Altria immediate access to a growing segment of the market to augment its brick-and-mortar distribution channel. But Green Smoke turned out to be far from a game changer. The company's cigalike product lineup turned out to be underwhelming, and with just $40 million in annual revenue, it remained a bit player in the burgeoning market. Green Smoke did little to move the needle for Altria, which further frustrated Willard.

By the time he became chief operating officer, he was actively searching for ways to better compete in the space. In a call in June 2015, just days after Juul launched, Willard was tasked with explaining to investors how Philip Morris was innovating in the space. Willard boasted about how the company had released a larger version of its cigalike that it called MarkTen XL, which was supposed to deliver a more satisfying product for smokers. But he acknowledged that the products currently on the market had "performance gaps" and that the market for e-cigarettes was "still developing." "We remain convinced that the desire adult smokers have for innovative tobacco products could one day be met with the right technology," he said.

With Juul starting to make more than a blip on the radar, it was by now part of Altria lore that the start-up's founders, Bowen and Monsees, had in fact visited Richmond several years earlier. Now the same two guys had come out with a product that was being written about in publications like *Wired*, under the headline "This Might Just Be the First Great E-Cig." The angst around innovation was rearing its head again. People couldn't help but wonder what might have been if Nelson and others hadn't blown off Bowen and Monsees that day so many years ago. Altria could have scooped them up for a song.

Willard had already grown uneasy about Altria's fit-and-start entrance into what was becoming a fast-changing market. He was also growing frustrated with Barrington's painstaking approach to decision-making. Watching Juul rise made Willard seethe. In no time, Juul would loom so large that Willard's pursuit of the company and its fancy device would become an obsession.

THREE THOUSAND MILES SEPARATE San Francisco from Richmond, Virginia, but the distance might as well be measured in light-years. The cultural lacuna between Silicon Valley and Big Tobacco was vast. Aside from the obvious fact that one was born of semiconductors and software and the internet, and the other from loamy soil and curing barns and plantations, Big Tobacco's vainglorious disposition clashed with Silicon Valley's holier-than-thou mindset when they came into contact.

For Altria, which had long viewed itself as the center of the universe, it was hard to accept that the company's gravitational pull was drifting away from them, out west, to an entirely new economy with companies like Facebook, Amazon, and Google. As the strategy group scoured the globe for new deals to be done, they were constantly baffled by some of their encounters. Altria executives were stunned, for example, when Apple refused to allow the new Marlboro app in its app store. "They were just not used to thinking that somebody else could tell them no," one insider said.

Nevertheless, as the chief operating officer and in effect the num-

ber two executive at the company, Willard started gently gauging people's interest in Juul. Given the history between the two companies,
Willard wanted to tread lightly. With so much at stake, Willard had no
compunction reengaging with Bowen and Monsees. But would Bowen
and Monsees feel the same way? By mid-2016 Willard had begun putting feelers out through the company's investment bank, Perella Weinberg, to get a sense of whether an overture would be welcome or
rebuffed.

Willard and Crosthwaite, along with others in the strategy group,
began dusting off Altria's dossier on the Juul founders: Stanford grads,
former smokers, founders of Ploom, met with Nelson years ago.
Meanwhile, various departments launched an intensive effort to figure
out everything they could about Juul and its product. Just like they did
with the Ruyan a decade earlier, Altria's scientists and engineers ripped
apart Juul devices and poked and prodded the thing to learn as much
as they could about it. How was the device designed? What kind of
plastics were used? What was in the aerosol? What ingredients made
up the nicotine formulation?

But there was one fact in particular about Juul that was the hardest
to explain to Willard and other top executives at Altria: "You've got to
understand the mindset of some of these tech founders," the insider
said. "They don't give a shit about us."

BUZZ FACTOR

The cave you fear to enter holds the
treasure you seek.
—JOSEPH CAMPBELL

I t "feels too young," Nick Pritzker said about the "Vaporized" campaign in the summer of 2015.

As Juul was rolled out to the masses in New York City and Los Angeles and the Hamptons, with stops in between, the "Vaporized" campaign
was turning into a coast-to-coast nicotine Bacchanalia. As a result it was
starting to draw unwanted attention. That was making some Pax Labs
executives queasy.

In particular, the flashing Juul ads in Times Square seemed like an
unnecessary taunt to those in the tobacco control community waiting
to pounce on anything of the sort. Tobacco companies were notorious
for deluging that very spot with billboards before they were banned by
the Master Settlement Agreement. In 1941, Camel erected a legendary
billboard in Times Square that blew two-foot-wide smokelike rings,

day and night. Later, the company stuck a seventy-two-foot neon Joe Camel there. For years, a giant Marlboro Man lorded over New York City's honking traffic below. Now, almost twenty years later, here in that same spot was a gargantuan Juul, looming over the throngs in spectacular triumph.

The print ads were also causing a little heartburn. The company had launched a "Vaporized" spread in *Vice* magazine, a scrappy, irreverent publication with a coveted millennial readership. Glossy magazines, of course, were another advertising format that tobacco companies had relied on for decades to win new customers before the tobacco settlement banned them. Now, just a few weeks after hitting Times Square, a young high-pony-tailed model Juuling was featured next to articles with titles like "Portraits of the Paradoxical Chechen Republic" and "Getting Drunk on Tea Infusions with Montreal's Underground Connoisseurs."

Juul's edgy ad campaign had already started to draw fire. Right after the launch, *Ad Age* ran an article about the Juul campaign, quoting a person from the Campaign for Tobacco-Free Kids who said the "Vaporized" campaign raised concerns about "irresponsible marketing of unregulated products such as e-cigarettes."

Over the past several weeks Monsees, Pritzker, Valani, and Alexander Asseily, the Jawbone cofounder and Pax director, had been having intense discussions among themselves about the "Juul approach." In early July, Asseily wrote an email to Valani and Pritzker, copying Mumby, the architect of the "Vaporized" campaign. Asseily was troubled by the campaign's allusions to the tobacco industry's much-maligned advertising tactics from an earlier era.

"Our fears around tobacco/nicotine are not going away," Asseily wrote. "We will continue to have plenty of agitation if we don't come to terms with the fact that these substances are almost irretrievably connected to the shittiest companies and practices in the history of business. . . . An approach needs to be taken that actively, if implicitly, distances us from [Big Tobacco]: what we say, the way we sell, the way we run the company, what we emphasi[z]e, who we hire, etc."

Sensing a looming problem and worrying about the consequences,

Mumby and others began scrapping elements of the "Vaporized" campaign, getting rid of the young faces and youthful images, and replacing them instead with images of simple bare hands holding the device. The triage wasn't enough to quell the rising furor and dampen the magic already at work on social media and in the streets of America.

Before launching Juul, executives at Pax had commissioned an in-depth competitive assessment that carefully studied the e-cigarette advertisements and social media strategies of its main competitors, including Vuse, MarkTen, and blu. One of the main conclusions of the report was that those brands hadn't done a good enough job using social media platforms. For example it said MarkTen and Vuse had no official presence at all on Twitter, Facebook, or Instagram. That left Juul with almost virgin territory to conquer. Without the same baggage or history harbored by the tobacco companies, or the inhibitions surrounding youth marketing, Pax Labs doubled down on the flashiest, coolest, sexiest tobacco marketing campaign America had seen in a generation, maybe ever.

Over the summer and fall of 2015 the company traveled up and down the East and West Coasts, handing out tens of thousands of free samples at parties hosted in a pop-up Juul Vapor Lounge. Some of the lounges were built inside a twenty-by-eight-foot steel shipping container finished in gleaming white paint, decorated with the brand's fluorescent-colored geometric patterns, and topped off with pink lounge furniture and a bar with brightly lit jewel boxes displaying the nicotine gadgets. After guests were handed a free Juul kit, they were invited to step in front of the Bosco animated "GIF booth" to have their pictures snapped and turned into silly moving videos designed to go viral on social media with an assortment of hashtags—#juulmoment. #juullife. #juulpod. #juulvapor.

As the sampling tour descended on cool bar after hip spot after club, models sometimes handed out more than five thousand free samples at a stop. Combined with other sampling events—on yachts, at art shows, at movie screenings, at wine tastings—Juul easily distributed hundreds of thousands of free Juul pods over the summer of 2015. Company documents showed that the so-called Container Tour was expected to "get JUUL into the hands of over 12,500 influencers subsequently introducing JUUL to over 1.5M people." Additionally, the marketing crew was encouraged to sign up people with their email addresses to help them spread brand awareness and to make them more likely to enlist in Juul's "auto-ship" program that delivered the product straight to the person's doorstep without their lifting a finger.

Juul was following a well-worn formula that had come to define new tech start-ups. Rather than plow a bunch of money into a traditional, expensive Madison Avenue ad campaign on television and radio, it had become more effective to deploy the boundless reach of social media with the help of influencers. So-called user-generated content, which relied on real people posting about the product on Twitter or Instagram, had become the go-to tactic for start-ups to give a brand an air of authenticity and generate an x-factor that money couldn't buy. It had been done masterfully by insurgent brands. While at Bonobos, Mumby had helped run contests on social media like the #Pantsformation challenge that had customers upload photos of themselves on Instagram for a chance to win a trip to New York City to be featured in one of the company's official marketing campaigns. Warby Parker, the trendy eyewear start-up, used #warbyparkerhometryon as a way to get people to share photos of themselves sporting the brand's eyewear.

The combination of old-school marketing practices, like the billboards and glossy ads, with twenty-first-century marketing tricks was a potent combination.

It's not that Bowen and Monsees were clueless of the tobacco industry's advertising past—they had spent enough time in the tobacco archives to know the ire generated by the companies' youth-oriented marketing practices. Several years earlier they'd even visited a Stanford professor named Robert Jackler who'd built an archive of old tobacco ads and was an expert in tobacco advertising. But the mindset of the Pax Labs executives was trained almost solely on one thing and one thing only: getting customers.

Asseily was warning that the tactic could backfire. "[T]he trouble with just doing 'what the others do' is that we'll end up as Nick rightly points out in the same ethical barrel as them, something none of us want no matter the payoff (I think). . . . The world is transparent and increasingly intolerant of bullshit. It's not about faking it—it's about doing it correctly . . . which could mean not doing a lot of things we thought we would do like putting young people in our poster ads or drafting in the wake of big players in the market."

But the Juul campaign seemed to be working. Not only was there a growing buzz about the brand, unmatched by any of its competitors, but the company was attracting another kind of attention that was very much wanted. Juul "could be a multi-billion [dollar] opportunity," read a presentation from the investment bank Stifel, in an August 2015 presentation to Pax Labs. The bank was pitching the company on strategic alternatives, which included a potential sale to a major tobacco company to "maximize Juul Growth Trajectory." The tobacco industry, the presentation noted, had "aggressively but unprofitably entered the vape category" and launched "products that are not compelling." As a result the industry's shortcomings in the e-cigarette industry presented a "prime opportunity" for Juul to own the market.

Just weeks out of the gate with Juul, despite the board's hand-wringing and the simmering controversy, Bowen and Monsees's nicotine start-up was already in play. And Big Tobacco, with its gloriously deep pockets, was an obvious suitor.

But then, something unexpected happened. By the end of the summer, despite the word-of-mouth social media barrage, the glitzy tasting parties, and the cross-country sampling tours, not to mention the flashing billboards in Times Square—no new orders for Juul came in.

The company had spent a ton of money expanding production to meet sales forecasts: Ramping up e-liquid production in North Carolina. Dialing up manufacturing in China. Landing Juul in gas stations, including at Speedway and Circle K. Yet after several weeks, the gas stations weren't calling back to refill orders. Customers weren't coming back for more.

Part of the problem was the quality of the Juul device itself. Customers complained that the batteries were failing, and that the little pods that snapped into the device were leaking, causing the nicotine liquid to seep into users' mouths. The company received so many complaints about the "JIM" or juice-in-mouth problem that the R&D team turned the acronym into a verb—"another one jimmed" or "if jimming occurs." While engineers believed the problems were related to manufacturing challenges, there was no obvious quick fix for what was a glaring problem for the sexy start-up.

A more fundamental issue was that the original sales forecasts for Juul were simply too aggressive. Monsees and the then chief financial officer, Tim Danaher, had cautioned the board from the outset that it might take some time for the business to develop, given that there were huge hurdles to overcome, including penetrating shelves in brick-and-mortar businesses that were often locked up by tobacco companies, and trying to convince skeptical retailers that despite any lackluster performance of other e-cigarette brands, Juul was different.

But there was another camp, namely the Pax Labs board of directors, which was eager to kick the thing into high gear and start making some money. The Pax board wasn't a typical corporate board that met periodically for perfunctory motions and to ensure basic controls were in place to keep the company from going off the rails. From the get-go, starting with Valani's short leash that he kept on Bowen and Monsees, the directors were unusually hands-on and exerted enormous control over the start-up in matters big and small, which progressively grew more intense as time went on. It wasn't uncommon for Riaz or other board members, or even board observers (those without voting rights), to wander around the offices and hit up employees while they were sitting at their desks or microwaving their lunch in the kitchen, firing off questions about the business, about their job, about industry trends, about sales forecasts.

"What other multi-billion-dollar company do you know of where board members just walk in the front door and sit next to some random line employee and just start asking them a bunch of questions?" a Juul insider said. "It was completely inappropriate."

One of the board observers at the time, a Rhodes Scholar named Zach Frankel who'd worked at Goldman Sachs and Founders Fund, the venerable San Francisco venture capital firm founded by Peter Thiel, was among those who were bullish on Juul and wanted to blow out the business. In the weeks leading up to Juul's launch Frankel, a close associate of Valani, and others pressured Monsees and Danaher to bake big numbers into the sales forecasts, making the argument that the product was so promising that it would no doubt perform. The two pushed back, but ultimately caved under pressure. As a result they were stuck with the blow-out numbers in the plan, and a seemingly impossible goal to reach.

So by the fall of 2015, as the company's warehouse in Fremont, California, sat stacked with unsold boxes of Juul and employees scratched their heads—*what happened?*—Monsees and others quickly realized there was no hope of meeting the overly zealous projections. Perhaps the numbers shouldn't have come as any surprise, but nevertheless, the board wasn't happy. Valani, in particular, was losing patience. As the earliest and largest shareholder in the company, he'd watched the Model One go down in flames. Then he stood by as the Model Two all but crashed and burned. The loose-leaf Pax marijuana vaporizer was doing relatively well, but Juul was the third nicotine product created by Bowen and Monsees in seven years and was the last shot that Bowen and Monsees had. And, unfortunately, in this moment it appeared that Juul might meet the same upsetting fate. "We thought it was Model Two all over again," said a former employee

Meanwhile, the company was in the final stages of reaching a resolution to the legal dispute with Philip Morris over the Juul diamond cutout shape, a problem that was ultimately going to cost time and money to remedy. Between the lawsuit, the lackluster sales, and the quality issues, in addition to the percolating controversy over the product itself, the situation was dire. And Monsees, as the CEO, had a target on his back.

Some members of the board had already grown piqued by what they perceived to be Monsees's brash attitude. The cofounder had a penchant for contradicting others, and for bluntly proclaiming his opinions about anything and everything from design to strategy. While that conduct might be in order for a high-flying CEO, Monsees at that moment was anything but.

In mid-October, Monsees was brought into a hotel room where

Valani and Pritzker and Frankel, and other members of the Pax Labs board, were waiting. They suggested that now was a good time for Monsees to step down as CEO. "It is very rare that an individual can grow as fast as a company needs to grow," said one person familiar with the Pax board's thinking at the time. "There are very few individuals—Bill Gates, Steve Jobs, Mark Zuckerberg—that make it from entrepreneur to being a head of a mega-company."

Monsees wasn't Jobs and it was clear he didn't have much say in the matter. He told the board that he was happy to hand over the reins of the company to the right person at the right time, and hoped it would be someone who could deliver on his and Bowen's original mission of displacing cigarettes. Who, he wondered, was his replacement? The board's answer was surprising, if not unsettling: They didn't *have* a replacement.

Not long after, with Monsees removed from the CEO chair (he stayed on as a director and assumed the role of chief product officer), Pritzker and Valani cleaned house. They axed anybody who wasn't in lockstep with them or who didn't display the willingness or an ability to keep pace. Dunlap, the chief operating officer, was fired. Alexander Asseily, the Pax Labs director who raised doubts about the marketing campaign, didn't last on the board. A bunch of engineers and other staff were axed.

In place of a CEO, the board formed an executive committee with Pritzker and Valani in charge, along with Hoyoung Huh, the doctor and biotech investor who'd worked with Gal Cohen at Nektar Therapeutics. The board launched a search to find Monsees's replacement, but the task ultimately took months. All the while the CEO's chair sat empty, at a time when the company was in desperate need of leadership.

By November, Philip Morris and Pax reached a settlement over the Juul design. While the terms were confidential, its ramifications were clear: The device had to be redesigned, and every last piece of hardware had to be reworked to remove the offending diamond cutout. That, combined with the sales slump, translated into retreat. Soon production lines in China that made Juul's pods and devices were dialed back to a near stop. A pod-filling production facility in North Carolina was shut down and its workers were laid off. The board diverted resources to the Pax marijuana vaporizer. Juul was in a nosedive. At one point, things became so bleak that the recently hired vice president of engineering, Bryan White, called together a group of employees in a conference room in the company's San Francisco offices to deliver bad news about Juul. "We're going to end of life the product," White said.

"THE FLAP OF A butterfly's wings can be instrumental in generating a tornado," said the famous MIT mathematician and meteorologist, and father of chaos theory, Edward Lorenz in 1972. By the beginning of 2016, not long after crisis, and then eerie calm, had befallen the company, Juul was starting to make a ripple. A funnel was forming.

Out of the blue, it seemed, Juul employees' phones started ringing. New distributors were calling, saying they'd heard about Juul and were interested in carrying it. Stores that already had Juul in their rotation called, saying they were sold out and wanted more. To employees, the surge of interest seemed almost suspicious, but Juul was simply beginning to reach an inflection point. As the product got into more and bigger retail stores, it reached growing numbers of people, who in turn spread the word in vape shops and at parties and on social media, until the product started to snowball.

Engineers furiously worked to finish designing a new pod and device that steered clear of the Philip Morris trademark. They settled on a hexagonal shape, which sat in the little cutout between the device and the pod. The fix wasn't big, but it also wasn't simple, since it required the design to be ironed out and the production lines to be retooled. By early 2016, production in China resumed. The pod-filling line in North Carolina was eventually brought back online, and by the spring it had doubled its production capacity and was running around the clock. A second pod-filling contract manufacturer was eventually brought on to help meet the demand.

Throughout 2016, Juul's supply chain became completely overwhelmed. Just as soon as the company sent out a shipment, retailers were sold out again. Soon, the warehouse that just weeks earlier had been brimming with Juul boxes was nearly empty. Employees were getting screamed at by retailers complaining the company wasn't restocking fast enough, and slapping them with late fees for not filling orders on time.

Customers were complaining that they couldn't find Juul anywhere. When they found stock, they'd buy it in bulk, scooping as much as they could off the shelf as fast as they could. Retailers couldn't keep Juul in stock for more than a day. The scarcity led people to track the product like a precious commodity, posting on social media when they found a store that had it. "PSA: speedway on bird and 81st will restock juul pods at 5 pm," read one posting on Twitter, drawing the reply "damn why so late."

The despondent mood inside Pax had dramatically changed. By now so many demands from customers and retailers were flowing in that employees would work over the weekend, ordering pizza as they stayed late. Bowen and Monsees often pitched in, personally answering customer tickets and responding to inquiries. Not surprisingly, Valani and Pritzker and other board members dropped in frequently, sometimes staying late into the night with a team that was running on adrenaline. There was a sudden electricity about the place.

"Everyone was so astonished that they wanted to be a part of it," one former employee recalled. Just months earlier Juul was on life support, but now there was a gathering sense that they were witnessing the birth of something big. "This was a once-in-a-lifetime company."

OF THE MANY REASONS for Juul's sudden popularity, one was indisputable: Juul was leaving its unique mark. It had crossed the blood-brain barrier of America and was starting to pump through a nation. Well before the product launched, back to the days when Bowen was in New Zealand giving his own blood, the company had been in pursuit of the perfect nicotine high. And it was becoming clearer by the day that they appeared to have found it. That combined with the compact, handy design of the hardware made the thing incredibly enticing, and hooking.

When Erica Halverson—a cheerful but blunt Pax marketing manager with a fast-talking charm—first started working for Juul in 2016, she was tasked with putting together a marketing plan for vape shops nationwide. While convenience stores were an important sales channel for Juul, the largely independently owned and operated vape shops were critical as well. But the vapers were a much different animal than somebody rolling up to a Circle K to pump gas. Vape shops were dominated by a steampunk culture filled with pierced guys with beards who'd typically kicked a lifelong habit of smoking through ripping monster nicotine hits on squonk mods. The hard-core enthusiasts hand-mixed liquid nicotine concoctions from glass bottles like mad scientists and tinkered with copper wires to tweak resistance. They expired streams of vapor from their nose like angry bulls. As one former Juul executive described them: "These are just a bunch of good ol' stoners that went along for the ride."

When Halverson first started showing up to the haze-filled vape dens, toting dainty little Juul in its precious little box, she got some side eye. Compared to the big box mods, a Juul seemed like a toy. And while the other devices would give off billowing vape clouds, Juul's plume was ephemeral and discreet. But when she'd set up her little booth in the shop and allow sampling, it didn't take long for the tough guys to discover Juul could knock them on their ass.

Its 5 percent nicotine concentration was by far the strongest e-cigarette on the market. It would always amaze people when Halverson told them that a single tiny Juul pod delivered an amount of nicotine equivalent to an entire pack of Marlboro Reds. Even with Juul's proprietary benzoic acid–nicotine salt formulation that made its hits smoother compared to others, its potency delivered a powerful zing. Before long even the most hard-core vapers were Juuling.

"That was part of the marketing message—we were trying to show that Juul was cigarette-like without being a cigarette," said Halverson.

Introducing Juul to the world was much more calculated than sauntering into a vape shop or a gas station. The company collected all kinds of data on adult smokers that would help inform the company's marketing strategy. It brought in beta testers to the corporate offices for in-house focus groups. They'd sit around a table and Juul while the marketing people observed them. How often did they puff? How long did it take somebody to take a puff? They hired data scientists to ingest information from as many sources as possible, including from beta Juul devices given to testers to log their usage patterns. They purchased third-party data on existing smokers and worked to segment it out based on geography and demographics. Where did smokers hang out in Chicago, for example. And how were they different from smokers in Los Angeles? They hacked vaping like a Silicon Valley company would.

Still, consumer research conducted by the company showed that even some heavy smokers found Juul to be too strong. Unlike a cigarette, the Juul had no beginning or end, so people could ingest large amounts of nicotine without even realizing it. "They were floored by the delivery and didn't really know how to control it," said the researcher hired to do the consumer tests. Some of the comments from the study subjects were that Juul was "overwhelming when I first inhaled" or "too much for me" or "it caught me off guard." There were internal conversations over whether the product's nicotine content was too strong and could be interpreted as "feeding an addiction faster," according to notes from a 2017 internal science meeting at Juul. "Given the current climate with addictions to OxyContin, how the data is presented needs to be considered carefully."

Halverson was tasked with teaching shop owners and patrons how it was completely normal when first using Juul for even smokers or experienced vapers to hack up a lung. She'd reassure them that it was only because of Juul's uniquely satisfying (read, high nicotine) formulation. Before long, any lung aggravation would subside, and they'd be coming back for more.

Sure enough, when she'd come back to the shop, say, two weeks later, she learned that the people who'd been coughing and taking hesitant hits were now Juuling with no coughing at all. "People were taking deeper and longer puffs the longer they had the device," Halverson said. "We found that people were—I don't want to say they were getting addicted, because it was more that the device itself was just so easy to pick up and use, but people would get so used to being able to use this thing anywhere and everywhere."

It didn't take long for anywhere and everywhere to mean exactly that.

IT WASN'T JUST ANYWHERE and everywhere, it was *anyone*. As the masses began clamoring for Juul, teenagers started realizing that the product was surprisingly easy to procure. Early on, there were lax age-verification requirements, so virtually anyone with a computer could pull up the website, order a box of Juul pods, and have them delivered to their front door. Customers soon figured out that a loophole in the system allowed for them to get *free* Juul sent to them. Because of the deluge in the customer service department, aspects of the customer service system were automated. Now customers calling in about, say, a leaky pod or a broken device would be directed to an online portal. From there the customer would be prompted to enter the warranty information and serial number to receive a free product replacement. The system wasn't built to double-check whether serial numbers were unique, which meant people could submit multiple warranty claims using the same serial number. One college student was able to use the same serial number to obtain more than 150 free Juuls, which they then resold.

Any start-up would kill to have the level of frenzy and viral online engagement that Juul was attracting. Running out of product and not keeping up with demand is the type of story start-up founders dream of telling potential investors. For some Juul employees it was exhilarating to see the product they'd worked so hard on reach pinnacles of success. The influencer strategy was working, as the company distributed Juul swag and heavily discounted product to key influencers—people who appeared on podcasts mentioning Juul, or popular fashion bloggers, for example. The company had been able to cultivate famous Juul users. It was a coup the day somebody happened to spot Katy Perry on the red carpet at the Golden Globes palming a Juul in her pink Prada gown as she whispered in the ear of Orlando Bloom.

But as sales were soaring, "on the backend there was no question of who was using the product," said a former employee. People were buying Juul with obviously fake names, like "Patricia Juul," and "John JUUL Kordahl," and "?zge FIRAT." Juul shipped forty-one packages of Juul pods to an individual in San Francisco named "Beer Can." Soon they could tell from the buying behavior on the website that it was riddled with nicotine-jonesing teens trying to get their hands on Juul at any cost.

"Kids were committing so many crimes," said another former employee. "Like stealing their parents' credit cards, using their parents' names, their grandparents' names. Like *grandmothers*! I mean, it was out of control."

By the summer of 2016, there was a nagging sense inside Juul that things were about to get ugly. One former employee recalled getting a sinking feeling after noticing Juul pods littering San Francisco streets like cigarette butts. Like a bad omen.

Another recalled initially being excited about all the online traffic and frothy engagement over the Juul brand. It was fun to watch the rise of Instagram pages devoted entirely to Juul—*look at these hip college kids using our brand!* But they couldn't help but notice that more of the accounts seemed to be drawing in an ever-younger demographic.

One Instagram account, in particular, was bothersome. It went by the handle @JuulBoyz, and it was gaining a large number of followers. Upon closer inspection the followers appeared to be teenagers who attended fancy private schools like Deerfield Academy, a prep school in Massachusetts, and The Hotchkiss School, a boarding school in Connecticut. Suddenly, it started sinking in. The brand had spread from the edgy warehouse parties of Chelsea, to the genteel townhomes on Manhattan's Upper East Side, to the wealthiest enclaves in America. It was becoming too cool. And too ubiquitous.

"Oh, fuck," remarked an employee, with face in palm, as they scrolled through the JuulBoyz page. "Those little fuckers."

10

THE EXPERIMENTS

The road to hell is paved with good
intentions.

—POPULAR PROVERB

Teaching the little adolescent squirrel monkeys to vape wasn't going
to be easy. But it was a scientifically important undertaking nonetheless that was already under way in 2016, albeit in the early stages.

A couple years earlier, a dozen male monkeys aged ten to fourteen
months, and another dozen of adult age, had been brought to a government laboratory nestled in the middle of a pine forest outside Little
Rock, Arkansas. The Food and Drug Administration's Center for Tobacco Products, which had been formed in 2009 by the groundbreaking law that gave the agency jurisdiction over tobacco, was undertaking
an ambitious project under the leadership of its new director, Mitch
Zeller, who'd been plotting ways to execute on what he called the tobacco "endgame" strategy ever since he arrived at the center in 2013.

Zeller had a long and glorious history of battling the tobacco industry. He'd been David Kessler's right-hand man at the FDA during the height of the Tobacco Wars. A brusque, brilliant lawyer at the agency, he'd been a protagonist in the agency's Odyssey-like intrigue, stalking through cigarette factories, unearthing secret tobacco industry documents, interviewing confidential informants, tracing smuggled tobacco seeds around the world. He'd resigned from the FDA just as the agency's tobacco jurisdiction was being challenged in the U.S. Supreme Court, but in many ways his journey was just beginning.

His experience made him a natural fit for his next job as executive vice president of the American Legacy Foundation, the nonprofit that had been funded by tobacco settlement money, and that had used that money to create shocking anti-tobacco ads such as the one with body bags being dumped in front of Philip Morris headquarters. Then he spent a decade with Pinney Associates, a consulting company started in the 1990s by the legendary anti-smoking advocate John Pinney, a former three-pack-a-day smoker who'd been both the director of the CDC's Office on Smoking and Health and cofounder of Harvard's Institute for the Study of Smoking Behavior and Policy. Pinney was a leading expert on smoking cessation, and when Zeller joined the firm he landed right in the middle of his boss's work with drug companies on early pharmaceutical nicotine products designed to help smokers quit.

Zeller was instantly enthralled with the potential public-health implications of getting smokers off combustible cigarettes and onto a nicotine-delivering substitute. He adopted as his patron saint a British psychiatrist and addiction scientist named Michael Russell, who became one of the earliest scholars to postulate that smoking "is really a very finely adjusted drug-taking activity." Russell went on to advocate the idea that delivering nicotine through less harmful means could help eliminate the deadly habit of smoking. "People smoke for nicotine but they die from the tar," is the phrase, or some variation of it, most often attributed to Russell.

It became Zeller's guiding mantra. While still at Pinney, he served as cochair of a global consortium of tobacco control experts called The Strategic Dialogue on Tobacco Harm Reduction that advocated for "policies that encourage tobacco users to reduce their health risks by switching from the most to the least harmful nicotine-containing products"—a concept they called the "continuum of risk."

Zeller advocated for implementing mandatory product standards that would facilitate the reduction of harm caused by cigarettes, which is exactly what the 2009 Family Smoking Prevention and Tobacco Control Act gave the FDA the authority to do. In 2013, Zeller wrote a paper for the journal *Tobacco Control* titled "Reflections on the 'Endgame' for Tobacco Control," in which he argued that government regulators must "pursue strategies that are designed to drive consumers from the most deadly and dangerous to the least harmful forms of nicotine delivery."

> There is a spectrum or continuum of tobacco and medicinal products that aim to do the same thing—deliver nicotine to the user. But the toxicity associated with those products varies dramatically. At one end of the spectrum is the conventional cigarette, which is designed quite deliberately to create and sustain an addiction to nicotine. . . . Cigarettes kill half of all long-term users and are expected to claim the overwhelming majority of the projected 1 billion deaths from tobacco in this century if trends continue.
>
> At the other end of the spectrum is the current generation of medicinal nicotine products such as gum, patches and lozenges. Made without tobacco (though the nicotine is derived from tobacco), these products pose significantly less risk and have been approved by regulatory bodies around the world as both safe and effective for tobacco cessation.
>
> Along the path of the continuum of risk are products that pose less harm to the individual than cigarettes but for which less is known about their population-level health impacts. Here, we would place smokeless and dissolvable tobacco products as well as the "e-cigarette."

Zeller's advocacy work had caught the attention of his old employer, the FDA. President Obama had just been reelected and there were pressing tobacco issues that needed to be tackled. Would he consider taking the job as director of the newly created Center for Tobacco Products? Given everything Zeller had been working on over the past decade, it was a no-brainer. It would potentially put him in a position to put his tobacco "endgame" into practice on a national scale.

In March 2013 he assumed his new role at the FDA, right around the same time his endgame article was published. A cornerstone of his plan entailed exercising the agency's newly acquired power to regulate the level of nicotine in cigarettes to nonaddictive levels, which would help adult smokers quit but, more importantly, fail to get kids hooked. At the same time, he argued that the FDA should create polices that encouraged the use of "the cleanest and safest form of nicotine delivery," such as nicotine replacement therapies (the patch or lozenges) and electronic cigarettes—a newer but promising technology that potentially could help adult smokers migrate off of cigarettes while still enabling them to obtain "satisfying" amounts of nicotine.

The problem was figuring out just what nicotine level in cigarettes would render them minimally addictive. Regulators couldn't just pluck a number out of thin air. How much nicotine *should* be allowed in a cigarette to render it nonaddictive? And how should the agency even measure it? And would that level also render the cigarette nonaddictive for teenagers?

The FDA set out to answer those questions. That's where the squirrel monkeys came in. On March 5, 2014, the agency approved Project # E0753701, titled *Aspects of nicotine self-administration in a nonhuman primate.*

A group of researchers enlisted by Zeller's Center for Tobacco Products, in conjunction with the agency's National Center for Toxicological Research, began a long-term study that would evaluate the threshold levels of nicotine that lead to initiation and cessation of addiction in adult and adolescent squirrel monkeys. The highly intelligent species, known for their long squirrel-like tails, teapot-shaped heads, and black marblelike eyes, were specifically chosen not only because their cardiovascular and central nervous systems are similar to those of humans but because they also undergo an extended period of adolescence. Also, the species has been known to live up to twenty-five years in captivity, which was ideal for the purposes of potentially gathering data over many years to demonstrate how nicotine changes the brain over time.

Upon arrival at the Arkansas lab, the twenty-four monkeys—twelve adults and twelve adolescents—were anesthetized and surgically fitted with an indwelling catheter in their jugular. They had initial blood draws and brain imaging to serve as a baseline for the experiments. Next they were acclimated to the chamber, a metal box containing a small plexiglass chair on which the monkey would be locked in a sitting position for a specified period of time every day in front of a series of levers. The monkeys were trained to press a lever, which at first dispensed little banana-flavored food pellets. Eventually the lever, when pressed by their tiny slender hands, would dispense doses of nicotine intravenously instead of pellets. Once the monkeys demonstrated reinforcing behaviors indicative of addiction—independently pushing the lever to receive a hit of nicotine—the researchers, donning white lab coats and powder-blue plastic gloves, began progressively lowering the dosage with each lever press, while monitoring their behavior, brain scans, and blood levels.

For about a year, the studies went mostly according to plan, but in the summer of 2015 one of the monkeys stopped breathing during a brain scan and died. But the researchers were collecting valuable data nevertheless and the experiments continued.

Meanwhile, as the FDA was experimenting with nicotine on monkeys inside its labs, there was an even bigger nicotine experiment unfolding across America. By the summer of 2016, there was growing concern about a new wave of nicotine addiction among American youth as they started using electronic cigarettes, in particular Juul. Ironically, almost no long-term research had been done on vaping, and there were countless unanswered questions even though, by the spring of 2016, the CDC announced that three million middle school and high school students reported using e-cigarettes. Was it safe? What effect did the vapor have on the lungs? What about flavored e-cigarettes— were the chemicals used to make the cherry or the cotton candy or the unicorn fizz flavors toxic? And were those more addictive than plain tobacco-flavored e-cigarettes?

The FDA's monkey researchers began figuring out how they might be able to augment their study to better understand the effects of vaping, by testing it on the monkeys. They already had them self-dosing nicotine into the vein, but it was vaping that increasingly seemed like the more pressing public-health question. Even though this iteration of the study hadn't yet received FDA funding, they began working with a company that could make specialized flavored vapor products. And another one that was in the early stages of designing an inhalation chamber for the monkeys to go into that could be modified to have a nozzle attached to a plexiglass window that would at first dispense water. Eventually, instead of sucking water, they would suck nicotine vapor. They were in the early stages of teaching the monkeys, effectively, to Juul.

ON MAY 10, 2016, the FDA published its much-anticipated final "deeming" rule. It had been seven years since the FDA won legal authority to regulate tobacco products, and about that same amount of time since the agency had been working to bring e-cigarettes under its jurisdiction. The time it took the FDA to issue the deeming regulation was about the same amount of time that it took Bowen and Monsees to start and finish grad school, write a business plan, raise venture capital, build Ploom, ditch Ploom, build and launch Pax, and then build Juul.

For the first time, e-cigarettes were "deemed" by the FDA to be a tobacco product subject to federal oversight, along with myriad other tobacco products that had fallen through the cracks in 2009, including cigars, hookahs, pipe tobacco, and novel forms of tobacco like dissolvables, orbs, and discs. The rule, which took effect on August 8, 2016, banned sales of the products to anybody under the age of eighteen, both in stores and online, and it halted the practice of distributing free samples. It also set up a series of deadlines over the next several months that the industry would have to meet, including a requirement that manufacturers place health warnings on their packages and that they report a list of their ingredients, along with potentially harmful constituents, to the agency.

For e-cigarette companies that had grown used to unbridled commerce, the deeming rule was a buzzkill. No more selling to anyone, anywhere, as long as they could produce a credit card number. No more sleek packages free from eyesore labels warning of the addictive nature of nicotine. No more unrestrained freedom to firehose the nation with nicotine.

There was one provision in particular that struck a nerve for the industry. Manufacturers of e-cigarettes would be required to submit an application to the FDA and receive authorization from the agency before their products could be sold. Only e-cigarettes already on the market before February 15, 2007 (a date unrelated to e-cigarettes; it was the date when the Tobacco Control Act was introduced in Congress), would be "grandfathered" in. But because almost zero e-cigarettes had been on the market in February 2007, it meant that every single product on the market would be required to undergo review by the agency and receive regulatory approval.

Rather than remove every single product from the market (as some tobacco control advocates wanted), the agency cut the industry a break. Manufacturers would be allowed to keep selling their products for two years, until August 8, 2018. By that date they'd be required to submit an application to the FDA for so-called premarket review to determine whether their product demonstrated that it met the agency's standard of being "appropriate for the protection of public health." If the standard wasn't met, the product would have to be removed from the market.

The retroactive review requirement was so controversial that for months leading up to the final deeming rule, lobbyists for Altria, R. J. Reynolds, and other tobacco and e-cigarette companies pressured lawmakers (unsuccessfully) to allow their products to be exempt from having to seek the agency's blessing. The companies argued that two years wasn't enough time to file the lengthy, and costly, applications. Smaller manufacturers argued that the applications, which required in-depth scientific studies and costly research, were too onerous and presented an unfair burden for them. Despite the lobbying efforts, the FDA didn't budge, teeing up a fight that would ultimately dog the agency for years.

There was another sticking point—the only products eligible for the two-year grace period were those that were on the market as of August 8, 2016. Any product introduced *after* that day would be considered by the FDA to be a "new tobacco product," which couldn't be introduced until it first received authorization. That meant that e-cigarette companies selling products at the time the rule went into effect, such as Juul and MarkTen and Vuse, were forbidden from introducing any new product to the market. Not only that—the agency would consider their existing product to be a "new tobacco product" if they made even the slightest design change or modification to it. The FDA was trying to limit a flood of new products onto the market before they had a chance to evaluate those currently being sold. But it was a potential nightmare for the companies that had imperfect products that might otherwise benefit from improvement—which was nearly all of them. Many e-cigarettes weren't well designed and suffered from design flaws, including the same leaking problem that Juul had. But as of August 8, 2016, the e-cigarette market was essentially frozen and manufacturers were stuck with what they had.

After the rule took effect, Zeller penned an op-ed that provided color on the agency's thinking. "The new rule moves us away from a largely unregulated marketplace of these tobacco products increasingly favored by kids—a marketplace that I have likened to the Wild, Wild West—and into an era of effective and reasonable science-based regulation," Zeller wrote. "The FDA's expanded authority under the rule is a pivotal foundational step in understanding this frontier of novel tobacco products and protecting Americans from premature death and disease."

Yes, the regulations were a step toward bringing order to a highly unordered market. But for all the companies' hemming and hawing, the practical effect of the rule meant that the products currently on the market, including Juul, could largely enjoy the status quo for at least two more years while they put together their marketing applications.

This was all part of a high-wire balancing act that the FDA was attempting. The agency was trying to foster the market for reduced-harm products, while ensuring they didn't promote initiation among non-nicotine users. But despite the hopes of die-hard harm-reductionists, like Zeller, a worst-case scenario was starting to unfold—the exact products that were ostensibly designed to reduce harm among adult smokers were being picked up by kids who likely never would have touched a tobacco product.

In December 2016, the surgeon general, Vivek H. Murthy, released a report titled *E-Cigarette Use Among Youth and Young Adults*. It concluded:

> E-cigarette use among U.S. youth and young adults is now a major public health concern. E-cigarette use has increased considerably in recent years, growing an astounding 900% among high school students from 2011 to 2015. These products are now the most commonly used form of tobacco among youth in the United States, surpassing conventional tobacco products, including cigarettes, cigars, chewing tobacco, and hookahs. Most e-cigarettes contain nicotine, which can cause addiction and can harm the developing adolescent brain. . . . It is crucial that the progress made in reducing conventional cigarette smoking among youth and young adults not be compromised by the initiation and use of e-cigarettes.

The nicotine gadgets were turning out to be a Pandora's box. And the FDA wasn't doing a very good job keeping a lid on it.

11

MOVE FAST. BREAK LAWS.

If you never break anything, you're
probably not moving fast enough.
—MARK ZUCKERBERG, FOUNDER, FACEBOOK

O ver the past few months, Pax Labs executives had been nervously anticipating the FDA's new rules. Just like everybody else, they knew that when the deeming rule took effect the playing field would dramatically change. Critically, no new products, or those modified to be rendered new, could be introduced to the market after August 8, 2016, which meant that Juul's innovation efforts would be suddenly hampered. That was a less-than-ideal situation. Telling a tech start-up to not innovate was like telling Pizza Hut to not make pizza.

Nevertheless, in anticipation of the rule, the company began churning out as many products as it could, to get them on the market before "the curtain fell," as some employees internally described the impending rule. Between December 2015 and August 2016, Juul spit out e-liquids in dozens of special flavors, including cinnamon snap, crisp pear, and ginger peach, to augment its existing product line that included fruit, cucumber, mango, mint, and crème brûlée. Juul executives were well aware of the potential regulatory arbitrage at play. In one email in mid-2016, Gal Cohen, the former Nektar executive, sent an email to Bowen, commenting on how since the old tobacco Master Settlement Agreement's advertising and other restrictions didn't apply to e-cigarettes, the company "should consider taking advantage of the FTO," or freedom to operate.

Two weeks after the deeming rule went into effect, and ten months after being left without a permanent leader, Pax Labs finally found its new CEO. They settled on Tyler Goldman, an executive who'd previously run Deezer, a French music streaming company. The company put out a press release touting the new hire: "PAX Labs Hires CEO Tyler Goldman to Handle Rapid Growth," it blared.

Ever since the board ousted Monsees, Hoyoung Huh had been acting as the company's CEO. While the man was undeniably smart, he simply didn't fit in with the hoop-in-nose, flower-vaporizing office culture that had come to dominate Pax. Plus, Huh rarely showed up at the office, and when he did, it seemed like the best leadership he could muster was a faux-inspirational adage about sports that made people want to roll their eyes. Plus, the company was suddenly starting to rattle like a freight train. Juul still made up only a tiny fraction of the market, but sales were picking up.

Still, the executive committee's choice of Goldman to replace Huh at such a critical juncture left some employees puzzled. A lawyer by training, earlier in his career Goldman had run a digital media ad platform that featured a stable of pop-culture content brands designed to attract clicks, like "Celebuzz" and "SocialiteLife" and "Go Fug Yourself." He'd also launched a network of sports-related websites, run a movie website that was sold to Blockbuster, and was in charge of new media for the publisher of *Hustler* magazine.

While he had experience in early-stage companies, it was less evident that he had the operational chops to actually scale a fast-growing tech start-up with a manufacturing supply chain that stretched around the globe. And from a social standpoint, Goldman wasn't much of an improvement on Huh. His unfocused, sophomoric demeanor didn't sit well with employees. Instead of talking shop, he'd boast about idiosyncratic details of his life, and on at least one occasion regaled underlings with a story of how he once dated Vanity, the one-time pop singer who was Prince's muse.

Even more damning, there was a sense that Goldman never really understood or got excited about Juul, the company's future growth engine. He'd arrived at the company enthusiastic about the cannabis space. In press interviews he'd plug Pax, but when asked about Juul, he'd gloss over it. "How much did you know about the vape market before joining Pax?" a reporter asked him. "I had heard a lot about Pax and knew it had a cult following. I knew less about Juul, since most of my team at Deezer still smoked combustible cigarettes."

Goldman walked into a hurricane. By the summer of 2016, there was a nationwide Juul shortage. Bodegas and gas stations were hoarding Juul and jacking up the price by almost double in some instances. Goldman tried to police it but quickly found that he was engaged in a game of Whac-A-Mole. Retailers were calling the company, angrily demanding more Juul, as much as they could get their hands on. Eventually, the sales team had to halt the addition of any new retailers at a time when the brand was only in a tiny slice of the retail market, compared to its Big Tobacco rivals who'd dominated store shelves for decades. The company had maxed out its pod production capacity but was still able to supply only half of the product demanded by customers.

Goldman increased prices, hoping that would slow demand, and tried to expand capacity by working on new machines to increase production speeds in China. But they kept falling short of the orders. No matter how much modeling they did based on other tobacco and e-cigarette products on the market, they were wrong. They needed to produce more and more and more, leaving Goldman constantly caught by surprise.

Industry data for the tobacco companies had said that of the users who tried e-cigarettes, about 10 percent would convert to using the product. But Goldman found out that Juul's "conversion rate" was closer to 60 percent—which would have been great had he been able to supply all those converters. Goldman also underestimated just how much Juuling people would do. Users, it turned out, were consuming four to five pods every single week. By the company's own calculations, that nicotine intake equated to a person smoking four to five packs of cigarettes every week, or about fourteen cigarettes a day. It soon became clear, if it wasn't already, that there was something extraordinary about Juul. As Goldman explained it, customers were displaying a "high attachment rate" with the product. That's a euphemism for addiction. Nothing, it seemed, could slow America's rapacious appetite for it.

IT WAS THE FALL of 2016. Kevin Brzuziewski had recently gone off to a local liberal arts college outside Cleveland, Ohio, called Baldwin Wallace University. He'd grown up in the Akron, Ohio, area and graduated the year before from Revere High School, where he played varsity baseball. Now he was studying business marketing and living in an off-campus house with three of his best friends. They did everything together—attending Indians games, going out to sports bars, and collecting and selling baseball cards. A friend of his had long tried quitting smoking and was experimenting with different e-cigarettes. Not surprisingly, he'd fallen in love with Juul. Brzuziewski had been an occasional smoker, and when he tried his friend's Juul he instantly enjoyed the buzz it gave him. He was hooked. So he went out and bought a Juul for himself.

Brzuziewski had always been a fan of social media and had in fact built up a cottage business for himself over the years by selling ads on the social media pages and websites he'd built. He made his first such site, a fan page devoted to the Cleveland Browns football team, at the age of thirteen, while still in middle school. Ever since, he'd maintained various websites devoted to anything from phone cases to baseball cards to sports jerseys. Sometimes he'd stay up all night tending to them.

One night, in the fall of 2016, Brzuziewski and his friends were hanging out, drinking beer and Juuling. As they perused the internet, looking at random social media posts and Juul memes, Brzuziewski was surprised that there didn't seem to be any Juul fan pages. So, knowing all he did about building fan pages, he decided to build his own for the product on Instagram. He named it @JuulNation.

Initially he did it as a kind of inside joke with his buddies. On his Instagram page he posted the hashtag, #JUULnation and #hellanic, and wrote "If U Ain't Got One.. Whatchu Doing??" One of his first posts was prompted by a rumor online suggesting that Juul was planning to release a new, limited-edition Juul flavor, coco-mint. He posted a picture of a box of the coco-mint Juul pods and wrote something to the effect of "Is this real?" It was real, and was one of Juul's limited-edition flavors. The post got a surprising amount of responses—or "engagement" in social-media speak, in which Brzuziewski was fluent. Encouraged by the response, he posted another picture of another new flavor, this time mango. He got more likes. At first, he had just a few followers, but he was slowly getting more and more with every post. He'd post pictures that people sent in of themselves Juuling. And get more followers. He'd post pictures of tall stacks of Juul pods, shaped into impressive pyramids. And get more likes. He posted pictures of the parade of rare Juul pod flavors that hit the market, like chestnut croissant or cinnamon snap, and the limited-edition colored Juul devices, like gold. He posted photos of himself and his friends Juuling.

Soon, one hundred followers turned into five hundred, then a thousand. Within just a few months, he was gaining a thousand followers every day. It was then that he realized that his @JuulNation page was much more than a joke. Vape companies started contacting him wanting to know if he'd be interested in getting paid to feature their ads. Upstarts that made "skins" or covers for Juul devices also reached out to him, wanting to partner with his Instagram page. Eonsmoke, a company that made Juul-compatible pods, sponsored him. Soon he was cutting deals worth several thousand dollars and turning his joke page into a business. *Wow, this could really be a career,* he thought.

By 2017, now with tens of thousands of followers, he'd dropped out of college to focus on growing @JuulNation full-time. The give-away contests were always a hit. "About to post the finalists for the custom juul contest . . . whichever one gets the most likes by midnight EST tonight will win a free pack of whatever flavor pods you'd like!" Photos flooded in of tricked-out Juuls. One had the word *Fiend* scratched into the metal body. One was spray-painted in Rastafarian red, yellow, and green. Another was covered in purple peacock feathers. "Tag fellow Juulers to join the Nation," he wrote.

He'd post pictures of people boating and Juuling. Partying and Juuling. Doing nothing and Juuling. He devised little surveys that asked his followers to tell him which flavors they liked the best. He even started making swag—black hoodies and baseball caps emblazoned with the JuulNation logo. It became a team effort, where everybody in his house would pitch in, helping box up the swag, or the free Juul pods, or other "prizes" that people won. @JuulNation became the largest Juul fan page on Instagram, with its postings garnering hundreds of thousands of views, and regularly generating more than one million likes.

Some days he'd be amazed to see dozens of people from the same college follow him—one day it would seem like an entire fraternity from Baylor would follow him; the next it would be students from Louisiana State University. He didn't give it a second thought when the pictures started flowing in from teenagers clearly not yet in college. "I could tell it was spreading through schools," he said.

He posted comments of teenagers griping about teachers confiscating their Juuls and a picture of a hand-made sign inside a high school hallway that said "Hitting the Juul won't make you Cuul." They Photoshopped Juul pods in Mountain Dew or Cap'n Crunch flavors. They shared memes that showed how to hide a Juul inside a secret cutout in a book.

The fall of 2017 was the fall of the Tide pod challenge, when young people eating Tide detergent pods and posting it online went viral. It also became the year of the Juul pod challenge, where teenagers would see how many rips off a Juul they could take before passing out, or how many Juuls they could suck on at once. Brzuziewski thought it was hilarious. So he challenged his own tens of thousands of followers to take the Juul challenge. One guy shoved fourteen Juuls in his mouth and vaped them all at once. He was the winner. That posting got nearly 275,000 likes.

AS JUUL SALES WERE mushrooming, the product continued to have glaring flaws, an embarrassment for a company that prided itself on quality design. The most problematic issue had to do with its pods. The liquid inside the little plastic pods that users inhaled into their lungs as a vapor was called e-liquid. It's a simple formulation comprising just five primary ingredients: nicotine, propylene glycol, vegetable glycerin, benzoic acid, and flavorings. At first glance the ingredients would appear harmless. While nicotine is addictive, it isn't a major carcinogen. Glycerin is the substance used in fog machines, like the kind used in theatrical productions. Propylene glycol is used as a deicing agent in industrial settings and as an emulsifier in salad dressings. Benzoic acid is an organic compound commonly used as a preservative in all kinds of foods.

While individually there was nothing alarming about those ingredients—most are generally recognized as safe for ingestion by the FDA—there was a lot yet to be understood about how they interacted with the body in the context of vaping. The product simply hadn't been around long enough for there to have been sufficient long-term clinical research to determine whether the very act of vaping was safe or not. Cigarette smoking typically doesn't result in lung disease until decades of use. What if the effects of vaping or Juuling would likewise be gradual, and only over decades would damage to the lungs become apparent? In recent years federal regulators and researchers had begun researching the topic, asking whether the act of inhaling the base ingredients of most e-cigarette fluids, delivered as ultrafine particles to the deepest reaches of the lungs over long periods of time, was as safe as its proponents claimed.

In particular the flavorings in the e-liquids had health experts worried. While a flavor, say, mint or strawberry, might seem innocuous, most flavorings contain dozens or more sub-ingredients, some of which when heated up can become potentially harmful or carcinogenic. At a 2015 presentation to the FDA, a CDC researcher warned that two ingredients sometimes found in some e-cigarette flavorings, diacetyl and pentanedione, were potentially harmful when inhaled. In the 1990s, diacetyl had been linked to a cluster of lung damage among workers at a microwave popcorn factory in Missouri who'd been breathing in the chemical, which gave the popcorn a buttery flavor. Juul maintained publicly that its flavorings didn't have these ingredients, but some internal correspondence cited in a lawsuit against Juul indicated that the company wasn't entirely sure. For example, a company memo from April 2018 with the subject "'POPCORN LUNG'—Regular Perspective and Diacetyl Risk Assessment" found that "small amounts of Diacetyl" were detected in its cool-mint-flavored pods, one of the company's most popular products. The lawsuit alleged that Juul simply ran the tests again using "less-sensitive equipment," and then reported its new finding for the mint product: "Diacetyl—Not Detected."

Meanwhile, Juul employees watched in real time as problems emerged. An internal database of customer complaints contained nearly three thousand reports from customers reporting adverse health effects after using Juul (a fraction of the overall complaints in the database), including pain in the mouth, burning sensation of the lungs, fever, chills, vomiting, and light-headedness. One woman reported to the company that after Juuling her throat started to bleed.

A common source of the problems was tied to the little plastic pods that held the nicotine liquid and served as a mouthpiece. Sometimes, as a user would suck on the device, the harsh liquid would leak onto their lips or inside their mouth, causing burns or blisters or numbness.

Health concerns aside, there were other problems. Not long after launching, customers began complaining that the mint flavor didn't always taste like mint. Or that the tobacco flavor didn't always taste like tobacco. Or that the flavor was simply "off." The company hadn't yet adopted strict manufacturing specifications for its e-liquid, and it didn't always have a complete handle on its serpentine ingredient supply chain, which stretched from high-end European flavor houses, to major chemical manufacturers, to the tobacco fields of India where raw nicotine was sourced. That made it difficult to immediately ascertain what exactly was causing any number of problems, or to unravel quality issues as they cropped up.

At the time, Juul had a single e-liquid manufacturer, a third-generation family-run company called Mother Murphy's Laboratories, based in Greensboro, North Carolina, whose motto was "Making the World Taste Better." Mother Murphy's evolved from mixing flavors for local bakeries in 1946, into one of the biggest suppliers of sweet essences and aromas and extracts for makers of everything from doughnuts and sugary cereals, to loose-leaf tea and chewing gum. It also had long provided big tobacco companies with flavors like raisin, chocolate, and rum that helped finesse cigarette "blends." As the e-cigarette market grew in the mid-2000s, Mother Murphy's launched a dedicated e-liquid manufacturing business called Alternative Ingredients, which grew to become Juul's primary supplier and was instrumental in developing Juul's trademark e-liquid recipes, including the popular mint and mango that ended up driving the brand's sales.

To figure out what was causing the off-tasting e-liquid, Juul launched an internal investigation that dragged on for weeks. Part of the challenge was that Juul had tried, but could never find, a machine at any price that could gauge flavor consistency. Often they'd instead employ human testers to simply vape batches of questionable e-liquid to determine whether it was good or bad. Flavorists at Mother Murphy's, and at Juul, would sit around tables and pass around a Juul, often using a mouth covering to prevent the spread of germs. They'd taste the batch in question and compare it with batches known to be good. *Did it taste good enough to sell?*

One former Mother Murphy's employee who was tasked with tasting Juul's batches described sitting around a table in a windowless room in the back of the company's R&D lab, which was adjacent to the company's redbrick-and-green-trimmed headquarters sandwiched between a Motel 6 and Greensboro Tractor Company. The job of sucking down the flavored liquids (which didn't have nicotine yet mixed in), took some getting used to. "The draw itself would choke me up some-times," said the former employee.

Eventually, Juul traced the problem to an off-spec ingredient that had gotten into some of the e-liquids and caused flavor variations. The company also determined that the ingredient posed no health threats. Juul stopped production of the e-liquid nonetheless and disposed of the bad batches still in production. That came at the worst time pos-sible. The company was already backlogged with sales. This added another dent in supply, exacerbating the Juul shortage.

At the same time, the company discovered that some of the off-spec product had already made it into pods and onto store shelves. Rather than issue a recall, the company brushed it under the rug, con-cluding that there was no reason to believe that it would sicken some-body. The marketing team was instructed to tell retailers that if they received complaints from customers about off-tasting pods, to just swap them out for a newer product that the company would send. Juul didn't tell retailers *why* they might want to send it back. Since retailers were already facing a severe product shortage, most opted to keep the product on the shelf.

While Juul downplayed the issue publicly, inside it was the compa-ny's first big *oh-shit* moment as people began internalizing for the first time that their hip, flashy device had at least the potential to cause harm to human health. They'd dodged a bullet this time. But without repeatable processes or procedures in place, what if the next time the bad ingredient was something actually bad?

"There were no checks and balances on anything," recalled a for-mer employee who was involved in the handling of the issue.

The haphazard way of running the business spooked employees who started dwelling a little longer in thought about the product they were selling. The company freely handed out Juul to employees. It even invited employees across the company to try some of the newest flavors concocted by the company's flavorists and chemists. Employ-ees, who were asked to sign consent forms before accepting a new blend from a lab in the basement, tested new flavors as if they were testing a new flavor of potato chip. Some loved that. OMG did you taste the *Snozzberry*?! Others were shocked that the company allowed such a thing. Shouldn't there be more quality control before allowing employees to in essence be guinea pigs for new products? Was Juuling even safe?

"There were the occasional hypothetical questions over beer, about how people thought smoking was safe for fifty years," recalled one former executive. "We'd say, 'We know that we have less carcinogens in what we do, but how can we know it's *safe*? Is it going to take fifty years to find out? Are we missing something?' It's not that long that people have been atomizing nicotine and inhaling it into their lungs."

IN JUNE 2017, THE Pax Labs board decided to split the company into two separate entities. Pax Labs would continue on in the cannabis vaporizer space, while a newly named entity, Juul Labs, was spun off to focus solely on nicotine. As the company's sales clocked upward, there was growing attention from investors wanting a piece of the action. Yet some investors expressed reservations about investing in a company that had potential legal exposure in the cannabis space since it was still considered a controlled substance in several states. To truly unlock the value of Juul, it became obvious that it made more sense to divorce the two businesses, unleashing the nicotine side of the business.

Employees at the company started getting divvied up. Some would stay at the Pax Labs building and continue working on the marijuana side of the business. Others would get moved to Juul Labs, which would be headquartered in a historic building on the waterfront in the Dogpatch.

Ever since Juul launched, the company's bankers had been near constantly circulating pitch decks to investors, including top-tier hedge funds, which, despite any initial misgivings about investing in a tobacco company, had a hard time averting their eyes from what was undeniably an extraordinary investment proposition. The business model was like that of Gillette razors or Keurig coffee machines, which required customers to first buy the device, and then purchase refills over and over again, which gave the companies a repeatable revenue stream.

Yet unlike razor blades, Juul contained a highly addictive substance. That presented a tantalizing, albeit controversial investment thesis that even inside Juul people didn't like to openly discuss: Once a user became hooked on Juul, they'd become a very "sticky" customer, as they call it in marketing parlance. As in you can't pry the thing from their hands with a crowbar. And with one billion smokers in the world, well, the potential upside was staggering. The company hadn't even made it into the international market yet. Even those who considered investing and passed for ethical reasons were rapt.

Juul was "one of the most impressive e-consumer companies I've ever seen," one potential investor told *The Information*. "Putting what they do aside for a second. High use frequency, good economics. Subscription-like business."

Juul in fact made for a perfectly packaged investment thesis that served the twin purpose of making investors salivate over the massiveness of the market, while also giving them the sheen of morality that would help deliver just enough cover when an inevitably wary partner had the gall to doubt whether it was wise to jump into the tobacco business. "But they are out to *kill* the tobacco industry," they'd retort. "Their product will *save lives*."

And those statements wouldn't be untrue. If somebody was presented with the option of smoking combustible cigarettes for life—an almost guaranteed death sentence—or a Juul for life—maybe a lifelong nicotine addiction, but probably not emphysema or cancer, and almost certainly, but not a 100 percent certainty, not a guaranteed death sentence—the choice should be clear. That was the calculus, and the rationale that almost every single Juul investor made. They were doing it for the good of the world. To save lives. To take down one of the most notorious industries in modern America. Of course, it didn't hurt that a Juul user could potentially become a customer for decades, if not for life, worth potentially tens of thousands of dollars or more. Why *wouldn't* they invest in Juul?

OF ALL THE PEARLS of wisdom bestowed by Silicon Valley's venture capitalists and founders on a world seeking insight into their overwhelming, world-beating success, perhaps the most renowned—and possibly infamous—came from the king of Silicon Valley himself, Mark Zuckerberg. In Facebook's investor prospectus ahead of its initial public offering in 2012, Zuckerberg outlined the core values of his start-up. "Moving fast enables us to build more things and learn faster. However, as most companies grow, they slow down too much because they're more afraid of making mistakes than they are of losing opportunities by moving too slowly. We have a saying: 'Move fast and break things.' The idea is that if you never break anything, you're probably not moving fast enough."

The cofounder of LinkedIn, Reid Hoffman, built on that principle and, in quintessential Silicon Valley fashion, advanced it to the extreme. His theory of rapid growth, which he called "blitzscaling," was not just moving fast and breaking things but rather a framework that allowed companies "to achieve massive scale at incredible speed. If you're growing at a rate that is so much faster than your competitors that it makes you feel uncomfortable, then hold on tight, you might be blitzscaling!"

It was this ethos that helped transform Silicon Valley into a place where Mark Zuckerberg's platform, once lauded for connecting the world, became a platform for psyops and murderous dictators; where Google's set of organizing principles became a modern-day panopticon; where Uber's friendly drivers were overshadowed by a platoon of bullies and lobbyists that ripped through city after city until the company suffused the world. No matter what wide-eyed vision or cheeky mission statement these companies might have had—Don't Be Evil, say—the coldhearted pursuit of profit always seemed to win out.

Juul might have started with a mission—Destroy Big Tobacco—but it wasn't long before it started to deeply internalize the mores of Silicon Valley. Move fast. Blitzscale. Ask forgiveness, not permission. Aggressively inundate the world with their products before regulators figure out what hit them.

The hard truth is that Silicon Valley investors are driven less by the idealized visions of the Valley's founders and more the nuts and bolts of the business model. Is the business model replicable? Is the product sticky? Perhaps most important, has the business achieved "product/ market fit"? That's the idea popularized by Marc Andreessen, the cofounder of Netscape, who went on to cofound the venerated Silicon Valley venture capital firm Andreessen Horowitz. "You can always feel product/market fit when it's happening," he wrote in a blog post in June 2007. "The customers are buying the product just as fast as you can make it—or usage is growing just as fast as you can add more servers. Money from customers is piling up in your company checking account. You're hiring sales and customer support staff as fast as you can."

Stanford professor Steve Blank, a prominent Silicon Valley entrepreneur and a creator of the business concept called the "Lean Startup," explained product/market fit this way in the context of Juul: "It simply means people grab it out of your hands and in this case stick it in their mouths and don't let go. It's when people say 'I've got to have it.' It's when people's eyes dilate, or in this case when their heart rates rise," he said.

There's a reason, Blank said, that the holy grail for start-ups had become to create a product that possessed one thing above all else: addiction. "Companies do two types of things. They either have a product that solves a problem, or they fulfill a need, like social media or entertainment. And they are addictive. Facebook is addictive. Playing Minecraft is addictive. Juul is the ultimate addictive start-up."

WITH THE NEWLY FORMED Juul Labs, it was more important than ever to fix the problems with the devices, not least because the company now was selling a single product. If the company couldn't optimize the Juul, that could be a big problem.

Perhaps the most pernicious problem was related to its leaky pods. The syrupy nicotine was not only leaking into users' mouths, but it was also seeping inside the circuitry of the device, causing the electronics to stop working. As the engineers researched the problem, they determined a few basic things. When the e-liquid trickled into the guts of the device, it would come into contact with a tiny pressure sensor inside. The sensor was designed to recognize the airflow when some-body sucked on the mouthpiece, and in turn trigger the battery to heat up the liquid, which in turn produced vapor. If the sensor was liquid-logged it couldn't detect the airflow and that meant the user couldn't take a hit.

Juul engineers had dealt with this issue since the very beginning, but now that the product had gone viral, it was becoming more than a minor headache. Customers were furious. Complaints deluged a cus-tomer service team that was nowhere near big enough to handle the onslaught.

Of all the problems that the company was facing, this was one of the more vexing. Sure, from a basic health-and-safety point of view the problem was less than ideal. And from a design and aesthetics stand-point, the problem was anathema to a company that fancied itself the Apple of e-cigarettes. But, more important for a scaling start-up in a highly competitive business: This could potentially imperil the com-pany's growth plans if its sole product was crapping out in the market-place.

The quality and engineering departments furiously worked to find the root of the leaks. They tested the viscosity of various e-liquid for-mulations. They conducted a series of tests by turning the pods on one side, then another, then another, to pinpoint the root of the problem. They observed the pods at different temperatures and at high alti-tudes—in the Rocky Mountains and on cargo airplanes—to gauge how heat and pressure were affecting the leakage, and even relocated ware-houses closer to production to avoid having to ship the pods long dis-tances over hot, mountainous routes. Even with the smartest engineers in Silicon Valley, the company couldn't figure out how to solve the problem.

Under normal circumstances a company like Juul would have sim-ply fixed the thing. But these weren't normal circumstances. Because the FDA's deeming rule had just gone into effect, there were all kinds of new rules governing how the company was supposed to operate to stay on the right side of the law. Importantly, the law said that no com-pany could modify its products in any way—including changes in the "design, any component, any part of any constituent"—otherwise it would be rendered a "new tobacco product" that would have to receive FDA authorization before it could be sold. That would require withholding the product from the market until the manufacturer submitted a marketing application to the FDA and received a decision from the agency as to whether or not the product review met the agency's standards. That entire process could take years. Yet violations of the law could result in civil penalties and the FDA pulling the product from the market.

There's a well-worn meme that shows a cartoon figure standing over a control board, sweating nervously, as he hovers a finger between a red button and a blue button. Depending on the issue at hand, the labels under the buttons usually signify two contradicting paths that could be taken depending on which button the guy pressed. Juul was like that guy. Red Button: Abide by the law, potentially lose the race. Blue Button: Skirt the law, make bank.

By the summer of 2017, even though the company was stealing market from its competitors, it was far from the dominant player. Reynolds's product, Vuse, still had a third of the market. Altria accounted for more than 20 percent with its MarkTen. Juul still had less than 12 percent of the market. Meanwhile, Juul was in the process of raising another round of venture capital funding. The company's future was on the line.

Juul was busy moving fast and breaking things. It decided to press the Blue Button.

Toward the end of 2017, the company quietly overhauled its faulty device, potentially running afoul of FDA rules and the law. The old device, which had an internal code name of Splinter—named after a Teenage Mutant Ninja Turtles character—was scrapped. The spiffed-up device, which was given the internal code name Jagwar, after another Ninja Turtles character, hit the market in the beginning of 2018. It featured a leak-resistant pod, a new sensor that wouldn't fizzle out if liquid got on it, a reorganized motherboard, and improved firmware. It was like releasing the latest, greatest iPhone.

But there was no fanfare for the release of Juul 2.0. The new device looked identical on the outside. Customers would never be able to tell the difference—other than being pleasantly surprised at how their Juul purred like a kitten. The FDA would never know.

MEANWHILE, TYLER GOLDMAN WAS losing his luster. By the end of 2017, the company was selling nearly five million Juul pods every month, up from 750,000 when Goldman took over. Juul was closing in on its top competitors. But the company was still meeting only half of all demand. Goldman had been at the helm of the company for more than a year and the company was still unable to meaningfully break free from the supply chain logjam. For a board focused almost entirely on growth, that was not acceptable.

There was friction between Juul's founders and Goldman. Bowen and Monsees, who lived and breathed Juul, were irked by Goldman's perceived lack of love for the device, combined with his inability to bring about true transformation. Goldman chafed at Monsees's know-it-all sensibility and relished in reminding others that Monsees had been ousted from his own company's top job. At one point, Monsees was furious when he heard that Goldman was sniping about him behind his back, calling him the "exiled King."

At the end of 2017, Juul was growing so fast that it needed somebody who could actually scale the company. The company had achieved more than $200 million in annual revenue, and its monthly sales were up 600 percent over the previous year. That didn't even account for sales occurring inside vape shops, a channel so new that it wasn't captured by mainstream retail data tracking services. It also didn't account for online purchases, the burning white-hot center of Juul's business, which were soaring. All of the company's tactics—the Instagram influencers, the sampling tour, yummy flavors, the low barriers to getting the product, the "stickiness" of its product—were paying off.

On December 11, 2017, Juul announced that it had replaced Goldman with a new CEO, Kevin Burns, a former private equity executive. A week later, the company raised its first round of venture funding as an independent entity in the amount of $111.5 million. Pritzker plowed money in through Tao Capital. So did Justin Mateen, the founder of the dating app Tinder. Other investors included Gregg Smith, an angel investor in companies including Sweetgreen and Beyond Meat, and Carter and Courtney Reum, Los Angeles i-banker brothers whose investment firm, M13, poured money into the splashiest start-up brands.

Juul even snagged Fidelity Investments, the diversified financial services company that was one of the largest asset managers in the world and managed retirement nest eggs (and provided other investment services) for more than thirty-two million Americans. Fidelity had long invested primarily in so-called blue-chip stocks—typically publicly traded Fortune 500 firms—but over the past decade it began investing more in firms that hadn't yet gone public, giving it upside exposure to start-ups waiting longer to file for an IPO. Getting money from Fidelity was like getting a gold stamp of approval. It telegraphed to other investors that the company was not only vetted by Wall Street's best and brightest but that it might be headed for an IPO of its own.

As the big names plowed money into Juul, it was a flare shooting up into the sky for all of Wall Street and Silicon Valley to see. And since investors have inveterate FOMO, the stampeding herd would inexorably follow.

A NICOTINE COMPROMISE

If men were angels, no government
would be necessary.

—ALEXANDER HAMILTON OR JAMES MADISON

On May 11, 2017, Scott Gottlieb stood in the office of the then secretary of Health and Human Services, Tom Price, for his swearing-in ceremony, smiling widely as a coterie of aides and staffers stood by. About two months earlier the newly inaugurated president, Donald J. Trump, had named Gottlieb the next commissioner of the Food and Drug Administration. With an annual budget of almost $6 billion, the agency oversaw nearly a quarter of all consumer spending in the United States and touched the lives of every single American with its oversight of everything from everyday food items like ice cream and hamburger, to prescription drugs, to medical devices, dietary supplements, and cosmetics. And tobacco.

This was a huge day for Gottlieb. As a twice-previous FDA official, he had a deep love for the institution and was eager to get started. The secretary had high hopes for him. "I am confident Dr. Gottlieb will make decisions that reduce regulatory burdens while protecting public health," Price said in a congratulatory statement.

The pressure to roll back regulations under the Trump administration pervaded all of Washington. No agency was spared from the new ideology. And as Gottlieb was sworn in, there was no avoiding it at the FDA either. Trump had recently signed an executive order aimed at reducing regulations, and during his first address to Congress he'd said that his administration would "slash the restraints" to allow the "slow and burdensome" FDA to bring forth "miracle" cures to patients in need. Rumors had been flying around that in his zeal to undo anything and everything enacted by his predecessor—the Affordable Care Act, the Deferred Action for Childhood Arrivals, the Paris Climate Accord—Trump might go after the landmark Obama-era tobacco regulations too.

At his confirmation hearing just a few weeks earlier, Gottlieb had been goaded by Republicans to promise that he'd speed up approvals for everything from nonaddictive painkillers, hearts rebuilt from stem cells, a universal flu vaccine, an HIV/AIDS vaccine, an artificial pancreas for diabetes patients, and more. But in order to bring that forth, the Republican committee chairman, Senator Lamar Alexander, warned that Gottlieb would have to usher in a "regulatory process that is efficient and effective enough to bring safe discoveries to patients in a timely way."

Gottlieb, a physician, had been chosen in part for his well-articulated views on exactly those things. Over the past decade he'd practiced medicine less, becoming a prolific writer of opinion pieces in newspapers and a frequent talking head on cable television advocating for deregulation in the health sector. A libertarian, he espoused his views from a perch as a resident fellow at the right-leaning American Enterprise Institute, in the editorial pages of *The Wall Street Journal,* and as an author of niche biotech investor newsletters at *Forbes* magazine.

Gottlieb also had unique experiences that made him well prepared for the job. His first stint in the FDA was as a director of medical policy development, and he had returned a few years later as deputy commissioner for medical and scientific affairs. He was a cancer survivor who beat Hodgkin's lymphoma in his early thirties, giving him a natural platform to champion so-called adaptive clinical trials to speed up drug development, and allowing patients easier access to experimental treatments. He also advocated for the repeal of the Affordable Care Act, one of Trump's pet campaign issues.

Amid the heightened air of tension and political division in the wake of the 2016 presidential election, there were plenty of opposing views about Gottlieb. Republicans appreciated Gottlieb's background as a medical policy expert who advocated less regulation in the drug industry and assailed Obamacare. Democrats frowned on his long career as a paid adviser to drug companies and made it a point to take digs at him for what one senator during his confirmation hearing described as his "unprecedented financial entanglements with the industries he would regulate as FDA commissioner."

"Dr. Gottlieb," said one Democratic senator, during the hearing, "you are a partner in an investment bank, a venture partner in a large venture capital firm, a CEO or co-CEO of two health companies, and an individual investor in more than twenty health companies. You have sat on various types of boards for sixteen companies including two of the world's largest pharmaceutical companies. You also publish regularly, make speeches, consult for a number of large drug companies, and practice medicine. . . . Your involvement in so many companies likely to have business before the FDA—including key decisions by the agency on the safety and effectiveness of the company's drugs, devices, and products—is unprecedented."

Gottlieb assured the senators that he would lead the agency with integrity and a sense of purpose, and recuse himself from any potential decisions that could pose any conflict of interest.

Gottlieb went into the job expecting that his biggest priority would be dealing with the rising toll of opioids in the United States. But on the back burner an epidemic of a different sort was in the making. E-cigarettes had grown increasingly popular among teens, in part because the FDA until the year before had lacked the authority to regulate them. While nobody at the time of Gottlieb's confirmation hearing was yet calling youth e-cigarette use an epidemic, there were wide-spread and growing concerns about the products' appeal to youth as companies churned out a dizzying array of flavors—cotton candy, gummy bear, lemonade, cheesecake, pop rocks.

"If you are confirmed, do you commit to wholeheartedly address-ing the clear public health risk posed by flavored e-cigarettes," asked one senator. Gottlieb's response was unflinching. "As a physician and a cancer survivor, I am not going to countenance a rise in adolescent smoking rates in this country under my watch."

GOTTLIEB'S VERY FIRST MEETING as the new FDA commissioner was with Mitch Zeller, from the Center for Tobacco Products. Gottlieb had just started the job and already he was in hot water. The administra-tion that had appointed him had just blindsided him on the way in.

In the year since the deeming rule had taken effect, multiple legal challenges to the new regulation had materialized, including one from e-cigarette manufacturers and another from the cigar and pipe tobacco industry. And in the weeks before Gottlieb took office, lobbyists in those industries had seized on the power vacuum by trying to roll back the deeming rule before the next set of deadlines kicked in. In particu-lar the cigar industry was facing an August 2017 deadline that required cigar makers to submit plans on how warning labels would be dis-played on their products. In its lawsuit, the cigar industry had been ar-guing that the agency's warning label requirement was "arbitrary and capricious."

In early May, just a week before the Senate was scheduled to vote to confirm Gottlieb, the Department of Justice quietly filed a motion in the cigar lawsuit siding with the industry that had requested a three-month delay in the enforcement of key deadlines for their products. "New leadership personnel," the brief read. Need "additional time to more fully consider the Rule and the issues raised in this case and de-termine how best to proceed."

Gottlieb hadn't been briefed ahead of time. And when he found out about the deal in *The Washington Post,* he was furious. He told people that he felt he'd been tossed a grenade just a few days before he was set to be confirmed. The *Post*'s article pointed out that Gottlieb had held a financial stake in a chain of vape shops, called Kure, which he'd earlier agreed to unwind once confirmed. It also mentioned that the acting assistant attorney general named on the court brief had represented R. J. Reynolds before his position in the Justice Department.

The article made it appear as if Gottlieb were teeing up an inside Beltway favor for his buddies, when in fact Gottlieb was blindsided by the decision and had intended to make tobacco use one of his signature issues.

The optics of the administration's deeming delay were terrible for Gottlieb and left a political mess for him to clean up the moment he walked through the FDA's door. Either he had to cave in to the pressure coming from the White House to walk back the deeming rule—risking an uproar from public-health advocates who'd worked for years to will it into existence—or he had to swim against the current of his own political party to defend it. Had the administration not intervened, he would've had clean hands. The rule had been plodding ahead, slowly but surely, for years now. It had already gone through a period of notice and public comment. It had a more-than-defensible administrative record. Now, he was stepping into a political quagmire.

While the Obama administration did deliver the deeming rule on its way out the door (after years of infuriating inaction by the agency), there was still a ton of bureaucratic work that needed to be done before the hotly contested rule could be fully implemented, including issuing guidance and regulations to give the industry a clear framework in which to operate.

The longtime FDA hand, Mitch Zeller, was well positioned to help smooth things over, and eager to use the opportunity of a new commissioner and a new political party to push for unfinished work on his tobacco "endgame" strategy. Under the Obama administration, he'd been met with resistance. Zeller had come back to the FDA hoping that the agency would exercise its new authority to reduce nicotine in cigarettes to levels that didn't create or sustain addiction, but it didn't happen, in no small part because Obama spent much of his second term fiercely defending the Affordable Care Act, his signature issue. And on e-cigarettes, the Obama FDA had tried to ban them outright with its policy of seizing imports, but the practice was killed in court.

Gottlieb was more than receptive to Zeller's ideas. As a physician, Gottlieb had seen firsthand the devastating effects of smoking. As a cancer survivor, he was sympathetic to those afflicted with the smoking-related variation of the disease. And as a parent, he was well aware that he would never want his own children to start smoking. Also, he was no stranger to the tobacco issue since he'd long worked as a paid consultant to GlaxoSmithKline, the pharmaceutical giant that made nicotine replacement therapy products, including patches, gums, and lozenges.

With the deeming rule's fate up in the air, Gottlieb agreed with Zeller that it was the opportune moment to go big—to hammer out a policy that would actually save lives while changing the way society viewed smoking.

Over the first several weeks of Gottlieb's new job, he and Zeller met routinely, sometimes multiple times a week. Zeller schooled the new commissioner in the tenets of harm reduction and tobacco control, and they naturally saw eye to eye on the promises of new technologies, such as e-cigarettes, that could deliver nicotine to addicts while weaning them off combustible cigarettes.

They discussed the youth usage issue but took comfort in a recent batch of data. Every year, the FDA in conjunction with the Centers for Disease Control and Prevention would gather survey data to shed light on how many kids and teens were using tobacco products. The National Youth Tobacco Survey was the gold standard in the public-health community to show the patterns and rate of youth tobacco use. Over the past several years there had been an alarming trend showing that more adolescents were not only adopting e-cigarettes but that e-cigarettes had become more popular than regular cigarettes.

Nevertheless, in June 2017 the results showed that while e-cigarette use was up when compared over a five-year time period, it had actually gone *down* compared to the year prior. Given the explosion of interest in Juul on the part of young people, it was a curious piece of news, but the decline was potentially due in part to the fact that the survey didn't ask specifically about Juul, and because many teens that used the product didn't identify themselves as "e-cigarette" users. Also, the data were imperfect; the survey was only conducted annually, and it reported results from data collected the year prior, which meant it wasn't a real-time snapshot of what was unfolding on the ground. Either way, Zeller and Gottlieb believed that the time was right to release a bold nicotine plan.

As a plan started shaping up, they kept it under lock and key. They didn't want anything to leak to the press beforehand, so they used an intermediary to brief the White House and kept it out of the hands of the communications staff until the moment an announcement was imminent.

On the morning of Friday, July 28, FDA employees gathered in the atrium of the main lobby to hear Gottlieb speak about what he called a "comprehensive approach to nicotine and tobacco," designed to be "a multiyear roadmap to better protect kids and significantly reduce tobacco-related disease and death."

The cornerstone of the plan, Gottlieb said, was simple: nicotine. "Why nicotine?" he asked. "Because nicotine lives at the core of both the problem and, ultimately, the solution to the question of addiction, and the harm caused by combustible forms of tobacco. Nicotine is astonishingly addictive. . . . But the nicotine in cigarettes is not directly responsible for the cancer, lung disease, and heart disease that kill hundreds of thousands of Americans each year. Yes, it got them all addicted and kept them addicted for the long term. And it got most of them addicted when they were still teenagers. But it's the other chemical compounds in tobacco, and in the smoke created by setting tobacco on fire, that directly and primarily cause the illness and death, not the nicotine."

The plan was largely written by Zeller and his staff at the Center for Tobacco Products. Part of it involved writing rules that would once and for all regulate nicotine in combustible cigarettes to levels that would "render them minimally or nonaddictive." This was exactly the kind of endgame that Zeller and other tobacco control advocates had been dreaming of. The day when "addictive cigarette" might be an oxymoron was finally nigh. On the day of the announcement, Altria's stock tanked on the news that their product might be effectively regulated out of existence.

The second part of Gottlieb's plan entailed creating an environment that would allow noncombustible nicotine products, including e-cigarettes, to thrive. To do that, the agency was going to foster an environment in which adult smokers had a choice of nicotine products along Zeller's "continuum of risk," with harmful cigarettes on one end and medicinal nicotine products—such as patches, lozenges, gum, sprays, and inhalers—on the other. The latter group hadn't seen much innovation in years and were widely considered to be ineffective at getting smokers to quit. Since those products were defined as having a therapeutic purpose—helping people quit smoking—they were overseen not by Zeller's Center for Tobacco Products but by the agency's Center for Drug Evaluation and Research (CDER), a division tasked with ensuring that drugs are safe and effective.

Gottlieb outlined plans for what became the Nicotine Steering Committee, a collaboration between the two FDA divisions that would "examine possible steps" to "address the performance of" medicinal nicotine products. These were largely designed to deliver slow-acting, nonaddictive levels of nicotine to lessen withdrawal symptoms over time, not higher or "satisfying" levels of nicotine to curb cravings. For years, lobbyists and consultants had been trying, largely unsuccessfully, to persuade CDER to approve more "effective" and powerful forms of medicinal nicotine. But the division had long bristled at approving products that had levels of nicotine that could sustain addiction or, worse, give rise to abuse potential among adolescents.

In the middle of Gottlieb's continuum of harm were noncombustible tobacco products, such as e-cigarettes and smokeless tobacco. "There are now different technologies to deliver nicotine, for those who need it, that doesn't bring with it the deadly consequences of burning tobacco and inhaling the resulting smoke," Gottlieb said.

It turned out that one of most consequential parts of Gottlieb's "comprehensive" nicotine plan was his announcement that he was going to "extend timelines" for e-cigarette companies to submit their applications to the agency. Under the original deeming rule the deadline was two years after the rule went into effect, so August 8, 2018. Now, Gottlieb was delaying the implementation date until August 8, 2022. That meant the companies had an additional four years from the deeming date to continue selling their products without obtaining regulatory authorization. *Four years.* Anything could happen in four years—most important in that time frame, the companies could make a lot of money.

Public-health officials were irate. More than four years had already passed since Henry Waxman begged Obama's FDA head Margaret Hamburg to regulate e-cigarette companies that seemed to be targeting children, and since forty attorneys general had written a letter stressing the same. The deeming rule may have had a better-late-than-never feel to it after such a lengthy gestation, but it was a necessary marker on the road to staving off a potential public-health crisis. And now it seemed like Gottlieb was blowing it up.

While Gottlieb said the delay was necessary to strike a "balanced" approach to America's tobacco problem, and to ensure that the FDA had "the proper scientific and regulatory foundation to efficiently and effectively implement" the law, it also seemed like a gift to the tobacco and e-cigarette industry. For years the companies had worked mightily to get the agency to exempt their products from regulation.

Gottlieb pointed out that while the agency would work to provide adults new nicotine alternatives, it would also set up a series of regulatory gates, such as possibly regulating the types of flavors allowed in e-cigarettes, and do everything in its power to ensure that the policy didn't wind up creating new nicotine addiction in kids.

But it was too late. Juul was already coursing through the veins of teens across America.

ON SEPTEMBER 7, A few months after Gottlieb announced his nicotine plan, he received an odd and distressing letter. It was from Jane Goodall, the renowned primatologist. A pro-animal group called White

Coat Waste Project had learned that FDA researchers in Arkansas had been performing experiments on baby squirrel monkeys to study nicotine addiction, and received a cache of documents showing how the monkeys were put in restraint devices and dosed with nicotine. The group enlisted Goodall to raise awareness on the issue and to pressure the FDA to stop the experiments.

"Dear Dr. Gottlieb," read the letter from Goodall. "I was disturbed—and quite honestly shocked—to learn that the U.S. FDA is still, in 2017, performing cruel and unnecessary nicotine addiction experiments on monkeys."

The timing of the letter couldn't have been worse. Gottlieb was already fighting one fire with his controversial nicotine policy, and now there was *another* one related to nicotine that threatened to tip off a new kind of potential public relations disaster. Gottlieb's dalliance with nicotine was going from bad to worse by the day.

On September 15, 2017, Gottlieb ordered that the experiments be immediately suspended and that the catheters be removed from the monkeys. It was later revealed that four of the animals had died over the duration of the experiments, three while under anesthesia during surgery to insert the catheters for nicotine injections. Under pressure, and feeling personally offended by the animal studies, Gottlieb terminated the monkey experiments and established an Animal Welfare Council that reported to the FDA's Office of the Chief Scientist. A few weeks later, Gottlieb flew to Arkansas to visit the lab, and not long after he put a permanent end to the studies. He also vowed to place the animals in a sanctuary.

In one fell swoop, the FDA had ended the bout of nicotine addiction in the monkeys. Teen vaping would prove another story entirely.

13

PROJECT TREE

Peacetime CEO always has a contingency plan. Wartime CEO knows that sometimes you gotta roll a hard six.
—BEN HOROWITZ, VENTURE CAPITALIST

On November 2, 2017, a group of analysts and investors filed into a makeshift convention center built on the front lawn of Altria's oldest cigarette manufacturing factory, in south Richmond. The center was located on the opposite end of town from the company's headquarters, through downtown, past the Altria Theater, past the old brick tobacco warehouses, over the James River. Visitors knew they'd arrived when they saw the towering cigarette monument standing alongside the highway like some hokey relic on Route 66, and when the smell of toasted tobacco hit the front of their noses.

All the attention in this pocket of Richmond was for Altria's much anticipated "Investor Day." This was the type of periodic event held by almost all public companies to give investors a reason to get excited about a company's stock, provide a deeper look at their corporate strategy, or tease their most ambitious and promising soon-to-be-released products. For Altria, a company almost singularly focused on the company's share price, Investor Day was like the Olympics. Employees had been planning for this day for months, complete with dress rehearsals and meetings across multiple departments.

Booths displaying the company's elite brands—Marlboro, Copenhagen, Black & Mild—were set up to give investors the chance to smoke, chew, and vape the array of products. They could see Marlboro's new resealable foil pack, which the company boasted was "the first of its kind in the U.S. cigarette market." (Some employees were sheepish about *that* being the big innovation. Adding adhesive to foil. *Really?*) The guests also got a first glimpse at the company's heated tobacco brand, IQOS, which it licensed from Philip Morris International after effectively giving away the technology to its sister-company a decade earlier. The gadget that heated up a small cigarette was displayed in a mock retail store to show how the slick-looking product would be merchandised once it launched in the United States. The brand had already been launched in Europe and Japan. It was now getting ready to be introduced in test markets in the U.S. There was also a booth for Nu Mark, the company's division focused on e-cigarettes, with its featured slogan, "An Altria Innovation Company." It was an open secret at Altria that there wasn't much innovative about MarkTen, a Chinese hunk of metal filled with meager amounts of nicotine.

That morning investors were looking for something to get excited about. *Anything*. It didn't even have to be the equivalent of the iPhone of the tobacco world. Just a bit of good news to reassure investors who were starting to get jittery. Altria's stock had been sagging recently—that morning it was down nearly 20 percent from the year's high—and investors had been growing anxious about the company's ability to compete in a tobacco industry metamorphosing before their eyes.

Naturally, stock analysts had been watching Juul with increasing interest and fascination. The company had ascended with stunning rapidity, becoming the number one selling e-cigarette brand by the end of 2017, and surpassing Altria for the first time. The old Marlboro maker was starting to look more and more like a sluggish goliath ill-equipped to compete in the agile world of tech start-ups. Executives were eager to prove that the company wasn't asleep at the switch.

Just after ten A.M., after Altria's guests had wrapped up their brand tour, they relocated to an auditorium inside where they were shown a slick film about the company. "Tobacco," said a resonant James Earl Jones–type voice. "No crop played a bigger role in the founding of our nation." The film kicked off a highly orchestrated presentation, with CEO Marty Barrington and Howard Willard and others taking turns reading, word for word, their crisply written presentations that gushed about the future of the company.

But it would be Jody Begley, a longtime Altria executive who'd taken over as the president of Nu Mark, who delivered one of the day's most anticipated announcements. Altria was expanding its offerings in the "e-vapor" category to better compete with pod-based products like Juul. Begley described how the current MarkTen was in sixty-five thousand stores and had "nearly tripled its market share" since it launched. "It is now one of the leading e-vapor brands," he boasted. "And we believe it has a solid runway for the future."

In reality, everybody knew that almost nobody was clamoring for the MarkTen cigalikes, and they certainly weren't any magical driver of growth for the company. All anybody wanted to talk about was Juul. About its brilliant minimalistic design that looked *nothing* like a cigarette. Its flavored liquid nicotine "pods" that effortlessly snapped into the device. Its mighty nicotine punch.

Today, Altria was about to change all that. Begley announced that the company was introducing its own line of pod-based products. It was called MarkTen Elite. The Elite looked nothing like a cigarette. It did, however, look *a lot* like something else: Juul. The new device was black, had a long, rectangular body that housed a battery, and used little nicotine pods that snapped in.

"To wrap up," said Begley. "We have an existing portfolio of products in multiple formats to meet the expectations of a range of adult smokers and vapers. And we have a promising pipeline of future e-vapor products in development."

———

AT ALTRIA, THE AMOUNT of planning that went into even the most mundane meetings was legendary. Employees scheduled to give a five-minute presentation, say, at a weekly executive meeting were expected to rehearse for days ahead of time, usually in a series of meetings ahead of the meeting, and circulate their remarks beforehand to ensure it contained nothing objectionable. Altria executives did not like, nor did they expect, to be caught off guard. Nobody would dare spring an idea during the actual meeting, and most certainly nothing controversial. There was an expectation that everything be vetted ahead of time so that by the time the actual meeting happened, it unfolded more like a well-rehearsed ceremony.

Which was all to say just how atypical and hasty things were inside Altria in the days leading up to that slick November 2017 Investor Day presentation. Altria had been backed into a corner. By the time the company realized that Juul was an actual threat, any hope of actually innovating on MarkTen to make it better, or more appealing, had slipped away. The FDA's deeming rule had made it all but impossible. Companies were no longer allowed to introduce new products to the market, and they were forbidden from improving on any existing device.

The company was in an impossible situation. Not only was it essentially stuck in an inferior market position, but executives had to constantly answer questions about it, internally and every quarter when Altria's executive team had to sit for its inquest before investors and the media. What was Altria doing to compete? Could the company stave off competitors? Were e-cigarettes going to cannibalize cigarette sales? With each passing day, the questions became more frequent and more intense. As stock analysts raved about Juul and its meteoric rise, they'd barely get around to mentioning MarkTen and its mediocrity. There was no way Altria could sit there and do nothing.

But finding apertures in government regulations was Altria's specialty. While the deeming rule prevented companies from introducing new products that hadn't been on the market when the rule went into effect, technically it would allow the sale of products that had been in commerce in the United States *prior to* August 8, 2016. That was all the toehold Altria needed.

By the middle of 2017, a few months before that year's Investor Day, executives had begun combing the globe for a pod-based product that had been sold in the United States, if only in a single store, and had an iota of a chance to put up a fight against Juul.

With no time to waste, they ultimately settled on two paths. For one, the company acquired the pod-based product Cync from a company based in Atlanta called Vape Forward. Cync had developed a decent following over the past several months with its variety of prefilled cartridges or "pods" like Juul. And more importantly, it was on the market prior to the deeming rule taking effect. But the problem was that Cync's design and technology needed more than a little work before it would present any meaningful threat to Juul.

Altria's other ace in the hole was across the globe, in China. The company's original MarkTen cigalike was already being made there by a contract manufacturer. Now executives were negotiating with a new Chinese manufacturer that was manufacturing pod-based products and that had a provable record of being sold in the United States prior to the deeming date. The company, Smoore Technology, had grown to become one of the world's largest e-cigarette manufacturers and had done business with some of the biggest tobacco brands, including Japan Tobacco, Reynolds, and British American Tobacco.

Throughout the fall of 2017, as Altria was engaged in negotiations with the manufacturer, the clock was ticking. Investor Day was now just weeks away and their innovation pipeline didn't look much better than it did a year ago. Cync wouldn't be enough to satisfy investors who would eviscerate the company if executives showed up with the equivalent of a knife at a gunfight.

Finally, on the very night before executives were due to give their big Investor Day presentation, Altria signed a deal with Smoore. With literally only hours to spare, Altria had the star of its "innovation pipeline" in hand: Elite, just in time to make it onto a slide for investors to see. Despite the grand videos and proclamations from its executives about innovation, here was MarkTen Elite, another cheap device born not from the company's fancy innovation center in Richmond, or from the hundreds of scientists recruited from around the world, but from a dime-a-dozen contract manufacturer in China.

"There was no reason to believe that we had the next Juul on our hands," recalled one executive.

ALTRIA ALWAYS HAD INNOCENT-SOUNDING code names for its internal projects—Project Beta was its heat-not-burn product that became Accord. Project Leap was its heated aerosols. Project Table was its overarching effort to spark innovation inside the company. Project Tree? That was the code name for Altria's top-secret project to get Juul.

By the end of 2017 the San Francisco start-up was eclipsing the market. MarkTen had been knocked down to third place, and Juul was now on top. While MarkTen sales grew by about 32 percent over 2016, Juul sales grew by nearly *700 percent*. At the beginning of 2017, Juul had just over 5 percent of the market. By the end of the year, it had reached nearly 30 percent, and it was growing by the day. By 2018, MarkTen's market share was in free fall.

Every week, Barrington, Gifford, Willard, and a rotating cast of employees would gather around the big oval table in the main conference room for a senior leadership meeting, where they'd pore over sales figures, sift through datapoints, and listen to presentations from across the various operating companies—one week it might be Marlboro; another Copenhagen. No matter what they were discussing, though, Juul would wind up dominating the discussion. The conversations only grew more agonizing by the week.

"This thing is a juggernaut," an executive quipped about Juul during one of the meetings. "It's just running away."

"We're never going to have a path to e-vapor with this brand," Willard would growl about MarkTen.

Willard was pushing for a deal with Juul. He thought it would be wise to try to buy the company as fast as possible. The bigger Juul got, the more expensive it'd be. Plus there was undoubtedly competition in any race to acquire Juul. And even though cigarettes were falling out of favor, Altria was still endowed with a seemingly eternal spring of cash that Marlboro generated. Willard had leveraged the company's balance sheet before to great effect, most notably a decade earlier when he helped land the $10 billion deal for UST Inc., a deal that wound up being not too shabby after all, since it put the company in play in the highly competitive smokeless business. He knew how to get big deals done and he'd been hankering to do another, in particular in the e-cigarette space.

Over the course of 2017, Willard rekindled a relationship with Juul, at first back-channeling through Altria's investment bankers at Perella Weinberg to gauge Bowen or Monsees's level of interest. On one occasion Willard flew out to the Bay Area for what he was expecting to be an informal lunch with Nick Pritzker. But when he arrived, he was somewhat flustered to learn that Pritzker wouldn't be available. In his stead he'd be meeting with one of Pritzker's sons, Joby. Starting in 2014, Joby had taken on a more active role at Tao Capital Partners, the family office started by his dad, but he had also become deeply involved in the marijuana legalization movement and was a financial backer of cannabis-themed companies. He also served on the board of a non-profit called the Multidisciplinary Association for Psychedelic Studies, which evangelized the health and therapeutic benefits of psychedelics, including magic mushrooms, LSD, and ayahuasca.

So, when Willard returned to Richmond and colleagues learned of the surprise meeting with Joby instead of Nick, they thought it was one of the most hilarious things in the world. At the time, Altria had barely tiptoed anywhere near cannabis, but Joby pitched him on co-investing in the space. It became a recurring joke in the office that Willard might have considered, even for a flash of a second, having buttoned-down Altria dabble in shrooms. The company was already, after all, looking at every other adult stimulant. Why not psychedelics?

Even though Willard was slightly annoyed by being effectively stood up by Pritzker, he had reason for optimism: He was in the game. "Howard came out of that meeting pretty confident that he would be able to start opening James's and Adam's minds," said a person familiar with the meeting.

Talks between the two companies progressed, with Willard bending over backward to build rapport. "You may think we're big bad evil tobacco," he'd tell Nick, who served as one of the lead Juul negotiators. "But let me try to show you through this process we're not who you think we are. We're very serious about our adult customers, and very serious about not letting this get into the hands of underage consumers."

The two parties began informally floating potential valuations for a deal. Altria was willing to pay under $10 billion to purchase the entire company outright. The Juul team sniffed. Don't bother trying to buy the company outright, they said—the whole company wasn't for sale, especially not at that price. It would, however, consider carving off some piece of it, as long as Juul retained a majority stake. Bowen and Monsees had long said, since the very beginning of their odyssey, that they wouldn't sell a controlling interest to any tobacco company. And that point remained a deal breaker.

It was partly the founders' way of telling themselves that a deal with a tobacco company didn't have to be all bad. There was a lot of upside—Big Tobacco had longstanding trade agreements with retail chains that would allow Juul instant penetration of the consumer market. Altria, in particular, had one of largest marketing databases in the world and if Juul had access to it, it would be like being handed the keys to the kingdom. Also, the founders started warming up to the idea that if they could partner with the enemy, they could break the evil from within by prodding the companies to move away from the deadly cigarette.

But undeniably there was another upside, and it was the color green. So Juul began throwing out sky-high valuations to indicate what Pritzker and others believed the company was worth. Such lofty prices might have seemed wildly unreasonable, at least to many tobacco executives not schooled in the Silicon Valley art of growth investing. But Willard didn't blink an eye. Despite the lacuna between the parties, and by what no doubt would be Juul's lofty sticker price, he'd come back to Richmond energized. Soon, he unleashed his team and had them start modeling financial scenarios that could justify the asking price, raising some eyebrows internally.

Now, Willard just had to open the mind of his boss. Barrington wasn't sold. In recent months he seemed to have developed an allergic reaction to any mention of Juul. Partly Barrington was convinced that Altria didn't need to acquire its way to the top. He hadn't gone to all that work shepherding Nu Mark and MarkTen into the world only to abandon the vehicle he'd chosen to steer the company into a post-cigarette future. The company just needed a little time to catch up. Barrington was clear: Exhaust every option that lived inside the Richmond headquarters before setting out on a unicorn hunt out West.

"I don't want to say he used the word 'toxic,' " said a former Altria executive. "But he was like 'Now is not the time.' "

Barrington had now been chairman and chief executive of the company for more than five years. He had deep confidence in his people and believed that the new suite of e-vapor products they'd put together showed promise, an opinion shared by plenty of other people internally. Barrington was known for being a consummate diplomat. He chose his words carefully, which made it hard to ascertain how he truly felt about an issue. Some people took his tact as a sign of good leadership, but others felt he simply had no spine. It wasn't gratifying to leave a meeting and wonder where the boss stood on a given matter.

Barrington also frequently pointed out to employees and investors alike that the nascent e-cigarette market was still in a state of flux. When a Goldman Sachs analyst asked him about Juul on an investor call, he replied with a message that had become a familiar refrain inside the company. "I have counted at least five brands in the e-vapor category that had very significant growth rates early and then fell back to earth over time," he said. "I think it's worth remembering the history that there have been some rockets before that haven't sustained their trajectory."

That was investor-speak for "Juul very well could be the next rocket to lose altitude." That was what Barrington and other Altria executives had been saying for months now. *Hoping* was probably a better word for it. They would have loved nothing more than to see Juul crash to Earth and vanish into the cloud of vapor from which it appeared.

———

"CAN YOU BELIEVE IT?" an Altria employee remarked to a colleague as they chatted in the hallway in mid-2018. "My eighth-grade daughter talks about all the boys passing Juul to each other on their way to the bathroom."

"Yeah, Juul needs to cut it out," the colleague responded. "They're going to ruin it for us."

Juul was poisoning the well.

That wasn't the first such exchange in Altria's hallways, around the watercoolers, or in meetings. By the beginning of 2018, Richmond area news outlets had started featuring interviews with high schoolers about the rise of Juul. "There is a dangerous new trend among teenagers," read one local article. "It's called 'Juuling.'" Another read: "Several greater Richmond area school systems are aware of a new vaping device that is getting into the hands of underage teenagers."

Juul was starting to become a problem. It was attracting the kind of attention that could crater the whole market. For Barrington, if he'd been reluctant to consider approaching Juul before, he was really starting to get a pit in his stomach now. The headlines were terrifying to him. And so was the consumer research data available to the company that hinted at a nascent problem.

Howard Willard pressed forward. Despite Barrington's reluctance, he had tentatively begun due diligence on Juul, which involved trying to game out a fair price based on a series of interlocking metrics—how big would the overall e-cigarette category become? How much was it going to cannibalize Marlboro? And what other emerging products might pose any real competition?

It was clear to those inside Altria that Juul was having some problems. Various teams across the company had already been tasked with doing counterintelligence, analyzing and dissecting every aspect of the company. Eagle-eyed employees had been tearing apart Juuls for a while now to monitor the device's inner workings. One thing they happened to notice was that Juul seemed to be having a lot of technical problems (something that generated a healthy dose of schadenfreude inside Altria). The devices often stopped working, and the pods leaked like sieves. At one point Altria sent employees into convenience stores across Richmond to buy up as many Juul pods as possible. They brought the boxes back to the company, sliced into the little blister packages that they came in, and counted how many of them leaked. An informal study showed that at least 20 percent of the pods had significant leaking issues, and as many as 40 percent were moderately leaky. Altria was obsessed with quality—god save the soul of any person at a Philip Morris factory responsible for a quality error, say, like tobacco leaf falling out of a cigarette. It was unfathomable to them that customers would put up with such a glitchy product for long.

Beyond the leaky pods, a close examination of the devices over time seemed to show that Juul had put a bunch of new parts inside its device. The circuit board was different from the one being sold a few months earlier, and it had new and different components. That was a potentially significant finding. Under the deeming rule, companies weren't supposed to be changing anything about their product, even down to the smallest change of components or packaging. Doing so might have meant they were illegally selling their product. If Juul had indeed modified its device, wouldn't that be a violation of the law?

Employees were taken aback that Juul would take such a risk. Altria had narrowly survived the ire of society at the turn of the millennium, in part by agreeing to strictly adhere to the new rules of the road. The company's compliance department didn't take lightly its commitment to following the letter of the rules, laws, and regulations set out for it. For Altria the ranking of priorities was essentially: Follow the rules. Follow the economics. Then worry about the customer. It took the company's executives a while to realize that for Juul, like other tech companies, the priorities were inverted: Worry about the customer. Follow the economics. Then follow the rules. The Altria employees snapped photos of the old and the new Juul devices and kept it for evidence, just in case.

Meanwhile, the consumer research group was looking to find out as much as they could about Juul users in the greatest level of granularity possible. From the outset, the research showed what most people already knew—the people using Juul fell into two buckets. The first were people between the ages of thirty to forty-five who were smokers and were switching to Juul, largely for its powerful nicotine salt solution. The other group were nonsmokers aged twenty-one to twenty-nine, who research showed would likely have initiated into the nicotine category one way or another, probably through cigarettes. Instead they were taking up e-cigarettes, and most of them had adopted Juul. And they were adopting Juul at a stunning rate.

As the group started unpacking that second demographic, they began treading on an uncomfortable question. The younger twenty-one-to-twenty-nine cohort might not be fully capturing what, or rather *who*, was driving growth in the category. This second group raised thorny issues for Altria. For years at Altria there was no higher taboo than to talk about, think about, even hint at anything having to do with underage smokers. It was the company's sacred covenant—the public would let Altria keep selling its deadly burning sticks, but shit would blow up again if the data showed that adolescents were using them in growing numbers. For more than two decades, the number of high school smokers had fallen every year and reached historic lows. That kept the public's ire at bay.

Even though skeptical outsiders might not believe it, Altria was deadly serious about the red line it had drawn inside the company after the Tobacco Wars, not least because it in theory insulated it from future legal claims that the company was targeting kids. Altria's massive marketing database had been meticulously scrubbed of users under the age of twenty-one, and the legal team went to great lengths to keep it that way. Even though some states allowed eighteen-year-olds to buy cigarettes, most of the tobacco companies, including Altria, had for the past decade imposed their own voluntary marketing codes that prevented their marketing materials from reaching anybody under the age of twenty-one.

For years, when Altria purchased advertisements, they made publications prove that the majority of their readers were over the age of twenty-one. When the company went into bars for promotions, they had to do the same. Practically the entire reason the company created the Marlboro Ranch after the Master Settlement Agreement, purchasing 18,000 acres of ranchland in the Crazy Mountains of Montana, was to have a dedicated, far-flung place where legal age users could go and celebrate their love for the brand, and for smoking, without risk of penalty or judgment.

So as the question of Juul and youth customers bubbled to the surface inside Altria, it caused a lot of uneasiness. Anyone with two eyes could read the news or, just as likely, hear about it from their kids around their kitchen tables. Juul was ripping through middle schools and high schools across the country. The brand was all over social media. And who by and large used social media? It wasn't adult smokers. These were new users initiating into the nicotine category who never otherwise would have. But nobody wanted to talk openly about that elephant in the room. At Altria, "talking about initiation into the category is horrible," said one former employee. "It is a red line you do not cross. . . . We didn't talk about it out loud. . . . An open conversation about underage stuff was a no-go."

But as the company's study of Juul went deeper, it was nearly impossible to avert their eyes from Juul's youth problem. One way Altria executives reconciled such an incredibly uncomfortable topic was by talking about the company's unique expertise in this exact area. Altria knew better than anyone the problem of youth usage and what needed to be done to rehab a company that was overcome by a youth epidemic. So instead of saying "Look at all the high schoolers Juuling!" they'd engage in circuitous vernacular contortions like "This is a product that seems to have been built by the internet." It was like they started speaking code. Everybody knew what one another was really talking about. "It was no secret," said one former executive.

Nevertheless, the unavoidable conclusion of it all was that Juul had gone viral, and Altria executives were terrified of what that might mean for the future of e-cigarettes, the ostensible heir of Big Tobacco. The conversations made people sweat. Altria perceived itself as a company that had spent years trying to get youth to stop buying its product. The idea of virality was antithetical to the careful, conservative culture that Altria had fostered over the years. As Willard plowed forth, some Altria insiders started to get spooked.

For Barrington and other executives and employees who'd been at the company long enough to remember the past, the Juul conversation triggered a kind of PTSD. They'd lived through the Tobacco Wars and endured the wrenching fallout when the once-secret internal tobacco documents showed the ugly truth that tobacco companies had aggressively targeted preteens for years. They'd helped the company peel itself off the ground by promising never to target youth again, and managed to get the company back to the position that Steve Parrish had fought for—having permission from society to exist. And then, as the harm-reduction conversation had started to gain meaningful traction, there was a sense that while they perhaps weren't yet on the side of the angels, they were at least, and for once, not on the side of the devil. No matter how callous or villainous tobacco executives have been made out to be over the years, they also had beating hearts, and many were relieved to see the long arc of the industry bend in a more virtuous direction. The cigarette business was, dare they say, becoming respectable.

But now, thinking too hard about Juul created a deep cognitive dissonance within the tobacco giant. "Juul did so much right and so much wrong at the same time," recalled a former Altria executive. On the one hand, those employees who'd long heard Altria's leaders glorify innovation looked to Juul with a sense of not only envy but awe. There was simply no denying it—Juul was the first and only product to have cracked the code. Bowen and Monsees had brilliantly developed a potentially less harmful nicotine product that delivered satisfaction on the same level as a Marlboro Red. In contrast, all the time and money that Altria had lit on fire over the years in pursuit of the future had amounted to little more than an empty ashtray. It was painful to admit, but Altria had gotten out-innovated. By Silicon Valley, no less.

But at the same time, the very reasons that were fueling Juul's rising success and provoking envy were the same ones that were suddenly thrusting Altria toward the brink of another youth usage quagmire. So, in the winter of 2018 as a foreboding sense descended over the company, and a chill quivered through the executive ranks, the past began to haunt Altria's halls.

"Yes, it was a successful product," said one former Altria executive, of Juul. "But the day of reckoning, of regulators and tobacco control people, was coming. And it was coming fast and coming hard. You couldn't ignore the fact that this would get ugly before it got better."

The executive paused.

"It scared the holy bejesus out of me."

"GET READY FOR MARKTEN Elite. Available soon on MarkTen.com," read an advertisement for Altria's new Juul competitor. By February 2018, Altria was preparing to blitz the market with Elite. They couldn't get Elite onto shelves fast enough. The product hadn't been able to make it to market earlier in part because the company's desired launch had coincided with Chinese New Year, a time when virtually every factory in the country was closed. There was no chance that Elite would even be on U.S. shores before February.

But once the new brand launched, it blitzed more than six thousand stores across the United States in just a matter of weeks and was offered in several flavors, including Hazelnut Cream, Strawberry Brûlée, and Apple Cider. For Altria, it was a miracle to have moved that fast.

The problem was that fast didn't mean good. It's fair to say that almost nobody who wasn't an Altria executive with their career riding on it really cared about the launch of Elite. Despite all the fanfare during its Investor Day unveiling, Elite landed with a thud. Sure, it was designed to compete directly with Juul as a pod product, and it even sort of looked like a Juul. But nothing could take away from the fact that it was clunky in comparison, and most definitely not built in Silicon Valley. And, it didn't even have the magical nicotine salt formulation that had made Juul such a hit.

Online, instead of viral Instagram memes and YouTube shows dedicated to the product, Elite garnered comments just short of ridicule. "I guess it's not horrible," said one reviewer on YouTube after testing MarkTen Elite. "Affordable and alright," said another.

Altria responded by flooding more convenience stores with MarkTen, leaning on its premier shelf space to get the products in front of consumers' eyeballs, and offering generous discounts and free offers mailed to Marlboro smokers in the hopes of browbeating customers into buying it. One Altria insider compared the company's MarkTen strategy to "pouring a small bucket of water on a forest fire."

Even people responsible for selling MarkTen on the ground recognized that their product was second-rate in comparison. Still, Barrington and others were acting as if MarkTen had a real shot at competing with Juul. He and his backers in the executive suite seemed to have a false sense of confidence about the company's superiority. There was a rationalization that the two products weren't so different after all and, given just enough time and enough of Altria's massive marketing budget, MarkTen would be able to catch up.

That made Willard, and others who'd seen the light about Juul, agitated. Any rosy talk about MarkTen's future seemed delusional, if only because the truth could be seen as plain as day. Elite had 1.8 percent nicotine, and it was in the inferior, harsh freebase form. Juul had 5 percent nicotine, and it was in the superior, smooth salt form. It was nearly a scientifically proven fact—Juul would hook more users than Elite. Juul was so clearly in a league of its own that it drove some people crazy when they had to explain to Barrington that "they're not even equivalent products." It seemed like hubris to think that MarkTen was anywhere in the same league as Juul. It was like a Yugo drag-racing a Bugatti.

ON FEBRUARY 1, BARRINGTON announced that he was retiring from Altria, after twenty-five years at the company. Typically, executives at Altria were expected to retire at sixty-five years old, and he was approaching that age. He also announced that Willard would be succeeding him as chairman of the board and CEO, effective May 17 at the company's annual shareholder meeting. Billy Gifford, the other executive who'd been in the running for the top spot, was appointed vice chairman of the board. The latest Altria horse race was over, for now.

Not long after his announcement, Barrington made it clear to his subordinates that he wouldn't be making any major, course-altering decisions, not about Juul or anything else. Suddenly, mere mentions of Juul would get instantly swatted down. Barrington had already started to get cold feet anytime Willard or anyone else would bring up Juul with him. The price that Juul wanted was a joke, for starters. As a publicly traded company, Barrington had a fiduciary responsibility and it would be hard to justify any such lofty price to the board, let alone to investors. Anyone who'd been involved in a potential Juul transaction was told, "Pencils down."

But as Barrington sat on the sidelines, Juul's growth went stratospheric. Data were showing that while Juul was only being distributed in a fraction of retail locations compared to MarkTen, its sales in those stores were growing rapidly and its product was constantly out of stock, a key indicator of a product's popularity. "Their demand was insane," remarked a former Altria employee. "Just when you thought, 'Oh it's going to level off, oh it's going to level off'—it never did."

In April, an equity researcher at Citigroup, Adam Spielman, wrote a report with this headline: "The New World of Tobacco—JUUL Starting to Disrupt U.S. Cigarette Industry." He cut the Altria stock down from a buy rating to a neutral rating, saying that he'd come to the conclusion that the company's ability to simply raise prices to offset cigarette declines was becoming untenable. "The U.S. tobacco market is beginning to be disrupted by JUUL—U.S. cigarette volumes fell 6% in 1Q18 according to Nielsen, about 1–2% worse than historic models would suggest. This is due to the rapid growth of JUUL. We don't expect underlying cigarette trends to improve much in the rest of 2018."

Around that same time, about a month before the official transfer of power inside Altria, Willard quietly started telling people around him that he wanted to restart talks with Juul as soon as he was in charge.

Back in April 2011, after former Google CEO Eric Schmidt retired and Larry Page took over, the venture capitalist Ben Horowitz blogged about the differences in their leadership styles. Schmidt, he argued, was what he called a "peacetime CEO" who oversaw the company at a time of rapid growth. In contrast, he argued that Page was taking over at a time when the company needed what he called a "wartime CEO."

"Peacetime in business means those times when a company has a large advantage vs. the competition in its core market, and its market is growing," wrote Horowitz, cofounder and partner at the venture capital firm Andreessen Horowitz. "In times of peace, the company can focus on expanding the market and reinforcing the company's strengths. In wartime, a company is fending off an imminent existential threat."

That's the best way to explain why Howard Willard had grown so impatient. Altria, after enjoying several years of relative peace, had found itself at war.

Just before nine A.M. on May 17, 2018, Altria executives and shareholders gathered inside the convention center in downtown Richmond. Even though the cigarette factories and tobacco warehouses of a different era were no longer in the vicinity, Altria was firmly ensconced as the crown jewel of Richmond, as evidenced by the Altria Theater, an old Shriner's temple that Altria donated $10 million to in order to secure its name on the multicolored marquee.

Inside the big ballroom, after the meeting was called to order and various shareholder proposals were heard, Barrington made his formal announcement. "The keen eye among you will have noticed that when we elected directors earlier, that I was not among the nominees," Barrington said. "That's because earlier this year, I did inform the board of my decision to retire as chairman and CEO because I'm turning sixty-five shortly and have completed more than twenty-five years of service."

Then, he introduced his successor. "Through its long-term succession planning process, the board has selected Howard Willard to serve as the company's next chairman and CEO. Howard is immensely qualified to lead Altria, having served in numerous leadership positions during his twenty-five-year career with us, including as chief operating officer and as chief financial officer. Further, the board has selected Billy Gifford to the executive position of vice-chairman of Altria while continuing his appointment as chief financial officer. . . . These appointments reflect the leadership and the valuable contributions each of them has made to our company. Both Howard and Billy are fully ready to propel our great company forward to even greater future success as I step down today. So I hope you'll join me in congratulating them both."

Applause filled the ballroom. And then the meeting was over.

With Willard now officially in charge, the gloves were about to come off. This was war.

14

ATHERTON

If one more kid calls Walgreens asking
if we have juul pods or fidget spinners
I'm fucking quitting

APR 27, 2017 · TWITTER FOR IPHONE ·
MATT—@MVTTCLARK

Atherton, California, was a quiet old whistle-stop along the Southern Pacific Railroad, just down the alluvial peninsula from San Francisco, through the flowering Santa Clara Valley and minutes from downtown Palo Alto. While fewer than ten thousand people lived there, many of them behind tall hedges, redwood forests, and castle-like gates, Atherton was ranked the wealthiest city in America. The average annual income was above $500,000, and the town has called among its residents some of the most famous tech titans in the world, including Eric Schmidt from Google and Sheryl Sandberg from Facebook. NBA star Stephen Curry bought a $31 million estate there. Microsoft cofounder Paul Allen had one worth $35 million.

In comparison, Kevin Burns's stately home in a neighborhood of Atherton, fittingly called King Estates, seemed modest. Toward the end of the summer in 2017, Burns was sitting in the kitchen with his son and some friends. They were students at Palo Alto High School. Paly, as it was known by locals, wasn't even the fanciest school in the area, even though most anybody who went there had a parent who was somebody known for something.

Burns had left Chobani, the yogurt company, about a year earlier after pulling off an operational miracle. He was brought in from the private equity firm TPG to right the ship of a company that had shown great promise before being nearly ruined by a crisis that saw sour, bubbling, oozing cups of moldy yogurt wind up in grocery store coolers, sickening dozens and leading to a nationwide recall. The feat solidified his reputation as a "turnaround guru." Now Burns was considering taking a new job, this time as the CEO of Juul.

In classic consultant fashion, Burns wanted to do his own market research. So he convened a meeting with his son and his friends and asked them about vaping. Three of them pulled Juuls from their pockets. Juuling had become a thing in recent months, with growing numbers of students huddling in bathroom stalls, in search of a quick nicotine rush between classes or during lunch. The bathroom by the art classroom at Paly had become the most popular location, and the best place for teachers—if they came in at the right moment—to catch students exhaling the evanescent clouds before they vanished into nothingness.

That fall, the Paly student newspaper, called *The Campanile*, conducted a survey and found that more than half of 269 students surveyed reported vaping. And of those, half used Juul. "Clearly, vaping has become a habit on campus," the September 2017 *Campanile* article read. "For many students, Juuling brings a very attractive social aspect. Students pass around the Juul and meet new people through this act, breaking the ice with a simple drag of the Juul."

Of course Burns's son and his friends knew about Juul. Over the kitchen table, after revealing their Juuls, the teenagers regaled the elder Burns with stories of vaping, how they'd procured the devices, and just how popular they'd become. The conversation put into stark focus one of the challenges that Burns would likely face if he took the job at Juul. For some people that might have served as a red flag. Not Burns. He'd been in the rough-and-tumble private equity business long enough to know that when you smell smoke, you run toward it, not away from it. That's where the money was.

"We could not be more pleased to announce Kevin as Juul Labs' new CEO," said Monsees in a December 11, 2017, press release. "He was a key contributor to the extraordinary operational and strategic success at Chobani that positioned the company for long-term growth, strong financial fundamentals and continued innovation. We fully expect that he will bring similar success to JUUL Labs."

BURNS ARRIVED AT JUUL Labs just as the company was moving boxes over to its new 30,000-square-foot warehouse on Pier 70 in the Dogpatch, a stone's throw from Bowen and Monsees's first offices in the old tin can factory. There were the same neighborhood haunts, but this time they had a better view of the San Francisco Bay. And instead of fewer employees than could be counted on a single hand, they had more than two hundred, and it was growing bigger by the day. There wasn't much fanfare when Juul signed the five-year lease in the raw, industrial redbrick Renaissance Revival building with rounded porticos where steel ship hulls were once fabricated. In fact, nobody at all seemed to notice, which was surprising since you could barely move a brick in that "historic core" without somebody raising a stink about it.

Burns was fifty-four years old when he took the reins at Juul. With closely cropped gray hair and a stocky build, he exuded an unyielding, rust-belt ethos. *The New Yorker* magazine described him as a guy with "a friendly dad-who-loves-his-vacation-house demeanor." A metallurgical engineer by training, he went straight from college to General Electric in the days when Jack Welch, the ruthless godfather of lean manufacturing, was still running the company. While there, Burns attended the company's prestigious manufacturing management program that set him on a path whipping ailing manufacturing companies into shape, Neutron Jack–style. He'd been doing it ever since, for tire makers and solar panel manufacturers and chemical companies, for more than two decades.

Unlike Goldman, Burns seemed born for the job of Juul CEO.

From the moment he landed, he constantly prowled Juul's hallways, bantering with employees and loudly proclaiming brash managerial ideas in meetings, as executives took deep drags on Juuls, exhaling white clouds of vapor. Even though he surprised employees when he took to showing up to the office in Adidas tracksuit attire, a look one employee described as "Lithuanian mob," there was no question that he knew what he was talking about.

When Burns first started, it looked as if he'd been dealt a series of fairly run-of-the-mill scaling challenges that any MBA could tackle: Problem: Demand for Juul devices and pods was vastly outstripping supply. Solution: Enlist new contract manufacturers and put foot on gas. Problem: Large amounts of e-liquid were being scrapped. Solution: Improve quality control. Problem: Juul could be found in only a few stores. Solution: Hire a sales force to ram distribution into big retailers. Problem: Juul was sold only in the American market. Solution: Blanket the globe. Problem: Social media marketing had reached its limits. Solution: Launch a national ad campaign.

None of these problems was too hard for Burns. While Juul was as far from yogurt as one could get, the two companies shared a common problem: They'd both scaled too quickly and couldn't keep up with all that the growth entailed. Plus, with the recent round of investment in Juul, not only did Burns have a plan but he had a war chest on his side.

But the true enormity of what Burns walked into at Juul made sour milk and moldy yogurt seem like a dream. The number of troubling incidents that had continued to plague the company were too numerous to count: The bad batch of benzoic acid that made the flavored pods taste weird. The shards of metal that accidentally got mixed into e-liquid. The mango pods that were sold with mint labels. The mint pods that were sold with mango labels. The batches of e-liquid that would turn brown over time, and nobody could figure out why. The long discussions about whether they should put expiration dates on pod packages, which raised dumbfounding questions about whether the pods sitting on shelves or in hot cars for long periods of time could potentially result in toxic chemical reactions. On that issue, nobody ever seemed to have a definitive answer. Short of pulling a date out of thin air, they simply didn't adopt expiration dates.

And then there was the human testing. Burns was astounded to find that employees were regularly vaping new product before comprehensive toxicology tests had been done. That was alarming because while one ingredient, say cinnamon flavor, may seem safe, it could become a dangerous chemical when subjected to heat. "Nobody tastes anything until that entire recipe has been through two different levels of toxicology testing," Burns declared.

In a company dominated by consumer electronics engineers and product designers, many of them from tech meccas like Apple and Tesla, these incidents were not a bug. They were routine features of a high-growth start-up. Rapidly iterating. Pivoting. Making mistakes.

Burns tried to solve for that problem by recruiting people who had experience in the highly regulated medical-device industry, from places like Boston Scientific and Abbott. As the company ramped up, those two cultures clashed over a topic that would come to dominate inside Juul: speed versus quality.

The rapid scaling exacerbated the existing quality issues that didn't always have clear-cut answers, which made the employees with the medical backgrounds squeamish. As the demand for Juul grew, so did the batches of e-liquid. Because the mixing and production had been designed for smaller quantities, as the size grew the consistency of the liquid changed. In the mint-flavored pods, the menthol oils would separate from the rest of the ingredients, leaving a salad dressing–like liquid. When employees and contractors raised concerns about the safety of using what appeared to be a defective product, large batches of the liquid were placed into quarantine and tested for toxicity. Instead of throwing away the product and losing money, top executives ultimately ordered the factory workers to instead suck out the liquid from the bottom of the giant tub until it reached the oily top layer. That way they only had to discard a portion of the suspect batch. The rest was released for sale. That so alarmed at least one person working in the factory, who unsuccessfully pushed to have the product discarded in its entirety, that they filed a complaint with the FDA. "I was like hey this seems problematic," the person told the agency. "If this were Liqui-Gels, they'd say scrap it. They knew it was bad product." A finance executive later filed a whistleblower complaint about the same batch of mint e-liquid and alleged that the company refused to issue a recall of one million pods with the stuff in them. While Juul later said that internal tests showed that the product wasn't toxic to human health, the incident underscored the haphazard nature of Juul's operation, even as its product was being consumed by millions of people every day.

Sometimes there were close calls. At one e-liquid supplier, a person in quality control noticed that there were black flecks suspended in the liquid. Upon closer inspection they realized that the flecks were metal shavings that, had they not been caught, could have been inhaled into human lungs. The series of incidents spooked employees, who were starting to wonder if things were moving too quickly. "This isn't the wristwatch you're wearing and you run to the Apple store if it breaks," one horrified former employee told others. "People can actually die." Another employee described the ramp-up, and all the ancillary calamities, as a stress-inducing "fever dream."

No matter how dysfunctional, Burns was equipped to handle supply chain problems. But he wasn't prepared for the company's biggest, most glaring liability.

KEVIN BRZUZIEWSKI, THE CREATOR of the @JuulNation Instagram account, couldn't have given two fucks about the legal threat he received from Juul. "Dear Mr. Brzuziewski," the October 12, 2017, letter read. "JUUL Labs, Inc. ('JUUL') has retained our law firm to represent it in connection with your unauthorized sales and giveaways of its JUUL-brand products from the Instagram account @juulnation. Unless you immediately stop selling and offering giveaways of JUUL products through your Instagram account (and any other websites or social media accounts), and remove all posts promoting such sales and giveaways, we intend to file a lawsuit against you."

Brzuziewski wasn't fazed. He had zero intention of taking down the site. He was making way too much money, sometimes thousands of dollars a month. Plus he and his friends were having a blast with all the attention his wacky hand-curated page was generating. Gen Z had taken to Juul's marketing campaign like flies to honey. At the beginning of 2017, there wasn't very much Juul-related content on Twitter. But by the end of the following year, the number of Juul-related tweets had increased by nearly seventy times over, with nearly one hundred thousand such tweets every week. Only a fraction of those tweets came from an official Juul social media account. Juul had touched off a user-generated content explosion. And it was clear where the interest was coming from. A text search of social media showed that between October 2017 and February 2018, there were a quarter million tweets mentioning Juul or Juuling, with thousands of them mentioning the word *cafeteria, campus, class, dorm, library,* or *school.* Despite the stated goal of getting smokers off cigarettes, there simply wasn't much talk on these platforms about quitting smoking. There were entire subreddits devoted to kids Juuling, including one titled UnderageJuul that gave tips on how to conceal the device from parents and teachers, the names of retailers that didn't card, and even older people offering "discreet shipping," for a Venmo fee, to minors' homes.

Even before Burns came on, Juul executives recognized there was a problem. Juul hired a crisis communications firm, Sard Verbinnen, to help chart a path forward. Richard Mumby, the architect of the "Vaporized" campaign, had departed. Burns pleaded with his social media team to start rehabbing the brand's online image. "We have to make this product only appealing to adult smokers," Burns started telling them.

The same Juul employees who had excitedly cultivated cute and sassy content were suddenly instructed to do a one-eighty. No more posts that made Juuling look like fun, because that could open them up to accusations that they were going after kids. No more posting images of Juul devices or pods next to things that could be perceived as being too youth oriented. No bright colors. No frothy lattes. They could show plants, but nothing with flowers on it. They could show a whole mango, but not a sliced mango. They actively began strategizing how to make the content they generated skew toward an obviously older demographic—glasses, books, and crossword puzzles were features of the newer posts.

But despite Juul's growing unease, social media companies like Instagram and YouTube and Snapchat were happy to continue providing a platform for the growing number of Juul influencers, like Brzuziewski's Instagram page that generated huge levels of "engagement"—the term of art for eyeballs that generate ad revenue. eBay was making a killing off reselling Juul pods, and since the site largely didn't age verify, it was another powerful vector landing Juul in the hands of underage users. Juul expanded its compliance and "brand protection" team to go after social media accounts that were illegally using its logo, but most of the time the company found itself without much legal ground to stand on. Nothing Brzuziewski was doing was technically illegal, so the platforms took a hands-off approach on his and other Juul-fan accounts despite Juul practically begging the platforms to shut them down.

For the time being, Brzuziewski kept posting memes and racking up millions of likes. He had a hunch that many of his fans were in high school. But he was too busy gaining followers to care.

STANFORD MEDICINE PROFESSOR OF pediatrics Bonnie Halpern-Felsher had been studying adolescent risk behavior for more than two decades. A developmental psychologist with additional training in adolescent health, she endeavored to understand the developmental, cognitive, and social factors underpinning why kids engaged in risk-taking behavior, studying a whole host of risky behaviors that teens engaged in—unprotected sex, reckless driving, binge-drinking. She became a junior faculty member at UCSF in 1997 and received a grant from the Tobacco-Related Disease Research Program, a California entity that received money collected from cigarette taxes to fund tobacco prevention and cessation research. She also began working with the university's Center for Tobacco Control Research and Education, the ancestral home of the tobacco-prevention movement that was started with the help of Stan Glantz, the longtime tobacco control advocate who'd helped galvanize California's anti smoking movement in the 1970s.

As Halpern-Felsher started researching youth tobacco use, she had an epiphany. For young people, it's possible, at least in theory, to have a healthy relationship with sex and alcohol, even if that wasn't exactly the behavior she'd advocate. In contrast, she realized, "There is no healthy relationship with tobacco or nicotine, period." Not only was smoking deadly, but the nicotine in it had few redeeming qualities for children.

Adolescence is defined loosely as beginning in the early preteen or teen years. The brain, however, isn't fully formed until around age twenty-five, including the prefrontal cortex region that governs cognition and impulse control. As the brain undergoes a process of "pruning" to improve the efficiency of signaling between nerves, it retains synaptic pathways that are used and eliminates those that are not. That's why if the nicotinic receptors that humans are born with are stimulated with nicotine use during adolescence, the brain comes to expect continued stimulation, which results in addiction.

Also, nicotine has been shown to cause a "misprogramming of brain cell development and synaptic function" that can impair learning, memory, and mood. And while chronic nicotine exposure during adolescence can have the long-term effect of diminished cognitive function as adults, it can also prime the brain for future drug abuse. "Even brief exposure to a low dose of nicotine can produce lasting change in the adolescent brain," found a 2015 study in *The Journal of Physiology*.

For all of those reasons and more, Halpern-Felsher decided to focus on youth tobacco use prevention and research. By 2010, less than 20 percent of high schoolers were cigarette smokers, compared to 36.4 percent in 1997. Through ad campaigns funded largely by tobacco settlement money, kids had become so desensitized to the allure of smoking, and attuned to the deceptive practices used by cigarette makers, that the habit had started falling out of fashion.

The unfortunate side effect of that success, however, was that the issue had largely faded from the front pages of newspapers, and smoking prevention programs weren't deemed a priority. Money that states collected from the tobacco settlement was increasingly diverted away from tobacco prevention programs and to other general purposes by needy schools, states, and localities, such as closing budget gaps or early-childhood education programs or issuing bonds backed by settlement money. That meant that there was less dedicated tobacco prevention awareness being taught inside schools, which Halpern-Felsher felt was unfortunate, and unwise. All her years of research told her that tobacco prevention was still necessary and she was loath to see it get demoted. After all, tobacco prevention inside schools had contributed to the historic decline in youth tobacco use.

In 2009 Halpern-Felsher got funding to put together what she called a tobacco prevention "toolkit" that included critical components that other programs didn't have, such as more information about the power of nicotine addiction, positive youth development messaging, and the need to bring parents into the conversation. "Parents said to me, 'I really want to talk to my kids about cigarettes but I don't know how,'" she said.

As she and her team set out to create the toolkit, e-cigarettes weren't on her radar. But a few years into its development, e-cigarettes started to appear on campuses and she was alarmed that even as cigarette smoking rates continued to fall, a new type of nicotine addiction was cropping up. She applied for more funding and, in 2014, she worked on a teaching module for her forthcoming curriculum that focused entirely on e-cigarettes. Two years later, The Stanford Tobacco Prevention Toolkit was launched.

In it, Halpern-Felsher had an entire section on the brain. Students were shown slides with titles like "The Adolescent Brain: A Work in Progress" accompanied by images of overlapping highways and a traffic jam to symbolize all those brain pathways still in formation. Another slide had a picture of wriggling termites to depict how nicotine worms its way into the teenage brain. Soon it was being widely adopted in schools, as both parents and teachers were pleasantly surprised to see students respond positively to its messaging.

Still, in her new toolkit, there was no mention of Juul. The product had just started to make its ripple. In October 2017, though, the company's name finally reached Halpern-Felsher's ears. As she toiled away in her office on the Stanford campus, just a stone's throw from where

Bowen and Monsees birthed their creation, she realized she needed to act fast. She'd just hired a new a project director and told him this: "There's this thing called Juul. Find out about it. Create a PowerPoint. And put it on our toolkit."

Just a few months later, on February 1, 2018, the new curriculum, called "What are Juuls?," went live. She knew it would be of interest. But she had no idea the level of swamped she would be by school administrators and teachers, practically begging her for the curriculum. It hit like a tsunami. Schools across the United States were being inundated by Juul.

WHILE BURNS SENT HIS kids to Paly, the public high school in Palo Alto, the neighboring hamlet of Atherton had its own private school on 64 serene acres in the middle of town, called Sacred Heart Schools. It was founded as a boarding school in 1898 by an order of French nuns and now hosted upper-crust children aged preschool to twelfth grade whose parents didn't sneeze at paying $50,000 a year in tuition, per kid, to have them reared inside the stately redbrick building capped with an elegant mansard roof and bell tower.

In early 2018, Emma Briger was a junior at Sacred Heart. She'd developed a reputation as an up-and-coming star goalie on the girls' lacrosse team, the Gators, and had been named a captain of the varsity team. She'd already been goalie of the year in the regional West Bay Athletic League and had been recruited to play for multiple national leagues.

A high achiever, Briger was set on leading her team to the championship that year. So she was disappointed and somewhat shocked to learn that several of her teammates had taken up vaping. And it wasn't a rare occurrence. They'd hit the Juul before and after practice, and sometimes even vape marijuana, showing up to practice high. This irked Briger, a stellar student who had no interest in, or patience for, such peccadillos. But she didn't know what to do. She didn't want to seem like a killjoy or a tattletale. One night, she turned to her dad, Pete, for advice. The two had developed a trusting and close relationship and bonded over sports. Pete drove Emma to lacrosse practice and would travel to tournaments wherever they were held, cheering on his daughter's team. As they sat around the kitchen table in their Atherton home, Emma poured her heart out, recounting her conundrum.

"That's impossible," her dad replied.

"Dad, I'm really worried about this," she urged. "It's affecting the whole team."

Pete Briger wasn't just any dad. He was the billionaire co-chief executive officer at Fortress Investment Group, the towering firm that had more than $45 billion of assets under management. Briger had made a career at Goldman Sachs as an elite trader in distressed debt, raking in untold sums of money for the storied Wall Street investment bank and becoming a pre-IPO partner before moving to Fortress and opening an office for the firm in San Francisco. Like any self-respecting mogul who lived in the area, he moved to Atherton, into a well-appointed home just down the street from Sacred Heart, where he decided to send his children.

It wasn't that Pete didn't trust what his daughter was telling him. He was just in disbelief. He'd walked this earth long enough to know that people did stupid things, but surely no kid who attended Sacred Heart would be so stupid as to show up to lacrosse practice *high*? But over the next couple of weeks, Emma kept coming home with stories, and Pete finally came around. He and his wife, Devon, called up the coach of the team, Wendy Kridel, and had a confidential conversation with her.

"Wendy, you know, my daughter is telling me that this is happening, and that it's a real problem," Briger told her.

"It's not happening, Pete," Kridel responded. Like many others at the time, Kridel was in denial. It's not that she was naïve. It's just that she, like Pete Briger, thought it inconceivable that these overachieving kids at Sacred Heart would be so reckless.

Briger and Kridel had a good relationship. "Just do me a favor," Pete asked her. "Can you just go check into this?"

Lo and behold, a couple of days later, Kridel came back. "I'm just amazed about this," she said to Briger. "But you're right."

Just a few weeks later, Kridel was preparing to take the entire Sacred Heart girls' lacrosse team to Denver over spring break to play lacrosse against some teams up there. She called a meeting with the girls and their parents one day after practice on the sidelines of the emerald-green field to discuss details of the upcoming trip. After talking about the travel itinerary and other logistics, Kridel brought up the vaping issue. She explained that not only was Juuling unhealthy and addictive, but it was also against school rules and she had a zero-tolerance policy. If any of the girls got caught vaping on the trip, they'd be immediately sent home at the parents' expense, no questions asked. They'd also risk being kicked off the lacrosse team.

"Don't do this," Kridel warned, in her booming coach voice. "This is really bad for you."

The following week the team landed in Denver, just as a snowstorm was getting ready to barrel down. Pete Briger accompanied his daughter on the trip, staying with family, while the girls all posted up at a local hotel down the street from the lacrosse field where they were scheduled to play. The very next day, Kridel was approached by three of the lacrosse players. "There were girls vaping in their hotel room," they said.

Kridel was beside herself. After a dramatic confrontation with the girls in the hotel room, it turned out that two of the players had been Juuling. Given that they were warned just days earlier about this exact scenario, Kridel had no choice but to send them home the very next morning.

When Briger learned from Kridel about the turn of events, he was dumbfounded. Not only had the girls been warned, but the trip was only for three days. "Wendy, that's crazy. How could they do that?" he asked her.

The girls were put on a plane the next morning back to Atherton and never played for the Sacred Heart Gators again. The entire rest of the trip was clouded by the event.

When Briger got back to Atherton, he couldn't stop thinking about what had transpired. Do these girls not have supportive parents at home? Were they simply that distracted? Or that reckless?

Then it dawned on him. These girls were so hooked on Juul that they were willing to risk everything they'd worked for to have more of it. *This* was addiction. It made him fume.

BURNS HAD NO CHOICE but to tackle the youth issue head-on. Around the beginning of 2018, Juul hired a former educator named Julie Henderson to be in charge of a new "Education and Youth Prevention Department." Among other things, Henderson set out to create a new anti-vaping curriculum that could be offered in schools across the country. She also reached out to a company called Soter Technologies that made an anti-bullying gadget that looked like a smoke detector and could be installed in school bathrooms to detect noise indicative of violence. It could also detect vape and would alert teachers or school administrators when it detected the faint presence of, say, Juul.

Burns was in an impossible position. Even as he was tasked by the Juul board to rapidly scale, he found himself frantically trying to contain the collateral damage of the company's ascent. Here was a tech company now in the position of having to beg and plead with customers to *not* use its tech. But the heat was intensifying. If Juul didn't rein in the youth usage problem, they could wind up being put out of business.

By the spring of 2018, Henderson and a team of educators started going around to dozens of middle schools and high schools across the country, with a curriculum designed to provide students with "vaping replacement approaches" through unusual avenues such as "mindfulness" and "loving kindness meditation." The company also developed a "Saturday School" program for kids caught vaping.

Juul was offering schools $10,000 to adopt its prevention program, a red flag that raised suspicions. "Good afternoon," wrote a representative of the California Department of Education, in a February 1, 2018, email to school administrators. "Our office has become aware of overtures from the manufacturer of Juul products towards schools. . . . Should you be approached by the representatives of the Juul company, keep in mind that our office considers Juul to be part of the tobacco industry. . . . Our office strongly recommends that [you] reject these overtures."

Juul was stepping on a nerve. Aside from schools not wanting Juul to teach their students about the very product that was causing such pain and upheaval, something else was nagging them. Many educators had been around long enough to remember Philip Morris's Youth Smoking Prevention program back in the early 2000s that had garnered so much negative attention for its curriculum that actually made smoking more attractive to teens. They'd never forgotten the ads targeting their kids—the smoldering hot Marlboro Man, the cartoonish Joe Camel that research showed was more recognizable than Mickey Mouse, the glamorous Virginia Slims women.

In March that year, Bonnie Halpern-Felsher, the developer of the anti-Juul curriculum at Stanford, had started getting strange feedback about the program that she and her team had developed. Some people seemed to be under the impression that she was collaborating with Juul on its program. That's because Juul, she found, had developed their *own* anti-Juul program, in which the company appeared to indicate that it had been developed with some sort of partnership with Stanford Medicine. She also obtained a copy of Juul's lesson plan, which contained a link to her toolkit. Not only that, but some parts of Juul's curriculum were a near replica of hers, with entire paragraphs lifted verbatim. Slides in the PowerPoint that she'd spent years developing based on intensive research had been simply dropped into Juul's presentation, complete with the exact images—the same picture of a little brain that said "Brain Background," her tangled highways symbolizing the reward pathways in the adolescent brain, even the squiggling termites she used to depict a nicotine-addicted brain.

Halpern-Felsher was flabbergasted. "This is bizarre," she told her colleagues. It was not only disturbing as an academic hyper-attuned to plagiarism, it also struck her as unethical. It seemed like her work was being twisted in the service of marketing, of all things, Juul. She affixed a disclaimer on the toolkit website, stating: "We have been informed that some companies that are in the business of selling products that contain tobacco and/or nicotine had either included links to our

Toolkit in their marketing materials, or implied that The Stanford Tobacco Prevention Toolkit or the faculty and staff involved in creating it
have some affiliation with them. This is simply not true. We are committed to preventing use of tobacco products, e-cigarettes, and any
other tobacco- and nicotine-related products and we do not receive any
funding from them or otherwise collaborate with them."

And then, in April 2018, she reported her findings to Stanford's legal
counsel. Within days, Juul received a cease and desist order from Stanford, Bowen and Monsees's alma mater.

MEREDITH BERKMAN LIVED ON Manhattan's tony Upper West Side.
She was married to a former Morgan Stanley banker and the founder
of a well-known private equity firm in the city. Berkman's son Caleb
had just started high school in the fall of 2017. Berkman was clueless as
to why she'd always hear him and his friends crack open the bedroom
window when they were together. She'd peek her head in but breathed
a sigh of relief when she didn't smell smoke or notice anything suspicious. She didn't give it another thought when Caleb asked her for an
incense burner. *He's so spiritual,* she thought, affectionately.

One day in early April 2018, Caleb came home and told his parents
that something odd had happened at school that day. A speaker had
come to the auditorium to give an anti-addiction seminar to the entire
ninth-grade class of his small private school. The teachers were told to
leave the room so the kids could have a safe space to talk about any issues on their mind. While the man was there to talk about a wide
range of related issues, including drug and alcohol abuse, he ended up
spending time talking about nicotine addiction and Juul. That was surprising since it turned out the man was also working on behalf of Juul.
The man said that Juul was not for them. It was for adults. Still, "it's
totally safe," he told the kids. He also mentioned that the FDA was in
the process of "approving it" as safer than cigarettes. For Caleb's many
classmates who had already long been Juuling, the presenter's words
delivered a sigh of relief for students who now believed they could
continue using the product without any concern.

After the seminar ended, Caleb and his friend Phillip approached the Juul representative. What should they do if they had a friend addicted to nicotine, they asked? The two boys didn't mention that it was in fact Phillip who was addicted, and that he was in fact addicted to Juul. The speaker mistakenly believed that the "friend" was addicted to cigarettes, and he replied, "He should use Juul, it's ninety-nine percent safer than cigarettes." The man then took a Juul out of his pocket and showed the boys how it worked. "This is the iPhone of vapes," he said.

Berkman was astounded at what she was hearing. She called Phillip's mom, Dorian Fuhrman. Berkman recounted the story and asked Fuhrman if she knew anything about Juul. It turned out she did. Not long ago, Phillip had gotten home from a party one night and she detected a faint sweet smell on him. She'd already grown suspicious because it seemed like overnight that her adoring son had gone from liking surfing and cooking and playing with his little sister to instead locking himself in his bedroom. Not long after, Fuhrman had found what she thought was a USB drive in his pants pockets. Only after she saw the word *Juul* inscribed on it and googled it did she begin putting two and two together. Meanwhile, Berkman also reached out to another mom, Dina Alessi, whose teenage son was also disconcertingly familiar with Juul. They were immediately compelled to get to the bottom of the force that had caused their children to fall under a dangerous nicotine spell.

That very week, the three alarmed and angered moms jumped down the rabbit hole. They began furiously reading articles on the internet and diving into studies about addiction. They stayed up late into the night talking to each other on the phone, and met at one another's ritzy Manhattan homes. Berkman called her pediatrician. Fuhrman reached out to someone she knew at the New York–based Child Mind Institute. Bit by disappointing bit, they learned more than they ever wanted to know about the thing called Juul. "The more we learned, the more shocked we were," Berkman said. "How was it possible that there had been a teen cultural revolution and most adults hadn't even noticed?"

They assumed that there must be some sort of advocacy group

along the lines of Mothers Against Drunk Driving but for vaping, and were surprised to learn there wasn't one dedicated to the issue. So, they decided to build their own. Along the way, Berkman stumbled across a Stanford Medicine website that had something called The Tobacco Prevention Toolkit. She was pleasantly surprised to find that it contained copious amounts of information about Juul and youth nicotine addiction. But then she noticed a mysterious little disclaimer on the bottom of the page stating that "This is simply not true" that the program was affiliated with "some companies" that sold nicotine. That's odd, Berkman thought. She had a hunch that there was more to the story. She navigated her cursor to the generic email address at the bottom of the page, and wrote that she'd like to speak to the creator of the program. Two weeks later, her phone rang. It was Bonnie Halpern-Felsher from Stanford Medicine.

The two women hit if off. Berkman told her everything—about Juul's school visit, about the other moms she was working with, about the new anti-vaping website they were just starting to cobble together. Halpern-Felsher explained her own strange run-in with the company. In that moment, Berkman asked the Stanford professor if she would consider working on the fledgling cause. They were in the process of assembling a group of top medical experts to confront the teen vaping problem. It wasn't long before Halpern-Felsher had flown across the country and was sitting in Berkman's kitchen as the first advisory board member to a group that finally had a website and a name: Parents Against Vaping e-cigarettes, or PAVe.

MEANWHILE, SCOTT GOTTLIEB WAS coming under growing pressure to do something about Juul. The FDA was receiving a growing number of complaints about the company, including from parents and teenagers saying they saw Juul advertising on websites for cartoons and homework, and accusations that the company had intentionally designed its e-liquid recipe and device to allow for a more inconspicuous vapor cloud to allow kids to use the device behind the backs of teachers and parents.

On March 19, Gottlieb announced that his agency was starting to look at whether it might regulate the flavors of e-cigarettes. There was growing concern that the array of dessert and candy flavors were tempting youth to start vaping in the first place. The agency's "advance notice of proposed rulemaking" was essentially the first step toward potentially regulating the flavors.

But rulemaking, as shown by the deeming rule that took nearly seven years to pass, was a notoriously tedious process and lawmakers and others were starting to lose patience. A group of pediatricians and a network of health organizations, including the American Academy of Pediatrics, the Truth Initiative, the American Cancer Society, the American Heart Association, and the Campaign for Tobacco-Free Kids, had recently sued the FDA in federal court for its decision to allow the industry an additional four years to continue operating without regulations.

About two weeks later, on April 18, Illinois senator Dick Durbin and ten other senators published letters to both Juul and the FDA, citing a *New York Times* article of a few weeks earlier that ran under the headline "'I Can't Stop': Schools Struggle with Vaping Explosion." "Dear Mr. Burns," the Juul letter read. "Your company's popular vaping device (JUUL) and its accompanying flavored nicotine cartridges (JUULPods) are undermining our nation's efforts to reduce tobacco use among youth and putting an entire new generation of children at risk of nicotine addiction and other health consequences."

The letter to Gottlieb demanding action was no less cutting. "We write today to share our deep concern that the significant progress we have made in reducing tobacco use among our nation's youth is at serious risk of being reversed because of the FDA's failure to take swift action against specific products that clearly appeal to youth and threaten to hook a generation of children onto tobacco products," the letter read. "If we wait four more years to act, we will have doomed countless more children to addiction and adverse health consequences at the hands of big tobacco companies."

Five days later, Gottlieb revealed that his agency had been engaged since early April in an undercover "blitz" on retailers across the nation

to crack down on the sale of e-cigarettes to minors. The sting operation netted forty violations for illegal sales of Juul to kids, including at
7-Elevens, Circle Ks, and Speedways across the country.

At the same time that he announced the sting operation, Gottlieb
also announced that his agency had asked Juul to hand over internal
documents that related to the company's marketing practices, product
design, and complaints in regard to adverse health experiences as a result of using its product.

"FDA is requesting these documents based on growing concern
about the popularity of Juul products among youth. . . . Widespread
reports of youth use of Juul products are of great public health concern and no child or teenager should ever use any tobacco product.
Nicotine affects the developing brain and youth may not understand
the nicotine or other characteristics of Juul. Juul products may have
features that make them more appealing to kids and easier to use, thus
causing increased initiation and/or use among youth."

Burns had been on the job only four months and his company was
spinning deeper into crisis by the day.

15

PLAN A

If anyone is going to take away our
business it should be us.
—BRITISH AMERICAN TOBACCO EXECUTIVE

It was a new day at Altria, but there was no sunshine. Over the weekend after the May 17, 2018, annual shareholders meeting, which formally installed Howard Willard as CEO, heavy rain pummeled the Richmond area, causing flash floods and the highest recorded precipitation levels since 1889. The rain carried into the following week as well, so at Altria's headquarters workers erected a tarp off the side of the main portico and set up rows of folding chairs facing a stage. Willard was preparing to speak to his ranks for the first time as the new board chairman and chief executive officer.

Willard was faced with a dilemma. The newly empowered CEO was ready to make bold moves in a rapidly changing industry that was imperiling the company's future. But making bold moves at Altria had never been easy or acceptable. Altria was a place that instilled a healthy dose of fear in its senior executives when it came to moving fast. It was the opposite of Silicon Valley. Move slow. Break nothing. Implement incremental change that revolved around the core business of selling tobacco. In fact, senior executives at Altria were often coached by mentors about the movement of time on the company's metaphorical clock. Imagine it's twelve o'clock. People inside the company spend their entire careers moving the small hand to three minutes after twelve, and that's considered progress. Anybody who'd ever tried to move the long hand from twelve to three didn't last very long. One could cite Michael Miles, who'd earned the notoriety of being the shortest-tenured CEO at the company. In 1994, Miles was pushed out after just under three years at the helm, in part for not prioritizing the cigarette business enough, and trying to break up the tobacco-food conglomerate that his predecessor, Hamish Maxwell, had built just a few years earlier. Maxwell was arguably one of the few former CEOs who successfully did move the long hand to three, when he boldly diversified the tobacco business by acquiring General Foods for $5.7 billion, bringing the Jell-O and Birds Eye brands under the Philip Morris umbrella, and then by acquiring Kraft for $13.1 billion.

Howard Willard wasn't Hamish Maxwell, by any stretch of the imagination, but he'd had a propitious career up until now, receiving promotion after promotion, carefully groomed by another legendary Philip Morris CEO, Mike Szymanczyk, and so there was no reason for him to believe that he was anything but destined for greatness. As he prepared to take on the CEO role, he'd been studying all kinds of leadership books, including Jim Collins's classic *Good to Great,* which had long been cherished within the company not least because Collins showcased Philip Morris for having once made the titular transformation. Willard had also been reading other modern business classics, such as *The Fourth Industrial Revolution* by Klaus Schwab, the founder of the World Economic Forum in Davos. Willard also turned to Harvard Business School professor John Kotter, the well-known business transformation guru whose eight-step process evangelized the need for marrying vision and strategy. He was so into Kotter that he assigned his senior team to read one of Kotter's books, *A Sense of Urgency.*

If anything, Willard had a sense of urgency. Over the past two years, there had been so much careful weighing of the future as the e-cigarette industry around them exploded. Right out of the gate, he decided to thrust the clock hand to three, to bring Altria into the twenty-first century, kicking and screaming if necessary.

When he took the stage, the audience was unusually quiet, as if there were a collective bated breath. There was a range of emotions and opinions about Willard. Some, particularly those who'd worked most closely with him, were eager for him to get started. He'd already displayed an impatience about meeting the future, a trait that some felt was lacking with the uber-polished Barrington. Others were sad to see the "man of the people" CEO go and remained circumspect about Willard. That's partly because Willard was something of an enigma to many. Even though he'd been at the company for more than two decades, and occupied a variety of offices across the company, he wasn't the kind of guy who made himself easily visible and knowable. While Barrington was omnipotent, not only in the company but also throughout the Richmond community, from the ballet to art museums to nonprofits for underprivileged kids, Willard didn't have that same kind of omnipotent mayoral nature. Willard made philanthropic donations to some of the same institutions, but he wasn't visible on Richmond's ribbon-cutting, check-signing, high-society circuit. And unlike the avuncular Barrington, who spoke with an eloquence and steadiness of a well trained politician, Willard tended to have a distant mannerism and a flat cadence. He seemed unmindful of the imposing nature of his six-foot-six-inch stature that some found intimidating, and he often struggled at small talk, which could make him seem inurbane.

Every chair under the tent was filled for his first speech. "I'm honored to be here," Willard said. He'd been preparing for this position for years and was ready for the challenge. But he was not going to rest on his laurels. There were substantial challenges ahead, he warned, in what was easily the most competitive tobacco market he'd ever seen. Cigarettes were under pressure from every side, from the oral nicotine products like on! and Zyn, to the pod-based e-cigarette companies like Juul that weren't cut from the same cloth as Altria. Juul's founders came from Silicon Valley and Altria needed to be ready to compete on their turf. Altria needed to be willing to "fail fast" and be able to "test and learn," he said. Willard, like others at Altria, was partial to the buzzwords of the moment, although some in the audience felt a little frustrated that senior leaders only now seemed to be adopting a sense of urgency. Where were they a decade ago when e-cigarettes were new and they had the luxury of time?

The company was undergoing a transformation, Willard said. Not only was the marketplace for products competitive but so was the marketplace for talent, which is why the company was working to build a more inclusive workplace. Altria employees of color had long felt marginalized, as did many women, who watched executives get picked from the same narrow pool over and over again. Willard had promised to build on Barrington's efforts to diversify Altria across the corporate ranks. Yet his top aides, Billy Gifford and K.C. Crosthwaite, were middle-aged white men.

Gifford and Crosthwaite were two of Willard's closest allies inside the company, and almost immediately after taking over, the three men could be seen walking the halls together, ducking into meeting rooms, whispering and huddling. Some took to calling them the Three Muske-teers. Some people found the Three Musketeers endearing, a mighty troika of master strategists looking to do right by the company. Others cringed at the company suddenly being run by a secretive en banc panel. Was the man at the podium up to the task? The speculation would end sooner than they could have fathomed.

One of Willard's first decisions as CEO was to reorganize the man-agement structure at the top of the company, an almost axiomatic move for any new CEO in corporate America. As part of the new structure, Altria would pursue a "dual strategy" to maximize income from its traditional tobacco brands while increasing revenue from the new suite of tobacco products, such as MarkTen. The company was split into two divisions—one oversaw the core tobacco products, like cigarettes and snuff, the other ran the "innovative tobacco products" like e-vapor or oral nicotine products. By making this split, Willard was sending a clear message to analysts and others that Altria was taking seriously the insurgent products in the tobacco market and wasn't going to sit idly by as Marlboro got battered.

Jody Begley, the executive who'd been in charge at Nu Mark, was moved to oversee the tobacco business. In his place Willard named Brian Quigley as the new president and CEO of Nu Mark. Up until then Quigley had served as the longtime CEO of Altria's U.S. Smokeless Tobacco Company, which churned out the Copenhagen and Skoal brands. Now, he was tasked with leading the "innovative products business" at the company.

At the same time, Willard announced that as part of the transformation, Crosthwaite had been named the company's new "chief growth officer," a fancy title that had become in vogue. In this instance Crosthwaite would "accelerate speed to market for innovative products and technologies" and be responsible for "building and acquiring the competencies, technologies and talent to achieve Altria's aspiration of being the U.S. leader in authorized, non-combustible, reduced-risk products."

Press releases and corporate restructurings always tend to be jargony, so observers could be forgiven for not initially understanding the motive behind what one analyst described as little more than "musical chairs." But behind the scenes the strategy was simple. What wasn't mentioned in the press release was that the thrust of the new structure was really designed to push forward two strategies that Willard called Plan A and Plan B. As chief growth officer, Crosthwaite was in charge of Plan A: Get a deal done with Juul. As the new head of Nu Mark, Quigley was in charge of Plan B: Try to out-innovate Juul. A thankless task. Willard was betting big on Plan A. But with each passing week he waited, it would have to be a bigger and bigger bet.

LOOKING IN FROM THE outside, assuming a willingness to accept the raw business proposition without asking any questions, Juul could have been viewed as just another tech start-up disrupting a longtime incumbent player. Silicon Valley was awash with such companies, which is why hedge funds and investment managers had long been opening offices out west, piling into the start-up game. Charles Payson "Chase" Coleman III, the secretive billionaire founder of Tiger Global Management, was one of the shrewdest, most astute investors in the world. Before he was thirty years old, he'd grown a sum of money he'd gotten from his mentor into one of the most star-studded investment firms in the world with $40 billion in managed gross assets. A descendant of Peter Stuyvesant, a noted historical figure on Wall Street, Coleman had become a legend in his own right in the city where he helicoptered to work and threw rollicking parties, including one at his $52 million Central Park co-op that was getting ready to undergo renovations and he invited his guests "to vandalize the French plastered walls with cans of spray paint as they partied into the early hours."

He was now also inextricably linked to Juul. The company fit neatly into an investment thesis at Tiger that had been reliably powering the firm's returns. Start-ups that were following the so-called direct-to-consumer, or D2C, model that was predicated on cutting out the middlemen and upending entrenched old-guard players in big consumer industries likely presented an attractive target. Like Warby Parker, the direct-to-consumer eyeglasses company that disrupted long-standing industry giants, like Luxottica. Or Peloton, the cycling start-up that disrupted large swaths of the fitness industry by merging its stationary bike with an online, on-demand cycling platform. Or Harry's, the men's shaving start-up that managed to disrupt the razor giant Gillette by using hip packaging and a direct-to-consumer subscription model. Tiger Global was an early financial backer in all of them.

The potential of disrupting Big Tobacco presented an opportunity orders of magnitude bigger than any of these other industries. The global razor market was worth about $10 billion. The global fitness industry was worth around a $100 billion. Eyewear, a nice $140 billion. Tobacco? Nearly $1 *trillion*. It made sense that Coleman would want to invest. Tiger originally placed a modest bet on Juul in 2017. But in July 2018, with the start-up mushrooming, Coleman's firm plowed $600 million into the company as part of a $1.25 billion "mega" investment round that gave Juul a post-money valuation of around $16 billion.

If Juul executives didn't already have a holier-than-thou attitude about their transcendent nicotine invention, now more than ever they could play hard to get. Their company, it seemed, was made of gold. This latest round of funding made Juul the fastest-growing start-up in all of Silicon Valley. The company wasn't only a *unicorn*. Now it was a *decacorn*! And it reached that insane milestone four times faster than Facebook. With investors piling in, Juul was like a red balloon that somebody let go of on a clear blue, breezy day. Up. Up. Up. Eyes strained as it floated away, turning into a barely visible speck on the horizon.

ON THURSDAY, JULY 26, when Altria released its second-quarter earnings and Willard was poised to give his first earnings call as CEO, the numbers couldn't have been worse. They showed that Marlboro volumes had declined by an unexpected 10 percent compared to the same time a year earlier, an acceleration beyond the more normal 2 to 4 percent declines that investors had come to expect as the cigarette industry slowly withered. Generally, as long as cigarette companies were able to increase the price of cigarettes enough to offset volume declines, revenue would stay even. But today, Altria's financials revealed that the price increases weren't sufficient to outweigh the decline.

That morning, Willard was barraged with questions by stock analysts who wanted to know how much Juul was to blame for the lackluster numbers. Juul had never been invoked so many times on any such Altria call. "I was wondering if you can talk about the acceleration in the e-cig category and to what extent you think that Juul's growth is coming from cigarette volumes," one analyst asked Willard. Another said, "So I wanted to go back to the e-vapor category and just wanted to get your assessment in terms of what you're seeing from Juul. . . . Clearly, that brand has maintained very strong momentum."

For the past couple of years, Altria executives had been able to spin the company's "innovation pipeline" into a believable tale and brush off suspicious questions about what the company was really doing to stave off insurgent brands like Juul. But that was becoming trickier by the day. Altria's stock dropped 2.5 percent that day, and it was already down 20 percent that year. *The Wall Street Journal* had a crushing headline: "Marlboro Sales Drop Sharply in a Shrinking Market: Altria CEO Plays Down Threat from Popular e-Cigarette Rivals like Juul."

Behind the scenes, Willard was getting ready to go big with an aggressive growth strategy. Now as both chairman of the board and CEO of the company, he was finally in a position to push through his vision and to lay to rest any doubt once and for all whether Altria could compete in the new world. Willard pulled certain individuals aside to tell them that they wouldn't have to scream into the void anymore. Plenty of employees were frustrated by the increasingly intense pressures on the company's core tobacco business and the clear need to do something about it, whether it was a move into energy drinks or alcohol or cannabis. Or Juul. "I want you to know we're going to get something done, and take real action," Willard told them.

For some Altria executives and employees, it was refreshing to see Willard step into his skin and embody a more aggressive posture than anybody imagined. He almost immediately became what one insider described as a bull in a china shop. If Barrington had been waiting—hoping—for the Juul rocket to crash, Willard wanted to try to catch the rocket by its tail.

BY AUGUST 1, THE cherry blossoms in Washington, D.C., were long gone, but in the lobby of the city's Park Hyatt they lived on in a glass-enclosed box containing photographs of the famous foliage. The Park Hyatt Washington D.C. was a crown jewel in the Pritzker family's luxury hotel portfolio, which boasted Park Hyatt properties around the world, from Zanzibar to Buenos Aires to the Changbaishan ski resort in China. This one, just a few blocks from the White House, often featured dignitaries as guests, and the restaurant inside, the Blue Duck Tavern, was where the Obamas celebrated their seventeenth wedding anniversary.

That day, among the guests was Nick Pritzker, whose late cousin Jay had founded the Hyatt hotel empire. Nick's time nowadays had been consumed less by hotels and more by his current love, Juul. Two days earlier, Pritzker had sent an email to Willard, including an opening term sheet for discussions about a potential deal. Now he, Riaz Valani, and Kevin Burns were waiting to meet Willard and Gifford. There were no lawyers present.

Until this day, aside from Barrington's opposition, the sticking point keeping the two parties apart had been largely about ownership interest. Altria had never been a fan of doing deals that didn't give the company at least a controlling stake. But by now, Willard had gotten the message loud and clear that Juul would never budge on the ownership issue, and that Altria would never be in a position to acquire a controlling stake, let alone the entire company. So, in mid-2018 Altria floated another figure: It would consider paying $6.4 billion for 40 percent of the company, which put Juul at about a $16 billion valuation. Juul informally countered with $9 billion for 40 percent of the company, which would have valued the company at roughly $22.5 billion.

It's not that Willard was trying to intentionally low-ball Juul. It was just that Altria wasn't used to doing business in the Silicon Valley space, where investors flush with tech money were supremely comfortable chasing lofty valuations, which were generally orders of magnitude higher than, say, a traditional consumer products company. Altria was simply not used to getting into bidding wars with growth investors who operated in a fantastical world of companies like WeWork and Uber and Theranos, where valuation was largely divorced from profit and the number of zeroes on a company's purported worth was tied less to fundamentals and more to magical thinking. Altria was a conservative company that traditionally didn't stomach risk well. After all, the company had become all about managing risk, primarily litigation risk. Not chasing unicorns.

By the summer of 2018, Juul's sales were doubling nearly every quarter, and investors were lining up to shoot bazookas of cash its way, which Juul was more than happy to receive. At Altria the gravity-defying warp speed of Silicon Valley was somewhat disorienting.

But Willard was resolved. "You know," Willard said at an internal meeting not long after the Tiger deal. "If we want Juul we're going to need to pay."

Beyond that, since Juul wasn't a publicly traded company, it was difficult to tell what was really going on behind the curtain. The e-cigarette category was simply so new that the company didn't have the reams of metrics that they were used to in the traditional tobacco category. Every single week Altria executives would go over the available sales data from the consumer research firms Nielsen and IRI, but they largely showed only what was happening inside brick-and-mortar retail establishments. The data didn't completely capture sales inside vape shops or, more importantly, online. What was going on inside the finances of Juul was a mystery. Altria couldn't see inside the black box, which made it hard to know whether all the investors plowing money into the firm were delusional or whether there really was a *there* there.

That left Willard and others essentially trying to read chicken entrails. They'd closely gauge the number of new stores Juul entered. They'd try to evaluate the company's supply chain to identify any kinks and how to take advantage of them if possible. They'd look at GlassDoor to see where Juul was hiring and use that as a gauge to try to target those markets with MarkTen. The (frequent) moments when they learned that Juul was out of stock in certain stores or regions MarkTen reps took as a much-needed reassurance that perhaps the company wasn't so golden after all. Then they'd blast those stores with MarkTen too.

In discussions with Juul, Willard tried to break down just how valuable a potential partnership could be. Despite any misgivings about doing a deal with the very tobacco company that Juul's cofounders had set out to destroy, Altria was in fact a perfect partner, he said. His company, he told them, would be able to lend its massive infrastructure, its sales force army, its kingdom of shelf space in practically every retail establishment in the known universe. When it came to the complex regulatory environment, Altria was like an old sage. And, Willard stressed, when it came to the issue of youth prevention, there was simply no company better situated to deal with the problem. Altria had been through it all.

———

BY THE TIME WILLARD made him head of Nu Mark in the spring of 2018, Brian Quigley had been at Altria for more than a decade, working at Philip Morris USA and then becoming president and CEO of the U.S. Smokeless Tobacco Company in 2012. Quigley, a career consumer products executive with experience in the food business as well as tobacco, had done an admirable job growing sales at the $2 billion smokeless company and helping Altria recast the debate about tobacco to embrace a harm-reduction component. Moist smokeless tobacco was Altria's first harm-reduction gambit after the UST acquisition. As its CEO, Quigley helped grow its brands, in part through events like "Men of Copenhagen," which sent burly guys who embraced "core values of masculinity, heritage, authenticity, and tradition" out into communities to do restoration projects like repairing a riverfront park in McKeesport, Pennsylvania.

But Quigley had just been put through the paces. In the winter of 2017, consumers started reporting that they'd found sharp metal objects in their cans of Copenhagen and Skoal. That's any executive's nightmare. The incident led to a massive voluntary recall of the products that resulted in a 3 percent hit to revenue and an investigation that pointed to "a deliberate, malicious act" from people inside one of its factories that had been scheduled to close down. But Quigley's handling of the recall earned him praise inside Altria and helped earn him the job running Nu Mark.

Right out of the gate, colleagues watched with intrigue as Quigley almost immediately got sucked into the Juul saga. Willard wanted Quigley to do a top-down review of MarkTen and figure out what needed to be done to improve its standing in the marketplace. As the person now in charge of Plan B—making MarkTen competitive against Juul—Quigley was in an especially unenviable position. By now Juul had more than 50 percent of the e-cigarette market, up from around 12 percent a year earlier. The MarkTen brand, in contrast, had just 12 percent, down from 23 percent a year earlier. The new MarkTen Elite pods had only been on the market for a few weeks and they'd barely had a chance to make a dent. But everyone at the company knew that no matter how much time they gave Elite in its current form, it would have a hard time competing. And to throw salt on the wound, Altria's hands were tied by the FDA's deeming rule. No matter how much innovation *could* be done by Altria, the law had them boxed in. There was no way to put a better product on the market before going through the monthslong FDA process.

Quigley did the best he could with an admittedly bad hand. His colleagues were surprised by how optimistic he was, but they figured it was simply in his nature to look on the bright side of things. Quigley wasn't your typical tobacco guy. Yes, he'd been at the company for more than a decade, but he hadn't lived through the Tobacco Wars, and he therefore didn't have the usual Altria chip on his shoulder. After he'd completed his initial review of the MarkTen business, he was blunt when he communicated his findings to Willard and other executives: If the goal was to take down Juul with Elite, it wasn't going to happen.

But it wasn't like MarkTen had no game. Its other primary competitor was Reynolds's Vuse, which was in just as big a free fall as MarkTen. That left the two tobacco companies scrapping it out for second place.

"This is what we need to do," Quigley suggested. Submit the pre-market review application to the FDA for MarkTen, keep investing in the brand, continue to outperform Reynolds, and grow market share and profitability. Sure, MarkTen might not be a rocket ship right now like Juul, but Altria was better positioned than almost anyone else to play the long game. In two years' time, it wasn't out of the realm of possibility that MarkTen could come out on top.

In one executive meeting over the summer of 2018, the perennial topic of Juul came up, and somebody wondered aloud, "Why, if Juul is growing so fast, weren't industrywide cigarette volumes declining equally as fast?" Quigley didn't miss a beat. If one really focused on *why* Juul was winning, it was clearly in large part a result of *who* was buying their product. The room fell silent. Nobody seemed to know quite how to respond. Quigley was treading too close to Altria's red line. But the answer was as obvious as the bright green tobacco leaves poking out of Virginia's walnut-brown soil. "It's because the company is bringing new users into the category," he finally said. Willard flashed him a steely glare, as if to admonish him for speaking a cursed truth.

At Altria, while talking about underage users was bad, even talking about new adult users was verboten. That's because they weren't supposed to talk about expanding the nicotine category to non-nicotine-users of any age at all. But in that moment, everybody in that room, just like most everybody inside all of Altria, knew the truth. Cigarette sales weren't falling as fast as Juul sales were rising because Juul largely wasn't taking away its adult smoker customers. It was adding new users to the category, including nicotine-crazed teenagers.

Nevertheless, inside Altria's executive suites, the unsaid became more self-evident by the day. And soon it gradually sunk in as Quigley and others started framing the issue from a strategy standpoint. The Silicon Valley start-up had a potentially fatal flaw. There was only so long that the FDA, and the broader public at large, would stand for a product that was being so recklessly abused by the same kids who were supposed to have escaped a lifetime nicotine addiction. If Altria just lay low, time would ultimately be on their side. Juul could very well self-immolate. And if Altria played its cards right, who would come out on top?

16

SAN FRANCISCO STRIKES BACK

> If you don't like what's being said,
> change the conversation.
> —DON DRAPER, AS PLAYED BY JOHN HAMM
> IN THE TV SHOW *MAD MEN*

As public-health officials were starting to zero in on Juul, Kevin Burns was putting his foot on the gas at the company. The start-up was growing so quickly that it could barely keep up as it slammed bodies into the office at Pier 70. With all the new hires it was easy to lose track of who was doing what. On at least one occasion, two people accidentally got hired for the same job. The company was in full-on blitzscaling mode.

In June 2018, Ryan Woodring happened to be job hunting when he received a call from a recruiter. Juul was looking for a global marketing operations director. Woodring had a long career in marketing, having worked at several advertising agencies in New York City, where he carved out a niche in managing budgets and resources for creative projects. In 2014 he moved to the Bay Area to take a job at Apple overseeing creative resources, and then later at John McNeil Studios, a big branding agency in the area. He'd heard about Juul and knew that it was somewhat controversial already. The company had been in the news and had a buzz in the city. Would people perceive him, he wondered, as the guy selling "baby smokes for babies"?

Woodring had also received an offer around the same time from another big tech company in the Valley. He talked over his options with his friends and his wife, an emergency physician, and he was intrigued by the range of responses he received. In general, they were of two mindsets. On the one hand, if Juul was a tobacco company in sheep's clothing, then why in god's name would you ever work for them? On the other, mainly from his friends in the tech or venture capital world, "This is all upside." One of those techie friends piled on. The older tech companies are "done," the friend said. "You're not going to make any money there. But Juul: 'This was an opportunity to go make a bucket of money, which is what everyone in tech wants to do.'" Right?

The company had already raised mountains of capital and was planning to go international, opening up what was becoming an increasingly rare opportunity in the Valley: to get in before a company scaled. Why wouldn't you do it? Woodring was left to decide between the two divergent themes, going to work for the modern incarnate of evil or jumping at the opportunity of a lifetime.

When he went in for the final interview at the new Juul offices in the historic Pier 70 building in the Dogpatch, the hiring manager gave him a tour and reminded him that Juul wasn't any old tobacco company. This was a company on a mission to stop Big Tobacco. Juul had the potential to save lives by helping people quit smoking. And with a billion smokers in the world, that meant there were a billion lives that Juul could potentially save. Hearing about the company's noble mission helped him warm up to the prospect of working there. He himself had struggled over the years to quit smoking cigarettes. Practically on the spot the hiring manager offered him a compensation package that beat his salary at Apple. The hiring manager said he should act fast. "You've got to get in quick," she told him. "The stock is good. I would say yes quickly."

It struck Woodring as odd that she seemed to be almost twisting his arm. And it didn't appear that anybody had even called his references. But ultimately the check was enticing enough to ease the empty feeling he had in his stomach. "Am I being that guy?" he asked his wife as he deliberated what to do. "Is that the banality of evil where I'm just looking at a number?"

He pushed it to the back of his mind and tried to focus on the mission that the hiring manager and others had impressed on him. One billion lives to save. Plus, he'd worked in advertising long enough to know there were gradients of morality. Woodring took the job.

Right before he was due to start, Woodring bought himself a Juul and some mango-flavored pods. As an on-again, off-again smoker he thought it made sense to give Juul a try, not least to familiarize himself with the product he'd be hawking in a matter of days. That night he puffed on it as he loafed around the house, doing dishes, watching television, just hanging out. He loved it. It tasted fantastic. And it didn't stink up the house. But with no on/off switch—to activate a Juul you just pick it up and start sucking—before he knew it, he'd inhaled an entire Juul pod. *Oh shit,* he thought. He'd accidentally absorbed a cigarette pack's worth of nicotine. Now he was sweating, his heart was racing, and he felt a little woozy. He had to sit down. The night before he started his new job, he had a pounding headache.

The next morning, when Woodring showed up to Juul, he was impressed with the grandeur of the space. Soaring ceilings. Views of the bay. A well-stocked kitchen with everything you could want— kombucha, beer, even the requisite Chobani yogurt. The place was bustling with people. There were around three hundred employees at the time, and more were showing up every day, he was told.

But immediately he felt that something was off. His boss, Ann Hoey, Juul's vice president of marketing who'd come over from Nike, was nowhere to be found. Not only that, there was no place for him to sit. They'd forgotten to assign the new director of marketing operations a desk. Somebody swept away some junk and steered him there. He walked around, introducing himself to others, since there was nobody there to do the honors.

As Woodring sat there looking around, he was struck by the scene. His fellow employees were Juuling as they went about their day, talking on the phone, sitting around tables in conference rooms, walking around. Little white poufs occasionally floated up from behind a computer. People were just sitting, puffing away at their desks. It was surreal—they all looked as if they'd been cut from the set of a twenty-first-century *Mad Men*, Woodring thought.

Soon enough, he was shown the little commissary that was unlocked once a week. Inside there were office supplies—paper, pens, and Juul pods. Employees would sign their name in a log and in return be given their weekly allotment consisting of five packages of Juul pods and two devices. That struck Woodring as odd. Why did anybody need two new devices each week? Also, since each package contained four Juul pods, that meant employees were given twenty free Juul pods a week. That's a lot of nicotine in one week for one person. Of course, he assumed lots of people shared them with friends. But maybe not? He remembered how easily he'd sucked down a single pod that night. He seemed to recall stories of tobacco companies handing out cartons of cigarettes to employees back in the day. This seemed weirdly similar, he thought.

Juuling was something that allowed him to fit in at the company, but it was also something he'd grown exceedingly fond of. He didn't like to think he was addicted. It was just woven into the culture of the place and that was his life now. Employees were offered the chance to test some of the new flavors before they ever hit the market in exchange for writing a little review. He tasted papaya, wild cherry, and something called royal crème that tasted vaguely familiar.

"It tastes delicious," he told the flavor expert responsible for mixing it up. "What is it?" "Cookies and cream," the man replied. It dawned on Woodring. It 100 percent tasted like Oreos.

Almost immediately Woodring got to work looking for an agency of record to handle Juul's advertising. Burns didn't think Juul was a real company until it had one, and he was desperate to get a national campaign under way immediately. At Chobani, the yogurt brand had become a household name in part through massive ads, like one that appeared during the 2014 Super Bowl. Yet ever since the controversial "Vaporized" campaign of 2015, Juul had largely relied on user-generated content on social media platforms like Instagram and YouTube to spread the word about the product.

While Burns was looking for more gravitas for Juul, he also had to walk a fine line. As reports of the youth vaping problem cropped up, things were becoming more precarious by the day for Juul. Burns was keenly aware that the issue risked imperiling the company, and he was eager to sidestep it.

Burns made a strategic decision that attempted to thread the needle. In June, he announced that Juul would stop using models on Instagram and other social media platforms. Instead, the company would only feature on social media "former smokers who switched from combustible cigarettes." No more youthful hipsters Juuling. No more cute girls in tight T-shirts exhaling clouds of vapor.

Juul was also ramping up efforts to get rid of social media accounts that were targeting underage users. In fact, the company had finally been successful, after months of trying, in getting Instagram to suspend Brzuziewski's @JuulNation account, much to Brzuziewski's chagrin.

Around the same time, Juul launched a national campaign called "What Parents Need to Know About Juul" that entailed full-page newspaper ads and radio spots that looked suspiciously like a sleek ad for the product, featuring blips like "Juul uses an intelligent heating mechanism" and "cartridges that contain a salt-based nicotine e liquid to satisfy smokers," but also had a big warning at the bottom that said, "Juul is for adult smokers. If you don't smoke or vape, don't start."

Burns fast-tracked efforts internally to turn stories, or "testimonials" as they called them, of real people who'd successfully used Juul to quit smoking into a national ad campaign that would emphasize adult smokers. He was desperate to divorce the brand from its insidious cool factor. In reality, he was trying to exorcise the original sin.

Ultimately, Woodring helped land DDB, the big advertising company owned by Omnicom Group Inc. that had clients including Volkswagen, McDonald's, Unilever, and Exxon Mobil. In just a few months

Juul would launch its first ever national advertising campaign, with ads airing thousands of times on television stations across the United States.

AS BURNS ROLLED OUT an aggressive expansion strategy in the United States, he pushed to expand distribution into major retailers, including Walgreens and Rite Aid and Sam's Club—a huge coup for the company that not that long ago had struggled to get into Circle K.

Initially the prospect of selling Juul was a no-brainer for major retailers. When sales managers pitched stores they'd bring along a slide showing a chart comparing the blood-absorption rate of Juul to regular combustible cigarettes and other competing e-cigarettes. That would demonstrate just how much Juul matched the nicotine delivery of regular cigarettes and exceeded its e-cigarette competitors, which would mean more customers. They'd also show just how profitable it would be to sell Juul. On a typical pack of Marlboros, which cost around $10, depending on the state, a convenience store would barely make a quarter on each transaction. For Juul, which cost $50 for a new starter kit that included the device and pods, or about $16 for a four-pack of refill pods, the margin for retailers was orders of magnitude higher.

By the summer of 2018, even though Juul was on its way to becoming one of the fastest-growing start-ups on the planet, the company still had just a fraction of the cigarette market in the United States and an even smaller share globally. Armed with a huge round of funding from Tiger, which was intended to help the company scale overseas, Juul had nothing but runway.

There were an estimated 34.2 million smokers in the United States, which represented a tiny percentage of the one billion smokers worldwide. With Juul already growing so quickly in the United States, there was no reason to believe that the dazzling growth story couldn't be replicated around the globe. Philip Morris had done the exact same thing a generation earlier, barreling into former Soviet bloc countries in the '90s with cargo containers of Marlboro Reds, and likewise in

Africa, Southeast Asia, and nearly every corner of the world. The cigarette company's growth into virgin markets—especially ones un-
touched by anti-smoking crusaders—had become an important hedge
against the besieged American industry.

For Juul, it was obvious enough that identifying overseas markets
would be an inevitable part of the growth strategy, not to mention increasingly important amid growing backlash in the United States. If
American regulators shut out Juul, the company would have other
profitable markets to fall back on.

But it was going to be much more difficult to enter many of those
markets. Even before Juul launched, countries around the world had
already started erecting barriers and regulations for the new nicotine
products. The European Union had passed strict regulations on the
products, restricting advertising of the products and capping the
amount of nicotine in the product to a 2 percent formulation (compared to 5 percent in the United States). Japan heavily restricted them.
So did Brazil and countries across the Middle East.

Israel didn't yet have any restrictions on e-cigarettes, which was a
key reason it became Juul's first international market when it launched
there in May 2018. Juul landed there like a conqueror, plastering its
logo and planting its product in shops across Jerusalem and Tel Aviv.

Next Juul announced its intent to enter Russia, another market that
hadn't yet implemented nicotine limits. The company hired Grant
Winterton, a former executive for Red Bull in Russia, to lead the charge
there and to plant Juul's flag across Europe and the Middle East. As the
company moved quickly to roll out the brand, it employed a regulatory-
arbitrage strategy favored by other start-ups, including Uber and Bird,
that entailed flooding the market with their products in places that
hadn't yet moved to implement rules. Those were exactly the foot-
holds that Juul was looking for—the company needed to get over the
moat before the drawbridge was pulled up.

But almost immediately, executing the international strategy grew
to be fraught with challenges. Within weeks of setting up shop in Israel, Juul found itself on the defense as the country's health ministry
launched a campaign against the product, saying Juul posed "a grave
risk to public health." In August, Prime Minister Benjamin Netanyahu

banned Juul pods that had nicotine levels higher than 2 percent. The EU had the same policy. These nicotine limits were turning out to be problematic. A not insignificant reason for the company's success in the United States was its comparatively high nicotine strength. With its pods that contained 59 milligrams per milliliter of nicotine, which is also referred to as a 5 percent by weight nicotine formulation, Juul by far delivered higher levels of nicotine than any other e-cigarette on the market. In theory, by delivering higher levels of nicotine, adult smokers would derive enough nicotine in a satisfying manner to entice them to switch over from cigarettes. In other words, it would get them hooked. Any less nicotine would translate into a lower "conversion rate" of smokers to Juul, and ultimately fewer users. It also wouldn't attract as many new users into the category because the product wouldn't be as sticky from the first puff.

Nevertheless, as Juul planned its international expansion, Burns and his executive team forecast foreign sales by essentially copying Juul's U.S. growth trends, which were based on the unusually high nicotine content, and pasting them onto markets outside the United States, many of which capped the nicotine at 20 milligrams per milliliter, or a 2 percent by weight formulation. These aggressive, and arguably flawed, forecasts underpinned the company's fundraising and expansion strategies.

That summer and over the next few months, Juul started moving into European markets, including the United Kingdom, Switzerland, and France. Faced with the nicotine limits, Juul deployed its engineering talent in San Francisco to develop a potential workaround that could help speed up adoption of its product in these more restrictive markets. The pod in the United States used a silica wick that would absorb the nicotine liquid as it was heated and turned into a vapor. The engineers realized that by using a cotton wick instead, it would absorb more of the liquid and therefore allow for a bigger hit on each draw. Internally they called this the "turbo pod" and it was supposed to be the company's secret weapon overseas. If regulators capped the nicotine levels at 2 percent, then the turbo pod would simply allow users to draw bigger hits that delivered a bigger nicotine "impact."

Many people inside Juul, including Bowen and Monsees, advocated passionately for the turbo product, arguing that it was the best way to ensure that more users would have the opportunity to enjoy what Juul had to offer, and therefore allow for more lives to be saved. But others felt like it was an unscrupulous gaming of the rules that seemed more like a tactic out of the old tobacco company playbook.

Of course, cigarette companies had for years been tinkering with the design of cigarettes to maximize nicotine delivery. One of the biggest controversies to emerge from the Tobacco Wars was the revelation that cigarette manufacturers had been selling "light" cigarettes that in fact delivered no less tar than the regular variety. That's because smokers of the light cigarettes often "compensated" by inhaling more deeply or more frequently, or by plugging ventilation holes on a filter to obtain a bigger nicotine "yield." The turbo pod in theory worked in a similar fashion. With the cotton wick, European users who could only buy the "light" (2 percent) nicotine pods could still derive a bigger "yield" of nicotine in each puff. That meant the pod would be drained faster, and the user in theory would wind up just blowing through more pods faster, and potentially ingesting similar levels of nicotine.

Some in the company were uneasy learning about the turbo pods. "From a mission point of view, is that great? Or is it insidious?" one former employee recalled debating with co-workers. "No one was ever like 'we're being evil.' It was always about how this was mission-based, and this was going to help the mission. It's easy to say that, but was there a closed-door meeting? You started to wonder, to think, are they actually talking about this at lunch and I'm just not privy to that?" Then the former employee had a thought that was hard to shake: "Maybe they are just no different than Big Tobacco?"

SAN FRANCISCO'S DOGPATCH NEIGHBORHOOD on its eastern waterfront is tiny but mighty. It's just five blocks long and five blocks wide and is nestled in between the San Francisco Bay and another neighborhood called Portrero Hill. People who'd lived in the Dogpatch for a long time were diehards like Katherine Doumani, who'd moved to the neighborhood two decades earlier, drawn by the funky industrial vibe

mixed with history, art, and what she called "decrepitude." Doumani
had been there long enough to see the area change from a working
shipyard into a gentrified tech haven.

By then, the packs of wild dogs that were potentially the namesake
of the neighborhood existed only in lore.

Nearly all Dogpatch residents agreed that the neighborhood was a
tiny village in a big city. Everybody knew everybody. People like Doumani were like little birdies, always hearing about the latest zoning
decision or the newest tenant first, and then spreading the news to
everybody else like an old-fashioned Pony Express. If Katherine Doumani didn't know about it, it probably wasn't true. For years, the neighborhood association had been holding meetings about the looming
influx of tech money and a new type of California gold rush. Ever
since 2008 when the city began a complete overhaul of its "Eastern
Neighborhoods" to improve sustainability in industrial areas and increase the number of housing units and public amenities, longtime
residents of the Dogpatch had been near-constantly shell-shocked by
the pace of development. The 2000 Census showed that fewer than
a thousand people lived in the Dogpatch. It shot up to more than six
thousand two cycles later. That brought a flock of land developers enticed by the stretches of abandoned fields, long-vacant warehouses,
and blocks of underdeveloped land.

Pier 70, a 69-acre site that jutted into the bay, had once been home
to the marquee Union Iron Works foundry that churned out battle-
ships during both world wars. As the development boom began, this
area was marked to be a historic cultural center but instead was slated
to be deemed a Production Distribution and Repair zone, the city's
nomenclature for smaller, niche industrial businesses—bookbinders,
flower arrangers, theatrical stage builders, furniture makers—that
needed to be fostered apart from major corporations and high-rise
residential developers. So, when the infant clothing company Tea Collection applied for a lease on Pier 70, it fit the mold. But it wasn't until
the summer of 2018 when Doumani and others learned that Tea Collection had decided to sublet and another company had moved into
the building instead: Juul.

When Doumani found out about it, she was shocked. She herself was the mother of a teenager and was well aware of the company's product. In addition to serving in the Dogpatch Neighborhood Association, she was also an appointed member of the Central Waterfront Advisory Group, a group that met on a monthly basis to have a say in development of the area. She never would have consented to having Juul occupy the oldest building on Pier 70. It was not only against the character and history of the neighborhood, but it was also seemingly against the rules. Juul didn't seem to fit the definition of a PDR business.

Doumani immediately called up her neighbor Dennis Herrera. Herrera had lived in the Dogpatch for more than a quarter of a century, and was considered the neighborhood's informal mayor. While he had a personality more befitting a cabbie or a fishing boat captain, he wound up being elected San Francisco's city attorney in 2001. But Dogpatch remained a true love, and Herrera could often be seen in his San Francisco Giants baseball cap, ducking into the neighborhood's coffee shops or chatting up the bikers that frequented the Hells Angels clubhouse near the same nineteenth-century Victorian home he'd lived for nearly three decades.

As city attorney he'd developed a reputation as being somewhat of a bulldog, fighting payday lenders and big health insurers. He'd succeeded Louise Renne, the famously dogged city attorney who'd spent fifteen years in the office going after companies and industries with a crusading gusto. During the height of the Tobacco Wars, in 1996, Renne had filed a lawsuit against the major tobacco companies, making San Francisco the first city in the nation to do so, even before some of the state attorneys general brought their own suits. Her legacy had left a lasting impression on Herrera, who felt an obligation to carry on the torch. Fighting Big Tobacco was in the DNA of the San Francisco city attorney's office. Herrera was already mad that Juul had been born and raised in San Francisco. *This* was what the tech boom had become? he thought. So, when Doumani called him up, he was aghast.

"Juul moved in *where?*" he asked her incredulously. How could this have happened without him knowing about it? Normally, companies were carefully vetted before being allowed to occupy such coveted city property, owned by the Port of San Francisco. Pier 70 was no exception. Especially Building 104, with its imposing red brick, its views of the San Francisco Bay, its towering wooden beams and soaring windows inside.

Herrera began sniffing around to see how this could have happened and what could be done about it. He also began learning more than he ever wanted to know about Juul: All the teens using it. How it had reversed two decades of progress on youth smoking. How it seemed to fly in the face of all that San Francisco stood for.

"This is a travesty," Herrera told his staff. He was girding for a fight. If he couldn't stop Juul, at least maybe he could evict them.

TWENTY-FIVE MILES SOUTH IN Atherton, David Burke settled in to write a scathing message. Burke was furious, and the object of his rage was his neighbor, Kevin Burns, who lived just a five-minute drive away.

Burke was a former managing director of the Stanford Management Company, where he oversaw private equity and venture capital investments for Stanford University's endowment. He'd had a long career as a cofounder and CEO of Makena Capital Management, a $20 billion investment management firm started with another Stanford alum. And he was a prominent individual who sat on numerous boards, including the Carnegie Endowment for International Peace, the University of Virginia, and Sacred Heart. His kids attended the private school with Pete Briger's daughter and, to his great dismay, he'd started hearing about the Juul problem rippling through the mannerly campus.

Not that long ago, Burke had started noticing something odd at his house. When his teenage children would have groups of friends over for hang sessions, he'd see these little devices plugged into the outlets by the basketball court as they were shooting hoops, or lying on the deck chairs as they were swimming in the pool. When he first saw them, he had no clue what they were—like so many others, he at first thought they were some sort of hard drive. But he quickly learned otherwise. Some of his kids' friends were so addicted to Juul that they couldn't go to a basketball game or a swim without hitting the thing.

Burke's own father had smoked cigarettes starting at the age of sixteen and struggled mightily until finally kicking the habit when he was in his forties. He died of esophageal cancer. Burke remembered watching with a sense of personal pride as smoking rates among kids had continued to tick down year over year. Now, he felt more than just betrayed. He felt duped. In a moment of fury, on the afternoon of June 23, 2018, he sat in front of his computer in his Atherton abode and banged out a note to Burns on LinkedIn:

Kevin,

I believe we're both in the same Atherton community near Stanford. I just wanted to let you know that your stupid fucking company has gotten my teenage kids' friends hooked on nicotine. From here on out, I'm going to go out of my way to fight the bullshit that you all are doing there and will be more than vocal about it. I have deep ties in the investment world and am from Washington DC and have deep ties there, all of which I will leverage to the max. I hope you feel really great about making lots of money for yourselves, under the guise of helping old conventional smokers kick the habit, while you hook a whole new generation on something that a decade from now we'll all know the truth about, just as things have played out with conventional smoking. Just like the Sackler family legacy with opiates, helping all those in pain while addicting millions and killing thousands. You'll have a beautiful, proud legacy for you and your family to celebrate in future generations.

Best,
Dave Burke

After a few days passed, Burke could see that Burns had opened his LinkedIn message. But he received no reply. That made him even madder. The coward didn't even have the balls to reply? He decided to take his anger public, and he banged out a post on Facebook.

Here is my vote for the most evil company in the world, making money hand over fist in large part by destroying the lives of what will prove to be millions of middle school students who get rapidly hooked on nicotine and cannot control their addiction. They know exactly what they are doing and where that revenue is coming from as they target their under age illegal audience with flavors like mango, bubblegum, and cool cucumber. Just like the now-exposed Sackler family which has destroyed the lives of millions from easy opiate access as their privately held company Purdue pocketed the cash and looked the other way. Don't believe the bullshit PR statements they put out and their pledge of $30 million to "fight underage use," which is a rounding error of their profits. I've seen the numbers and it's appalling.

Not long after his Facebook post, he got a call from his other neighbor, Pete Briger, who'd seen Burke's post. Briger was still fuming from the Denver lacrosse trip incident from a few weeks earlier, not least because he'd also since found Juul in one of his sons' bedroom. Briger shared the incident with Burke, who in turn revealed his own story about Juul infiltrating his kids' peer groups. The product was showing up everywhere. As the two men talked more about it, Burke and Briger grew angrier.

"We've got to stop these people," said Briger.

"Burns, this goddamned asshole, can you believe how despicable he is?" Burke replied. "I mean, they're pumping massive amounts of nicotine into kids."

"These people should go to jail," Briger replied.

Knowing that Burns, like most people who lived in Atherton, had more money than they knew what to do with, they started thinking about what they could do to *really* make him pay. "The only way is to play hardball with them," Briger said. "To make it uncomfortable for them. To let everybody know that people in our community are making money off this."

Dave Burke knew someone they could ask for help. Toward the end of the 2018 summer, the Stanford football season was just getting under way. It was Friday night, one of the last before school started, and the first home game at Stanford Stadium. The up-and-coming quarterback K. J. Costello was up against San Diego State. He had a banner night, bringing the team to a win on home-opening night. Burke was a die-hard Stanford football fan. He'd had season tickets—and the same seats in the upper deck—for years. And for as long as he could remember, the same person had season tickets with seats right in front of him: Jim Steyer.

Many people knew Steyer because of his younger brother, Tom, the billionaire founder of the San Francisco hedge fund Farallon Capital and a former member of Stanford's board of trustees. But Jim was eminent in his own right, also in the Bay Area, as a well-respected civil rights professor at Stanford and longtime child advocate who pioneered the field of digital literacy. A believer in the power of early education to beget a just and thriving society, Steyer had founded a children's advocacy group called Children Now in 1988, which helped shape policy in California and across the nation around children's issues, such as access to health insurance and immunizations. He worked on the intersection of media and children and became one of the early advocates focused on the dangers of youth overexposure to sex-and-violence-and-commercialism-laden media, the importance of childhood privacy, and the adverse health effects of what is today known as "screen time." Steyer's nonprofit, Common Sense Media, had started in 2003 as a movie and media ratings system for parents to help guide them to appropriate content, but had since grown into a grassroots "advocacy army" of 150 million parents and other concerned citizens that drew on Steyer's deep connections in the power centers from Wall Street to Capitol Hill to Sand Hill Road.

Just before kickoff, Burke and Steyer were catching up—about their summers, their families, the kids' plans for the year. Not surprisingly, Juul came up. Burke hadn't been able to stop thinking about it.

"Jim, have you heard about Juul?" Burke asked.

"Yeah, of course. I have four children. They're like the new Big Tobacco."

They began swapping their own stories, about their kids, about their peers, about the Juuling problem in their kids' schools. Burke told

Steyer about how Pete Briger had gotten involved. Briger and Steyer, of course, knew each other through the hedge fund world.

"Well, you run the biggest child advocacy group in the country," Burke urged. "Do you want to get involved?"

That night, Steyer went home and called up a colleague, Matthew Myers. Myers was the longtime president of the advocacy group Campaign for Tobacco-Free Kids, and his career fighting the tobacco industry spanned his role as a key negotiator of the historic Master Settlement Agreement to his early efforts pushing for FDA regulation of e-cigarettes.

Myers explained that Juul was not a fad. It was an insidious problem. Millions of kids were getting addicted to nicotine. It was reversing the two decades of declines in youth tobacco use. The once tobacco-free kids were increasingly not nicotine-free.

"Why can't we go after Juul like you went after Big Tobacco?" Steyer asked him. "Like get all those plaintiffs' lawyers that had a feast on the tobacco industry, and won. Can't we get them involved?"

"We can," Myers replied.

Steyer decided to ask his own children about Juul. How big of a deal was this? At the time he had a high schooler and three older children, one attending Stanford, the other two already graduated from Stanford. The high schooler not only confirmed that Juul was a big problem but that he had in fact tried it himself. Steyer's blood boiled "Do you understand how bad nicotine is?" he chided. His older kids almost chuckled at the naïveté of the question. "You have no idea, Dad," they said. "People Juul in your class at Stanford, and you don't even know it."

Steyer already had little love for the Silicon Valley companies that made a killing off addicting kids to all sorts of things—videogames, social media, YouTube. In 2012 he wrote *Talking Back to Facebook: The Common Sense Guide to Raising Kids in the Digital Age,* a cutting critique of Facebook before the company's fall from grace made it a popular punching bag symbolizing all that was wrong with Silicon Valley. In it he lambasted videogame and social media companies for rewiring kids' brains and subjecting them to a lifetime of distraction and frivolity.

"Video games and social networks are more than a pastime," he wrote. "They're a compulsion, a consuming adrenaline rush that can crowd out other aspects of a healthy life. . . . Digital technology threatens the quality of relationships, creates attention and addiction problems, and can invade our kids' privacy."

Now, here was another Silicon Valley company addicting kids. It was a company born at Stanford, to boot. Steyer was in.

By the fall of 2018, a formidable group of wealthy parents whose children had fallen prey to Juul, from Atherton to San Francisco to New York City, began forming a coalition to stop the company.

17

THE JUULIONAIRES

Greed clarifies, cuts through, and captures the essence of the
evolutionary spirit.

—GORDON GEKKO, AS PLAYED BY MICHAEL DOUGLAS
IN THE MOVIE *WALL STREET*

On August 2, the day after the secret meeting between Juul and Altria at the Park Hyatt, Gottlieb and Zeller were celebrating the one-year anniversary of their nicotine plan, which they'd elevated as the solution to the nation's tobacco problem. Gottlieb's allies over at the American Enterprise Institute published a blog post titled "Happy birthday, FDA tobacco plan!" Gottlieb and Zeller co-authored their own post on the FDA website to mark the one-year date of the comprehensive nicotine plan. "Over the past year, we've taken important steps toward fully implementing this plan as part of our overarching goal: a world where cigarettes can no longer create or sustain addiction, and where adults who still seek nicotine could get it from potentially less harmful sources." The bottom half of the post brought up the rising youth usage issue. "We look at the marketplace for tobacco products today and see increasing concern from parents, educators, and health professionals about the alarming youth use of tobacco products like Juul and other e-cigarettes," they wrote. "Our mission at the FDA is to protect the public's health, and we want to assure the public we're using all of our tools and authorities to quickly tackle this public health threat. We will not allow our efforts to . . . become a back door for allowing products with high levels of nicotine to cause a new generation of kids to get addicted to nicotine and hooked on tobacco products."

Still, the gravity of the youth problem hadn't yet fully sunk in at the otherwise quiet FDA headquarters in Silver Spring, Maryland. Yes, Gottlieb had announced the sting operation against retailers illegally selling e-cigarettes to underage youth, and issued the document request to Juul. But the Silicon Valley giant appeared to be aggressively taking advantage of the deferential treatment by regulators, running roughshod over Washington and the nation.

As the product was getting more popular by the day, Gottlieb was holding private meetings with Juul and other tobacco companies—more than any other industry. From the time he stepped into the commissioner's office and announced the new nicotine policy, he'd made clear to Juul and tobacco companies that he'd be willing to keep an open door to his office. In addition to inviting them to submit comments and written petitions, he gave them the opportunity to come into FDA headquarters for a series of sit-down meetings with him, his top aides, and career staff at Zeller's Center for Tobacco Products. At the time, almost no other industry in America had such unfettered access to the FDA commissioner. Gottlieb felt that he owed them the courtesy of what he wanted to be an open, fair process, since his agency was undertaking such a huge regulatory shift that would fundamentally alter their business.

The companies jumped at the opportunity. Over 2018, Gottlieb and his staff held multiple meetings with Juul's executives and legal counsel, either in person at his FDA office, or at the Center for Tobacco Products, or via teleconference. By the beginning of August, Juul had taken part in at least half a dozen meetings with FDA officials. It had also flooded the agency with comments urging it to tread lightly on the regulatory front. For example, over the spring and summer of 2018 Juul sent the FDA several submissions that pressed the agency to hold off on any policy that would restrict flavored tobacco products. Juul's most popular products by far were its flavored pods, including mint and mango. The company wanted to ward off any regulatory action that would see those products removed from the market, which was exactly what tobacco-prevention groups like Campaign for Tobacco-Free Kids were pushing the agency to do. In one submission Juul wrote that as Gottlieb moved forward with his grand nicotine plan Juul's flavored products could in fact be part of the solution and would "help increase the success of programs to reduce nicotine content in combusted cigarettes." In another, the company argued that "overly restricting" flavored e-cigarettes "would be a significant public health detriment."

Juul also used the opportunity to build a conciliatory rapport with Gottlieb and his staff. On a call with FDA career staff, a Juul executive gushed about their willingness to work with the agency to address the youth issue and promised that the company was "on track" collecting the documents requested by the FDA and that they expected "to provide a comprehensive response by the requested due date."

Over the past year, Juul tripled its spending on lobbyists and hired a cadre of Washington insiders to help shape its message, including Tevi Troy, a former White House adviser under George W. Bush, and Josh Raffel, a former senior aide in the Trump White House who'd worked closely with Jared Kushner and Ivanka Trump. Juul worked to lay other groundwork inside the White House.

AFTER THE PARK HYATT meeting in D.C., Willard gathered with top Altria executives to discuss options. Juul talks were in a near-constant state of flux, with one week a deal seeming to be imminent, and then the next the deal being called off, with people lamenting how insufferable the Silicon Valley set was.

Originally, Quigley seemed to have buy-in from Willard and other executives to go full steam ahead with making Nu Mark as competitive as possible with Juul, despite Elite's current limitations. But it soon became clear that Willard was becoming more interested in Plan A. At one meeting, Willard casually raised the possibility of shutting down Nu Mark. MarkTen's sales numbers were embarrassing. In August 2018, Juul's brick-and-mortar retail sales amounted to nearly $200 million. MarkTen sales were less than $20 million.

"Maybe we should just exit the entire business," Willard suggested.

It looked like Quigley had been punched in the gut. Not only did he just take the job as the head of that business, but he was outspoken about how he thought exiting the business was fundamentally the wrong thing to do. But he wasn't one of the Three Musketeers, so he wasn't privy to details about where negotiations with Juul stood.

"No, you can't do that," Quigley replied. "What are you going to tell investors?" He reminded the group that just a few months earlier, at Altria's Investor Day presentation, the company's top executives had gotten up onstage and bragged about Nu Mark's thriving innovation pipeline. If they pulled the plug now, they'd be virtually empty-handed.

Willard was confronting a frustrating pattern. When little cigars started doing a brisk business, Altria started work developing its own branded product but wound up springing to buy John Middleton Inc., the maker of Black & Mild cigars, for nearly $3 billion. When smokeless tobacco grew in popularity, Altria tried to innovate with its own Marlboro branded smokeless products—Marlboro Snus, Marlboro Tobacco Sticks—before giving up and paying $10 billion for the leader in the category, U.S. Smokeless Tobacco Company. No matter how many Clayton Christensen or Klaus Schwab books its executives read or John Kotter consulting sessions they attended, Altria simply couldn't move much beyond rolling tobacco in paper.

So acquiring its way to leadership in the e-cigarette market wasn't a completely farfetched idea for Altria. It's just that by now, it would almost certainly come with a dizzying price tag. But, Juul was only growing bigger with every passing day. Time was of the essence. Willard had been in on again, off again negotiations with Juul for months now and was eager to close a deal.

Meanwhile, the Juul team was turning up the heat on Willard. If talks were to continue, they'd need reassurances that they were dealing in good faith. Not surprisingly there was mistrust between the two parties. How could they trust Altria to be a partner when the company was also selling a product designed to compete with Juul? There wasn't room for both products on the market. As Pritzker sent his July 30 opening term sheet to Willard, one important point was communicated, according to a later Federal Trade Commission complaint: "Continued competition from Altria's e-cigarette products was the only option clearly off the table." The message was loud and clear. If Willard wanted a deal with Juul, he might have to get rid of MarkTen.

MEANWHILE, IN SPITE OF the growing youth usage problem, there was growing competition for Juul. Other tobacco companies had expressed interest in a potential deal with the company. So did other investors. Juul's annual revenue for 2018 was on track to exceed $1 billion, up from $200 million in 2017, while the company sold a record 450 million packs of Juul pod "refills," up 600 percent. Juul shareholders received calls and emails almost every single day from investors offering to buy their shares at prices that put the company at ever higher valuations, $18 billion, $20 billion, and more. Inside Juul, employees who'd been at the company for years were amazed as they watched the potential value of their shares soar. They drank beer and talked about how lucky they'd been to land at the company as it made its meteoric ascent. And how the company's valuation would only likely continue to go up from here, reaching who knows, $60 billion? $80 billion? *$100 billion?* Nothing, it seemed, was out of the realm of possibility. The cognitive dissonance of the situation— kids vaping vs. hypergrowth wonder story—bothered some, but certainly not all.

By the beginning of the fall, as talks between Altria and Juul dragged on in fits and starts, Juul's bankers had already begun preparing for another big round of fundraising to follow on the heels of the $1.2 billion "mega" round from a few weeks earlier that had valued Juul at $16 billion. This one was on track to potentially value the firm at $30 billion. There was a feeding frenzy for the new nicotine giant.

OVER THE SUMMER, GOTTLIEB and Zeller's nicotine plan became gradually more precarious. But there wasn't widespread panic yet inside the agency. That was partly because the most recent National Youth Tobacco Survey, which reflected trends from 2017, had been released in June and showed another year-over-year *decline* in e-cigarette use. By now, though, there were enough indicators of a problem: Between anecdotal reports and weekly retail sales data that showed burgeoning sales of Juul, there appeared to be problems with the government's data. The nation's top public-health officials were relying on numbers that didn't fully capture the reality of what was unfolding on the ground.

As a result, Gottlieb and Zeller were still focused on the grand vision behind their plan—dial down nicotine in combustible cigarettes to minimally addictive levels, while at the same time encouraging smokers to either quit altogether or migrate from the certain-death products to others less deadly on a "continuum of risk" like the patch or gum, medicinal nicotine or e-cigarettes.

But to outsiders it increasingly seemed like the FDA was out of step. More people started asking questions. Where was the FDA? How was it possible that Juul was doing business without a shred of government regulation? On July 17, *PBS NewsHour* aired a special about the growing number of teens using Juul. "It looks like a flash drive, can be hidden anywhere, and doesn't create tell-tale smoke. Across the country, the use of these e-cigarettes is spiking among youth, but parents often aren't even sure what they are and many teens mistakenly believe there are no serious health risks."

"I will tell you, straight up, this is one of our top concerns right now," Gottlieb told PBS correspondent Kavitha Cardoza. "If all we do is end up hooking a whole generation of young people on nicotine by making these products available, we won't have done a service from a public health standpoint. And so we need to be very aggressive in trying to take steps to crack down, prevent the youth use of these products."

Zeller tried to remain calm and reassure Gottlieb. He'd seen the models showing the potentially huge public-health benefits of migrating people away from cigarettes and was committed to his career-long goal—millions of lives could be saved if the plan worked, was his mantra. He'd long remembered a talk more than two decades ago by one of his idols, an Australian tobacco harm-reduction expert named Nigel Gray who explained that in the field of harm reduction—with vested interests among powerful tobacco companies who resisted change— the measure of success or failure came over decades, not months or years. He kept reminding himself, and Gottlieb, of that. They were just one year into this new nicotine experiment and they needed to take the long view.

But one morning in mid-August, that sense of hope and longevity was shattered in an instant. Zeller had a regularly scheduled meeting with Gottlieb, but this one was going to be different. He'd received early data from the latest National Youth Tobacco Survey, which wasn't supposed to be released publicly until months from now. When he saw the numbers, he rushed all the way across the FDA campus, from Building 75, where his office was in the Center for Tobacco Products, to Building 1, home of the commissioner's office. He was practically out of breath by the time he reached Gottlieb. Gottlieb could tell by the look on Zeller's face that there was a problem. He'd gotten to know him well enough over the past few months to tell that the normally Zen look on Zeller's face was now scrunched up in a state of either vexation or shock.

"That bad?" Gottlieb asked him, trying to lighten Zeller's obviously tense disposition.

Zeller wasn't in a joking mood. Instead of responding, he just started rattling off the preliminary findings. More than three million high school students were current users of e-cigarettes in 2018, up nearly 80 percent over the previous year, with more than 20 percent of them now using the products. That meant that one of every five high schoolers in America was vaping, mostly Juul. It hit Gottlieb like a bomb.

"Holy shit," Gottlieb finally mustered.

"Holy shit," Zeller replied.

Gottlieb felt like he'd been punched in the stomach. This was his worst day as FDA commissioner.

A CROSS BETWEEN PANIC and outrage swept over Gottlieb's office, and then beyond Building 1. Gottlieb had immediately called Alex Azar, secretary of Health and Human Services, and Andrew Bremberg, Trump's assistant at the White House and director of the Domestic Policy Council.

Gottlieb and Zeller's nicotine plan was not only at risk of vanishing before their eyes, but the data were gut-wrenching. Even worse, Gottlieb wanted to hold a press conference immediately, to sound the alarm on an issue that he was worried he'd badly miscalculated. But he couldn't. The CDC data weren't finalized and the agency didn't initially support an early public release. Gottlieb was furious. There was a gathering wave of youth vaping clearly getting worse by the minute and he was being told to sit on his hands. Gottlieb and Azar, a former executive at Eli Lilly, had known each other from mutual pharma circles. Now, with Azar as Gottlieb's boss, they were in frequent communication and they both agreed that the information needed to get out to the public. Over the next days, they formulated a plan. No matter how much Gottlieb had wanted the nicotine strategy to work, this was a five-alarm fire. On September 11, Gottlieb put out a statement, for the first time calling the youth usage of e-cigarettes what it had become.

We didn't predict what I now believe is an epidemic of e-cigarette use among teenagers. Today we can see that this epidemic of addiction was emerging when we first announced our plan last summer. Hindsight, and the data now available to us, reveal these trends. And the impact is clearly apparent to the FDA. Unfortunately, I now have good reason to believe that it's reached nothing short of an epidemic proportion of growth.

As part of the statement, Gottlieb also announced additional actions against the e-cigarette industry. Expressing concern about the role of flavored e-cigarette products in youth initiation into the category, Gottlieb said the agency was "seriously considering a policy change that would lead to the immediate removal of these flavored products from the market." At the same time, he said that he'd sent letters to five of the largest e-cigarette manufacturers, including Juul, Vuse, and MarkTen, giving them sixty days to respond with "robust plans on how they'll convincingly address the widespread use of their products by minors."

"They're now on notice by the FDA of how their products are being used by youth at disturbing rates," Gottlieb said.

Over the next forty-eight hours Gottlieb appeared on national television, angrily chastising the companies for causing this new "epidemic" of teen vaping.

"A lot of this youth use is being driven by one manufacturer in particular: Juul," he said on *Squawk Box*. "We're creating a whole new generation of addicted young people . . . that's simply not tolerable."

Desperate to share the CDC's not-yet-finalized data more widely, rather than wait for the wheels of bureaucracy to turn, Gottlieb and Azar wrote an opinion piece in *The Washington Post* that flagged the gravity of the problem and provided snippets of the data to the public. "We are deeply concerned," they wrote. "From 2017 to 2018, according to new preliminary data from the National Youth Tobacco Survey, the number of high-school-age children reporting use of e-cigarettes rose by more than 75 percent. Use among middle-schoolers also increased nearly 50 percent. That is an epidemic."

Gottlieb was on the warpath. And Juul was squarely in his crosshairs. He was growing frustrated with the start-up to which he'd given open access since the day he stepped foot in the commissioner's office. The company's executives and lobbyists embodied a holier-than-thou attitude that rubbed FDA officials the wrong way. They often came across as if they were deserving of special treatment and exempt from the need to be regulated because they were a flashy tech company from Silicon Valley on a mission to save the world. At the same time, Gottlieb and his career staffers began to sense that Juul was playing games with them. On the one hand in meeting after meeting Juul's top executives gave slick presentations on how they planned to help reduce youth use of their product. But then Gottlieb would get wind that Juul had been quietly lobbying the White House to snuff out any actions to rein in the exact youth problem they promised they were working to help end.

Gottlieb had given the company every opportunity to flourish, and in return they'd tossed a youth nicotine epidemic in his lap. They'd promised to respond with documents but they seemed to be purposefully dragging their feet. Gottlieb wanted to act.

THE ANNOUNCEMENT BY GOTTLIEB about the "epidemic" started rippling through Juul. People who'd managed to convince themselves that they were on the righteous path started to have doubts.

One day, Burns stood up in the wide-open kitchen area–slash–communal workspace where he had his weekly all-hands meeting. Not long ago, there was ample room in there to kick back and Juul. Every week, it seemed, the meetings grew more and more crowded as Burns continued to scale the company.

There were now more than one thousand employees, up from just two hundred at the beginning of the year, and more than one hundred people joined each month while the company had hundreds of openings in locations around the world, from Tel Aviv to Singapore to Brussels. Despite Burns's sometimes brusque personality—"With Kevin, you knew instantly whether or not he gave a shit about what you were saying," one person said—he had a knack for building bridges to the rank and file. At every meeting he'd always take questions from the employees, and never discouraged or shied away from tough ones. At this meeting one person raised their hand. "If we want people to quit smoking with Juul, why are we pushing to be in so many major retail locations like Walgreens?" Burns didn't miss a beat. "Simple," he said. "I want market share." That the answer surprised anyone was perhaps more surprising, but it left some people with a sour taste in their mouth given everything that was going on.

Meanwhile, Ryan Woodring was struggling to stay positive amid the flurry of bad headlines. He focused on the mission to get adult smokers off cigarettes, but little things started to bother him. In marketing meetings, somebody from the legal team was almost always present and involved in decisions. *Get rid of this person in the ad—she looks too young. This person appears to be having too much fun—scrap him.* In previous advertising jobs he'd occasionally interfaced with the legal department, usually to ensure they had copyright to an image for a campaign, but he'd never encountered anything like this. Not only did lawyers sit in on creative meetings, but they began sending out periodic reminders to not write anything down or store documents.

What the fuck is happening here? Woodring thought.

But he went about his work, helping with the impending rollout of the national television campaign, collecting his weekly ration of pods. His favorite flavor was mango, but those were usually snapped up first, so he'd settle for crème brûlée. Some days he found himself believing in the mission, and he felt proud that he was actually helping people. But then he'd make the mistake of bringing it up with the wrong colleague. "Are we doing the right thing?" he'd ask. Often the response he got was disheartening and somewhere along the lines of: "Well, you know how rich we're going to be?"

There were too many of those moments that he couldn't square in his head. He started struggling with cognitive dissonance that he couldn't shake. Increasingly he'd come home and feel despondent, walking around the house, Juuling, wondering how he'd ended up here. He began Juuling more and more, all through the day, and at home after work, eventually getting to the point where he was imbibing two pods a day. All the nicotine had the effect of keeping him up at night. The next morning he'd wake up exhausted. So, he'd Juul all day again to help him get through. And the cycle would continue. He felt awful. And disillusioned.

But nothing prepared him or others at Juul for that late September morning when a team of federal inspectors in navy-blue windbreakers emblazoned with AGENT in yellow filed into Juul's offices. Over the course of four days, the inspectors camped in a conference room. A Juul executive was always in the room with them. As stenographers took notes, employees were brought in to answer questions. When the inspectors wanted a document, someone would message people in a pair of rooms that had been set up with computers and printers, and it would be delivered.

The agents were polite, and there was some small talk, but the environment was tense. Among other things, employees and executives were fretting over the company's risky decision to overhaul its subpar Juul device in potential violation of the law. Should they come clean with the FDA? If they did, would the FDA yank Juul off the market? But if they didn't, would the FDA find out that they were hiding something from them? With the FDA inspectors now inside Juul, there was a heightened sense of panic that they'd be found out.

Over the past several weeks, Burns and others had been bracing for a visit from the FDA. As a result, they'd been engaged in coaching sessions designed to teach executives how to interact with the federal officials and respond to their questions. Several Juul employees and executives were schooled using a technique called "hats on hats off." During hats on, a designated person would play the role of an FDA inspector, asking probing questions. That was followed by hats off, in which the person evaluated the performance of the employee and offered tips on doing better. Employees were coached on specific FDA techniques they were told might be used to try to get them to talk more than they should. In at least one coaching session that included Juul's chief quality officer, Joanna Engelke, employees were instructed on how to respond to questions about device modifications. If asked, acknowledge the changes, they were told. But don't volunteer any information.

By the end of the multiday inspection, the FDA carted off boxes of documents and hard drives filled with information. But they never learned about the full extent of Juul's modifications. The inspectors didn't ask the exact right question or pull on the exact right thread, so under the heat of the feds, Juul's executives simply didn't tell.

THE FDA'S BELLICOSE POSTURE sent shock waves through the e-cigarette industry. In particular, inside Juul, Gottlieb's threat that the agency might remove its only product from the market became uncomfortable. One Juul executive recalled being "terrified" that Gottlieb possessed the power to annihilate the industry. Not only that, but Gottlieb's cage-rattling had had the unfortunate effect of torpedoing upcoming rounds of private investment that had been in the works and had the potential to be the next bucket of cash. Investors got spooked. That, in turn, touched off a series of dominoes, the first being that, suddenly, Altria seemed like a more attractive suitor.

It wouldn't be long before Juul and Altria were back at the negotiating table, but for now their talks had stalled.

MEANWHILE, AS WILLARD AND his team worked to meet Gottlieb's sixty-day deadline to report a plan to stop youth use of its products, Altria's internal discussions became much more intense. There was a core group inside Nu Mark, including Quigley, advocating to keep MarkTen on the market. And now the FDA's newly tough stance presented Willard a new opportunity. If he couldn't buy Juul, maybe he'd at least be able to hasten its demise.

Just as Juul had a serious Achilles' heel, Altria had critical advantages. The company had spent decades fortifying relationships in and around the FDA. They'd already been a key player in helping solve one youth smoking crisis. There was no reason they couldn't help solve this one too, especially since it wasn't even a problem of their own making. If Willard played his cards right, he might be able to persuade Gottlieb to take sides. *His* side.

Already, Altria had taken one swipe at Juul, when its threats in 2015 over the Marlboro trademark had played a role in pushing the company to the brink. The company also had in its possession theoretically damaging information about Juul's risky modifications and had even floated the idea of whether to weaponize it. What if they ratted out Juul to the FDA? The idea never gained much traction, but one Altria insider referred to that as the "nuclear option"—a radical kill shot if all else failed. "Go to FDA, cause a shitstorm, and your competitor is gone," was how the person described the speculative thinking.

But the youth usage issue offered an entirely different opportunity. In fact, it was low-hanging fruit, and required much less bloodthirstiness, albeit a dose of risky statecraft. Plenty of Altria executives were already miffed by Juul and its undisciplined marketing strategy. Even in the throes of courtship there was little love lost for the company that had arguably sullied the marketplace for what was supposed to have been the first meaningful, and profitable, future of smoking.

"Let's actually make life hard for them because of this youth usage issue," one executive suggested to Willard and others. The company could cozy up to the FDA, buy some time to work on submitting all the necessary regulatory submissions, and focus on growing its own organic market. All the while it could pressure Gottlieb to take action against an undeniable culprit in this spiraling crisis—Juul. And then, Altria would be perfectly positioned to come back and win another day.

But by now, Willard was stuck on the idea of just shutting down Nu Mark altogether, which not surprisingly made multiple people inside that arm of the company bristle. Quigley, in fact, had become so outspoken against that strategy that he'd alienated himself from Willard and his inner core. And he ultimately got pushed out.

Rather than settle on a single decision amid the swift-moving situation, by mid-October Willard simply decided to play all sides. He wasn't going to shut down Nu Mark, at least not immediately. Instead, he'd voluntarily take just the MarkTen Elite nicotine pod product off the market, while leaving the other MarkTen cigalikes. By publicly acknowledging that it was the pods that were the problem, Willard was simultaneously portraying his company as the responsible actor—the adult in the room—while indirectly putting Juul in a vise.

It was a potentially masterful hedge, and at the very least a high-stakes game of poker. If Gottlieb ended up banning pod-based products, Altria would gain credibility in the eyes of the FDA while simultaneously kneecapping its frenemy and leveling the playing field. If Gottlieb didn't take pods off the market, well, Altria wouldn't have lost much, since MarkTen was already flailing. And there was a third benefit to that strategy: By taking his competing product off the market, he was removing a key roadblock to a deal with Juul should it materialize.

The timing involved in pulling all of this off was precarious. By late October, Willard had been meeting with Juul's deal team on a regular and intensifying basis and had obtained tentative approval from his board to consummate a deal. Executives debated a rather interesting question: What would happen if Willard successfully convinced Gottlieb that pods were the problem, but then turned around and reached a deal with Juul? Willard's response took some people off guard by its nonchalance: "Well, that would be a good problem to have," he said.

ON OCTOBER 18, 2018, Willard set out to execute his wire-walking plan. He and four other Altria executives traveled to D.C., where they met in Gottlieb's office with Zeller and more than a dozen other FDA employees at 10:15 in the morning. Gottlieb kicked things off by saying that he was still committed to the potential opportunity for e-cigarettes to help adult smokers. "But we cannot allow that opportunity to come at the expense of addicting a whole new generation of kids to nicotine," he said.

Willard said that he shared Gottlieb's concerns and that he and everyone at Altria considered youth tobacco prevention a serious problem, and a priority. His company was willing to take bold action as a result. A week later, on October 25, Willard announced in a formal letter to Gottlieb, and to shareholders, that the company was taking MarkTen Elite off the market.

Dear Commissioner Gottlieb,

On behalf of Altria Group, Inc. and our subsidiary Nu Mark LLC ("Nu Mark"), I write in response to your September 12, 2018, letter raising serious concerns about underage access to and use of e-vapor products. We share your concerns and believe kids should not use any tobacco products. Importantly, we are alarmed about the reported rise in youth e-vapor use to epidemic levels, and we are concerned that these youth issues may jeopardize harm reduction for adult smokers. . . . We believe that pod-based products significantly contribute to the rise in youth use of e-vapor products. Although we do not believe we have a current issue with youth access to or use of our pod-based products, we do not want to risk contributing to the issue. To avoid such a risk, we will remove from the market our MarkTen Elite and Apex by MarkTen pod-based products until we receive a market order from FDA or the youth issue is otherwise addressed.

Sincerely,
Howard A. Willard III

THE PRESSURE ON JUUL only intensified through the month of November. Burns was all-consumed by the task of coming up with a plan to respond to Gottlieb's demand for a strategy to reduce youth use of its product. Employees and executives had exhaled a sigh of relief after FDA inspectors left the building following the four-day raid. But the incident had left people on edge. Even as the company was being investigated for practices that incidentally hooked millions of teenagers on its product, it was simultaneously reaping the rewards of doing just that. That made for a somewhat mystifying air at Juul. There was a heady excitement that pervaded the place, but there was also a nagging fear that somebody might get arrested.

In San Francisco, anti-tobacco activists continued to dog the company. Katherine Doumani, the neighborhood activist, and her neighbor Dennis Herrera, the city attorney, had made it their personal mission to drive Juul out of Pier 70. Doumani showed up at the company's offices, sneaking upstairs to snap photographs of the interior.

Doumani also connected with other San Francisco anti-Juul activ-

ists, including Christine Chessen, a mother who'd discovered Juul in
her son's backpack and had written her own letter in desperation to
Kevin Burns, going so far as to march down to Juul's offices to make
sure it reached him, along with a plastic baggie containing her son's
contraband. On November 13, the two women showed up at a San
Francisco Port Commission meeting, pleading for the city to evict Juul.
"That the expansion of private use on public land is for Juul Labs, a
tobacco company that has come under fire by the FDA, the CDC,
UCSF and Stanford, and whose core mission is nicotine addiction, is
unconscionable," Doumani said in the public hearing.

The Port Director, Elaine Forbes, said at the meeting that there was
nothing that could be done. Juul had entered into the sublease legally
and was abiding by its terms. "There is nothing in city code or city
policy that would exclude Juul from being a subtenant," Forbes said.

After the meeting, which appeared to foreclose any action against
Juul, Chessen and Doumani urged Herrera to do something, anything,
to get Juul out of San Francisco. Herrera began an official city investigation into Juul's tenancy.

Meanwhile, the billionaire Fortress executive, Pete Briger, connected
with Meredith Berkman, the cofounder of the website Parents Against
Vaping e-cigarettes. Briger happened to be talking with Berkman's husband, an old friend he'd known from the investment world for years.
Upon learning about Meredith's website, Briger called her up. By the
end of their conversation, Briger was so impressed with her zeal on
the issue that he encouraged her to aim bigger than just a website. If
she really wanted to help hobble Juul, she should consider formalizing
an advocacy organization that could have more of a national reach to
pack a bigger punch. Ultimately, she followed Briger's advice and officially organized as a 501(c)(4) nonprofit organization. Briger was the
group's first donor, writing her a check for $100,000, which he followed
up not long after with another $150,000. Berkman in turn introduced
Briger to Bonnie Halpern-Felsher, the Stanford youth tobacco expert. Briger wrote Halpern-Felsher a $250,000 check, this one to help
fund her anti-vaping work at Stanford. Dave Burke kicked in some
money too.

Meanwhile, Jim Steyer and Matt Myers began attending or sending policy staffers to roundtables with state attorneys general, as a conversation was percolating among some of the same players who'd helped bring about the tobacco Master Settlement Agreement. Steyer's longtime friend was Josh Stein, the attorney general of North Carolina, who'd already watched in dismay as Juul invaded schools in his own state and soon launched his own investigation of Juul. The attorney general of Massachusetts, Maura Healey, was deep in her own investigation into the company's marketing practices.

Meanwhile, Burns and other executives scrambled to contain the growing furor. On November 13, Burns announced Juul's "Action Plan" in response to Gottlieb's request. "Juul Labs and FDA share a common goal," Burns wrote in a press release. "Preventing youth from initiating on nicotine. To paraphrase Commissioner Gottlieb, we want to be the off-ramp for adult smokers to switch from cigarettes, not an on-ramp for America's youth to initiate on nicotine. . . . Our intent was never to have youth use Juul products. But intent is not enough, the numbers are what matter, and the numbers tell us underage use of e-cigarette products is a problem. We must solve it."

The company announced that it was removing its crème brûlée, cucumber, fruit, and mango pods from brick-and-mortar retail stores, although it would continue selling them online. It also said that it was shutting down its social media accounts in the United States to "remove ourselves entirely from participation in the social conversation."

Juul was in damage control mode. But since talks with Altria were now back on, at least the company's owners had a potential payday on the horizon that would entail enough zeroes to make anybody's head spin.

TWO DAYS LATER, GOTTLIEB finally publicly announced data from the National Youth Tobacco Survey that he'd been forced to sit on for so long. And it was no easier to confront them on that day than it had been nearly three months before when he first got them from Zeller. "Today, the FDA and the Centers for Disease Control and Prevention are publishing data from the 2018 National Youth Tobacco Survey (NYTS). The data from this nationally representative survey, conducted of middle and high school students, show astonishing increases in kids' use of e-cigarettes and other [electronic nicotine delivery systems], reversing years of favorable trends in our nation's fight to prevent youth addiction to tobacco products. These data shock my conscience. . . . These increases must stop. And the bottom line is this: I will not allow a generation of children to become addicted to nicotine through e-cigarettes."

It was too late.

IF ANYBODY EVER DOUBTED that Howard Willard was a gambler, the fall of 2018 proved it. As he'd been deep in the throes of negotiating with Juul, he'd also been orchestrating a deal in the cannabis industry as well. On December 7, Altria announced that it had invested $1.8 billion for a 45 percent stake in a Canadian cannabis company called Cronos Group, which had been started by a group of investment bankers. At the time, Cronos carried a lot of cachet—it had become the first weed company to be listed on a major U.S. stock exchange earlier in the year. The same day, Altria announced that it was shutting down the entire MarkTen business, not just taking the pods off the market temporarily as Willard had announced earlier, and also discontinuing the production and distribution of its other products under the Nu Mark umbrella, including Green Smoke e-cigarettes and the Verve nicotine discs. "We do not see a path to leadership with these particular products and believe that now is the time to refocus our resources," Willard said in a statement.

Willard was in the final stages of clearing another path.

ON THE NIGHT OF December 7, 2018, hundreds of Juul employees arrived at the San Francisco Giants stadium in the China Basin neighborhood overlooking the bay. Every year Juul had a holiday party, but this one was unusually epic. Champagne flowed freely from an open bar, and the buffet was stacked with shrimp and roast beef and turkey. Employees got to tour the dugout, batting cages, and locker rooms. They snapped selfies as they walked out onto the perfectly manicured field aglow in the night with floodlights, walking the same earth as Major League Baseball Hall of Famers. Music bumped as they toured the area that displayed Giants trophies and diamond-encrusted rings from the team's World Series championships and photos of Willie Mays.

Partly the bash was held in a baseball stadium because the company had outgrown the cozy restaurant-bar it had bought out the year before for its holiday party. But the special location was also because it had been a monster of a year at Juul. Annual revenue exceeded $1 billion, and Juul could now be found in the biggest mass retailers in America and in more than a half dozen international markets. Let alone the fact that Juul had become a verb, a notable if not hubristic badge of honor among the Silicon Valley set. If this year wasn't deserved of a party, when would it be? Plus, 2018 was getting ready to end with a bang. Fittingly, a dazzling firework display crackled through the sky at the end of the night.

Just a few days earlier, *The Wall Street Journal* had reported that Juul and Altria were in talks about a potential deal that could give the tobacco company a minority stake in the San Francisco firm. Ever since, people had been whispering nervously about it. A tobacco company buying Juul? Enough people had speculated about that potential over the years, but it had always been seen as a somewhat unlikely doomsday scenario, one that was spoken about in whispers, traded like a piece of salacious gossip or treated like a sacrilege. The only way Juul had been able to recruit top talent from the likes of Apple and Uber was by hewing closely to the founding mythology of the company, which depicted Bowen and Monsees as anti-smoking crusaders devoted to saving lives and destroying Big Tobacco. Vanquishing the cigarette was Juul's raison d'être. It was that construct that allowed scores of Juul employees—many who had reluctantly taken the job—to sleep at night.

On the morning of December 20, 2018, Juul Labs employees gathered in the kitchen area for a company-wide meeting. Others around the world tuned in from satellite offices via Zoom. That morning, Burns stood in the kitchen area, flanked by Monsees and Bowen, neither of whom were known for rousing rallying calls. Microphone in hand, Burns laid any rumors to rest: Juul had reached a $12.8 billion deal with Altria Group Inc., giving the nation's largest tobacco company and maker of the Marlboro cigarette a 35 percent ownership stake. It was the largest sum ever raised by a U.S.-based venture-capital-backed company. And with the deal valuing Juul at $38 billion, it made the e-cigarette company one of the most valuable start-ups of all time, more than SpaceX or Airbnb. Even by Silicon Valley standards, it was massive. Juul had become a unicorn on steroids.

The news elicited audible gasps in the room. Bewildered employees looked around at one another, searching eyes and faces for emotions to help inform their own. Just like that, the start-up that had vowed to strike a dagger through the heart of Big Tobacco suddenly was Big Tobacco.

"The glass house was shattered," said one employee.

Juul's executive team was smart enough to know that probably none of their employees had ever aspired to work for a tobacco company. And Altria executives knew that they'd be potentially received with open hostility. So, as part of the deal, Burns said, Altria would pay out $1 billion in bonuses to the employees. That averaged out to more than $600,000 per employee, although the actual amount was based partly on tenure, meaning some got more than $1 million. That elicited more audible gasps. One employee who was tuning in remotely recalled having to sit down upon hearing the news. But there was a catch. A big reason Altria paid a king's ransom for a stake in the company was for the talent and they couldn't afford to have the entire staff jump ship. The full sum of the bonus would be doled out over two years with a check coming every six months or so. In other words, if you wanted to get paid, you had to stick around and suck it up.

Monsees was unabashedly bullish on the deal. Yes, he understood that there might be dismay, and that the partnership seemed counterintuitive, he told staffers. But this was not a sign of capitulation in

Juul's fight against the tobacco industry. It was in fact the exact opposite. This deal, he said, amounted to the most resounding signal yet that Juul was winning the war to get people off of cigarettes. That the tobacco industry was conceding that its future rested with noncombustible products, which could translate into a meaningful public-health opportunity. Plus, Altria didn't get a controlling stake in the company and its executives had promised to be hands-off.

Monsees's monologue struck some as self-serving at best, not least because the deal had just made the man filthy rich. After the announcements, the floor was opened for employees to ask questions. Some were about the mechanics of the deal. Others were softballs. One long-time employee raised a hand and asked a question that crystallized what had likely been going through everybody's minds. For all the shine that was being put on the deal, in that moment things became real.

"A $13 billion investment like this doesn't happen in a week. Have you been lying to us this whole time?"

It's not that Juul's founding myth was a lie, necessarily. Monsees and Bowen had been true believers in their cause. They were so committed to transcending the sins of the tobacco industry that at one point Bowen hired a small team to investigate whether it might be possible to derive nicotine—an alkaloid found in other plants of the flowering nightshade genus like eggplants and tomatoes—from synthetic sources instead of the tobacco leaf. Big Tomato had a less sinister ring to it. It's just that it turned out that, like most things in Silicon Valley, the founding myth was at the very least fungible.

By Christmas, as the Altria checks rolled in, Juul employees were genuinely astounded by the life-changing nature of the deal. That was especially true for those who were among the first hundred or so employees at the company. The bonuses were in part based on tenure, which meant that a bunch of millennials who'd started at Juul barely out of college had made out like bandits. A company secretary who'd worked there from the beginning became a multimillionaire. A long-time junior program manager suddenly was wealthier than his seasoned executive boss. Employees carried boat magazines to the office.

There was almost a kind of baffled air of disbelief. Like, what was the catch? It all seemed incredible. Altria had minted millionaires and billionaires. Some people took to calling them *juulionaires!*

But no aspect of the deal was more incredible than the payoff for the founders and the investors. In fact, it was one of the most gobsmacking deals ever made in Silicon Valley. Normally, when a big investor comes in, they do one of two things with the funds. They either buy out early investors to allow them to take chips off the table while streamlining the shareholder structure, or they use the money to grow the business or pay off debt. But in this instance, the funds were structured as a "special dividend." That meant that almost all of the $12.8 billion was paid out essentially in the form of a cash bonus, leaving only around $200 million on the balance sheet. Existing Juul shareholders got to keep their shares *and* receive a $150 dividend for each share.

Altria has long been referred to in the investing world as the Dividend King, for its unwavering commitment to paying out its regular dividend to shareholders over fifty years, through thick and thin, no matter what. That's why investors have continued to stick by Altria's side despite the unpopular nature of its business. But not even the Dividend King had ever before paid out such a princely dividend. At the time of the transaction, Valani, the single largest individual shareholder in the company, owned an estimated 20 percent of the company, and so was positioned to rake in around $2.6 billion on the deal. Pritzker owned about 13 percent of the company, and pulled down around $1.7 billion. Bowen and Monsees together had around 10 percent of the company, with Monsees holding a slightly larger stake, which translated into around $640 million apiece. The Stanford grads were made. Chase Coleman's Tiger Global investment firm pulled down what amounted to a $1.6 billion *windfall*. Fidelity made its money back and more. Even the smaller investors in some instances doubled or tripled their money. The Silicon Valley unicorn that ran roughshod over a nation was raining money.

"It was one of the biggest wealth creation opportunities in the history of the world," said a person familiar with the deal.

One longtime employee perhaps best described the transaction. "We basically punked a hundred-plus-year-old, hundred-billion-dollar tobacco company out of thirteen billion dollars," the person quipped.

ON THE OTHER SIDE of the country, on the same day, on the outskirts of Richmond, the mood was entirely different. Employees were gathering to hear their own leaders' announcement about the development they'd heard about through an early-morning company-wide communication as the markets opened, or on the news, depending on which they happened to read first. A podium similar to the one that had been set up in the Altria headquarters for Willard's first town hall a little more than half a year ago was being set up again, in the same place underneath the covered breezeway, off the main courtyard. But the differences in the circumstances were stark.

Not only was it a lot colder outside, but there was nothing celebratory about the mood that morning. It fact, it was downright somber. For weeks employees at Altria had heard rumors about a potential Juul deal. But now the details were being unveiled for the first time. Willard announced the top-line news. "We are taking significant action to prepare for a future where adult smokers overwhelmingly choose noncombustible products over cigarettes," Willard said. "We have long said that providing adult smokers with superior, satisfying products with the potential to reduce harm is the best way to achieve tobacco harm reduction. Through Juul, we are making the biggest investment in our history toward that goal. We strongly believe that working with Juul to accelerate its mission will have long-term benefits for adult smokers and our shareholders."

He discussed the terms of the deal—that Altria was paying $12.8 billion for a 35 percent stake in Juul at a $38 billion valuation. It was the single largest deal done in Altria's history. As Willard went deeper into the content in the news release, his demeanor visibly changed. Everything comes with a price, he said, and this was no exception. To offset the cost of the Juul investment, Willard announced a "cost reduction" program that would deliver up to $600 million in savings by the end of

2019. To achieve those savings, the company was planning a round of layoffs that would likely entail hundreds of jobs being cut.

As Willard got to that part of his talk, he started to well up. He stopped for a moment to compose himself. Then he began talking about how much he'd appreciated the past six months as CEO, and how much he'd learned from all the people around him. As he talked about the personal connections he'd made with people, he teared up again.

Nobody expected the corporate embodiment of the Marlboro Man to cry. It simply wasn't routine behavior, at least not so publicly, for the usually impeccably polished senior leaders at Altria, and it took employees off guard. It also added to the stress of the moment. If Willard, a guy who raked in $15 million in annual compensation and faced no immediate threat to his job, was crying, just imagine how a midlevel hourly employee who was the sacrificial lamb for a lavish deal with Juul was feeling.

After his remarks, Willard agreed to take questions. An older man stood up and took the microphone. That morning, as the news of the deal circulated, CNBC published a story outlining how Juul's fifteen hundred employees were receiving a $1 billion cash bonus from Altria that made some of them millionaires. The guy was clearly pissed. "Can you explain to me why these employees at Juul are getting millions in bonuses and you're laying off your workforce?"

Willard seemed like a deer in the headlights and stumbled over his words before finally eking out a response that sounded like something he would have delivered back in the day as a Bain consultant. And it did not go over well. "We had to," he in essence replied. "They also work hard and are owed compensation."

The next question came from another employee who was not as much mad but sad. "I can't help but feel doing these things is you giving up on us," he said. Willard choked up again and could barely manage to respond. There were so many people at Altria who were essentially lifers—they'd worked in the cigarette factory for decades, or they'd worked their way up through the corporate offices over their entire careers. Despite any negative view that outsiders might have of

Philip Morris employees, there was a deep love for the company inside. Finally, Willard marshaled a response: "This isn't us giving up," Willard tried to explain. "This is us trying to forge a new path."

Altria had been trying to forge a new path for a generation. Now, here on the precipice of doing just that, no amount of explaining could take away the truth. As bonuses rained down on Juul employees, Altria employees were getting hosed—five days before Christmas.

18

THE TAKEOVER

We don't live with angels; we have to put up with human nature and forgive it.

—SAINT MADELEINE SOPHIE BARAT, FOUNDER OF THE
SOCIETY OF THE SACRED HEART OF JESUS

Let us see how high we can fly before the sun melts the wax in our wings. —SUBRAHMANYAN CHANDRASEKHAR, ASTROPHYSICIST

The Four Seasons Silicon Valley, in East Palo Alto, sat in a glass-enclosed building, just off the edge of the Stanford campus, and alongside Highway 101 that snaked north along the bay to San Francisco. Given that rooms started at more than $500 a night, and thousands more for the luxury suites, it was somewhat of an awkward spot that January for the two alpha-male CEOs of Juul and Altria to appear before a large audience. Sure, they'd just inked the biggest venture-capital-backed deal in Silicon Valley history. But only one of those parties had walked away feeling relatively flush.

Willard was still in the middle of executing his "cost reduction" plan to pay for the 35 percent stake in Juul, and the layoffs were under way. In January 2019 the company cut nearly one thousand salaried jobs, amounting to more than 10 percent of Altria's workforce. The savings were designed to offset interest from the loan taken out to fund the Juul deal. As Juul employees were paying cash for boats and Bay Area homes, Altria employees were being asked to pack up their desks.

Inside the Four Seasons, Burns and Willard climbed up onstage and spoke to the more than two hundred Juul executives in the room, extolling the virtues of their newly minted partnership. "I believe that in five years, 50 percent of Juul's revenue will be international," Willard said, according to *The New York Times*. Burns interrupted him, joking: "I told the team to accomplish that in one year!"

While the two appeared chummy onstage, behind the scenes tensions were already building. To those around him, Burns projected the swaggering attitude of someone who'd helped pull off the deal of the century. He had made clear to colleagues that he had no intention of taking orders from a glorified cigarette salesman. Plus, Willard's company only had a minority stake in Juul so Burns saw no reason to genuflect before anyone at Altria. How the tables had turned since Bowen and Monsees had dragged their way across the country to Richmond a decade ago to have the privilege of pitching Ploom to the most storied cigarette company in the world.

Altria, meanwhile, hadn't spent nearly $13 billion to hold its tongue. Already Willard's top lieutenant, K.C. Crosthwaite, had been given an observer seat on Juul's board of directors, which was designed to convert to a regular seat with voting power once the transaction was approved by regulators. Like most deals of its size, this one still needed antitrust clearance by the Federal Trade Commission before Altria could exercise any legal control over matters of corporate governance.

Crosthwaite had become intimately familiar with Juul and its leadership team over the course of negotiations between the two companies. His stature inside Altria had risen, alongside Willard's, and employees speculated that the CEO chair might one day be in his stars.

On the day the deal was announced, Willard painted a sanguine portrait on a special "Business Update." "Just imagine," Willard said. "The combination of Juul's leading market position, brand equity and deep innovation pipeline with our strong retail presence, our ability to connect directly with adult smokers on our company's databases, while avoiding unintended audiences, our leading sales organization, which covers approximately 230,000 stores and our deep regulatory affairs expertise." He went on to preempt some expected questions about the steep price of the deal, saying that it represented "the fastest and most sustainable opportunity to generate significant income in the e-vapor category." Translation: *MarkTen was a flop and thank god for Juul; we'll finally be able to make some money in e-cigarettes.*

The problem was, investors were spooked. The price tag, and restrictive deal terms, left some woozy in the knees. On the day the deal was announced, Altria's stock suffered one of the biggest drops in years. *The Wall Street Journal* published a column titled "Marlboro Maker Is Paying a Desperate Price for Juul." Two credit ratings agencies, S&P Global and Fitch, downgraded the company's credit grade to BBB, the lowest level for investment-grade companies, because of the high amount of debt Altria incurred to finance the deal.

On the investor call, an analyst asked about the "standstill agreement" that prohibited the company from acquiring any additional shares above its 35 percent state for six years from the time the deal closed. "I'm a little bit surprised that there is no pathway to control given the size of the check and the valuations," she said.

"You're right," Willard replied. "Given the strong performance of the business and its expected upside, we felt even without a pathway to control, this was an attractive deal for us."

Willard carried on throughout the call, explaining that the company had been modeling Juul's financials and expected growth trajectory "for quite some time" and that they were continually surprised by how they exceeded their most optimistic projections. And as far as the $38 billion valuation? Willard acknowledged there might be some "disruption" as Juul worked with the FDA to solve the youth issue, but "we actually are quite comfortable with the valuation and expect there to be upside over time."

But not everybody was as sanguine. Altria's stock was typically an attractive investment proposition because of its steady and dependable returns. If investors wanted exposure to high-flying tech stocks, they'd put their money elsewhere or go to Vegas. Citi analyst Adam Spielman recommended that investors sell Altria's stock after concluding that the deal signaled a potentially worrisome underlying weakness. If the company was willing to pay such a high price for Juul, what did that say about the future of Altria's cigarette business? Altria "is effectively signaling it is doubtful about the future of its core business," he wrote. And with Juul now having access to Altria's massive customer marketing database, wouldn't that just allow the San Francisco start-up to cannibalize Altria's cigarette business even more? Plus, since Juul was a private company, investors simply didn't have enough visibility into the financial inner workings of Juul on which to base an informed opinion. They had to take Willard's word for it.

ON THURSDAY EVENING, JANUARY 10, 2019, scores of parents strode across the campus at Sacred Heart School in Atherton, atop the intricate stone labyrinth modeled after one at Chartres Cathedral in Paris, past the Our Lady of Lourdes grotto, into the Campbell Center for the Performing Arts, which was named after Silicon Valley legend Bill Campbell, the former CEO of Intuit, an Apple board member, and guru to countless tech executives, including Steve Jobs, Larry Page, and Sheryl Sandberg. Campbell's children had attended Sacred Heart and he'd been a longtime beloved coach for the school's eighth-grade boys' and girls' flag football teams. When he died in 2016, a memorial was held on Sacred Heart's football field, attracting the Valley's upper crust, including Tim Cook and Jeff Bezos.

Inside the 350-seat auditorium, there was a shared sense of anger and frustration. Ever since the girls' lacrosse team incident last spring, the Juuling problem at Sacred Heart had only grown worse, approaching the "epidemic" levels that Gottlieb had declared just a few months earlier. So many Sacred Heart students now Juuled that on any given day during lunchtime, if a parent drove the campus's leafy perimeter, past the rows of heritage olive trees, they'd be able to catch a glimpse of kids sitting in cars, clouds of vapor escaping from their windows.

One Sacred Heart parent likened it to going down an inner-city street and seeing drug addicts shooting up in broad daylight. Richard Dioli, the longtime head of Sacred Heart, had grown so exasperated by the expanding piles of confiscated Juuls that he brought in dogs to sniff students' lockers.

That night, Dioli sat in the audience as Pete Briger climbed up onstage. Briger and Dioli had started working closely together after the Fortress executive came to him in a fit of desperation as Juul invaded his personal life. Over the winter, the two had skipped over to the Stanford campus, a ten-minute drive from Sacred Heart, to meet with Bonnie Halpern-Felsher, the youth tobacco prevention expert, who showed them charts and data and told them everything she knew about nicotine addiction, the adolescent brain, and the uniquely powerful potion inside Juul. She told them that nicotine was more addictive than heroin. It wasn't until that moment that Briger and Dioli began to realize the gravity of the problem. Addicts were walking Sacred Heart's hallowed halls.

Now, the no-bullshit finance titan steeped in the world of distressed debt, complex rescue financings, and Bitcoin, was preparing to get up in front of three hundred parents to speak about a deeply personal issue. Briger and Dioli had invited Halpern-Felsher to come present to the Sacred Heart parents about the Juuling problem. When Dioli asked Briger to open the meeting, Briger was at first reluctant. He'd never done anything like that before at his kids' school. And he didn't love the idea of publicly airing family drama. But what he loved a lot less was Juul. And he also felt a moral obligation to be a leader on the issue that he'd come to embrace so deeply.

Briger was known to be a blunt but exceedingly thoughtful man who carefully chose each word before letting it leave his lips. That night in the performing arts center, with barely a seat empty, he laid it all out there. How he'd found Juul in his own home. How nicotine addiction had upended his daughter's lacrosse team. How he'd begun working with a grassroots anti-vaping organization that was growing into a nationwide advocacy group with powerful sway. Then he introduced Halpern-Felsher, who shared with the parents everything about nicotine addiction that she'd shared with Briger and Dioli, and which she'd also been sharing at schools across the country. She flipped through slides on the giant movie screen that showed charts depicting the surge in adolescent vaping, how nicotine addiction rewires kids' brains, and ways parents could identify vaping paraphernalia.

The conversation shifted to how Juul had recently linked up with Altria, the big cigarette maker, in the $13 billion deal done just a few weeks earlier. It was exactly what Briger and others had been saying. Juul was a tobacco company masquerading as a tech start-up and all the company cared about, they said, was selling more and more of their nicotine devices at the expense of their children's future.

Sacred Heart parents were furious by the end of Halpern-Felsher's talk. "People like me had no clue what it was," said one Sacred Heart dad who attended the meeting. "I thought it was a hard drive. And then it ran through like a cancer ripping through a body. It took hold and raced through these classes. And there was about a year there where even switched on adults were totally clueless." The dad grew angry just talking about. "Their little brains got hooked overnight!"

What really upset parents was when they learned that Kevin Burns lived right down the street. That the CEO of the very company crashing like a wrecking ball through their homes and locker rooms and schoolyards lived a five-minute drive from the school was blood-curdling. "We should go march down right now and picket his house," one of the parents said. Passions grew so heated that if at that moment, Burns had shown up on the campus founded in 1898 by nuns in devotion to peace and justice, he might have gotten mobbed.

Tensions simmered long after the meeting was over. "If I saw that guy Kevin Burns," a parent who attended the Sacred Heart meeting said. "I always think in my life that I never want to do something out of anger that is going to put me in the worst place. But if hitting him with a baseball bat were legal, I'd crush him right in the face."

KEVIN BURNS GOT HIS long-standing wish. Just after the New Year rang in, in the second week of January, Juul announced that it was planning to launch its first ever national television ad campaign. The $10 million campaign featured interviews, or "testimonials," with older men and women, some with pronounced wrinkles, others in their oversize sofas wearing cozy sweaters, one in a rambling old house in Harlem. There was the barber, the Israeli soldier, the film producer, a federal government worker, a crossing guard. In all of them, they casually held a Juul as they explained their personal struggles overcoming cigarette addiction. There was "Pat's Story" and "Mimi's Story" and "Carolyn's Story." And there was absolutely nothing sexy or attractive or hip about most of them.

This was Burns's attempt to thread the needle. Get the brand out there in a big way. But do it while deflecting the rising furor over the product. "It's clear that we're focused on the mission of the company to convert people off combustible cigarettes," Ann Hoey, Juul's vice president of marketing, told CNBC.

The launch of the TV campaign made for its own strange juxtaposition inside Juul. Employees saw a company forging ahead in what it had always done, but nothing was the same. After the Altria deal, a cloud gathered atop the company. Employees started asking more questions and having conflicted feelings about Juul's so-called mission to end cigarettes. After all the executives' missionary zeal, could they be trusted? Bowen, who'd arguably been the more strident anti-smoking flag bearer of the two founders, made a point of telling people that now, with the pile of Altria cash, Juul would be able to save *even more* lives. That struck some as a well-rehearsed line coming from somebody with a guilty conscience. Yes, at the end of the day there were one billion smokers in the world, which meant one billion potential lives to be saved. But it also meant that there were one billion people who could hypothetically buy Juuls.

And even though the founders were not running the company on a day-to-day basis, when employees saw them around the building, they looked at them differently. If they weren't immoral for the deal they'd cut with Altria, some argued that they were at least *amoral*.

It didn't take long for a collective existential crisis to settle over Juul. Employees who had joked gleefully about the "bags of rubies" Altria was handing out, using them to buy new houses, new cars, new wealth advisers, now found themselves with a sinking sense that they had instead taken blood diamonds. One former employee described falling into a deep depression, wondering how they'd ended up in such a "dystopian nightmare." Another employee left after the Altria deal and went on to devote his time to building cricket fields for underprivileged California children.

Ryan Woodring, the marketing head who worked under Hoey, had left just a few weeks before the Altria deal, after becoming increasingly fraught with guilt. Some people might have kicked themselves—*I should have stayed for the paycheck of a lifetime!*—but the thought barely crossed his mind. He'd grown so disillusioned by working for the company that it all became too mentally and psychically taxing.

On Woodring's last day in the office, an office manager packaged up a little farewell bag for him filled with some mango pods. As he walked out of Pier 70 on his last day, onto the gritty Dogpatch streets, he snapped one in his Juul and took a deep hit, letting the satisfying vapor roll deep into his lungs, and then out of his mouth. He felt relieved.

The Altria deal only made things worse. Any moral high road Juul had been able to claim as it recruited new hires evaporated almost overnight after the Altria deal. It was hard to argue that people should come work for a company whose mission was to destroy Big Tobacco when it was now owned in part by Big Tobacco. But that almost didn't matter anymore. Juul had a steady pipeline now directly from Altria. Within weeks of the deal closing in December, people who'd worked at Altria started quietly being hired by Juul. Everyone from low-level salespeople, to midlevel executives in regulatory and compliance divisions. It wasn't long before Altrians were folded into the fibers of Juul.

SCOTT GOTTLIEB WAS SITTING at a Bluestone Lane coffee shop in downtown Washington, D.C., on the morning of December 20, 2018, just around the corner from his apartment, when a news alert popped up on his cellphone. The headline announced that Altria had invested $12.8 billion in Juul. As he scanned the article, he could feel his blood pressure rising. He was shocked. Just a few weeks earlier, Willard had looked him in the eye and told him he wanted to work together to stop the youth vaping crisis. And then he followed up in writing with his commitment, saying that he believed so strongly that pod-based products were the problem that his company was taking its own such product, Elite, off the market in a show of good faith. At the same time, Burns had outlined a plan that entailed dramatically scaling back sales of its products in retail establishments to contain the spiraling epidemic. Now, these very same companies were announcing this monster deal that gave Altria a stake in not just any pod company but the biggest one in the world. And it gave Juul access to not just any company but one with nearly unmatched retail distribution in 230,000 stores that would allow the Silicon Valley start-up to blow out its sales.

Gottlieb dialed Mitch Zeller. "Did you see this?" he asked Zeller. "We need to respond." Gottlieb told him that he wanted to put out some sort of a public statement or a condemnation that immediately put them on notice. Zeller had seen the news and he was equally miffed. But he tried to talk Gottlieb off the ledge. Zeller knew that Gottlieb had picked up the habit of his boss, President Trump, often taking to Twitter to air his grievances. But Zeller told him tweeting in this moment was not a good idea. Gottlieb had never commented specifically on any business transaction, Zeller reminded him, and doing so in the heat of the moment would only raise suspicions about his objectivity. He urged him to take a deep breath. They'd figure out a more deliberate response.

Gottlieb deferred to Zeller, but he was less than thrilled about it. He felt immediately betrayed and, frankly, used by Willard and Burns. He'd bent over backward to give the two companies fair representation before his agency. He'd let them inside the commissioner's office for sit-down meetings. He'd listened to them and accommodated their requests. He'd let them present their plans, and seek advice, and angle for their carefully honed requests. They'd reassured Gottlieb that they were on the same page as the FDA. That they wanted to solve the problem together. They were all on the same team. All the while, the two had been secretly negotiating this blockbuster deal that made a mockery of it all.

On January 18, the audience in the FDA's Great Room applauded as Gottlieb walked up to the podium. He gave the opening remarks at a public hearing about the role that drugs could play in pediatric tobacco cessation programs, a topic that reflected just how bad things had gotten.

"I am deeply troubled by the fact that we find ourselves at this crossroads today," he said. "In recent years we've appeared poised to slay one of the most pernicious public health challenges of our times—the death and disease caused by cigarette smoking. Significant strides had been made to reduce conventional smoking among both youth and adults. . . . Sadly, this progress is being undercut, even eclipsed, if you will, by the recent and dramatic rise in youth vaping. A few years ago, it would have been incredible to me that we'd be here today discussing the potential for drug therapy to help addicted young people quit vaping."

At the public hearing all kinds of experts and pediatricians and advocates spoke, who pointed out that there were no FDA-approved nicotine replacement therapies for youth. Gottlieb, along with a growing number of pediatricians and public-health officials, were facing a troubling situation that just a year ago would have been unfathomable: Millions of kids now were potentially in need of a cessation product to get them off Juul.

Meanwhile, Gottlieb was scrambling to figure out an appropriate response to the Juul-Altria deal that still made his blood boil. Every day that passed without a public denouncement made it easier for the whole issue to fade into the noise. Gottlieb didn't want the issue to fade into the noise. Within days of the transaction, he'd written a scathing four-page letter to Burns and Willard demanding from each an explanation for why they appeared to have misled the FDA. But before he had a chance to send the letters, the White House heard about them through the grapevine and intervened, requesting a chance to review them first. Special assistant to the president and deputy White House counsel Steven Menashi immediately took issue with Gottlieb's harsh tone. He disagreed with how in his view Gottlieb was trying to use the pulpit of a federal agency to publicly browbeat a company. So, he marked up the letters and sent them back to Gottlieb. Then, Gottlieb's office made the requested changes and sent them back to Menashi. This back-and-forth between the FDA commissioner's office and the White House carried on for the next six weeks. Gottlieb was livid.

The White House, meanwhile, was being pressured by a growing political force made up of pro-business groups like Grover Norquist's Americans for Tax Reform, the Club for Growth, and others in the so-called liberty coalition that were lining up to support Juul and the e-cigarette industry. Altria had already been lobbying the White House and the FDA in 2018, and Juul was actively beefing up its army of lobbyists. Juul's federal lobbying expenditures swelled to more than $1.6 million in 2018, thirteen times more than the year before. In 2017, the company paid two outside lobbyists. The following year it paid sixteen. And throughout 2019, the company continued to bring on more Washington players with close ties to the Trump administration, including Rebeccah Propp, Vice President Mike Pence's former director of media affairs, and Johnny DeStefano, a former White House aide. Tevi Troy, Juul's top internal communications adviser, had worked for Alex Azar in the Bush administration and was now a frequent presence at the White House, lobbying on behalf of the company.

At his wit's end, Gottlieb picked up the phone and called Azar. "I've had it," Gottlieb told him. "This is absurd, these edits from political appointees trying to soften this letter." Finally, on February 6, Gottlieb sent the letter to Burns, and one to Willard, saying that the deal appeared to "contradict the commitments you made to the FDA." He also summoned representatives from Juul and Altria to his office for a meeting the following month. But it wasn't the letter Gottlieb had wanted to send. It was only a single page with four terse paragraphs, and much less biting.

Meanwhile, some of the same state attorneys general that Steyer and Myers and others had spoken with earlier had begun investigations into Juul. There'd been a widening number of conversations about the potential to pattern a legal strategy against Juul off the state attorneys general who'd so successfully deployed an avalanche of litigation against cigarette companies, bringing the industry to its knees. Since there had already been a tobacco Master Settlement Agreement, which funded decades' worth of tobacco-prevention programs that led to declining youth smoking rates, was there a possibility of using litigation—and potentially ultimately some sort of an e-cigarette Master Settlement Agreement—to help fund programs in schools and communities to cope with e-cigarette addiction?

On March 5, Gottlieb gave a speech to the National Association of Attorneys General about this exact topic—the role that state policies and actions could play in combating the youth e-cigarette epidemic. He climbed onstage at the Capital Hilton in Washington, D.C., and stood at a podium in front of royal-blue drapes and an American flag. "Time and again, state attorneys general have used the power of their office, whether the bully pulpit or litigation to address deceitful or unfair practices that harm consumers," Gottlieb said. "State attorneys general have made important contributions to reducing the death and disease from the use of tobacco products. Some of you in this room were probably part of one such effort. I'm referring, of course, to the lawsuits brought by state attorneys general against the tobacco industry in the mid-1990s. . . . As a result of the litigation, millions of pages of internal memoranda, reports, and other tobacco company documents were made public. The documents revealed significant inappropriate marketing practices, including marketing towards youth and young adults. . . . As this epidemic has emerged, I've heard the echoes of history repeating itself."

Gottlieb went on to outline the problem of the new tobacco products, which had 3.6 million students using e-cigarettes—"We've stigmatized smoking. But, many kids don't even associate e-cigarettes with smoking. Instead, they think they're just 'Juuling,'" he said—and urged the attorneys general in the audience to consider how they might tackle the problem. "I want to see how state enforcement action and state efforts can support our shared goals, and how we can be

working with you better to advance efforts that achieve these purposes."

Gottlieb's speech struck people in the audience as not only groundbreaking but invigorating—this was the dawning of another historic
moment in tobacco control. Twenty years had passed since the Master
Settlement Agreement. There was so much outrage on behalf of parents and teachers and others across the country, about how Juul had
marketed its product directly to a youthful audience, how it had designed the device in a way that made it easy to inhale with its smooth
nicotine salt formulation, and also highly addictive with its potent
amounts of nicotine. And on top of all that, the company used the best
flavor chemists in the world to make it taste like candy. There was a
rising sense that a new fight might be on the horizon.

After Gottlieb's speech was over, former Mississippi attorney general Mike Moore, an architect of the 1990s tobacco settlements, made
his way into the hallway outside the ballroom. Moore had arranged a
meeting with Gottlieb and several attorneys general to talk about Juul.
But when he got out there, Moore was told that the meeting was canceled because Gottlieb had to handle a pressing matter.

Only a few hours later, it was all over the news. Gottlieb had
abruptly resigned, citing his desire to spend more time with his family,
who still resided in Connecticut. His last day would be in mid-April.

ON MARCH 13, WITH only a few weeks left at the agency, Gottlieb announced a proposed policy to step up enforcement against manufacturers of flavored e-cigarettes and require brick-and-mortar retailers to
keep flavored e-cigarettes in a separate, walled-off area unreachable by
minors. The proposal stopped short of banning all flavored e-cigarettes,
which had been floated by the FDA. It also didn't include mint or menthol flavors, which public-health experts had long argued were the
most popular "flavors" among youth.

That same day, Gottlieb held one of his final official meetings as
FDA commissioner. It was with Willard and three other Altria executives, and Burns and three others from Juul. From the FDA, along with

Gottlieb, were Mitch Zeller and a dozen other career staffers. They all gathered in the large conference room in the commissioner's suite. In total there were around two dozen people in the room.

Gottlieb had been waiting weeks to really lay into Willard and Burns, and his anger had not abated. For fifteen minutes at the meeting's open, he let it fly.

"There's no other company or industry that we deal with who in their interactions with the agency have behaved this way," he said, leaning onto the oak table, staring directly at Willard, and then Burns. "I've given you more access than any other company. Not only have I met with you multiple times, but my staff take all your phone calls, return all your phone calls, reply to all your letters. We have been more responsive to you than perhaps any other industry. . . . Don't come here today and tell me that you want to work with us!"

Everybody in the room was silent. Gottlieb's staffers looked a combination of shocked and proud. The industry executives looked sheepish as they were called to the carpet. Willard and Burns defaulted to slick lobbyist mode, explaining the respect they had for the agency and how everything they'd done was in the spirit of fixing the youth epidemic. The rest of the meeting was largely perfunctory.

It was fitting that the meeting with Juul and Altria was among Gottlieb's last as FDA commissioner. He'd started his tenure as FDA commissioner confronting nicotine. Now, less than two years later, he was ending it confronting nicotine. And once again, a quarter century after nicotine had engulfed the FDA under David Kessler, America's most fraught substance had left the agency in tatters.

When the meeting was all over, Gottlieb got up and walked toward the door. Before he exited, he turned around and faced Willard and Burns.

"I'll see you on the other side," Gottlieb said.

SAN FRANCISCO CITY ATTORNEY Dennis Herrera's first swing at Juul had been a whiff. At the urging of Katherine Doumani and Christine Chessen, Herrera had pursued an investigation into Juul's lease on city property. The Port Commission hearing had made it clear that Juul had legally entered into its sublease, and that there was nothing the port could legally do to evict the company. The city's own internal investigation turned up no evidence that Juul had run afoul of anything. Since Juul's sublease was in effect for at least five years, and with another five-year extension, that meant that not only was Juul not going anywhere, but it was potentially going to be at Pier 70 until at least the year 2027.

Over his nearly two decades as city attorney, then serving his fifth term, Herrera had taken on—and won—hyper-controversial issues, from California's ban on same-sex marriage, to Uber's treatment of drivers, to gun law reforms opposed by the National Rifle Association. But Juul made him see red. He saw the company as not only a moral affront to the kids of San Francisco but also as a stain on the city he'd lived in for three decades.

On March 19, Herrera and Supervisor Shamann Walton stood at a podium in city hall, flanked by a small army of city officials. They were there as part of the city's latest attempt to stop Juul. "It's up to local governments like San Francisco to protect their children," said Herrera. "These companies may hide behind the veneer of harm reduction, but let's be clear; their product is addiction."

Walton had just been elected to the city's Board of Supervisors for District 10, which encompassed the Dogpatch neighborhood. With deep support among the highest ranks of San Francisco politics, Walton beat out five other candidates and immediately tackled progressive issues, like working to close the city's juvenile detention center. He immediately agreed to help Herrera take on the Juul problem.

That day Herrera and Walton introduced city legislation to put a moratorium on the sale of any e-cigarettes that hadn't yet undergone FDA review. Since no e-cigarette at that point in time had undergone FDA review, that meant the proposal was in effect a ban on e-cigarettes in San Francisco—the first of its kind in the nation. The year before, San Francisco had in fact enacted a ban on all flavored tobacco products, including e-cigarettes, but this legislation took it a step further. It was an unmistakable message to Juul.

"We don't want them in our city," Walton said.

It was a shot across the bow in what would become one of the most expensive political brawls in the city's history. It was also a turning point for Juul, as it was now forced to defend itself against the very city from which it had been born.

JUST BEFORE NINE A.M. on May 2, Howard Willard arrived at the Grand Hyatt in downtown San Francisco, along with his two top executives, K.C. Crosthwaite and Murray Garnick, the longtime Altria general counsel who'd been deeply involved in the Juul negotiations. By now Willard had gotten used to the cross-country trip from Richmond to San Francisco, and it was he who'd called this morning's meeting. Barely five months into Altria's single biggest investment ever, he was getting nervous.

Willard knew that solving Juul's youth problem was the key to unlocking the full value of his investment. If kids kept using Juul in droves, there was no way the FDA would ever reach the conclusion that the product was "appropriate for the protection of the public health"—the agency's standard for authorizing a tobacco product. And with a group of public-health organizations challenging the generous deadline the FDA had given manufacturers to submit their "premarket tobacco product applications," there was no time to waste. It was a real possibility that the judge in that case might move the deadline to an earlier date. Everything was riding on the PMTA (premarket tobacco application) process. If Juul didn't get the FDA's blessing, there would be no Juul. And if there was no Juul, Willard may as well have taken the $12.8 billion, rolled it in cigarette paper, and lit it on fire.

The truth is, at the time Juul didn't really need Altria's money, and likely could have cashed out in any number of ways. "Nobody at that point in time thought you weren't going to get filthy rich by investing in Juul," said a person familiar with the transaction. "This wasn't deciding between two billion dollars or nothing. It was do I make $2 billion today or $3 billion next year." What Juul needed, though, was the intangibles that Altria could provide, not least of which was direct access to the billions of packs of Marlboro sold every year inside which the company would now be able to stuff Juul coupons. It also gained access to a laundry list of services that Altria would provide to the company, including lobbying, Altria's massive customer database, usage of its byzantine network of distribution logistics, legal services, trade marketing, and more. In addition, Altria would cooperate with Juul on developing initiatives to prevent underage use of its product. It was this last issue that Willard wanted to discuss with Juul executives on that May morning.

The headlines about Juul's youth problem had only gotten worse. Just a few weeks earlier, a group of nearly a dozen Democratic senators had sent a scathing letter to Burns, chastising his company's recent deal with Altria and announcing that they'd launched a congressional investigation into the company. "By accepting $12.8 billion from Altria—a tobacco giant with such a disturbing record of deceptive marketing to hook children onto cigarettes—" the letter read, "Juul has lost what little remaining credibility the company had when it claimed to care about the public health. While you and your investors may be perfectly content with hooking an entire new generation of children on your tobacco products in order to increase your profit margins, we will not rest until your dangerous products are out of the hands of our nation's children." At the same time, the city of San Francisco was working overtime to ban Juul from the city, while a network of attorneys general across the United States was quietly rekindling the anti-tobacco work they'd done two decades earlier that sparked the tobacco settlement.

Going into the meeting, Burns had a bad attitude. He'd preferred to limit interactions with "Richmond" as much as possible and now he and his entire executive team had been summoned here. Burns made it no secret that he'd developed somewhat of a recalcitrance toward the Altrians. He constantly ribbed Willard behind his back for getting Big Tobacco to fork over Silicon Valley money. And to Willard's face he didn't much bother changing his tone. The day before the meeting, Burns called Willard multiple times, only to have his assistant repeatedly tell him he was busy. Finally, Burns dialed Willard's cellphone directly and left a voice message: "I can save you the time. Cigarette sales are down. Can you talk?" If Willard was coming here to get Burns to bend the knee, he was sorely mistaken.

Burns strolled into the swanky Grand Hyatt boardroom in his usual tracksuit zip-up, jeans, and Allbirds. Willard wore a houndstooth sport jacket, Oxford shirt, pleated khakis, and loafers. Crosthwaite and Garnick were likewise sporting your typical mid-'90s East Coast corporate attire. The hoodie memo hadn't reached Richmond yet.

Over the course of several hours, the meeting unfolded around a big U-shaped boardroom table, with the three Altria executives and more than a dozen people from Juul and Juul's board, including Nick Pritzker, his son Isaac Pritzker, Riaz Valani, Zach Frankel, and others. As Willard listened, he'd occasionally puff on a Juul, a habit he'd apparently picked up over the course of the past year during talks with Juul. Some people wondered whether he was Juuling just for show. But the manner in which he hit the thing seemed authentic.

Burns was visibly annoyed to be in the room. His staff had been working overtime to get prepared for this meeting. The plan had been to blow the Altrians out of the water with all the steps Juul had taken to rein in the youth problem, as a way to get them to back off. They regaled Willard with details about Juul's "secret-shopper" and "track and trace" programs designed to ensnare retailers selling to minors. They explained a pilot program that integrated technology into retailers' point-of-sale systems to prevent the sale of Juul to anybody who couldn't be age-verified. They had data to answer every question. And charts that summed it all up. If this wasn't enough to signal to Willard and Co. that Burns had things under control, nothing would be.

But instead of receiving praise and accolades, Burns was met with circumspection. During the meeting he stared at his phone. Anytime he was asked a question, his answers were halfhearted. He was visibly annoyed that he had to even answer questions from anyone at Altria.

"Is any of this really going to have an impact?" Willard asked at one point. The mood coming from the Altria camp was that this was a deadly serious topic, and not some cool Silicon Valley beta test. The numbers in the National Youth Tobacco Survey needed to go down, he said, and if they didn't, none of these flashy strategies and technologies would ever work. Some of the strategies Juul presented were great, but they needed to be put into warp speed. *Bigger. Faster. Now.*

That wasn't at all what Burns wanted to hear. In his own mind, he'd taken the youth problem more seriously than anybody. He'd taken the hugely popular fruit- and dessert-flavored pods out of retail stores, sacrificing a huge chunk of the company's revenue ("I've never seen a brand work so hard to hurt its own sales," said one former sales executive); he'd committed to spending $30 million on "youth and parent education, and community engagement efforts"; he'd shuttered the company's Instagram; he'd personally made the case to regulators and lawmakers.

The coming-to-Jesus moment that Willard desired fell flat. It was abundantly clear that Burns just wanted his guests to get on their corporate jet back to Virginia as fast as possible and leave him the hell alone. That was a strategic miscalculation on Burns's part. The three Altria executives in the room, in fact, had more experience dealing with the exact type of crisis facing Juul than everyone else in the room combined. Here they were making a peace offering, albeit a self-interested one, to throw every resource Altria had to help Juul dig its way out of the ditch. And in return, Burns had all but snubbed his nose at them.

Burns may have been the CEO of Juul. But it was abundantly clear that it was Juul's board of directors that held ultimate sway. In the days after Burns's spectacle toward the deputies of a company that had just written a check bigger than (most) anybody in the room had ever seen and likely would never see again, the board was not happy.

BUT THERE WAS ENOUGH dissatisfaction to go around. Willard's people weren't happy either. Namely, his shareholders. On May 16, Altria's annual shareholders meeting was getting under way again, at the downtown Richmond Convention Center. The previous year, Willard had just been introduced as the company's new CEO, and he didn't speak at the meeting at all. So much had changed in just a year. This year, Willard had a lot to account for. The day before the annual meeting, the North Carolina attorney general, Josh Stein, became the first in the nation to sue Juul, alleging that it had intentionally marketed and designed its products to attract youth, by using colorful ads and social media and potent nicotine solutions, while misrepresenting the addictiveness of its products. And there was a growing number of lawsuits by parents suing Juul for addicting their kids. That meant that in theory, Altria could now have liability exposure in those cases. Meanwhile, Altria's stock had taken a hit after the deal, and shareholders were questioning the wisdom of tying up with a company in the middle of a raging firestorm.

As Willard entered the convention center, he walked past groups of teenagers carrying giant signs shaped as various colored Juul pods that said "Who do you think these flavors are targeting?" and other signs that said "Big Tobacco is Back to their Old Tricks" and "We will not be FUULed 1 Pod = 1 Pack."

Inside the big ballroom, shareholders—one after another—brought up the recent Juul deal. One longtime shareholder, who'd held Altria stock since the 1960s, traveled to Richmond with his brother, stood up, and addressed Willard directly:

"I'd first like to begin by expressing some disappointment and some criticism that relates to the Juul transaction. You're aware of the three main criticisms of the deal: one, that we paid too much. Two—and more bothersome to me—is that there's no path to control; and lastly, we're restricted from distributing any other nicotine vaping systems. . . . That prohibits our ability to build a diversified portfolio in that space. My criticism and disappointment is that I believe that the deal negotiated was a consequence of the failure on the part of management to reach certain conclusions and act on those conclusions sooner, conclusions that I feel could have been made by mid-2017, if not sooner."

Willard pivoted deftly, but several other questions followed that reflected a similar sentiment. Was the Juul deal wise? Willard's decisions were being second-guessed.

The mood in Richmond had been somber for weeks now, as employees finished packing up their boxes from the now-defunct Nu Mark offices or other divisions of the company that had been hit by layoffs. Those who stayed struggled to come to terms with what had happened, because it all happened so fast. For the first few months after the Juul deal, Willard tried to maintain a sense of normalcy. At an investor conference in Boca Raton, he was confident telling attendees that despite concerns about Juul's future, he and the company had done "a deep strategic, operational and financial analysis" of Juul beforehand that took into account a wide variety of scenarios, including one in which the market for Juul slowed "due to disruption by regulatory or other action." They'd concluded, Willard said, that even in that type of a scenario, Altria could fall back on its "traditional tobacco categories" that he expected "would perform in line with their historic dynamics, and our core tobacco businesses would generate the strong returns you've seen from them historically."

In other words, the assumption was that if Juul got knocked off its pedestal for whatever reason, they'd still have cigarettes. That was an aspect of the 3D chess that Willard had been trying to play. If Juul was successful, Altria would cash in. If Juul was a failure, Altria would *still* cash in, since the assumption was people would go back to smoking cigarettes. "We believe Altria is better off with an investment in Juul across a variety of futures than we would have been without," he said. No matter what, Marlboro would still be standing. And most importantly, the company could continue to pay out its dividend to shareholders.

Undeterred by the noise, Willard kept pushing forward with his checkbook strategy to dominate the market for novel, reduced-harm products. Between Juul and Cronos he'd already spent $14.6 billion on alternative products. Now, on June 3, Willard announced that Altria had invested $372 million to purchase an 80 percent stake in a Swiss company that made a brand of nicotine pouches called "on!" Two months later, he announced that the company's cannabis investment,

Cronos, had just expanded by spending $300 million for a cannabis company with a brand called Lord Jones, which made luxury CBD body lotions, gel capsules, and tinctures.

Willard was still pushing into Altria's brave future.

OVER THE NEXT SEVERAL weeks, as Dennis Herrera and Shamann Walton pressed ahead on the proposed e-cigarette ordinance, Juul began its own lobbying campaign. The day after Herrera announced the legislation, a team of four Juul executives had made their way to the ornate Beaux Arts city hall building, into the city attorney's office in Room 234. They tried to level with Herrera, explaining that Juul was doing everything in its power to stop kids from using its product, from secret shoppers to point-of-sale retail monitoring. "This isn't about restrictions being put on storeowners," Herrera said, in his blunt New York accent. "This is about *you*." He was annoyed that Juul kept trying to make it seem like the problem lay solely at the feet of irresponsible retailers, instead of owning up to its own role in the problem.

A few weeks later, in mid-May, CEO Kevin Burns came to see Herrera. He tried to fast-talk the city attorney, impressing on him how committed he was to working with the city to solve the youth addiction crisis together. Juul was for adult smokers only, he said, and the product stood to help millions of people. He told them all the things Juul was doing to make sure the product no longer would get into kids' hands: The retailer restrictions. The secret shoppers. The public awareness campaigns.

Herrera had zero sympathy. At that very moment, Juul was still rippling through the city's schools, kids were still hiding it in their backpacks, teachers were still struggling to keep it at bay. Even more troubling, parents were now desperate to help their kids wean off a newly acquired nicotine addiction. Herrera retorted by rattling off statistics—how 3.6 million kids were vaping and Juuling. How almost a quarter of American high schoolers were current users of the products. How youth tobacco use had surged since Juul hit the market.

Burns grew defensive. "Look, I have kids myself," he snapped.

"That's not what we're about." He was in the unenviable position of trying to convince people to look ahead to an idyllic future, where Juul wasn't a bane to society, but all anybody could see was the conflagration in front of them.

Despite all of Burns's diplomacy, Juul was preparing for war. With the looming vote on the proposed ordinance to ban Juul in the city, the company tried to make an end run around it. On May 15, Juul had filed a notice with the San Francisco Department of Elections that said the company intended to collect signatures for a ballot initiative designed to moot Herrera and Walton's ordinance, and set up a new framework that would provide for the sale of e-cigarettes. Juul had no intention of being locked out of its home turf. Political consultants immediately began knocking on doors across San Francisco in an effort to collect the 9,485 signatures they'd need to get the measure on the ballot.

A few days before the final vote, Burns sat down with the editorial board of the *San Francisco Chronicle* as part of a final effort to make his case for Juul. He said that the company could have done a better job communicating with city officials and acknowledged that his company bore responsibility for the youth nicotine epidemic. "We have eighty percent of the marketplace. How can we not be responsible for this?" Burns said. "I don't think it's intent, but we are responsible and we've got to take action on it." But he also made clear that Juul was not going to be driven out of town on a rail. "Yes, we're staying," he said, "San Francisco is our home."

On the afternoon of June 18, the San Francisco Board of Supervisors spent all of twenty-five minutes debating the proposed ordinance.

"We spent the nineties battling Big Tobacco and now we see its new form through e-cigarettes," said Supervisor Walton, wearing a black pinstripe suit, light blue tie, and goatee. "I hope you support this legislation to protect our young people from being addicted to nicotine and a lifetime of addiction."

The body passed it unanimously. San Francisco became the first city in the United States to effectively ban e-cigarettes. Juul was shut out from its home market.

Some companies might have acknowledged defeat, humbly. Not

Juul. On that very day, the company announced that it was not only *not* leaving the city but had just spent $400 million to purchase a sky-scraper in downtown San Francisco that would serve as its new head-quarters. The address was, aptly so, 123 Mission Street. It was 363,000 square feet of some of the most valuable real estate in all of San Fran-cisco, in a building twenty-eight stories tall. It may as well have been a twenty-eight-story-high middle finger to the city.

19

PANIC

We're conducting a big, uncontrolled and poorly documented set of chemistry experiments inside people's lungs.
—ALAN LOUIS SHIHADEH, AEROSOL SCIENTIST AT
AMERICAN UNIVERSITY OF BEIRUT

When Mike Meyer decided to move to the suburbs of Milwaukee, it was specifically so he could send his children to Arrowhead High School, one of the best public schools in the state of Wisconsin, offering everything from an advanced robotics program to a winning football team to a robust musical theater program straight out of the TV series *Glee*. The school, which spanned two idyllic campuses—one for the lower classes and one for the uppers—was perfectly situated so his job at Children's Wisconsin hospital in Milwaukee was just a quick drive away.

Meyer had a long career in pediatrics, starting at Children's in 1998 as a fellow while on active duty in the military, and returning to the hospital in 2008, where he's practiced as a pediatric intensivist ever since. Children's, as it was simply called, was one of the largest pediatric hospitals in the state of Wisconsin and was one of only a few in the United States that was independently owned and operated. It first opened in 1894, after a group of Good Samaritan women rented a Victorian house in Milwaukee and offered ten hospital beds for children. Since then it'd grown into a sprawling campus in downtown Milwaukee with nearly three hundred hospital beds to treat patients from across the state. It was featured in *Time* magazine as one of the most advanced hospitals in its treatment of premature babies.

Meyer had known about vaping for a while. His teenage daughter's boyfriend used a "mod," the larger, more advanced vaping implement that was popular in certain circles. Meyer was furious when he found a vape pen in his daughter's room. He'd also been hearing tales of Juul for months beforehand at Arrowhead High, which had recently implemented a new policy for the suspension of any student found in possession of an e-cigarette. Already, several student athletes had been suspended after they were found vaping in the back of the bus after a tournament. The school ultimately had to install electronic vape detectors in the school bathrooms that would send email alerts to the principal's office. But by the summer of 2019, that was about the extent of Meyer's (frustrating and maddening) experience with Juul.

One of Meyer's colleagues, Louella Amos, a pediatric pulmonologist at the hospital, had already been on high alert over e-cigarettes. She'd been speaking to schools in the Milwaukee area about the dangers of nicotine—how overnight nicotine withdrawals could cause irritability in the morning. How it could interfere with concentration. How it could do lasting damage to the teen brain. She'd been worried that kids were showing an inability to even recognize the fact that they were addicted to the products. Some of them said they had no idea that nicotine was even in the pods. In February 2018 Amos gave an interview to a local television station about the dangers of teen vaping. "There's a false sense of security that this is a harmless, safe way to get your nicotine buzz," she said. "My biggest concern is that we will find some adverse lung effects in the future in studies that will involve the teens that are vaping today."

In hindsight, it seems like a premonition.

———

MEYER'S FOURTH OF JULY week in the summer of 2019 involved his usual rounds at Children's Wisconsin as the medical director of the pediatric intensive care unit. Other than it being a holiday week, there was nothing extraordinary. It was just another beautiful summer day in Milwaukee near the shore of Lake Michigan, which glittered its usual seasonal shade of cerulean. It was also the final days of Summerfest, the twelve-day-long music festival on the lakefront that attracted people from around the world.

Meyer had almost forgotten about the patient from about three weeks earlier who'd come to the emergency room with fever, wheezing, and shortness of breath. He did recall thinking it was an odd time of year to see what he assumed was some form of interstitial pneumonitis. In summertime, kids didn't usually show up in the intensive care unit with respiratory illnesses; it was more common in the fall and winter, when viruses were raging. Summertime tended to be the slower season, when kids were overall pretty healthy, and those patients who did show up needing urgent care more typically presented with the broken bones or twisted ankles or dehydration that came along with waterskiing or hiking or summer sports.

Meyer immediately put the boy on antibiotics and steroids, and put him on breathing treatments since his oxygen saturation was lower than he would have expected. Even with supplemental oxygen, though, the kid just wasn't turning the corner. He and his colleague Lynn D'Andrea, the medical director of pulmonary services at Children's, ordered a CT scan, which showed odd opacities on the lungs that formed a pattern like ground glass. "Oh, this looks bad," Meyer said to D'Andrea. They ordered a full workup for the boy, which cost more than $200,000 and entailed engaging an army of specialists— immunologists to determine if it was an autoimmune disease like Wegener's disease; oncologists to determine if it might be cancer; even infectious disease experts to see if, as a dirt bike racer, the boy had inhaled some mold-saturated particle from the plumes of dust, which in very rare instances could cause a serious infection called sporotrichosis. Meyer even began wondering whether the boy had HIV. The Milwaukee area still had a reasonably large HIV-positive population and so he began pondering whether intravenous drug use was potentially at play.

During the course of just over a week, the boy began recovering by default, and ultimately he was discharged. Neither Meyer nor D'Andrea felt great about letting the patient go in the absence of a clear diagnosis. But they had at least ruled some serious things out.

About two weeks later, on June 28, a second teenage patient came in with similar pneumonia-like symptoms. By then, so much time had passed that there wasn't more than an inkling that they could in some way be related. Just a twinge of *huh, that's odd.*

But when patients started coming in on the Fourth of July week, Meyer and his colleagues could no longer avoid making the connection. On Tuesday, July 2, Meyer was doing his rounds in the ICU when D'Andrea brought him a *third* teenage patient with the same pneumonia-like symptoms. D'Andrea was on call, as she was that entire holiday week, along with a pediatric pulmonary fellow named Brian Carroll, and the patient's arrival—while the second case was still in the hospital being treated—was unnerving. *We're in the middle of summer, this is not the time for pneumonias,* D'Andrea thought.

The third patient's chest X-ray looked similar to the others—like a significant pneumonia affecting both sides of the lungs, along with wheezing, weight loss, and gastrointestinal issues. She initially decided to send the third patient to the OR for a bronchoscopy, in which a thin tube is inserted down the airways to allow for closer inspection and to obtain a fluid sample. If this was pneumonia, there should have been thick mucus and puss in the airways. But there wasn't. Rather, what D'Andrea saw was that the airways looked red and irritated, and they were marked by little brown spots that looked like burns, like from a fire or from some chemicals.

But that wasn't all, she told Meyer. Later that same day, on July 2, yet another teen had shown up. Carroll, the fellow who'd been doing the initial consults of the patients, started recounting the details of the latest patient to D'Andrea.

"This is a teenager, who is having trouble breathing, and who . . ."

D'Andrea stopped him. "Why are you repeating the same thing?" she asked, puzzled.

"Well, no," Carroll replied. "This is *another* patient who has the exact same thing." The fourth patient was in critical condition, so D'Andrea brought the patient to Meyer while letting him know that the third was in the OR, undergoing a bronchoscopy.

Three days later, the day after Fourth of July, a fifth teen showed up, with the same symptoms.

"This is not infectious," D'Andrea said to Meyer.

"No kidding," he replied. "It's gotta be something else."

By the end of the long Fourth of July weekend, now with a cluster of five teenage patients with bilateral lung injuries, Carroll, the pulmonary fellow, couldn't stop thinking about the patients and their puzzling symptoms. He walked from the hospital across a skyway to the pulmonary offices where his desk was located. As he sat there, he started reviewing the charts of the five patients, looking for any clue that might inform a medical opinion. He began going over their history and physical exams, or H&Ps as they're called, which are essentially the beginning of a patient's story that details why they showed up to the hospital, their symptoms, their medical history, as well as social history. For years doctors had asked their teenage patients whether they smoked cigarettes. Only recently, with the emergence of e-cigarettes, had they started asking a new question: "Do you have a history of vaping?"

As Carroll began putting together a Word document with the key pieces of information for each patient, it just popped out at him.

They all reported vaping.

AT AROUND THE EXACT same time, just about forty miles south of Children's Wisconsin hospital, twenty-year-old Tyler Huffhines was busy cranking out vape pods from a lovely brick condo in the new Bristol Bay housing subdivision, on the outskirts of Bristol, Wisconsin.

The condo was situated on a plot of land with expansive green lawns and was located just down the road from the Kenosha County shooting range and the Mars Cheese Castle, a tourist destination off the side of Interstate 94 that sold bratwurst and beer and beef jerky and more. About a year earlier, Tyler had graduated from Westosha Central High School, where he was an MVP football player for the school's Falcons. He'd signed a letter of intent to play football for Lakeland University, a private liberal arts school affiliated with the United Church of Christ, just north of Milwaukee. But he'd gotten sidetracked. Around the beginning of 2018, Tyler, a serial entrepreneur, had turned his business selling random items, including used cars and collectors' Air Jordans, into an entirely different sort of venture— selling vape pods filled with tetrahydrocannabinol liquids.

A swift-moving and profitable black market for these THC-laced products, which were illegal in Wisconsin, had popped up alongside e-cigarettes. While nicotine vape pens and products like Juul were growing in popularity, so were their THC counterparts that were being sold on the street, at music festivals, on Instagram, over Snapchat, and in a rainbow of flavors—gummy bear, sour watermelon, vanilla wafer, and more.

Tyler didn't live at the condo in Bristol Bay. He actually lived in a neighboring town with his mother, and only used the condo as a makeshift vape pod factory with people he hired to hand-fill the cartridges, clocking in and out on a timesheet, and earning 30 cents for each one. Inside the condo, thousands of the THC cartridges littered the place and were stuffed in large boxes, garbage cans, anything big enough to contain his increasingly large stash. There were tote bags filled with marijuana buds, jars filled with a honey-sticky liquid, and stacks of money on the counter. Tyler had buzzed blond hair, sharp blue eyes, and a wide, youthful smile, features that easily could have depicted a college-going, football-playing version of himself. Now, he drove a white BMW and carried a Springfield XD semiautomatic pistol at all times.

AS THE DOCTORS IN Milwaukee were in triage mode, so was Kevin Burns in San Francisco. The furor over kids using his company's product had grown to a fever pitch. And the problem wasn't limited to kids. Data from Wells Fargo showed that upward of 20 percent of Juul's users were new to the nicotine category, a figure that was likely an understatement. The once avoidable was becoming more unavoidable by the day: The product wasn't only attracting adult smokers looking to switch from combustible cigarettes. It was enticing kids, young adults, and adults who'd never smoked but who nevertheless began using Juul, thereby adopting a brand-new nicotine addiction. In the eye of public-health experts, teen nicotine use was bad. But so was the initiation of anybody into the nicotine category who hadn't been there before.

On July 15, CNBC aired a special documentary about Juul and vaping. In it, reporter Carl Quintanilla interviewed Burns inside one of Juul's pod-filling factories in Wisconsin, the first time the company had allowed television cameras inside. Burns wore a hairnet and safety glasses and a bright orange jumpsuit over his blue jeans, as he showed Quintanilla around the facility, past huge machines injecting nicotine liquid into the tiny pods, boxes of Juul zipping over a conveyor belt, massive hoppers overflowing with the colorful plastic pods.

"If we did this tour today with a parent of a teen who had been using or who had been addicted, how would you sort of defend all this, all this scale, all this production, all this growth?" Quintanilla asked Burns, who nervously wrung his hands. His answer: "First of all, I would tell them that I'm sorry that their child is using the product. It's not intended for them. I hope there was nothing that we did that made it appealing to them. As a parent of a sixteen-year-old, I'm sorry for them and I have empathy for them in terms of what—the challenges they're going through."

The answer was not only surprising for its mea culpa manner amid what was still a worsening problem, but it was a reminder of the deeper concerns that had been plaguing Juul since its inception, and that had grown increasingly worrisome over time. Tensions between executives grew over how little the company had been doing to rigorously analyze whether its ingredients contained potentially harmful constituents. There were concerns about whether traces of the heavy metal chromium detected in Juul's vapor, which were a potential by-product of the nichrome heating element in the Juul pod, were high enough to warrant concern.

It was within that context and swirling concern that Quintanilla asked Burns whether he was concerned about risks of chronic Juuling— a question whose answer would hit too close to home just as the public was starting to grow increasingly uneasy about the chemistry experiments being done on America's lungs.

"Frankly, we don't know today," Burns said. "We have not done the long-term longitudinal clinical testing that we need to do."

ALMOST IMMEDIATELY, D'ANDREA INFORMED Meyer about the apparent vaping commonality among the patients. It wasn't a conclusive determination, but it was the only thing that seemed to connect them all. Another bothersome fact was that more than one of the patients had attended Summerfest. Was there a batch of poisoned vapes circulating at the music festival? The two immediately reached out to the chief medical officer of Children's Wisconsin, a physician named Michael Gutzeit.

"Something's going on," D'Andrea told Gutzeit. "We've now had five of these kids and I don't know who we call. I don't know if we need to call the health department or the police."

Did this cluster of kids have some sort of novel infectious disease? Had they been poisoned by a bad batch of e-liquid? Or could it be that the very act of vaping was so injurious to the lungs that it was causing this?

Like others, Gutzeit had heard about Juul and vaping largely through an informal network of parents who'd encountered it firsthand with either their own children or their children's peer groups. The tobacco control community in the Milwaukee area had also become more attuned to the issue as alarm grew that the decades of success in reducing youth tobacco use seemed to be evaporating before their eyes as their children took up vaping in droves. Gutzeit had seen the charts showing the line for youth tobacco use sloping down, juxtaposed with the line for youth vaping sloping up in a hockey-stick fashion. That image remained emblazoned in his mind. As he quickly did his own internal research and got up to speed on all the patients, he concluded they had no choice but to alert the public. This was a potential public-health emergency.

When Gutzeit reached the Wisconsin Department of Health Services, he got Jonathan Meiman, the state's chief medical officer, on the phone. Gutzeit explained everything, about the teens showing up gasping for air. About their lungs so damaged they had to be put on ventilators. About the vaping connection.

Meiman couldn't believe it. Wisconsin had already been battling back-to-back public-health emergencies. Barely a year ago dozens of people had shown up at area hospitals with bleeding stomachs. It took only a matter of weeks for the state's health department to figure out it was a batch of K2, or spice, that had been laced with rat poison. Before that, the state had been struggling for years to get a handle on the spiraling opioid addiction crisis, which hit Wisconsin particularly hard. Meiman was no stranger to public-health emergencies, having responded to the Ebola outbreak in Sierra Leone and treated MERS patients in Saudi Arabia. He saw firsthand the heartbreaking toll of opioid addiction. But what he was hearing from Gutzeit was uniquely upsetting. Kids were showing up with what looked like smokers' lungs after a lifetime of smoking. He offered any help the Children's Wisconsin doctors needed.

On July 25, Gutzeit and Amos stood before a podium inside the hospital, with news reporters and television cameras. It had not been an easy decision for Gutzeit to call a press conference. Doctors are accustomed to dealing with emergencies all the time, and keeping their composure through it all. They're not prone to panic. But there was clearly something bigger happening in their community. Even worse, it appeared to be squarely hitting children.

"We're here today to warn you about what we believe is a significant health issue," Gutzeit said. "We've had eight teenagers who have been hospitalized at Children's with severe lung damage in a short period of time and all have had the common thread of vaping. We're working with the Wisconsin Department of Health Services to better understand what the cause of this is and what the potential long-term effects on these teenagers might be."

The same day, the Wisconsin health department put out a warning letter to clinicians: "Severe Pulmonary Disease Among Adolescents Who Reported Vaping," it said, requesting that they "remain alert for potential cases among persons presenting with progressive respiratory symptoms who report a history of inhalation drug use, particularly vaping." They also asked that physicians report any such cases to the department of health.

Things cascaded from there, and fast. Meiman reached out to the CDC and shared everything. Then, on July 31, Meiman received a call from a physician in the state of Illinois who'd seen the letter and was seeking guidance on a clinically ill patient they'd been treating.

Meanwhile, Brian King, the deputy director at the CDC's Office on Smoking and Health, was one of the first people brought into discussions about the lung illnesses. By the time he and his colleagues learned that the lung injuries were being reported in more than one state, the agency mobilized a multidisciplinary team of subject matter experts and sent an epidemiologic assistance field team to Wisconsin and Illinois. The CDC also began working with the FDA to send agents into the field to help with the collection of product samples, such as vape pens or Juul pods or THC cartridges, from critically ill patients. Those samples were in turn sent to the FDA's Forensic Chemistry Center in Cincinnati, Ohio, to screen for potential toxicants or identify commonalities to narrow down the nature of investigation.

Then on August 23, the state of Illinois reported the death of an adult who'd had a vaping-related lung injury. It was the nation's first vaping-related death. That day, the CDC also announced that there were now nearly two hundred cases of potential vaping-related lung injury in twenty-two states. For the first time, there was what seemed like a nationwide panic. Vaping was causing death and sick kids. And unfortunately for Juul, Juuling had become shorthand for vaping.

20

THE BELLAGIO

The question is not merely whether or not to surrender, but on what political conditions that surrender is to be based.
—PAUL KECSKEMETI, *STRATEGIC SURRENDER: THE POLITICS OF VICTORY AND DEFEAT*

When a San Francisco nonprofit announced in July 2019 that it had collected more than twenty thousand signatures to ensure its measure "An Act to Prevent Youth Use of Vapor Products" would appear on the ballot in November, one could be forgiven for thinking that the tobacco-control community would celebrate. Preventing youth from using vapor products like Juul was what Dennis Herrera and Shamann Walton and a bevy of San Francisco anti-tobacco advocates had been fighting for. But they weren't celebrating, because the measure was actually sponsored by a nonprofit created and funded by Juul.

A month after the city of San Francisco had passed Herrera's law effectively banning all e-cigarettes from being sold in the city, Juul (and by default its major investor, Altria) was fighting back. In the eyes of the city's graying tobacco-prevention advocates, this was just the latest iteration of the same fight they'd been at for decades. But there was something about Juul's tactics that seemed *uniquely* disturbing. The company not only named the ballot measure "An Act to Prevent Youth Use of Vapor Products," but it created and funded the Coalition for Reasonable Vaping Regulation, and plastered the city with TV ads and billboards and door hangers that advocated messages like "Stop Youth Vaping" and "Let's Create the Strictest Regulations in the Nation." Contrary to the measure's proposed name, it was actually designed to *overturn* the citywide ban on e-cigarettes that had passed just weeks earlier. In the annals of *Alice in Wonderland* moments attributable to tobacco companies, this one stood out.

The city had seen big money campaigns before, from the battle against Airbnb and Big Soda and Big Oil, but Juul's strategy was unprecedented in its size and tenor. With enough signatures collected to put the measure on the ballot, Juul began spending money "like a drunken sailor," as the *SF Weekly* put it. The company hired Tony Fabrizio, a veteran GOP strategist who was Trump's pollster during the 2016 presidential campaign and a business associate of Paul Manafort. It also snapped up nearly every political strategist in town, like "pieces of See's Candy," *SF Weekly* said, including former dueling campaign advisers and consultants from both sides of the aisle, in an effort to lock up political talent and flood the city with money and influence. One person described it as Juul unleashing on San Francisco a "political den of lions."

If it seemed excessive for a battle in a single city, it was because Juul understood the stakes. If the San Francisco ban was upheld, it could tip off a domino effect across the United States, just like what happened back in the '70s and '80s as the anti-smoking movement took root in the same city before cascading across the U.S. and fundamentally shifting the balance of power against Big Tobacco. For tobacco policy, it's long been understood: What happens in California, so goes the nation. The company was already under attack from many sides. It couldn't afford to have its markets choked off, one by one, by more cities and states across the country. For the ever-hardening anti-Juul army, that was exactly the point.

———

THE FLUSH FEELING IN the wake of the Altria deal pervaded Juul, despite the growing health scare and the backlash from federal regulators. Burns was still a freightliner going at full speed. He remained laser-focused on executing his plan to turn Juul into a multinational company rivaling the world's best consumer products brands. For the past year or more, executives had boasted how Juul could someday be not just a $38 billion company, but a *$100 billion* company, or even bigger. They included slides in internal corporate presentations suggesting that, on the current sales trajectory, five years from now Juul could be more valuable than Apple. Sure, the company was coming under a lot of heat, but Burns was of the mindset, shared by many others at Juul, that the best was still yet to come.

By the end of 2019, Juul's annual revenue had more than doubled the previous year's to just over $2 billion—and that was despite Burns pulling the most popular flavors off the market, shuttering its social media accounts, and taking other steps to slow its raging popularity among teens. The company mushroomed to more than three thousand employees around the world. It had barreled into new international markets like a real-life game of Risk, adding Spain, South Korea, the Philippines, and Indonesia to its growing global empire. Bowen and Monsees were jet-setting around the world for these launches, often holding press conferences in the new markets, and giving talks onstage to new employees.

The company's European executives cut the ribbon on a "Global Business Center" in Gdańsk, Poland. They feted employees with glasses of champagne and Juul-emblazoned balloons when they moved into a new headquarters in a tony London neighborhood with a rooftop deck overlooking the city. They hired a fancy architectural firm to redesign their Zurich offices. In the spring of 2019, more than seven hundred Juul Labs employees from around the world descended on Berlin for a lavish three-day party to celebrate the launch of the product. At the capstone "Think Big Berlin" event, held beneath hanging chandeliers in a ballroom at the Ritz-Carlton, special guest Arnold Schwarzenegger gave a rousing speech as tuxedoed waiters passed glasses of champagne. With seven nationalities in attendance, complete with simultaneous translation as needed, the three-day party was a showcase of just how global the San Francisco start-up had become.

The ribbon cuttings were in stark contrast to what was happening back home in the United States. On July 25, 2019, Monsees was called to testify before Congress, where he was subjected to a barrage of tough questions from hostile lawmakers.

Throughout 2019 the price of Juul shares on the privately traded market only went north, reaching close to $300 per share, more than double what Altria had paid just a few months earlier. Nothing was going to stop Burns. He acknowledged on *CBS This Morning* in an August 28 on-camera interview that the lung injuries were "worrisome" and he even urged nonsmokers in no uncertain terms not to use his product: "Don't vape. Don't use Juul," he said. "Don't start using nicotine if you don't have a preexisting relationship with nicotine. Don't use the product. You're not our target consumer." Still, he maintained that his company had no intention of slowing or stopping production as the CDC scrambled to pinpoint what exactly was causing the lung illnesses.

"If there was any indication that there was an adverse health condition related to our product, I think we'd take very swift action associated with it," Burns told Tony Dokoupil in the CBS interview.

"So, you feel confident enough to keep selling despite these reports? That Juul is not contributing to these, more than a hundred now, dozens of cases?" Dokoupil followed up.

"At this point," Burns said. "Until we see some facts . . . yes we do."

But the breakneck pace was starting to catch up with Burns. If the company was growing fast before the Altria deal, it had been kicked into warp speed after. The reality of operating in Silicon Valley means that when a company gets pegged with a unicorn-level valuation, the people running the company are under unicorn-level pressure to achieve financial metrics to justify that valuation. To fuel the growth and beat expectations, Burns was shoveling as much money as possible into the firebox as fast as possible.

While Burns was already under heat from the board for his flip attitude toward Willard during their youth prevention meeting, people inside Juul started questioning what seemed not only like unchecked spending but sheer recklessness. As Juul rushed into new markets, executives expedited everything from merchandise to machinery to routine contracts, which wound up costing the company double or triple for everything. They spent millions on several pieces of manufacturing equipment intended to transform the supply chain in Europe, but which were never put into production. They tested production of a line of multicolored Juul devices that never saw the light of day. They held executive retreats at the Ritz overlooking the Pacific Ocean. What should have cost $10,000 cost $30,000. What should have cost $100,000 cost $300,000. "That was just the attitude," said one employee. "It was like 'Oh, can it be done in a day? Well, yes, but it's going to cost a lot. I don't care.' . . . We were spending so much fucking money on stupid shit."

EVER SINCE THE OLD Italian deli on California Street had closed down about two years earlier, the corner storefront in the upscale Laurel Village neighborhood had sat vacant with a FOR LEASE sign in its window. The crimson awning with the deli's name, A. G. Ferrari, still adorned the brick building, as did cursive script etched in the window that said SINCE 1919.

Christine Chessen, a San Francisco mom, thought the location was perfect for her needs. It was late August and she was still fuming after learning that Juul had been successful in getting its measure certified to appear on the ballot. She was in the midst of doing grassroots work to galvanize the support of other parents and San Francisco residents who would vote down Juul's measure on November 5. The former deli was about to become their war room.

A few months earlier, Chessen had cold-called Meredith Berkman, the cofounder of the New York–based Parents Against Vaping e-cigarettes, or PAVe, and eventually became the point person for the group in San Francisco. The two women had been swapping stories about their kids and sharing information about how best to fight Juul, with Berkman occasionally flying back and forth between Manhattan and San Francisco to help organize the grassroots effort. They strategized with Louise Renne, the former city attorney who'd battled Big Tobacco in the early days before Herrera took over the job. Renne put the two women in touch with a political consultant who in turn suggested they'd have to raise nearly $4 million to even stand a chance against Juul.

That was before the Campaign for Tobacco-Free Kids got involved. The group had grown worried that if Juul's measure passed, it would potentially result in the repeal of an important flavored tobacco ban that the organization had worked hard to see enacted in the city the year before. Annie Tegen, the campaign's western regional director, helped reinstate the committee that backed the flavor ban a year earlier, called SF Kids Vs. Big Tobacco, and set out to build a coalition, of which Chessen and Berkman were a part.

It didn't take long for funding to start rolling in, including from the American Heart Association and the Kaiser Foundation. Christine and Kevin Chessen each donated around $25,000, as did the cofounder of The Gap and prominent San Francisco resident Doris Fisher, and Pete Briger. One of the earliest large donations came from the legendary Silicon Valley venture capitalist Arthur Rock, who had learned about Juul in part because of his deep involvement and financial backing of charter schools across the United States. Juul had flooded those schools too. "I consider Juul immoral," Rock said.

By early September, the Chessens had rented out the deli to serve as a canvassing office for the "No on C" campaign. They hired a cleaning crew to come sweep out the cobwebs, draped a cloth over the meat slicer that had been left behind, and taped campaign literature to the deli case that was once used to keep the frozen lasagnas they'd buy for school potlucks. A chalkboard still displayed the handwritten A. G. Ferrari menu. A left-behind wooden table was repurposed for volunteers to gather around when they came in on weekends to help nail together signs and organize door hangers, like the one that said "Don't be fooled by Juul. Vote NO on Prop C."

Soon, the "No on C" coalition grew to include parents across the wealthiest enclaves of San Francisco whose own children were addicted to Juul, along with other public-health groups and prominent San Franciscans. Stan Glantz, the UCSF professor and anti-tobacco instigator from the old days joined the coalition. Jim Steyer's organization, Common Sense Media, spearheaded key on-the-ground support and backing.

By then Juul was blanketing San Francisco with "Yes on C" billboards, blitzing campaign text messages to residents' cellphones, and releasing an army of canvassers onto the streets to knock on doors and hand out flyers that said, "Stop Youth Vaping" and "Keep Vaping an Option for Adults." The Juul campaign had enlisted a prominent campaign consulting firm called Long Ying International, Inc., to carry out the day-to-day affairs of the campaign. The firm was run by David Ho, a lobbyist and consultant with deep political ties in San Francisco's Chinatown. Ho oversaw some 450 workers, who were paid $25 an hour to make phone calls and knock on doors. The pro-Juul operation was staged out of two offices in the city, one in a WeWork building off Market Street and the other across town, just down the street from their "No on C" rivals working out of the deli. Sometimes the two camps would run into each other on the street and would hang a "No" door hanger on top of a "Yes" one, and vice versa.

The "No on C" camp had passion, and at times it got personal. At one point, after a legal battle between the city and Juul over specifics of the ballot language, city attorney Dennis Herrera lashed out. "I wonder if it ever crosses Kevin Burns' mind that his child could be the one hooked up to machines in a hospital room struggling to breathe because of vaping," he said in a press release.

The "Yes on C" camp had money. Even though internal polling was showing that voters would likely vote against the measure, Juul was still wildly outspending its rivals. Then, on September 10, the game changed when former New York City mayor Michael Bloomberg joined in.

New York City under Mayor Bloomberg, who served from 2002 to 2013, had become one of the most progressive large cities in the fight against tobacco. In 2002, Bloomberg signed a law banning smoking in restaurants and bars, and then a decade later the prohibitions were extended to outdoor areas like beaches and parks. In 2013, New York became the first large city to require customers to be twenty-one years old to purchase tobacco products. One of the last things Bloomberg did as mayor was to extend the city's existing public smoking bans to include e-cigarettes.

Given that Juul had launched its ill-fated billboard ad campaign in Times Square so many years earlier, there was a twist of irony that Bloomberg himself was now coming out of his stomping grounds to haunt them. For the past several weeks Bloomberg's top aides had been in regular contact with people on the ground in San Francisco working to stop Prop C. They were incensed that Juul's ballot measure would have potentially overturned the flavor ban, which Bloomberg—a fierce and growing force in the anti-tobacco movement—had spent more than $2 million to protect. But they were also worried that the kind of moratorium that San Francisco had enacted risked going too far and turning off voters who might have viewed it as governmental overreach.

Some of the influential backers of the "No on C" campaign began personally pressing for Bloomberg to join the cause. "We need you," one of them told Bloomberg's top aides. "You guys are the most important funders of this. We need to beat them in San Francisco. If we win here, we'll win everywhere."

For Bloomberg, the founder of one of the world's largest financial data firms, data reigned supreme. Eventually, New York City's ex-mayor had seen enough. Not only did the data continue to show that Juul's product was imperiling decades of anti-smoking progress made in the United States—including a 35 percent reduction in smoking rates in New York City that had followed after his smoking ban—but the polling data was becoming clearer by the day. As the number of vaping illnesses ticked higher, so, it seemed, did the polls in favor of stopping Juul's ballot initiative. This was not only a cause that Bloomberg personally believed in but one that he became confident would prevail. Plus, there was already an immense grassroots operation on the ground. Ultimately, the former New York City mayor concluded: "We can't afford to let Juul win." He committed to going big to stop Juul. By the end, Bloomberg spent more than $7 million to back the "No on Prop C" campaign.

That was a lot of money, even for a billionaire. But Juul, to the astonishment of even seasoned San Francisco politicos, was spending even more. By the end of the campaign, Juul had spent nearly $20 million to support Prop C. If they'd been spending like drunken sailors before, now it was like the entire navy had gotten shitfaced.

WHEN KEVIN BURNS TOOK the stage in front of the several-hundred-strong Juul sales force in the ornate ballroom of the Bellagio, underneath chandeliers hanging from a crown-molded ceiling, he appeared in his trademark tracksuit garb, this one in the blue and yellow of the Golden State Warriors. While his attire wasn't necessarily unusual for Burns, it was certainly a contrast to the other executives who showed up in sharp suit jackets. His vibe, as one person described it, was "DGAF"—*don't give a fuck*.

It's of course not uncommon for companies to have over-the-top annual retreats to celebrate the hard work of their sales teams. But it seemed like a particularly odd time for Juul to be celebrating anything. By the time the event kicked off on Monday, September 9, the company was roundly under siege. Its hometown was trying to kick it out. Multiple state attorneys general were investigating the company for its marketing practices. Hundreds of lawsuits brought by trial lawyers on behalf of Juul-addicted teens alleged everything from improperly marketing the product to kids, to selling a product that caused lung injuries, to deceptively labeling the nicotine content of the product. Multiple federal agencies were conducting their own investigations, including at the FDA, the Federal Trade Commission, and the Securities and Exchange Commission. Federal prosecutors in the Northern District of California had started a criminal probe that touched on marketing strategies and Juul executives' representations to federal officers. On top of that, the number of vaping-related lung injuries was climbing every day, had already affected nearly five hundred people, and resulted in five deaths. Since the CDC had not yet reached any conclusive determination pointing to the cause, the agency warned people to simply stop using e-cigarettes.

None of that stopped Burns from throwing a killer party.

Some of the events were low-key. There were seminars and trainings that touched on the importance of Juul being a good corporate citizen—employing appropriate marketing practices, diversity training, the role of women in leadership positions. There was a youth prevention seminar that featured Ben Jealous, the former president of the NAACP who'd lobbied for Juul in Washington and had temporarily been named the company's "Chief Youth Prevention Officer." Every employee at the seminar received a 122-page book called *Prevention by Design*, which reminded them of Bowen and Monsees's original mission to "improve the lives of the world's one billion adult smokers by eliminating cigarettes," and the need for "Reflecting on our own past" and recognizing "the existential challenge of youth usage." The content had echoes from the days of Philip Morris's penitent past.

During the evenings, employees were treated to live entertainment. At one event, Burns handed out "Golden Juul" trophies (trophies shaped like large golden Juul pods) to top performers. A cocktail reception was held at Spago, the upscale restaurant squished between the Louis Vuitton and Bottega Veneta shops, and overlooking the Bellagio fountains.

The entire affair, which easily cost several million dollars, seemed tone-deaf at best. JUUL LABS signs were plastered throughout the lobby of the Bellagio, making some employees wonder whether it was a good idea to be so flashy. *Maybe Juul should just lay low for a while? Until the heat subsided?*

But the heat was only about to get turned up. On the morning of Wednesday, September 11, just as the Juul employees were waking up, some shaking off hangovers and settling into their morning seminars, they got some startling news. It was just after lunchtime in Washington, D.C., and President Trump was giving a news conference in the Oval Office. He was sitting in front of the fireplace next to his wife,

Melania, who'd tweeted the night before that she was "deeply concerned about the growing epidemic of e-cigarette use in our children."

"We have a problem in our country," Trump said. "It's a new problem. It's a problem nobody really thought about too much a few years
ago, and it's called vaping. And we're going to have to do something
about it." He later mentioned that Melania had grown worried in part
because their son, Barron, was in the exact age demographic that had
been attracted to vaping. "Don't vape," they told Barron at home.

After his remarks, Trump invited Secretary Azar, from Health and
Human Services, to speak. Azar said the agency had gotten an early
look at the latest figures from the National Youth Tobacco Survey—the
same one that had given Gottlieb a near heart attack the year before.
The situation had grown even worse. There were now more than 5.4
million high school and middle school students using e-cigarettes, a 50
percent increase from last year. Nearly 30 percent of high school students in the United States were current users.

"An entire generation of children risk becoming addicted to nicotine because of the attractiveness, appealability, and availability of
these vaping products," Azar said, from the couch next to the president.

Then he dropped the bomb: "With the President's support, the
Food and Drug Administration intends to finalize a guidance document that would commence enforcement to require that all flavors,
other than tobacco flavor, would be removed from the market. This
would include mint and menthol flavoring, as well as candy flavors,
bubblegum flavor, fruit flavor, alcohol flavor. You get the drift."

Trump, a business-friendly, tobacco-friendly Republican, was taking what appeared to be the most aggressive stance any president had
ever taken against e-cigarette companies. His FDA was going to remove all flavored products from the market.

The announcement caught everybody by surprise. "Oh shit," said
one Juul employee sitting in the Bellagio ballroom seminar as he got a
text message with the news. While Burns had pulled its fruit and dessert flavors from the retail stores almost a year earlier, the company
had continued selling them online and they remained a big driver of

sales. Trump's threat would have entailed removing all flavors, including the popular mint and menthol, from the full stream of commerce. This was some of the worst possible news any sales force could hear— that they'd no longer be able to sell the vast majority of their product line. Juul was thrust into a heightened crisis.

Amid the opulence of Vegas, it was the quietus for Burns.

ON SEPTEMBER 12, LOGAN Krahn started feeling really ill. The sixteen-year-old was a sophomore at Fort Atkinson High School in Fort Atkinson, Wisconsin, about an hour west of Milwaukee, ground zero of the lung-injury crisis. Krahn was a healthy teenage boy who enjoyed fishing for walleye in French Lake, playing *Call of Duty* with his friends, and shooting hoops, a sport he'd played since he was young. About a year earlier, he was at a friend's house when somebody offered him a Juul. He tried the mango flavor and loved it. He was hooked almost right away. Never a smoker, he believed that Juuling was, if not harmless, at least safer than cigarettes.

Shortly after that gathering, he obtained his own Juul pods, after asking somebody older to buy him a device and some pods. He started off vaping just one pod a week. Then it increased. He'd rotate between mango and mint, and within a few months he was blowing through a four-pod package of Juuls almost every other day. Eventually he started using a non-Juul vape pen too, which he'd load with a THC-laced liquid.

Krahn's mother, Rebecca, was a single mom raising four boys, and a certified nursing assistant at a home for Alzheimer's patients. She had been born and raised in Fort Atkinson, a town of just twelve thousand people, as had all her children. Logan was her oldest child and Rebecca looked to him as a rock in the family. She originally had no idea about her son's new addiction. Partly she was too busy working long hours at her job while doing her best to keep on top of her children. But over the past several months she noticed that Logan's behavior had changed. He'd stopped playing basketball as much and was moodier than normal. Eventually she started finding little green and orange plastic caps lying around the house.

"What is this?" she wondered. She picked up the little plastic things and threw them in the trash.

Eventually she wised up to the little colorful caps and learned about his vaping habit. She didn't like it, but there was only so much she could do. She had no idea just how hooked her son had become until the summer of 2019. At one point, Logan had run out of Juul pods, and also out of money. So he asked his mom if she would buy some for him. Rebecca was floored. She had no idea that Logan's casual vaping habit had turned him into a fiend. And she also didn't know that he'd begun vaping THC as well. "Absolutely not!" she cried, exasperated.

More red flags emerged. Logan had started losing weight, coughing, and having bouts of diarrhea. In recent days he'd been throwing up. Rebecca was worried. Logan was one of those kids who never got sick. That evening, she took him to the emergency room at the local Fort Atkinson hospital. Doctors thought his appendix was rupturing, so they removed his appendix and sent him home not long after. But when he got home, he continued vomiting, so on September 15, Rebecca brought him straight back to the hospital. Doctors ran some tests, concluded that he was dehydrated, and gave him medication for nausea. Rebecca had a bad feeling that it was something worse. Logan had developed a fever and she noticed that her son's breathing had become labored. She requested that he be seen by a new doctor, who ended up listening to his lungs and taking a chest X-ray. The results were alarming. His lungs were filled with fluid, as if he had severe pneumonia.

By that afternoon, Logan was in respiratory distress, and his condition was deteriorating. The doctor called over to the nearest pediatric hospital, American Family Children's Hospital at the University of Wisconsin–Madison, about forty miles away. Specialists there were well aware of the vaping injuries unfolding across the country. Logan displayed all the symptoms of it, they said. If the boy wasn't immediately transferred to the pediatric ICU, he could die. So, sixteen-year-old Logan was wheeled into an ambulance and whisked off into the dusk.

When Logan arrived at the pediatric hospital, the ICU staff immediately put him on a breathing machine and monitored him overnight. The next morning, he saw Vivek Balasubramanian, a pediatric pulmonologist, who said if Logan's condition didn't improve he'd need to be intubated and placed on a ventilator. Rebecca's first question to him was: "Is my son going to make it?" His response was sobering: "I'll tell you in twenty-four hours."

UNBEKNOWNST TO TYLER HUFFHINES, the vape-pod bootlegger outside of Milwaukee, he and his apartment had been under surveillance by area police starting in July 2019, and a confidential informant had been feeding information to law enforcement. Tyler, the informant told the cops, was the head of a drug-dealing operation, with the help of his brother Jacob, that was churning out THC-laced vape pods from his condo. The informant showed the cops Tyler's Snapchat account, which appeared to substantiate the tip. There were photos and videos showing large boxes piled in a garage and a walk-in closet stuffed with what appeared to be thousands of pods, tote bags filled with marijuana buds, and stacks of money.

The confidential informant then tipped off police that Tyler would be flying to California soon to procure a bulk order of jars filled with pure cannabis oil. Sure enough, on August 28, 2019, the detective was able to view Snapchat videos that Tyler posted of himself sitting in first class on an airplane and footage of him in California. He'd taken $300,000 in cash to buy THC oil. Not long after, Tyler was back home filling up to five thousand pods every day with the golden oil.

On September 5, the Kenosha Police raided Tyler's condo, which turned up a loaded .12-gauge shotgun, bags of cocaine, nearly twenty pounds of marijuana, prescription drugs, and money-counting machines. They also found what appeared to be an industrial-grade vape pod operation, with nearly one hundred thousand empty plastic pods, thirty-one thousand filled THC pods, and fifty-seven mason jars filled with THC oil, which were worth $6,000 each. The THC pods were packaged in colorful boxes and came in candy flavors—grape, sour patch, peaches and cream, and bubble gum. The police valued the entire operation at nearly half a million dollars.

Tyler and Jacob were arrested. When the police met with Tyler, they asked him why he had started this operation. He told them that it was simple: There was a demand for the THC vape pods and he seized on a business opportunity. He at first sold a hundred THC pods for $15 apiece, netting up to $800 of pure profit, after paying workers he hired 30 cents per pod to fill them. After demand soared, he increased his minimum sale to five hundred pods. "You invest more, you make more," he told police detectives. "No risk, no reward."

After the bust, *The New York Times* asked, were the Huffhines brothers the "Walter Whites of THC oils"? More importantly, did their operation have something to do with the outbreak of lung injuries across Wisconsin? And, god forbid, across the nation?

BY THE MIDDLE OF September, the federal government was kicking its investigation into high gear, as it scrambled to find out why people were being hospitalized and sometimes dying after vaping. On the sixteenth, the CDC activated its Emergency Operations Center, the agency's way of bringing together the CDC's top experts, health communicators, clinicians, and technology into a single location to ensure a rapid and coordinated response to public-health emergencies. By then there were more than five hundred cases of vaping-related lung injuries, and seven deaths, across thirty-eight states, and yet still nobody knew what was causing it.

"I want to stress that we at CDC are very concerned about the occurrence of life-threatening illness in otherwise healthy young people reported from around the country," said Anne Schuchat, the agency's principal deputy director, who'd taken to giving weekly press briefings on the matter as a sense of urgency and fear rippled across the nation. "This is a complex investigation. It spans many states, involves hundreds of cases, and a wide variety of substances and products."

Mitch Zeller, the man who'd for so long pushed for e-cigarettes as a solution to the nation's smoking epidemic, now awkwardly found himself embroiled in the investigation. His comprehensive nicotine policy hadn't just resulted in a new youth nicotine epidemic. Now, it was being dragged into a public-health emergency that was killing people.

"We are leaving no stone unturned in following all potential leads regarding any particular product, constituent or compound that may be at issue," Zeller said on the press briefing call.

At the time, the CDC had already activated another Emergency Operations Center to respond to an outbreak of Ebola in the Democratic Republic of Congo, which at the time was the second-largest outbreak ever recorded. As a result, the Emergency Operations Center to triage the unfolding vaping-related crisis was set up at the agency's secondary campus in Atlanta, in the building that housed its experts in noncommunicable diseases, such as chronic disease injury, birth defects, and environmental health.

The CDC's Brian King was thrust into the center of the investigation. He helped set up command in several rooms across multiple floors, organized by proximity to the experts, whether it was epidemiology surveillance, laboratory work, or communications. Over the next several months the group would eventually swell to four hundred people and would hold multiple briefings every day so that updates, new findings, or breakthroughs could be reported in a relatively uniform fashion. King's office was in the neighboring building, so every day he found himself running back and forth between the two, riding up and down elevators.

At the same time, the FDA was a key partner. The agency that was responsible for containing and responding to food-borne illness outbreaks and adverse drug reactions had long wrestled with the exceedingly difficult task of trying to pinpoint in serpentine global supply chains the "bad" ingredient responsible for causing Americans to fall ill, whether it was tracing E. coli to a worker in an Iowa meatpacking plant, or Salmonella on a spinach farm in California's Central Valley, or deadly blood thinners to a pig intestine factory in China. The vaping-related lung injuries posed a similar problem. While there were typically only a handful of ingredients in store-bought nicotine products, the ingredients originated from all over the world, and the flavorings often had dozens of "sub-flavors" with their own ingredient supply chain.

Early research from across the United States, both inside the federal government and also in state labs, was showing that the majority of lung-injury patients had been using products containing THC. That made the task of tracing the ingredients even harder, since most of those products were being sold illegally because of laws prohibiting the sale of marijuana in most states. Many of the THC-containing products were potentially being sourced from the street, which came from black-market operations like the one being run out of Tyler Huffhines's condo.

As the FDA continued analyzing product samples, they tested for everything, including heavy metals, pesticides, and toxins. Some laboratories had already begun showing that many of the THC products contained thickening agents, including a popular one called Honey Cut that was made of vitamin E acetate. The golden, syrupy oil, which was typically used in skin creams or shampoos, was increasingly being used to thicken the THC liquid in vape cartridges. It could also be used to "cut" the THC liquid to make it go further and allow more profit per cartridge.

In early September, the New York State Department of Health reported that its own testing showed the presence of vitamin E acetate in nearly all of the products tested that were submitted by patients, and that it was issuing subpoenas to three manufacturers of the product, including the Santa Monica–based Honey Cut. The investigation was starting to produce answers, even as teenagers continued to fall severely ill.

THE FIRST THING THAT struck Vivek Balasubramanian about his patient Logan Krahn wasn't necessarily that the boy was having trouble breathing. As a pediatric pulmonologist with a specialty in treating chronic lung disease in children as young as newborns, he was used to seeing that. There was something about Logan's disposition that struck him as curious. He was edgy and the nurses had discussed potentially having to sedate him to keep his oxygen mask on.

As Balasubramanian examined his intake, he was alarmed by how much Logan had reported Juuling—around two pods every day. He did the calculation for the amount of nicotine in each pod. *That's an immense of amount of nicotine that he was using on a daily basis,* he realized. Logan was having nicotine withdrawals. So, Balasubramanian did something that he rarely had to do before: He put the teenager on nicotine replacement therapy. After being on the patch for about six hours, Logan finally calmed down, and that, combined with steroid treatment, helped him take a turn for the better.

Over the next two weeks or so that Logan was in the hospital, he tried to complete as much schoolwork as he could while recovering. He made as many phone calls as he could to his friends to warn them about vaping, urging them to stop. His mom, Rebecca, cut back her hours at work to be with Logan as much as possible, and drove to the hospital every night to stay with him. She did everything to keep life as normal as possible for him. When his younger twin siblings celebrated their birthday, she brought them to the hospital, along with a birthday cake and homemade chicken alfredo. They sang "Happy Birthday."

Balasubramanian and other doctors from University of Wisconsin Health gave a press conference to raise awareness about the problem—they'd seen now almost a dozen teens like Logan. They asked Logan to make a statement, which he agreed to do. On the day of the event at the hospital, they blew up photos of a normal lung and what they called a "vaping lung." Balasubramanian spoke about the problem of nicotine addiction and the danger of vaping. When it was Logan's time to speak, he struggled to carry his wiry frame up to the microphone, with his mom standing next to him. He held in his hand the statement that he'd written. He stood at a podium in front of a stone hearth in the hospital, with television cameras capturing his pale face offset by his shoulder-dusting jet-black hair.

"Good morning," he said, his frail voice raspy and trembling. "My name is Logan Krahn. I am a sixteen-year-old. I am just one of many teenagers that used to Juul. I thought that Juuling was safer than smoking regular cigarettes. I was wrong." He paused as he labored to inhale. "I came very close to dying. And I have suffered lifelong damage to my lungs . . . this experience has changed my life tremendously. If you don't smoke or vape now, please don't start. But if you do, I urge you to stop and get some help immediately. While quitting might seem really difficult, going through this is far worse. Thank you."

While it wasn't possible to pinpoint whether Logan's illness was caused by Juul or the THC vaping products he was also using, it was likely the latter. The evidence would soon become clearer that while Juuling was commonplace, it was likely bootlegged cannabis products that had been the culprit of the lung injuries. Still, it at least wasn't inconceivable that but for Juuling, the boy might never have taken up vaping other substances. Either way, the damage to Juul's reputation had been done—vaping and Juuling had become synonymous in the eye of the public. In fact, the barrage of bad news was stunningly bad for Juul. Just as the public was realizing how widespread youth vaping had become, the sudden rise of the vaping-related lung injuries seemed suspicious. Nobody yet knew that Juul wasn't principally responsible for the lung injuries, so in the mind of the public Juul was not only addicting its kids, but it might also be killing them. Juul's stars were suddenly crossed in a very bad way.

When Logan was discharged in the fall of 2019, he limped out of the hospital wearing a 30-milligram nicotine patch.

JIM STEYER HAD BEEN upping his level of involvement in the "No on Prop C" campaign. He and his brother, Tom, had long had a rule—never get involved in local politics in the city they live in. But ever since he'd talked to his friend Dave Burke, Steyer hadn't been able to let go of the Juul issue. It made him upset. Plus, the company was squarely treading on his territory at Common Sense Media. The nonprofit had a group of more than one million teacher members nationwide who received its curriculum materials pertaining to, among other things, media's effect on child health and manipulative and deceptive marketing online.

For Steyer, Juul was not only creating a public-health crisis among youth, but he also felt it was employing the same kinds of manipulative and deceptive marketing that had long been used to addict kids to other unhealthy products, whether it was soda or sugary cereal or violent videogames or hateful social media platforms. "They were just trying to re-addict America's kids to nicotine," Steyer said about Juul. And the icing on the cake for him was that it was also coming from what he perceived to be an irresponsible firm in Silicon Valley. "What was the motto at Facebook? Move fast and break stuff. That was the great Zuckerberg motto," said Steyer. "Really? Well, move fast and break stuff doesn't work for kids. In fact, it's terrible. And the actions of Juul and Big Tobacco were also move fast and break stuff. It's exactly the same behavior that you saw from Facebook and the same kind of manipulative, addictive stuff that we've seen—hook kids in with no regards for health consequences."

In addition to helping the "No on C" campaign, Steyer used his organization's massive reach to parents and teachers to spread the word about the dangers of Juul. The group created classroom materials, such as the "Juul Ads and Media Literacy" that instructed teachers to print out an old cigarette ad and one of Juul's early ads as a "great case study on the persuasive tricks and deeper meaning of advertisements and commercials."

Steyer also happened to have a deep Rolodex of media executives whom he'd worked with over the decades in his capacity as a child advocate and through his ratings that media companies licensed for their content. On September 18, Steyer wrote letters to the top executives at major media outlets, including Viacom CEO Robert Bakish, iHeartMedia CEO Robert Pittman, and YouTube CEO Susan Wojcicki, asking them to boycott Juul ads. By then, Juul had already spent more than $30 million on television commercials on nearly ten thousand national ad spots featuring its testimonials from former smokers. A few days earlier the head of CNN, Jeff Zucker, had said that his company would no longer accept Juul advertising dollars. After Steyer's letter, more companies followed suit. Bakish wrote a personal note to Steyer in response to his letter, thanking him for his advocacy on the issue. The same day, Viacom announced that it would pull all its Juul ads.

The dominoes fell. In the United States, Walmart announced that it would stop selling e-cigarettes in its five thousand U.S. stores. Within a few weeks, Kroger and Walgreens followed suit. China had recently pulled Juul from major e-commerce platforms, effectively halting the company's planned entry into the world's largest tobacco market. A few days later, India followed suit with an effective ban on Juul.

JUUL WAS IMPLODING. BURNS and others grew irate as they watched news headlines tacitly implicate Juul for the lung injuries even as the investigation increasingly pointed to black-market THC-laced vape juice. They were angry that the CDC wasn't doing more to make it crystal clear that Juul didn't appear to be the culprit, that black-market counterfeiters were to blame. But that was lost in the noise. The fact of the matter was vaping was killing people and by now, most people in the world associated vaping with Juul. The company's brand preeminence was coming back to haunt them.

On September 25, two weeks after the Bellagio sales retreat, Burns called an all-hands meeting at Juul's headquarters. With several hundred employees packed into the main kitchen area, the same place where he'd given dozens of pep talks and town halls for nearly two years, he announced that he was leaving the company.

Since at least the meeting where Burns had conveyed his utter disdain for Altria's input on Juul's affairs, there had been a growing sense inside the company that he was the wrong person to build the broad tent needed to span stakeholder groups and to win over its critics. Burns was a relatively blunt instrument who was gifted at one thing: scale. While that strategy had gotten Juul its paycheck, it was also now imperiling the company's survival. "There was a joke that Kevin's the type of guy who probably read Jack Welch's memoir when he was twelve-years-old," said a person familiar with his tenure at Juul. "But he had the view of Altria that the man on the street has—that it's an evil company that sells a deadly product."

Even though Burns collected a fat payday from the Altria deal, ironically he simply refused to buy into the idea that a cigarette salesman somehow held the ticket to the company's salvation. He didn't grasp that to run a tobacco business you had to deeply internalize regulations and be willing to hold your tongue and deploy the much more subtle, albeit not less powerful, tactic of convincing rather than cajoling the public to buy into your brand. The reason he couldn't internalize it was simple. Burns never could swallow the pill that Juul, despite all its shine and Silicon Valley pop, was at the end of the day the very thing that he loathed: a tobacco company. Ben Horowitz's distinction between wartime and peacetime CEOs didn't quite hold in this moment. Juul was at war, but it was a war that no amount of aggression could win. Juul needed someone who could engineer a strategic surrender. Burns was not that man. He knew it, and so did everybody at Juul.

Bowen and Monsees stood next to Burns in the kitchen, as did Burns's chosen replacement: K.C. Crosthwaite, the former Altria executive and close colleague of Howard Willard who'd helped negotiate the Juul deal a year earlier. The Juul founders praised Burns for all he'd accomplished—scaling the company from three hundred employees to more than three thousand; launching Juul into twenty markets around the world. "Kevin transformed our start-up into a global business," they said.

Crosthwaite knew that he was walking into a tough crowd. There was no sugarcoating it. Juul was now being run by a tobacco executive. In an email the day he was announced he didn't sidestep the issue:

"As many of you know, I have spent most of my professional career at Altria. In much the same way that I know many at Juul Labs were skeptical about Altria's investment in the company last year, I suspect some of you may have questions about how my background there prepares me to drive forward our mission. . . . The answer is simple. At Altria, I had the opportunity to learn a great deal about adult smokers and about the ways in which companies that sell nicotine delivery products must earn their place in society. For over a decade, I have believed that the future lies with alternatives to combustible cigarettes. I have personally heard from far too many adult smokers expressing their interests in alternatives to believe that the combustible cigarette cannot be displaced."

That same day, Crosthwaite announced that Juul would immediately suspend "all broadcast, print and digital product advertising in the U.S." and refrain from lobbying the Trump administration on its recently announced flavor ban. This was Crosthwaite effectively signaling retreat on the areas that had recently generated the most furor.

As usual, the Juul executives, including Crosthwaite, took questions from the kitchen audience, as many of its member struggled to process the news. "How can we believe in the mission of this company to eliminate combustible cigarettes when you've been at the head of Altria?" was one type of question asked. "Are we Big Tobacco now?" was another. Crosthwaite, the consummate diplomat, had neatly organized answers about how Juul and Altria were independent companies, and how he was committed to Juul's original mission. As he praised that mission, and lamented the "unacceptable levels of youth usage" and "eroding public confidence," he started sounding like a ghost from the past.

Few people likely picked up on it, but Crosthwaite's words were frozen in time from another era, the days of Philip Morris when Steve Parrish was helping the company at its nadir, fumbling toward an indeterminate future, adopting terms like "societal realignment" and exhorting the public to trust the most reviled company in America once again.

"We must strive to work with regulators, policymakers and other stakeholders," Crosthwaite said. "And earn the trust of the societies in which we operate."

The ouroboros was complete. For a company born from its stated desire to drive a stake through the heart of Big Tobacco, it was no longer clear where Juul began and Big Tobacco ended.

On the very day that Crosthwaite was named CEO, many Juul employees updated their résumés and commenced a job hunt. "That was the beginning of the end," one former employee recalled.

21

A BLOODBATH

*Vapers spend more time vaping than
people in monasteries spend praying.*
—GROVER NORQUIST

On October 1, just a month before Election Day, Juul abruptly
pulled out of its own campaign to overturn the e-cigarette ban in San
Francisco. Chessen and her team, and the rest of the anti-Juul cam-
paigners, were in disbelief when they heard the news. "This could very
well be yet another of a series of lies and exaggerations from Juul and
Big Tobacco," said Larry Tramutola, the "No on C" campaign director,
on the day the decision was announced.

Even the campaign staff hired by Juul's own coalition was blindsided by the announcement—not only had they not been informed of
the decision ahead of time, but now they found themselves suddenly
out of work.

Juul had already dumped a fortune into the campaign, and the San
Francisco streets and airwaves were blanketed with "Yes on C" mate-

rial, so it's understandable why people might have been skeptical. But Crosthwaite was desperate to move the ball forward. For him and for Altria, this fight wasn't personal in the way it was for Juul or Burns, an existential struggle in the city of the company's birth. The rich "No on C" backers weren't Crosthwaite's Atherton neighbors, as they were Burns's, and so he and Richmond saw no reason to throw good money after bad in a fight that polls showed they would clearly lose. In a statement, the new Juul CEO said this: "I am committed to seeing that Juul engages productively with all stakeholders, including regulators, policymakers and our customers." In other words, Crosthwaite, like Parrish, was waving the white flag. Juul had gotten buried so deep in the Prop C fight that it had no choice. It could either die fighting or surrender alive—with the hopes of rising again another day when the heat had died down. Exactly like Philip Morris did before.

To continue pouring money into a bitter political fight that had a perilously narrow path to victory was irresponsible. Not to mention that running a campaign that championed more vaping at a time when vaping was killing people was stupidly bad optics. The Prop C campaign was an absolute boondoggle that was only making Juul's black eye even blacker. It was an obvious first thing to go.

Even though Juul had backed out, the vestiges of Prop C lived on like a zombie. Prop C ads still ran. Prop C billboards were still up. Prop C flyers still littered the city streets. Even with the Bloomberg war chest behind them, volunteers for the "No on C" campaign kept knocking on doors. Making phone calls. Staging rallies in front of Juul headquarters.

GROVER NORQUIST WASN'T THE first person most people would have picked to be a champion of vaping. But he also wasn't the first person people thought of when they thought of Burning Man. Both actually made perfect sense. The longtime anti-tax, small government icon who founded the Washington group Americans for Tax Reform during Ronald Reagan's presidency relished bucking the status quo. He'd originally been invited to attend Burning Man in 2014 by its cofounder

Larry Harvey after the two bonded over gripes about the Big Bad Government. Harvey had allegedly grown troubled by the Bureau of Land Management's overbearing presence in Burning Man's affairs. That was music to Norquist's ears.

That year Norquist and his wife traveled to the Nevada desert, where they set up camp in the area reserved for the festival's founders and graybeards. It was love at first sight. As Norquist himself explained in a *Guardian* piece titled "My First Burning Man: Confessions of a Conservative from Washington":

> Some self-professed "progressives" whined at the thought of my attending what they believed was a ghetto for liberal hippies. Yes, there was a gentleman who skateboarded without elbow or knee-pads—or any knickers whatsoever. Yes, I rode in cars dressed-up as cats, bees and spiders; I watched trucks carrying pirate ships and 30 dancers. I drank absinthe. But anyone complaining about a Washington wonk like me at Burning Man is not a Burner himself: The first principle of Burning Man is "radical inclusiveness."

Burning Man had long been a spiritual home for futuristic tech. And for vaping. Bowen and Monsees had not only beta tested Ploom there, but they also befriended Harvey and set up Pax Labs in Burning Man's San Francisco offices. Norquist's "don't tread on me" predisposition melded nicely with Burning Man's penchant for a lack of rules—and taxes.

Norquist had been making the anti-tax argument on behalf of big tobacco companies for the past two decades, ever since he rolled out his Taxpayer Protection Pledge, which he induced lawmakers to sign as a promise that they'd never raise taxes and allow government to become the usurping, Hobbesian Leviathan that unjustly ruled dominion over Americans' lives. As the tobacco industry came under increasing fire in the late 1990s, one of the main weapons used by anti-smoking advocates, and by corollary state and local lawmakers, had been to advocate higher taxes on cigarettes to disincentivize consumption and to raise revenue to pay for healthcare and tobacco prevention programs.

Norquist was enlisted by Philip Morris, and other tobacco companies, to discredit such fiscally liberal "sin taxes" by organizing anti-tax conferences, giving grants to think tanks to write white papers, writing op-eds in state and local newspapers, and using his "blast fax" to carpet bomb media outlets with messages about beating back bureaucracy and resisting a creeping welfare state.

Whether or not Burning Man had anything to do with it, Norquist immediately embraced vaping as a new frontier in his long war against sin taxes. "This is Grover Norquist here with *The Grover Norquist Show,* and we're going to be talking taxes," he said in a January 2015 episode titled "Leave Vapers Alone!" "For many years, the state legislators, congressmen would go after taxing tobacco or cigarettes, then they would go after beer, wine, and spirits. Or they'd go after gasoline, or your cars with the car tax. And the new sin that they want to go after is . . . e-cigarettes or vaping, which don't have the health challenges of tobacco and yet the politicians want to tax that."

Norquist's guest on the show that day, a colleague from Americans for Tax Reform named Paul Blair, explained just how big the vaping community was and how its members could be harnessed. "There are probably about six to seven million daily vapers," Blair said.

Norquist's mouth practically watered. "A new addition to the Leave Us Alone coalition," he stated with satisfaction. "A new phalanx for the taxpayer movement, vapers."

As the number of vapers grew, so did the number of vape shops across the United States. These were often independently owned shops that were sensitive to minor disruptions in the business calculus. For years, as the e-cigarette industry operated virtually without regulation, it had become a decently profitable business. Not to mention that many vape shop owners had become true believers. Vaping wasn't just a habit or an indulgence, it was a form of counterculture that sprang from the notion that a nicotine fix no longer had to come from Big Tobacco. Instead, it could come from Billy or Betty cooking up e-liquid in the back office. All you had to do was buy the gear, squirt in the juice, and crank up the battery.

When state legislators, backed by public-health advocates and tobacco control groups, began pushing for new taxes on e-cigarettes, it was these vapers who got pissed. One vape shop owner in Caledonia, Michigan, told a reporter that such taxes and regulations threatened his business. He "just wants his shop to stay open. He feels betrayed that people with heroin addictions can have a safe place to use drugs and that flavored alcohol is still on the market, but not the blueberry maple syrup–flavored vape juice he uses."

The fanaticism of vapers became religious. Here was a product that vapers and vape shop owners viewed as safer than cigarettes, one that could have a net benefit on the public health of society, yet the government was trying to make it harder to get that very thing into the hands of the people who needed it most—smokers. And so, the battle lines were drawn: The Vapers against The Man. Their swords were drawn, and Grover Norquist was there to lead them into battle.

Soon enough, so were a host of other free market–supporting individuals and organizations. Together, they turned out to forge vapers into a voting bloc. Among them was the Libertarian National Committee, which formed the "I Vape I Vote" coalition (not to be confused with a different "We Vape We Vote" coalition); the American Vaping Association, which worked to train vapers on how to participate in politics (not to be confused with the Vapor Technology Association, which hosted two events at Trump International Hotel in Washington); and the Smoke-Free Alternatives Trade Association that ran a "Save the Vape" campaign (not to be confused with the Consumer Advocates for Smoke-Free Alternatives Association). Veteran political operatives got involved, including Mark Block, chief of staff for Herman Cain, who started the Vape PAC. Big voices backed the movement, including that of Sean Hannity, Trump's "shadow chief of staff" who ran Juul ads on his network and, reportedly, vaped himself. Influential lobbyists got involved. Social media saw a proliferation of pro-vaping bots that flooded Twitter with pro-vaping, anti-tax messages.

The Vaping Army was locked and loaded by the time Trump wandered into the fight.

———

RIGHT UP UNTIL AUGUST, Howard Willard had been sounding an optimistic tone about his Juul investment. He'd expressed excitement
about the company's expansion into international markets, including
Ireland, South Korea, Austria, and the Philippines. The company had
been named in a few Juul-related lawsuits, but so few that they required
little more than a footnote in corporate disclosures. "Our 2019 plans
remain on track," he said on Altria's second-quarter earnings call,
which was held on July 30. "I think that Juul has performed quite admi-
rably in the first half of this year."

But by the time the leaves started changing color, the mood began
to change too, as the lung injury situation morphed into a public-
health crisis. After that it didn't take long for a collective sense of anxiety to descend over Altria's C-suite. Willard, like everybody else, could
see the onslaught of unforgiving news every day that was simply refus-
ing to let up. It was like waking up from a nightmare only to realize
that the nightmare was, in fact, real.

On October 1, Altria received a civil investigative demand from the
Federal Trade Commission. The agency had opened an investigation
into Altria's investment in Juul, marking the agency's latest foray into
the tobacco industry. A few years earlier it had challenged the $27.4
billion merger between Reynolds American and Lorillard, and had required the companies to divest portions of their cigarette portfolio before allowing the deal to be finalized. Now the agency was interested
in whether Juul and Altria had violated federal antitrust laws when Altria pulled MarkTen off the market weeks before doing the deal with
Juul, thereby lessening competition in the e-cigarette market.

While Willard maintained that he discontinued sales of MarkTen
out of an abundance of concern over kids using pod-based nicotine
products—and had his letter to Gottlieb to prove it—the FTC wanted
to know whether he had in fact used MarkTen as a bargaining chip in
the Juul negotiations. The FTC was also probing Crosthwaite's resignation at Altria and subsequent appointment as Juul's new CEO, which
the agency was concerned might have been further evidence of anti-
competitive conduct, since the two companies hadn't yet received the
agency's approval to finalize the deal. If the agency brought a formal

challenge to the Juul investment, it could result in drastic measures, including a requirement that the colossal deal be revoked.

CROSTHWAITE HAD SWOOPED INTO Juul like a redeemer. His high-profile departure from his longtime employer Altria wasn't that of just any old corporate executive leaving for greener pastures. The tobacco giant had gifted Crosthwaite a $2.5 million "special recognition payment" on the way out the door. Employees at Juul assumed he was some sort of an intelligence asset sent by Altria to protect the company's high-value investment.

By then, morale at Juul had already hit rock bottom. Juul employees had been able to stomach the Altria deal, largely because of the checks they'd gotten. But they lamented the days when their start-up was on the cutting edge. When they were the vanguard of a mission-centric future. When despite all the doubters and haters, they could walk with their heads high, believing that they stood as at least an unconventional bearer of hope. Now, it was like they'd been tarred and feathered. Some people refused to put the company on their résumé because they believed it now conveyed such an odious stench.

In Burns's short and fiery tenure at Juul, he'd done his best to salvage the image of the company, to shrug off the vestiges of the ill-fated "Vaporized" campaign, and for that, many of Juul's employees had been grateful. Sure, he'd been somewhat of a prick, but he was widely viewed as a more-than-competent leader who had their backs. More importantly, ever since the December 2018 deal, he'd served as at least a metaphorical firewall between Juul and Voldemort. Now, with Burns gone, Voldemort was in the building.

Crosthwaite's arrival touched off a freeze that snapped over all of Juul. It didn't help that he appeared to be building a bridge between his old employer and his new one. On October 1, Juul announced that it had hired Joe Murillo, Altria's former associate general counsel and president of Nu Mark, to be Juul's new chief regulatory officer. Over the course of the next few months, half a dozen former Altria employees would be hired by Juul, adding to the dozen or so who had joined since the deal.

From day one, Crosthwaite brought to a grinding halt the rattling momentum that Juul had amassed over the past two years. When he opened Juul's hood to get a look at the motor, he found an absolute beast. In just two years, the start-up had grown from fewer than two hundred employees in a single market to more than four thousand employees across nearly two dozen countries. Throughout 2019, Juul had been growing around the world so quickly that it hired on average three hundred people every month.

Crosthwaite's first task was to oversee a top-down review of the entire company, from its operating expenses to its strategy, to identify inefficiencies. He started pulling the plug on projects big and small, from advertising to digital marketing to R&D. Efforts that had long been under way suddenly were stopped. Every day was punctuated by bated breath as employees anticipated that layoffs were around the corner. For weeks, scores of Juul employees had no projects to work on, so they just fucked around and waited for the next shoe to drop. There was a gingerbread house–building competition. People looked at jobs online. Employees stopped showing up to the office on Fridays. Every day sucked more than the last.

But Crosthwaite had a focus that was ruthless in its singularity: the FDA. As expected, the federal judge in the case challenging Gottlieb's decision to grant e-cigarette companies four years to file their applications to the FDA had ordered the agency to move up the deadline. "Given the uncertainty in the efficacy of e-cigarettes as smoking cessation devices, the overstated effects that a shorter deadline may have on manufacturers, the industry's recalcitrance, the continued availability of e-cigarettes and their acknowledged appeal to youth, and the clear public-health emergency, I find that a deadline is necessary," the judge wrote in July.

Instead of having to file its application by August 8, 2022, Juul now needed to file by May 20, 2020. That was just months away, putting Crosthwaite under an extraordinarily tight deadline to finalize the company's premarket tobacco application. This all-important document would need to be scientifically rigorous and packed with data demonstrating to the FDA that the company's product met the agency's "appropriate for the protection of public health" standard. The company's FDA application ultimately was more than 125,000 pages and cost in excess of $100 million.

Now, at Juul, almost nothing else mattered. What difference would it make if Juul's fancy Silicon Valley engineers designed flashy new nicotine gadgets if the FDA wouldn't allow any of them to even be sold?

With the FDA's deadline months away, the gravitational pull of Juul was clearly shifting away from San Francisco toward Washington, D.C. Any spare time was focused on salvaging the company's standing in Washington and in the eye of the public, by lobbying in favor of Tobacco 21 legislation that raised the federal age for purchasing tobacco products to twenty-one from eighteen years old, and by helping roll out point-of-sale technologies to inhibit underage purchases at retail establishments.

Meanwhile, pressure was building in Washington to rein in the e-cigarette companies once and for all by forcing them to remove flavored products from the market. The e-cigarette moratorium and flavor ban that had passed in San Francisco were already now spreading to dozens of other cities and states, just as the company had feared, and state legislatures and city councils were hammering out growing numbers of restrictions on e-cigarettes. Trump's promise to remove flavored e-cigarettes from the market was turning political.

Crosthwaite decided to preempt the administration by making a series of announcements explaining that Juul was voluntarily removing all its fruit and dessert-flavored products—mango, crème brûlée, fruit, and cucumber—from the U.S. market. While Juul had stopped selling most of these flavors in retail stores several months earlier, the company had continued selling them online. No more. Then, a few weeks later, a study in the *Journal of the American Medical Association* found that Juul's mint pods were actually the most popular flavor among its teen users. Two days later, Crosthwaite announced that he was yanking those too, a cutting wound into the company since mint pods comprised 70 percent of Juul's business. But in this moment in time, it wasn't about the money. Juul was in survival mode. And Crosthwaite, desperate to appease Washington and an enraged public, was retrenching.

Toward the end of October, Crosthwaite sent out a company-wide email announcing major changes on the horizon. In addition to a reorganization of the Juul executive leadership team, the company was going to be shrinking substantially.

"I know that the question on everyone's mind is whether we are laying off employees, and how and when these layoffs will happen," Crosthwaite wrote. "The short answer is yes, we are going to right-size our business and our operating budget to align more closely with our strategic framework. . . . This will unfortunately mean a 10 to 15 percent reduction in employee headcount along with significant cost reductions in other areas to align spending with our strategic priorities." By mid-November, it was publicly announced that Juul was laying off 650 workers, or 16 percent of its global workforce, as part of a restructuring of the company that would reduce spending by $1 billion.

Meanwhile, Crosthwaite announced that Bowen and Monsees would be leaving the company's day-to-day operations and forming a "Founders' Office" where they'd still be on the board of directors and serve as "direct advisers" to Crosthwaite.

The bloodbath was beginning.

ALTRIA'S THIRD-QUARTER EARNINGS WERE released on Halloween, and they were appropriately ghastly. The number revealed the looming land mines buried in Altria's Juul investment. The company reported that market conditions surrounding Juul—lower volumes, state and city bans, adverse publicity, vaping-related lung injuries, and regulatory uncertainty at the FDA—forced it to write down the value of its $12.8 billion investment in the company by more than a third. Just like that, $4.5 billion on Altria's books had turned into vapor.

Warning signs had been cropping up in the past several days. A hedge fund had slashed its own internal valuation of Juul by $14 billion, to $24 billion. The day before Altria reported its earnings, Fidelity cut the estimated value of its Juul holdings by nearly half to $386 million. Now, Altria's $4.5 billion impairment charge resulted in Altria posting a $2.6 billion quarterly loss, compared to a $1.94 billion profit a year earlier.

"How do you feel about having to so materially reduce your estimate of such a large investment so quickly after being completed?" a stock analyst with Morgan Stanley asked Howard Willard.

"Of course, we're not pleased to have to take an impairment charge on the Juul investment," he replied. "And certainly, while we had a range of scenarios when we made our investment in Juul, we did not anticipate this dramatic a change in the e-vapor category. Certainly, the lung injury was something we had not predicted."

THE CDC'S BRIAN KING was sitting at the airport in Ottawa on November 5 when his phone rang. He'd come as part of an international delegation meeting with the Canadian counterpart of the United States' Health and Human Services. They discussed a variety of topics. King was there to talk about the outbreak of vaping-related lung injuries. The number of cases had swelled to nearly two thousand, with cases in almost every U.S. state and a total of three dozen deaths. The spate of lung injuries had become so worrying as the case count continued to rise that the CDC in recent days had given the malady its own name: EVALI, or "e-cigarette or vaping product use-associated lung injury."

King had been working around the clock alongside the now four hundred or so federal government employees tasked with the complex lung injury investigation. Because the investigation covered such a large number of states, and because it was complicated by the wide range of e-cigarette products in the marketplace, including many sold illegally on the black market, things could only move as quickly as the data allowed.

The government's investigation had come under an increasing onslaught of scrutiny from a worried public demanding to know what was causing adults and children alike to fall, mysteriously, into severe respiratory distress. The House Committee on Oversight and Reform in Congress had convened an emergency hearing, calling a CDC official to testify just two months after Monsees himself had testified on Capitol Hill about the youth epidemic of vaping.

But perhaps nobody was more desperate for an answer than Juul. If there was an alibi for its product, the public needed to know about it. Already, Juul sales were starting to slow after near-continuous growth for almost two years, and industry analysts were attributing it to the drumbeat of negative news related to the lung injuries.

Panic had swept over the entire e-cigarette industry, as vape shop owners and e-cigarette companies watched in horror as a once-booming industry spiraled into crisis and as the public lost faith in products they'd promised would be a silver bullet to cigarettes. Instead, kids who'd never smoked a day in their lives were showing up to the hospital with lungs of the Marlboro Man.

As Juul watched its valuation sink and its products and reputation get demolished in the media, there was a sense of helplessness inside the company. Juul employees passed along stories they'd heard of customers getting so spooked by the lung injuries that they'd reverted to smoking cigarettes. It drove Juul executives crazy that people were trying to extinguish opportunities for smokers to have access to a less bad product even as deadly cigarettes remained widely available. But it was difficult for them to make their case when the ostensibly less bad product was entangled in the health crisis.

There was an intensifying divide between those in the public-health community who increasingly believed that vaping of any kind was bad—*see, people are dying, nobody should inhale anything into their lungs other than air, ever!*—and those in the e-cigarette industry desperate to preserve the industry for adult smokers—*only an idiot would try to cut off access to e-cigarettes while leaving deadly Marlboros freely available!* Under the cloud of a public-health crisis, any hope of finding common ground between the two camps was proving to be more distant than ever. Complicating it all was the fact that Juul was now part-owned by Big Tobacco. Anything Juul did was seen with even greater suspicion than before.

It didn't help that as the lung injuries added up, Juul poached talent from the tobacco control community, angering people who thought it evoked the "white coats" strategy that had been a tried-and-true tactic long used by the tobacco industry. The company hired Erik Augustson, a former behavioral scientist at the National Cancer Institute, and

Mark Rubinstein, a longtime researcher who'd worked with Stan Glantz at UCSF's Center for Tobacco Control Research and Education. Jed Rose, the co-inventor of the nicotine patch who for years received funding from Philip Morris, had started doing research for Juul. Pinney Associates, the tobacco harm-reduction consultancy that the FDA's Mitch Zeller worked at for several years, began exclusively working with Juul. Instead of lauding a company for taking reasonable steps to hire the foremost experts, Juul was lambasted by critics who accused the company of cloaking itself in a guise of public health and co-opting the tobacco control movement by showering experts with money.

When King picked up the phone, he got a much-needed break-through. For the past several weeks, his laboratory staff had been collecting samples of bronchoalveolar lavage, or lung fluids, from EVALI patients, and had gathered samples from twenty-nine patients in ten states. The initial data had just come back. Every single one of the samples tested positive for vitamin E acetate, the golden, syrupy additive found almost exclusively in THC cannabis vaping liquids. While the New York health department had zeroed in on vitamin E acetate as a likely candidate several weeks earlier by identifying it in suspect cartridges, this was the first set of data confirming that the substance was also found in the lung samples of patients.

"We need to get this out immediately," King told his CDC colleague, overcome by a sense of urgency as he sat in the airport waiting to fly back home to Atlanta. Over the next seventy-two hours, King and his team began furiously writing up the findings.

IN SAN FRANCISCO, CELEBRATION was in the air. It was Halloween as the sun set, and a sliver of the moon rose in the sky. Costumed children out for trick-or-treating walked past a yard that had a skeleton emerging from the grass next to two tombstones. One said "Here lies Juul" and the other said "Vaping Kills, No on Prop C." Down the street, music blared from a speaker as steam from a fog machine filled the air. A bright orange candy bowl sat on the stoop of the Chessens' grand townhome. Behind the bowl stood a life-size coffin with a bloody corpse wearing a suit. As children approached the bowl to fish out a piece of candy, they couldn't see Christine Chessen off to the side with her finger on a hidden button attached to an air compressor. As they reached down into the bowl, she'd press the button, and the corpse would jump out. Screams and laughter filled the air. The children likely missed it amidst the fog and candy-induced frenzy, but if one looked close enough at the bloody skeleton, they could see a name tag pinned to its lapel. It read: *Hello, my name is K. Burns, ex-CEO Juul Labs.*

Just five days later, on November 5, that celebratory mood among the fierce anti-Juul activists continued as San Francisco voters headed to the polls. By now, it wasn't a question of whether Proposition C would get voted down but by how much. Almost every poll showed that Juul was poised for defeat. That evening, around nine P.M., as the polls closed and the election results started coming in, "No on C" activists started gathering at the Hotel Zephyr, a quirky boutique hotel overlooking Fisherman's Wharf. Among others, Annie Tegen from Tobacco-Free Kids was there, along with lawyers who'd helped the campaign, Christine and Kevin Chessen, Shamann Walton from the San Francisco Board of Supervisors, and city attorney Dennis Herrera.

They toasted with beer and wine to what was by now an inexorable victory, swapping stories about the strange campaign that had unfolded over the previous twelve weeks. By the end, 82 percent of San Franciscans voted against Proposition C. Even though Juul had pulled out of the campaign a month before, this was still an undeniable referendum on the company. It had tried to overrule the city at the ballot box and failed. That meant that in just a few weeks, the original ordinance that passed over the summer would finally take effect: Juul would no longer be sold in the very streets that birthed the product.

WHEN THE CDC'S *Morbidity and Mortality Weekly Report* was released on November 8, it was the fastest publication King had ever been involved in. "This is the first reported identification of a potential toxicant of concern (vitamin E acetate) in biologic specimens obtained from EVALI patients," read the report, which was authored by two dozen CDC researchers and dozens more from across the public-health community. "These findings provide direct evidence of vitamin E acetate at the primary site of injury among EVALI patients."

Vitamin E acetate, the CDC later reported, likely interfered with the lung's surfactant, causing it to "lose its ability to maintain the surface tension that is necessary to support respiration" and leading to "respiratory dysfunction." The other potential problem with vitamin E acetate was that while the ingredient was widely known as being safe for ingestion or used topically, inhaling it via an e-cigarette posed potential safety issues because the heating of the substance could create a new reactive compound called ketene that "has the potential to be a lung irritant."

The breakthrough came with mixed reactions. The problem for Juul was that the CDC's conclusions didn't give them a total pass. While the data clearly showed that bootlegged THC products containing vitamin E acetate were the likely culprit, they weren't conclusive. The CDC's data were consistently showing that about 15 percent of lung-injury patients reported using only products containing nicotine.

All of that led the agency to conclude that the vaping lung injuries had what's called a multifactor etiology, meaning that there was likely more than one factor leading to EVALI, even though the primary factor was likely vitamin E acetate. That meant the agency believed that at least some EVALI cases were attributable to nicotine-only products. No matter how badly the e-cigarette industry wanted to put this whole matter behind them, the agency stood its ground: It simply didn't have sufficient data to exonerate anybody or anything. And so the agency continued to urge caution with e-cigarettes.

That drove the e-cigarette industry mad. They'd started to lose patience with regulators whom they saw as gatekeepers out to doom their product. Groups like the American Vaping Association started going on news shows in a desperate bid to defend the industry, accusing the CDC—without merit—of intentionally withholding information in order to put political pressure on the government to ban flavors and to strike a dagger through the heart of the vaping industry.

"The CDC is weaponizing a health crisis that is clearly linked to illicit street vapes in order to scare the public about nicotine vaping products," said Gregory Conley, president of the group.

Meanwhile, as the vaping injuries became more prolific, more politicians were pressured to take action, either by moving to pass flavor bans in cities or state legislatures, or to seek more aggressive moratoriums on vaping like the city of San Francisco. That made the pro-vaping crowd even more desperate to lash out. In the days and weeks after Trump announced that his administration would ban flavored e-cigarettes, Norquist and others in the pro-vaping lobby turned up the heat on Washington.

Norquist's Americans for Tax Reform circulated a document to lawmakers with #WeVapeWeVote on it warning them that flavor bans could jeopardize not only their own political careers but that of their standard-bearer. "A flavor ban will cost Trump the 2020 election," it read. "To ignore that these adults have used e-cigarettes to quit smoking cigarettes, something that they're proud of and strongly believe in, would be among the biggest political miscalculations of the presidential campaign in 2020."

The Vapor Technology Association hosted a lobbying day in Washington, D.C., where hundreds of vaping advocates and vape shop owners from across the United States descended on Capitol Hill to pressure lawmakers to push back against any proposed legislation that would ban flavors. The group also took out ads that aired on Fox News in an attempt to speak directly to the president, a cable news fiend. And they flooded the White House comment line with pro-vaping messages.

Even as First Lady Melania Trump continued to speak out against vaping, including in a White House Blue Room event with teens associated with the Truth Initiative, Trump was wavering. His then campaign director, Brad Parscale, had warned him that polling showed that moving ahead with the flavor ban would be a grave political risk. Norquist's call to stop taxes and regulations on vaping drew support from a deep bench of conservative, small-government groups, including the Koch brothers–linked American Legislative Exchange Council, the Competitive Enterprise Institute, and the Goldwater Institute, who all cosigned a letter to Trump.

Dear Mr. President,

We urge you to preserve access to life-saving alternatives to cigarettes for the millions of adults who rely on electronic cigarettes
and vapor products to quit smoking in the United States. . . . Adults
like flavors. That's precisely why everything from vodka to ice
cream comes in a variety of flavors. When it comes to vaping, this
holds true. . . . We urge you to immediately halt the FDA's planned
actions that will limit choices for millions of American adults who
rely on flavored vaping products to quit smoking. More than
100,000 jobs and the lives of 34 million adult smokers are on the
line.

Sincerely,
Grover Norquist

ON NOVEMBER 22, MORE than a dozen people sat around the oval
wooden table in the Cabinet Room of the White House. Trump presided, with Health and Human Services Secretary Alex Azar sitting to
his left. Sitting to his right was Senator Mitt Romney, a critic of flavored e-cigarettes. Kellyanne Conway, also a critic of the products, sat
next to Romney.

Trump had come under an avalanche of political pressure to walk
back his earlier announcement on flavored e-cigarettes. The president
of the United States had called this listening session to gather all the
stakeholders in one room, and to hopefully arrive at some sort of compromise.

While the issue had erupted into a multifaceted political and public-
health explosion over the past several weeks, stretching from Washington to Virginia to San Francisco, now the bang was contained here, in
this single room. Among the nearly two dozen participants: Howard
Willard from Altria; K.C. Crosthwaite from Juul; Matthew Myers from
Tobacco-Free Kids; Harold Wimmer from the American Lung Association; George Conley from the American Vaping Association; Robin
Koval from the Truth Initiative; Christopher Butler from Americans

for Tax Reform; Joseph Fragnito from Reynolds American; Meredith Berkman from Parents Against Vaping e-cigarettes (PAVe).

This was supposed to be the place where progress would be made. Where everybody got along, at least for a day, to work together toward a common goal. After all, shouldn't everyone be able to agree that no one wanted teens vaping or smokers dying?

Word had gotten around already that the president was leaning toward reversing course and backing away from his earlier announcement to ban flavors, a policy that just a few weeks earlier had been on the one-yard line with Azar and the FDA ready to go. But the political pressure had grown too intense. Norquist's coalition appeared to have gotten under Trump's skin, leaving the president to fret that moving forward with a flavor ban might pose too big of a political risk. As everybody by now knew, Trump often made policy decisions based on the last thing that had been whispered into his ear. Today in the Cabinet Room, a week before Thanksgiving, everyone along the spectrum of the issue would clamor to be the last whisper in the president's ear.

As Trump took his seat, and before the event officially kicked off, he made a final wisecrack before the news cameras were allowed into the room.

"This crowd's going to be more difficult than a meeting between the Israelis and the Palestinians," the president quipped. "Bring in the fake news!"

As the media filed in, sounds of snapping cameras filled the room. The guests took their seats around the table, with public health advocates plopped right next to industry players, perhaps a deliberate strategy to build camaraderie but nonetheless a tense and sometimes awkward elbow-to-elbow arrangement. They began introducing themselves. "I have been working on reducing death and disease from tobacco for thirty-five years," said Matthew Myers, "and I've never seen an epidemic this serious, this rapid, and this intense as caused by the flavors of e-cigarettes among our youth."

"And you think you have a solution?" the president asked.

"I think that we do have a solution," Myers replied. "And I think, in

September, the solution that you posed is an extraordinarily powerful step in the right direction."

"Okay. We'll take a look at it," Trump said.

Next up.

K.C. Crosthwaite was seated right next to Myers. "Mr. President, thank you for having me here," he said, in a calm, professional tone, his hands folded neatly atop his brown leather folio on the table. This is a very serious issue to discuss, and thank you for hosting us to have the discussion. I am honored to be a part of it, and I look forward to engaging with everyone in the room on a solution to the problem."

"So, did you know it was going to be so controversial?" Trump asked Crosthwaite.

"Yes, sir," he acknowledged. "I knew I was stepping into a pretty intense environment, but am happy to lead the company and honored to offer solutions here to this problem."

As the introductions continued, participants bantered with the president as he peppered them with questions. Some used honey, others vinegar. Opponents of the flavor ban reminded the president that he could lose political support if he moved ahead with the controversial policy. "We are concerned about the public policy implications of this for adult vapers," said Butler from Norquist's Americans for Tax Reform. "But, also, we view it as something as a prerequisite of keeping people in the Liberty Coalition."

Meredith Berkman was smooshed in between Ryan Nivakoff, CEO of NJOY and Joseph Fragnito, president at R.J. Reynolds. She came to the meeting carrying a giant binder filled with emails and letters from parents whose children had become addicted to e-cigarettes, which she had positioned in front of her. She wore two necklaces—one that was a butterfly pendant and the other that said "Mom"—and a PeptoBismol–pink dress, an intentional sartorial choice that was designed to scream *concerned parent!* and to stand out in what she figured would inevitably be a sea of drab gray-and-black suits and ties.

This was a huge moment for Berkman. Two years earlier she hadn't even known what vaping was, and now here she was, sitting at the Kentucky Derby of vaping. She knew going into the meeting that she'd have to struggle to have her voice heard over the big industry players, but never a shrinking violet, Berkman was ready to rebut what she expected would be carefully crafted messages from industry titans. By now she'd turned PAVe into a nationwide organization with parent volunteers from coast to coast, and she was fighting battles in state legislatures and city councils across the country. This meeting would not only put her organization on the map in an even bigger way but she saw it as a make-or-break moment that could further her goal of getting e-cigarettes out of the hands of youths.

Berkman knew that the president was prone to flattery, and determined to speak directly to him, she did her best to stroke Trump's ego, while keeping her eyes from rolling. "You know, Mr. President," Berkman said. "It is no secret that you have great instincts, and your first instinct solving this problem of the youth vaping epidemic, we think, and I think many people in this room, believe is the right one. And that is ridding the market of all of these flavors, including menthol flavor and mint flavor, because it's the flavors that have hooked the kids and that kept the kids from perceiving harm in these products and the presence of nicotine."

Trump grilled the participants, repeatedly asking them for their opinion, or their proposed solution. *What do you suggest?* he asked Gary Reedy, the CEO of the American Cancer Society. *What are they saying about the vaping phenomenon?* he asked the CEO of the National Association of Convenience Stores. *What is your solution?* he asked Berkman. *So, what are you recommending with flavors?* Trump asked George Conley, from the American Vaping Association.

Conley, a well-spoken New Jersey attorney, was one of the most strident opponents of vaping regulations, constantly going on cable news to tout the alleged harm-reduction benefits of vaping, and to admonish what he saw as the industry's foes. One of his targets was former New York City mayor Michael Bloomberg, who'd recently jumped into the San Francisco fight as part of a wider announcement that his philanthropy would spend $160 million to ban flavored e-cigarettes in states and cities around the U.S. and more broadly work to end the youth-nicotine epidemic. Conley was a bulldog and wasn't afraid to take the fight into ad hominem territory. "Right now," he told Trump, "it's important that you know, Michael Bloomberg, who is no friend to your presidency, he is funding $160 million to try to ban these flavors, and many people in this room are the recipients of those monies. So they are not here with the position of 'we can come to a compromise,' they have money specifically to get these products banned."

"So what would you do?" Trump responded.

"We want smokers to be able to access these products everywhere they can purchase a pack of Marlboros," said Conley. "We can't forget about the adult smokers in this debate."

Trump turned back to Matt Myers, whose Tobacco-Free Kids received funding from Bloomberg. "So what would you do, Matthew?"

"Having worked on this issue for thirty-five years, I would, in fact, eliminate the sale of any flavors that haven't been approved by the Food and Drug Administration," Myers said. "We have seen an epidemic among our kids that I haven't seen ever before. We now have more kids using nicotine products than at any time in the last twenty years. And what's more disturbing about it is that thirty-four percent of the kids who use these products use them more than twenty days a month, which means they're hooked. They can't quit. We have stories of young people who say, 'I started it because it was cool and literally, within days, I lost control.' Kids sleep with these products because they need to wake up in the middle of the night."

Trump turned to Crosthwaite.

"You're the head of Juul?"

"Yes, sir."

"So what do you say?"

Crosthwaite had been with the company barely two months and here he was sitting in the burning white-hot center of the vaping controversy, just an arm's length away from the president. This was the exact type of moment the life-long tobacco executive was trained to inhabit, perhaps one that Valani, Pritzker, and the Juul board had in mind when they brought him in to replace Burns. Crosthwaite had been gaming out for months, even before arriving at Juul, how the Trump administration would ultimately treat e-cigarettes. And since the day he arrived at Juul, he'd acted accordingly by taking flavors off

the market, a move designed to placate the government, while blunt-
ing the bevy of angry spears pointed at the company. Now, in this
meeting, every ounce of his tobacco-industry persuasion and innate
choir-boy mannerism was on display. Crosthwaite wasn't here to be a
rogue player or a bomb-thrower. In true tobacco executive fashion, he
was here to be the conciliator who came bearing an olive branch flowering with solutions.

"Well, when I came into the job," Crosthwaite said, "we decided
that action needed to be taken. We agreed this was a serious issue, so
we have already removed our flavors from the market. Most recently,
we removed mint, and for us, that was seventy percent of our business.
So, it was a big step for us, but we felt it was the right thing to do with
this youth data that came out."

From there, things quickly escalated into a crescendoing free-for-
all. Berkman knew that she'd have to do be bold in the meeting, but
still she struggled to be heard as the alpha males began raising their
voices and talking over one another. Suddenly she felt like she was sitting around her dinner table with her four children on a particularly
acrimonious night.

Romney butted in at one point, in exasperation. "The kids! How
about the children? We've got almost six million kids addicted to nicotine, and they are getting addicted to nicotine because of flavors. . . .
It's a health emergency!"

The table erupted with people clamoring to speak over one another. Romney pounded on the table and continued: "The adults have
access to menthol products through Juul. They have tobacco-flavored
products. By putting out cotton candy flavor and what is it—unicorn
poop flavor?—I mean, look, this is a kid product. We have to put the
kids first."

But what about the smoking adults? the e-cigarette backers wanted to
know. "They don't want to admit that if an adult smoker switches to
vaping, that they greatly benefit their health," said Conley. "The Royal
College of Physicians, Public Health England, even your own former
commissioner, Scott Gottlieb, has stated smokers who switch improve
their health."

Myers interjected. "But the difference is the kids who are using these products are not kids who are smokers, and they are very often not kids who would have become smokers, so that the measurement of the risk for these kids . . ."

"That is just not accurate," interrupted Tony Abboud, from the Vapor Technology Association.

"It is consistent with all the government studies," rebutted Myers.

"All right," said the president. "Go ahead, Tony."

"I'm sorry that's just not an accurate statistic," Abboud said. "Most of the kids who have tried this product have already tried cigarettes or some other tobacco product. These are kids that have at-risk behaviors."

He stepped on a land mine by insinuating that kids Juuling were somehow already troublemakers who would have taken up nicotine one way or another, an assertion not backed up by facts. The data clearly showed that before e-cigarettes came around, youth tobacco use was at all-time lows.

"They *don't* have at-risk behavior," yelled Berkman as she leaned into the table, obviously personally offended given her own experience with all the kids vaping in her son's school.

"I'm sorry but that's a completely false statement," interjected Azar, the health secretary, rejecting Abboud's claim and raising his voice over several others who tried to speak over one another.

Romney was aghast. "Utah is a Mormon state," he said, laughing in disbelief. "Half the kids in high school are vaping. All right? They wouldn't have used these products." He sat back in his chair and threw up his hands.

In the entire meeting there was one person sitting around the raucous table who said not a single word beyond his earlier formal introduction: Howard Willard. It was clear that while Altria had a big dog in the fight, Willard wasn't the one tapped to be the front man. That job was now left to his longtime former colleague Crosthwaite.

After another half hour or so of bickering, Trump concluded the meeting.

"Thank you very much, everybody. We are going to be announcing very soon."

———

WHEN THE SUN ROSE over San Francisco on January 1, it was a new era. In just days from now Bowen and Monsees, or anybody in San Francisco for that matter, would no longer be able to buy Juul in their own city. The city law affirmed by voters in November was slated to take effect later in the month.

The following day, on January 2, President Trump announced his much-awaited final vaping policy. Almost nobody was happy. Trump's policy allowed vape shops to continue selling flavored vape juice for the clunkier "open systems" of the refillable nature, which, the logic went, weren't the products teens were clamoring for.

At the same time, the policy effectively banned most flavored e-cigarette *cartridges,* like the kind sold by Juul, from being sold any-where in the United States until the products received marketing au-thorization from the FDA. No more unicorn milk pods. No more cherry lollipop cartridges. No more rainbow of fruit flavors. Impor-tantly, however, the policy exempted menthol, angering public-health groups that had pressed the administration to remove that flavor as well, since it remained one of the most popular products. Vape shops were furious that the administration moved ahead with any version of a ban whatsoever.

Amid the noise, Juul was sanguine. Ever the cunning tactician, Crosthwaite had already planned for exactly that scenario. Which is why for the past month, almost every day, at around seven A.M., a semi-truck rumbled to a stop in a remote Arkansas outpost near the border of Louisiana, leaving a frosty cloud of exhaust in the air. Its doors swung open, revealing pallets stacked as high as the truck's ceiling with stickers bearing a skull-and-crossbones and the word "Toxic." A closer look revealed more details. "Flavored Re-fill Kit," read one of the boxes. "Cucumber 5%," read another. "Juul Labs, Inc." was stamped all over them.

Over the final weeks of 2019, dozens of semitrucks just like this one—filled with $20 million worth of Juul pods—had been steering into this remote incineration facility. Since the company had taken all

376 THE DEVIL'S PLAYBOOK

its flavored products off the market, it was now faced with the task of destroying them, so the product didn't escape into the black market.

Over the next several hours, men unloaded the sea of pallets, containing thousands of boxes of Juul pods stacked on top of one another. They were wheeled onto a forklift and steered into a nearby warehouse where they awaited their fate in a holding facility. Soon, they were moved to the destruction site, loaded on a conveyor belt, and fed toward a big metal door that opened like the yawning jaws of a monster. The door opened into a massive funnel, and the boxes were dropped down into it. After the machine's teeth ripped apart the material, it was fed into a second shredder. Finally, the Juul remnants were sent to a kiln that was fired up to 2,600 degrees, hot enough to be a stage of hell in Dante's inferno. Barely an ash was left behind.

22

VENI VIDI VICI

> According to unicorn lore the animal was so swift, wild, and strong that it could not be taken alive.
>
> —HELMUT NICKEL, CURATOR, THE METROPOLITAN MUSEUM OF ART, ON THE UNICORN TAPESTRIES

I'm highly disappointed in the performance of our Juul investment," Willard said on a January 30, 2020, call with investors.

The company had just reported its most recent financial results and they were even worse than the last. Altria wrote down the value of its investment in Juul for a second time, this time in the amount of $4.1 billion. That meant that in just over a year, the value of the cigarette company's original $12.8 billion investment in Juul had been devalued to just $4.2 billion. Willard trying to bag Juul like a trophy kill was backfiring on him in a big way.

Shareholders had started filing lawsuits against Altria, demanding that the board investigate how its internal controls could have resulted in such a monumentally terrible outcome. They wanted to know in what universe Willard could have justified making the deal? And how could the board of directors have allowed it?

Litigation had long been the Achilles' heel of the tobacco industry. Nearly four decades since the housewife named Rose Cipollone dying of lung cancer sued Philip Morris and other tobacco companies, triggering an avalanche of litigation that engulfed the industry, Altria had been successful in being able to resolve many of the cases brought against it in a manner that allowed the company to continue being profitable. Any pending litigation was largely chalked up as a cost of doing business and any settlements paid out were largely already baked into the company's stock price. Shareholders had come to expect that investing in Altria entailed litigation risk. And for years the risk had been abating as the number of pending lawsuits against Altria related to cigarette smoking had declined, from about 425 in 1999, compared to fewer than 100 in 2019.

But now, the exposure to Juul was raising the specter of potentially damaging litigation risk again. Every month, the number of lawsuits mushroomed. By the end of October, the company had reported being named in nearly forty Juul-related lawsuits—twelve class action lawsuits and twenty-six individual lawsuits. Now, Altria was named as a defendant in more than one hundred Juul-related lawsuits.

As Willard announced the second impairment charge, he blamed it on mounting litigation. "This impairment is primarily due to the increased number of legal cases pending against Juul," Altria said in its financial disclosures, "and the expectation that the number of legal cases against Juul will continue to increase."

IT WAS A BLUSTERY morning in Washington, D.C., on February 5, 2020, as K.C. Crosthwaite, along with his longtime colleague at Altria, and now Juul, Joe Murillo, ducked inside the marble-encased Rayburn House Office Building, in the heart of Capitol Hill. Crosthwaite, along with four other CEOs of the largest U.S. e-cigarette companies, had been asked to testify before a House Energy and Commerce subcommittee in a hearing titled "Vaping in America: E-Cigarette Manufacturers' Impact on Public Health." Its purpose was to "give the American public the opportunity to hear directly from the captains of the five largest e-cigarette companies on their marketing practices, the public health implications of their products and their responsibility in addressing the nation's youth vaping epidemic."

Not a single seat in the hearing room was left empty—a testament to the furor that e-cigarettes had generated in recent months in the wake of EVALI. More than a dozen of those seats were occupied by advocates wearing bright orange T-shirts emblazoned with #DITCHVAPE across the front and that stood out against the backdrop of the room's wood-paneled walls and royal-blue carpeting. Just down the hallway, a hearing on the emerging coronavirus would soon be under way. The virus had ripped through China but hadn't yet registered in the United States as a credible threat.

If it seemed familiar that the hearing was being held in room 2123, that was by design. A quarter century earlier, the room served as the setting for the famous hearings that called CEOs of the largest tobacco companies to testify before a House Energy and Commerce subcommittee. The CEOs had stood up, raised their right hands, and stated their belief that nicotine was not addictive—the historic moment that had haunted the tobacco industry ever since.

Now, on this morning so many years later, the subcommittee chair, Diana DeGette, asked the five CEOs to stand up.

"Please rise and raise your right hand," said DeGette, a Democrat from Colorado.

The five men stood up.

"Do you swear that the testimony you're about to give is the truth, the whole truth, and nothing but the truth?"

The five men answered in the affirmative.

"I want to clear a couple of things up with this panel," she said. "These questions should be able to be answered with a simple yes or no answer. So, my first question is, isn't it true that nicotine is addictive? Mr. Crosthwaite?"

"Yes, nicotine is addictive," he responded, as did the four other men, one by one.

The remainder of the hearing lacked fireworks. No bombshells were dropped. Nothing more than mild discomfort ensued as the legislators questioned the executives. It all seemed a much tamer affair, compared to the hearings that took place a generation earlier. There was no smug Philip Morris executive attempting to upbraid the committee members for insinuating that he, along with the millions of American smokers, were drug addicts. There was no equating the executives' products with Twinkies or chocolate or cheese, as the tobacco executives in 1994 had done. There was no combative skewering by committee members who incredulously dismissed the tobacco executives as "fanatical" for maintaining with a straight face their stated positions that cigarettes were neither addictive nor cancer-causing.

But the simple existence of the hearing, and its accompanying theatrics, was loud and clear. A generation later, the tobacco industry was alive and well.

Which also meant that the plaintiffs' bar was alive and well. Over the past twenty-five years, plaintiffs' attorneys had made a killing off of lawsuits that successfully extracted large sums of money from punitive damages, or other awards tied to adverse verdicts or settlements. Whether class-action cases from the earlier years, or ongoing litigation in the Florida courts against tobacco companies, the practicing attorneys that brought lawsuits on behalf of smokers had dialed their art of advocacy into a well-paid science. An entire industry of expert witnesses on both sides had thrived as well, with some of the same experts being used over and over again for various cases. It's fair to say that ongoing tobacco litigation, tied to the harms of cigarettes, had developed into a well-oiled machine. Not surprisingly, it didn't take long for that machine to be turned on and fired up for Juul cases.

By the start of 2020, the number of lawsuits brought by individuals against Juul had mushroomed to thousands. School districts across the country also brought their own cases, alleging a variety of issues, including that Juul had caused the districts to divert money and resources to contain the nicotine problem. Many school districts demanded that Juul fund nicotine addiction treatment for the nation's youth. There were so many individual cases that eventually they were consolidated before a single federal judge in San Francisco.

At the same time, since North Carolina attorney general Josh Stein brought his case, and also Massachusetts attorney general Maura Healey, a growing number of state attorneys general began bringing their own lawsuits against Juul. The cases were in part aided by a network of lawyers working on ongoing litigation against drugmakers for their role in creating the opioid epidemic, and others who'd participated in the tobacco Master Settlement Agreement, including former Mississippi attorney general Mike Moore, now a board member at the Campaign for Tobacco-Free Kids. By the end of 2020, nearly forty states were investigating or had sued the e-cigarette company. There were discussions of whether there might be a new kind of master settlement agreement.

Between the congressional hearings and the mounting litigation, and rising ire of a nation, the Juul matter was starting to look more and more like the quagmire from the days of the Tobacco Wars.

Which meant that it was a good time to get out of Dodge. On March 12, Monsees sent an email around to the entire company announcing his departure from Juul, even as Bowen remained the company's chief technology officer.

"After 15 years on this tremendous journey, it is with a great deal of thought and consideration that I have decided it is time for me to move on from Juul Labs," he wrote. "As both a founder and a major shareholder, I could not be more proud of the thoughtful actions that are being taken and the people in whose hands I'm leaving the company for its next great chapter."

THE EARLIEST PHILIP MORRIS logos featured a gold heraldic crest flanked by a rampant lion on one side, and a unicorn (later a horse) on the other. Underneath, a banner read VENI VIDI VICI, the Latin phrase attributed to Julius Caesar, meaning "I came, I saw, I conquered."

Howard A. Willard III endeavored to embody the spirit of the company's great conquering tradition. He'd devoted his life to the cigarette maker, and fought in some of its most searing battles. But in this moment in time, the high-flying executive who over a quarter of a century had reached the pinnacle of the Fortune 500 firm, was on the precipice of succumbing to his own ambitions.

By mid-March the coronavirus had started metastasizing in the

United States. For an industry dependent on selling a product inhaled into the human lungs, it seemed an odd fate that *another* respiratory illness of an entirely different nature was befalling the nation. As if lungs hadn't been in the news enough. Now there wasn't only talk about whether vaping was safe, there were questions anew about whether people who vaped were at higher risks of contracting coronavirus.

Cities had started implementing lockdowns, and other restrictive measures, but not fast enough. The virus was starting to burn through communities like wildfire. Still it came with a level of surprise when on March 18 Altria announced that it had detected the first case of coronavirus internally. The following day, the company announced a second case and said that it would shut down its Richmond cigarette factory—halting the company's only domestic cigarette manufacturing plant, which produced half of all the nation's cigarettes. That evening, even more bad news. Murray Garnick, the company's longtime general counsel, sent out an email to all its employees with the subject line "Important News about Howard."

> Dear Employees,
>
> I'm sorry to inform you that today Howard was diagnosed as positive for COVID-19. Howard has been out of the office for several days, and we have notified those who were in close contact with Howard and asked them to self-quarantine for 14 days.

This did not bode well for Willard, to say the least. The board had just recently denied him his annual bonus, a rare measure taken by corporate boards, citing "the significant impact that Altria's 2018 minority investment in Juul Labs, Inc. has had on shareholder value." Now, with Willard sidelined on medical leave, Billy Gifford, the chief financial officer who'd been at the company since 1994 and who himself helped negotiate the deal with Juul, was put in charge temporarily until Willard was healthy enough to come back. Over the next two weeks, as Willard battled his illness, his fate, along with that of his most monumental deal, only worsened. On April Fool's Day, the Federal Trade Commission filed a complaint that sought to unwind the deal in its entirety.

The agency alleged that the two companies violated federal antitrust laws by entering into a series of agreements that resulted in Altria ceasing to be a competitor in the e-cigarette market "in return for a substantial ownership interest in JLI, by far the dominant player in that market."

If the FTC proved its case, the most draconian outcome could result in the agency requiring Altria to divest its stake in Juul, and reverse the deal in its entirety. It was hard to imagine that happening, if only because, well, the $12.8 billion that Altria gave to Juul—it was long gone into the pockets of Valani, Pritzker, Bowen, Monsees, and Burns, along with other board members, investors, and employees. There were a range of other less severe actions the agency could take, including the appointment of an independent monitor to oversee aspects of the arrangement, or a requirement that the companies file periodic reports with the agency. A trial was set for April 2021.

ABOUT TWO WEEKS AFTER the FTC suit was filed, the curtain fell on Altria's CEO. "Mr. Willard, who was recovering from COVID-19, decided to step down following 28 years of distinguished service to Altria and its subsidiaries," the company announced. Willard never even made it to his second annual meeting in Richmond. Instead of bringing glory to his former employer with his bold promise to usher in change to the tired old cigarette maker, Willard instead brought unwanted controversy to a company that had worked tirelessly for two decades to avoid exactly that. To stay out of the limelight. To quietly go about its deadly business without raising too many hackles. Now it was in the center of the most unseemly limelight. Willard violated Altria's cardinal rule: He tried to move the long hand to three o'clock.

In the pantheon of deals gone sideways in corporate America—from Quaker Oats's $1.7 billion purchase of Snapple in 1994 to Bayer AG's ill-timed $63 billion acquisition of Monsanto in 2018—not to mention the flameouts and scandals that have perennially tarnished lustrous Silicon Valley such as WeWork, Uber, Theranos—Willard's Juul deal ranked near the top. The words of Willard's predecessor, Marty Barrington, may well have been prescient: "I think it's worth remembering the history," he'd once said about e-cigarette companies. "There have been some rockets before that haven't sustained their trajectory."

Silicon Valley has a brightness to it. It has the power to polish old monoliths, to liberate them from their heirloom inventors, and to make them new again—Big Taxi (Uber), Big Hotel (Airbnb), Big Auto (Tesla), Big Fitness (Peloton). It has the ability to package ideas and concepts inside flashy gadgets and slick apps, and turn mundane businesses into gallant unicorns. Yet Silicon Valley's sheen can be so glaring that even the most seasoned of humans transfixed by it can be blinded by its brilliant light.

Which is what happened when Willard was cast in its glare. Altria was in the throes of a careful regeneration and was paranoid about protecting its moated ramparts, long under siege. Altria's previous leaders resisted the lure of what was an undeniably tantalizing opportunity. Watching Juul grow ultimately became unbearable for Willard. He became convinced that he could bring to bear all the experience and knowledge that he and his tobacco company had acquired over decades. That he could swoop in and with the snap of his checkbook fix the intractable problem that was ultimately born of the weight of the company's own historical burden. It was, after all, the deadliness of the product it sold that was causing its customers to take flight from the product, if not from the earthly realm. Howard Willard too was blinded by Silicon Valley's light.

It wasn't only that. Willard got to Juul too late, after the damage had already been done. Rather than investing in an asset that could round out the cigarette company's core business, he bought a grenade, with the pin already pulled. Surely, his advisers and the board of directors knew what they were getting into, and it was always possible that down the road Willard would come out looking like the smartest guy in the room. But in the short-term at least, it's unfolded about as badly as his skeptics feared: When Willard took over, Altria had a market capitalization of more than $100 billion. By the end of 2020 it was clocking below $80 billion, and soon Altria had written down the value of its Juul stake to just $1.6 billion.

Also by the end of 2020, Altria was named as a defendant in more than one thousand lawsuits involving Juul, including charges ranging from fraud and unjust enrichment, to violating Racketeer Influenced and Corrupt Organizations, or RICO, laws. The company's own shareholders sued the company, alleging that Willard and the Altria board breached their fiduciary duty in the course of executing the Juul deal by failing to disclose the deal's inherent risks. It was unclear how much liability Altria could ultimately face in those lawsuits, but nonetheless it was a suboptimal situation for a company that has strategically avoided incurring new legal risks.

Some of Willard's allies pointed out that he had no choice. Was he to stand by and watch as its business got eviscerated by two kids from Stanford? Shareholders wouldn't have stood for that either. He was in between the proverbial rock and a hard place.

Others were less generous: "It's a mess," said one former Altria executive. "He has made a huge mess."

"I think he was in a hurry to make a mark," said another.

A third former Altria executive summed it up perhaps perfectly: "If he's guilty of anything, he's guilty of being obsessed with being a new chairman and wanting to rock the world, and it blinded him."

Yet despite it all, Altria still managed to keep churning out a profit. Thanks to the company's built-in lever, the company could simply increase the price of cigarettes, banking on the product's inelasticity of demand, to offset volume declines or rocky patches, and continue to churn out ever more profit. Even a penny increase in a pack of cigarettes could move the needle on the balance sheet. That's why even with the stunning write-down of Juul, the public's ire over the teen nicotine epidemic, and the FTC's threat to unwind the entire deal, Altria was still powering along. It still delivered annual earnings growth, and spit out its quarterly dividends to shareholders like it had done for half a century. The cow was still being milked, as they say, and likely would be for some time to come, even in the shadow of the calamitous Juul ordeal.

That was the magic of the cigarette business—no matter how bad things got, no matter how many people loved to hate Big Tobacco, nearly 40 million Americans still smoked, and millions of Marlboros still rolled off the factory line in a white blur every single day.

Willard did notch one lasting achievement. He became the shortest-tenured CEO in the tobacco company's history.

WILLARD'S FORMER DEPUTY, K.C. Crosthwaite, wasn't having much of an easier time over at his new gig. Not long after he took over as Juul's CEO, one of his first official visits had been to Seoul. Juul had landed in South Korea a few months earlier, with Bowen and Monsees appearing as prominent guests at a launch event. The company later opened a brick-and-mortar store in a ritzy area of the Gangnam neighborhood that sold the device in slate and silver colors, along with flavors that went by the names Crisp, Delight, Fresh, and Tropical.

South Korea had been Juul's first Asian market, followed (however briefly) by China, Indonesia, and the Philippines, and was supposed to have been a crowning outpost that would cash in on a nation where up to half of all adult men smoked. Korea represented the tip of the spear of the company's international expansion story, one that had enticed investors, including Altria, who were eager to share in an unprecedented-in-size bounty as the company blanketed the globe with its product and landed in the hands of the world's one billion smokers. Uber had done it before, and so had Airbnb—two Silicon Valley start-ups that predicated their sizzling growth strategy on bulldozing their way around the globe, a strategy fraught with risks as regulations and rules and influence centers vary from market to market. As Uber pointed out in its financial disclosures ahead of its 2019 initial public offering, "Our business is substantially dependent on operations outside the United States, including those in markets in which we have limited experience, and if we are unable to manage the risks presented by our business model internationally, our financial results and future prospects will be adversely impacted."

When Crosthwaite went to tend to Juul's South Korean investment, the company had already begun falling prey to exactly those types of risks. Amid the lung injury outbreak in the United States, in late October the Korean health ministry abruptly issued a warning to consumers to stop using e-cigarettes until the science showed them to be safe. Hours later one of the nation's largest convenience store retailers, GS25, pulled Juul's flavored products from its stores, dealing a blow to the company.

Meanwhile, sales of Juul were far from taking off in South Korea. To anybody familiar with the popularity of the product in the United States, that might be puzzling. But for those inside Juul, it was a no-brainer. Because of strict regulations on the products, the company's Juul pods there contained less than 1 percent nicotine, compared to the usual 5 percent in pods sold in the United States. It didn't take a rocket scientist to know that Juul's success in the United States was based on its potent nicotine salt solution that easily hooked its users. That had been a key element of the business model—make a product strong enough to entice smokers. A product with barely any nicotine simply wouldn't catch on.

In South Korea, as in other international markets, that much was becoming painfully clear: Juul's optimistic sales forecasts underpinning its international expansion had been badly miscalculated. "They knew the product they had wouldn't convert as many people as the five percent," said a former executive. "We all told them it wasn't going to, but they built their models based on this crazy fucking idea that somehow this product that had less nicotine in it would attract as many people."

Between the weak nicotine, the lack of any careful strategic dialogue with regulators before entering these markets, and a patchwork of restrictive local regulations around the world, the company's once-ambitious international expansion was about to tank. China had already pulled Juul from online retailers. India had banned e-cigarettes in September 2019, citing a concern over potential youth abuse. The Philippines president, Rodrigo Duterte, called for the arrest of anybody vaping, saying in a November 2019 speech that "nicotine is an addictive devil."

Under the cover of the lung injuries hit, and then the coronavirus, Crosthwaite took a hatchet to the company. There was no time to waste. On May 5, Crosthwaite called a company-wide meeting to an-nounce a second round of layoffs. This time he was laying off a third of the company's remaining three thousand employees and ceasing operations in South Korea. Several more overseas markets would likely follow, including Austria, Belgium, France, Portugal, and Spain, all coun-tries that Crosthwaite said were no longer sustainable. The bottom was falling out of Juul's international market. "We will no longer scale for the sake of expansion," he said in an internal company memo.

And then, Crosthwaite announced that Juul would be relocating its corporate headquarters from San Francisco to Washington, D.C. Now Juul would be closer to the regulators who held the company's fate, which was hanging by a thread.

All of these moves were designed with surgical precision, the kind that only a tobacco executive knows how to execute best. They were intended to subdue the company's worst Silicon Valley impulses. To eschew the company's growth-at-all-costs ethos that gave rise not to just any unicorn but one with the blood of a raging bull. Crosthwaite knew that righting Juul's ship wouldn't be as easy as relocating its cor-porate home, or even publicly disavowing its viral internet roots. He needed to rip out any rot from beneath the ground. Ultimately, for the business to succeed it needed to foreswear the flashy, growth-obsessed philosophy, and embrace what his old-cigarette company had become: a boring, mundane business that quietly went about servicing addic-tion.

There's always been an art to running a tobacco company, a com-pany that sells a product that is almost guaranteed to kill its customer. While some might believe it involves brute force, it's much more com-plicated than that. It's not enough to simply make bold public pro-nouncements about, say, stopping youth addiction. It's about deeply internalizing the idea that you need buy-in from society to stay in busi-ness. About demonstrating that you're not just slinging nicotine hits to anybody with a pumping heart but being a responsible steward of a portfolio of highly addictive products.

It entails quietly flexing muscle with guile. It requires not iron-fisted diplomacy or coercive threats but the type of soft power wielded

behind closed doors in the halls of Congress, in stuffy offices of government regulators, and in the text of byzantine rules and regulations.
It's the kind of power that the famous Harvard political scientist Joseph Nye articulated, saying, "seduction is always more effective than
coercion." Tobacco executives have long known that without it, you'll
get your head chopped off.

It's the grand bargain that Philip Morris learned the hard way how
to execute after the Tobacco Wars. Silicon Valley has always been about
asking for forgiveness rather than permission. Crosthwaite was well
aware that in the addiction business that maxim needed to be inverted.
You must first obtain permission from society, and only then can you
go on, under the cover of societal grace, to make shit-tons of money.
It's the slightest tweaks in strategy that make all the difference. It is
about Steve Parrish's concepts of "societal alignment" and "constructive engagement" that he taught his employees in San Juan so many
years ago under threat of a hurricane. Or that he wrote about in an
article in the *Yale Journal of Health Policy, Law, and Ethics* titled "Bridging
the Divide," in which he quoted Ralph Waldo Emerson: "If you meet
a sectary, or a hostile partisan, never recognize the dividing lines; but
meet on what common ground remains,—if only that the sun shines,
and the rain rains for both; the area will widen very fast, and ere you
know it the boundary mountains, on which the eye had fastened, have
melted into air."

The irony is that when Willard and Co. were initially contemplat-
ing a deal with Juul, they spoke candidly about how the potential
"ownership risk"—the simple association with an "evil" tobacco
company—could irrevocably tarnish Juul's reputation, and therefore
touch off regulatory or market reactions that would undermine the
business and send the valuable talent that had flocked to the company
packing. The Altria executives also talked in a surprisingly self-reflective
way about the potential perils of "culture risk." In essence, Willard
warned that in the event of a deal with Juul, the cigarette company
should ensure that Altria's stifling hierarchical culture was kept at bay
as much as possible so as not to ruin the San Francisco start-up's magic.
"Howard's words specifically were 'if we run it, we're going to fuck it

up,'" said a former Altria insider. "We said we'd clean it up with guidance and process, but the company should be kept on the west coast to
keep it as far from the mothership as possible."

But Crosthwaite had no choice but to bring Juul deeper into its
embrace. The company had run into the ground in such a profound
way that it needed to be rescued, lest Altria's biggest investment get
completely flushed down the drain. The company simply didn't have
the bench of talent needed to dig itself out of the ditch, and there was
no better prescription in its darkest moment of crisis than Altria's dis-
tinct genre of managerial expertise. As a result, with every passing day,
Juul would morph ever more into the likeness of Big Tobacco.

Three days after Crosthwaite's jarring announcement, there came
another one. The company's finance department had recently conducted an appraisal of the fair market value of Juul. After taking into
account updated financial forecasts and projections in the United States
and overseas, the latest valuation of the company was $13 billion. The
estimated worth of Juul was now a sliver of what it had been at the
time Altria invested.

Every day throughout 2020, dozens of new lawsuits were filed
against Juul, adding to the hundreds of individual plaintiffs that had
already joined the massive multi-district litigation in federal court in
San Francisco. There were more lawsuits filed on behalf of minors
who'd become addicted to Juul. There were more lawsuits filed by
adults who claimed Juul contributed to lung injuries or chest pains, and
users who claimed the defective product design caused nicotine poisoning. To represent the company in this complex litigation, Juul hired
David Bernick, a renowned trial attorney who defended the Sackler
family in the OxyContin litigation and W.R. Grace & Co. in the government's landmark asbestos poisoning criminal trial. Bernick also had
a long history representing the tobacco industry. He represented Philip
Morris USA in a cigarette class action, and served as general counsel of
Philip Morris International. In the Department of Justice's racketeer-
ing case against Big Tobacco, Bernick represented Brown & Williamson and cross-examined David Kessler.

A Juul shareholder sued the Juul board for allegedly breaching its fiduciary duty. "After the huge investment by Altria," the complaint read, the board and executives "breached their duties of loyalty by using the money disproportionately to pay themselves massive bonuses. They also failed to invest sufficient capital in the company to strengthen Juul's internal controls, R&D, and other projects, which, had they been made, would have protected the company from the recent events that resulted in lawsuits, governmental investigations, and a . . . decrease in the value of the company."

At the same time, some of the state attorneys general cases were preparing to go to trial. Meanwhile, multiple government agencies continued to pursue various probes into actions by the company that potentially violated federal law, including potentially lying to federal investigators and withholding information from investors.

By the end of 2020, Juul's valuation had notched another decline to $10 billion, a stunning fall from its lofty $38 billion just two years earlier. At the same time, its sales were on a downward trend, having been left with just a fraction of its once-robust portfolio of flavors. That was partly a function of new products gaining popularity, and potentially a function of a declining youth market. The 2020 National Youth Tobacco Survey showed that there were 1.8 million fewer middle school and high school students using e-cigarettes, a reflection perhaps of the negative attention surrounding e-cigarettes alongside the deadly lung injuries that might have scared teens away from them. However, the same data showed that those remaining 3.6 million youths still using e-cigarettes were using them more frequently—almost a quarter reported using them daily—indicating that current users had a strong nicotine addiction.

Meanwhile, the fancy San Francisco office tower at 123 Mission Street that Juul bought at the peak of the company's frenzied expansion was becoming a stone around its neck. Juul put the building up for sale, just five months after the company paid $400 million for it. With the market downturn that hit alongside the coronavirus, there were few potential buyers. Two had already fallen through. It wasn't going to be easy to unload the twenty-eight-story tower at a price anywhere close to what Juul originally paid. So, 123 Mission stood largely empty, a towering totem to the promises Bowen and Monsees made. The promise to make the world a better place with their product. The promise to kill Big Tobacco. The grandiose promises, like so many others made in Silicon Valley.

DESPITE ALL THE RANCOR sparked by Bowen and Monsees's nicotine creation, the founders and the investors undeniably made out like bandits. Around the time Monsees left Juul, he purchased a $24 million home that sat at the top of a hill overlooking all of San Francisco. The sale broke the record in the city for the highest price per square foot in a single-family home. The newly renovated house was filled with modern art and described as a contemporary and architectural triumph. Its architect described being inside the light-filled house, with views of the fog-shrouded Golden Gate Bridge, as if you were floating over the entire city of San Francisco. That was fitting for Monsees, because in a way, he had risen up above the city, for better or for worse.

He'd recently gotten married and when he left Juul he'd said he was "looking forward to spending more time with my family." Normally when a corporate executive or politician says they are stepping down for family reasons, it's a euphemism for being fired. In this case, people who knew Monsees said he truly wanted to move on. And why not? The company he and Bowen built was no longer the same place. It was occupied by the sworn enemy. He no longer had to fight anymore. Monsees was leaving the company orders of magnitude richer than when he started this odyssey from the back patio of Stanford's design school. His company had become a unicorn. He'd attained peak Silicon Valley tech founder status. He came and saw and conquered, just like the old Marlboro logo said.

Bowen, meanwhile, remained at Juul, serving as an adviser to Crosthwaite in the Founders' Office, but largely giving up day-to-day control. He spent time traveling back and forth to Argentina, where he had family. The company he had started ended up being even more gravity-defying than the "vomit comet."

Nick Pritzker remained on Juul's board of directors, and, at least before Covid, could be found at Burning Man or hosting epic camp-outs under the stars for friends at a family compound and cattle ranch deep in the rolling grasslands and fields of wild hyacinth and clover in Marin County. With all the fiery fallout from his Juul investment, the Pritzker family's reputation might have taken a hit, but its bank account most definitely did not.

Riaz Valani is living like a king. Before Juul, he was scrapping for deals anywhere he could, from David Bowie's pockets to the garages of Silicon Valley. Now he was a billionaire many times over. In 2020 he paid $40 million in cash to purchase Johnny Carson's old estate in Malibu, landing the understated investor a slice of paradise overlooking the glittering Pacific Ocean, where dolphins could be seen cresting in and out of the waves in a rhythm as the sun set each day, leaving behind smoldering peach and lavender skies.

Not everyone could sleep so well at night. In the days after leaving the company, the former Juul employee Ryan Woodring meditated on the past half of a year that he'd spent at Juul, and all the years before in the advertising industry. He couldn't help but feel at least in part personally responsible for the endemic problems roiling San Francisco, the rising wealth inequality, the homelessness, the fractured value system that prioritized profit over all else. And then the youth nicotine crisis on top of it all. He needed his life to change. He decided to quit advertising altogether, and began pursuing a degree in social work instead. He also decided to quit Juuling. He felt compelled to cleanse himself of Juul and everything it entailed. He wanted to get rid of it all. The guilt-inducing memories of selling the product. The muscle memory of bringing the nicotine delivery device up to his lips, throughout the day, day after day. He started chewing nicotine gum, which satisfied him enough and didn't leave him with heart palpitations. A year after leaving Juul he was counseling homeless people in San Francisco, helping them connect with social services, find housing, and cope with the dire and harsh needs of living on the streets while billionaires walked past them. For Woodring, working for Juul had undone him in a way no other job ever had. It had affected him on a much deeper level. Juul had a way of doing that. It, in fact, coursed through people's veins.

———

FOR PETE BRIGER, TALKING about Juul, even years after his first run-in with the product, still makes his blood boil. After the Altria deal, he realized that the game had changed in a significant way, and making an impact would require forces much bigger than even his and his friends' resolve and substantial resources.

"Tobacco companies are in the business of litigation. They go home to their husband or their wife after a long day at the office and they say, 'Hey, honey, how you doing?' And then they move on from there thinking that they're good people, even though they're involved in litigation where the result is, they can infect more people if they win," Briger said. "These guys have tens of hundreds of millions of dollars to litigate. So, you have to figure out whether or not you're throwing buckets of water into the ocean and whether you really want to compete against the ocean." Still, Briger has vowed to keep fighting the ocean in his own way. He joined the board of the UCSF Foundation. He and his wife, Devon, made a $1.65 million donation to UCSF's Center for Tobacco Control Research and Education, which funded a new research position called the "Briger Fellow" focused on eradicating tobacco use around the world.

Eradicating nicotine addiction won't be an easy task. There are a growing number of new nicotine products that have figured out how to game FDA rules to stay on the market, like Puff Bar, a disposable e-cigarette that wasn't categorized as one of the "pod-based" products that were banned and so can still be purchased in vape shops in a dizzying array of flavors, like Blue Raz, Lychee Ice, Café Latte, and O.M.G. (orange, mango, grapefruit). Also widely available still are berry-flavored nicotine pouches, and nicotine gums like Lucy, which is sold in brightly colored boxes and has the tagline "Tastes like real fruit not nicotine." Regulators simply cannot keep up, and the market is now fueled by the new generation of nicotine addicts that Juul helped birth.

Chenyue Xing, the chemist that helped develop its proprietary nicotine solution, left the company about a year after it hit the market, and has gone on to launch her own e-cigarette company called Myst

Labs, which makes a nicotine salt pod product similar to Juul that she is targeting toward adult smokers in China.

Since leaving the FDA, Scott Gottlieb has gone on to be a vocal critic of Juul, using his favored mode of communication, Twitter, to lambast the company. "The youth vaping crisis was always a Juul crisis," he tweeted in the months after he left the agency. "I believe they primarily created it. One company, bent on pursuing top line growth at almost any cost, may have wrecked the entire concept of harm reduction in the U.S."

Meanwhile, Mitch Zeller at the FDA's Center for Tobacco Products is in the process of reviewing the hundreds, if not thousands, of applications that it's received from e-cigarette companies seeking the agency's all-important authorization they need to continue selling their products. The agency's task is an impossible one—no matter which way it rules on Juul, or other products, there will undoubtedly be anger from either side, and potentially litigation that could hamstring the agency for years. If Juul doesn't receive marketing authorization, the company will be left without a product to sell. It's hard to see the agency rendering a decision that would single-handedly annihilate an American company. But no doubt public-health advocates would be furious if the agency concluded the product that arguably bears the most culpability for creating the youth nicotine epidemic met the agency's standard of being "appropriate for the protection of the public health." Of course, adult smokers would argue that it should meet the definition since what better way to protect the public health than to get people off deadly cigarettes?

The surviving squirrel monkeys that had been subjects in the FDA's youth nicotine experiments in the Arkansas research laboratory, and which Gottlieb had vowed to save, indeed landed in a primate sanctuary. Poppit and Gizmo and Pip, and others from their research cohort, can be found at Jungle Friends in Gainesville, Florida, swinging from tree branches and munching on banana leaves as they live out their new life. Music is piped over speakers into their new habitat. On one day when a reporter visited them, they were listening to "Joy to the World."

———

IT TOOK SEVERAL MONTHS for Logan Krahn, the teenager from Wisconsin, to wean himself off nicotine with the help of the nicotine patch. But a year after the lung injury he sustained from vaping, he still hadn't fully recovered. Even the smallest of physical activities winded him. Krahn's pediatrician had warned Rebecca that her son might suffer from decreased pulmonary function for some time, perhaps forever.

Over the summer of 2020 he was with his mom and siblings at the family cabin on French Lake. At one point, Rebecca glimpsed Logan swimming in the lake. Her heart raced. It looked like he was huffing and puffing as if he'd swum the entire length of the lake. He was fine, but Rebecca was still getting used to seeing her previously healthy son gasping for oxygen.

There's a bright side, she said.

"You know how teenagers don't like to say I love you in front of their friends and family?" she asked. "Now it doesn't matter who he's with—he takes that second every time to tell me, 'I love you.'"

AFTERWORD

I find it somewhat fitting that it was a sixteenth-century Parisian alchemist who was likely the first to isolate nicotine from tobacco, a
surprisingly lovely flowering nightshade plant native to America that
produces spring-green leaves and dainty pink blooms before it is heat-
blasted to a burnt umber and subjected to fire.

All along humans have been transfixed by the plant's powerful
elixir, and in seemingly eternal pursuit of its wonders with as much
furor and devotion as an alchemist's quest to turn base metals into
gold. It speaks to the power of the drug that these simple leaves have
long since been the root of such tempestuousness and divide, as kings
and colonizers, and then regulators and lawmakers, have struggled to
contain it.

Enslaved people were brought in chains to colonial America to grow a crop from the loamy Virginia soil, forming the bedrock of a nascent nation. Hogsheads filled with tobacco were rolled from inland farms to wharves, literally carving out new roads from the land. Shipping routes were mapped by tobacco traders plying the seas between America and Europe. The British army burned colonizers' curing barns and tobacco fields during the American Revolutionary War. Tobacco grew into a mainstay of the southern economy, whose farmers and merchants wielded immense power in state legislatures and Congress, where they continue to hold vast sway.

It was why when David Kessler's Food and Drug Administration asserted regulatory jurisdiction over tobacco in the 1990s, he ran up against a formidable foe. Tobacco had been so enmeshed in American life that when the U.S. Supreme Court ruled on the matter, Sandra Day O'Connor cited in her majority opinion "tobacco's unique political history" as a reason why the FDA had overstepped its bounds. Surely, she stated, Congress never tacitly intended for the agency to regulate, potentially out of existence, "an industry constituting a significant portion of the American economy." *That* is the cornerstone of the devil's playbook—all those centuries of amassed power and deeply rooted tradition woven into every last fiber of American society.

To understand the fate of Juul, it is imperative to also understand those roots. Adam Bowen and James Monsees were modern-day alchemists. More than four hundred years after nicotine was known to man they too retreated into labs and toiled over the oil of tobacco. They too were seduced by the plant, so much so that they turned their lives over to it. They too were caught in a firestorm engendered by its very existence. And on top of everything, they got swept up in powerful forces contained in another storied place, Silicon Valley.

So much of Silicon Valley is built on storytelling. Its start-up founders are notorious for spinning wild tales that are just believable enough that a venture capitalist will bite. Unicorns are born out of these stories. Indeed, the Valley gives its raconteurs wide latitude and a more than generous benefit of the doubt. Aswath Damodaran, a professor of finance at the Stern School of Business at NYU, and an expert in corporate finance and valuation, calls these tech start-ups "story companies." "As we saw with Theranos, in its rapid fall from grace, there is a dark side to story companies," he wrote. "And it stems from the fact that value is built on a personality, rather than a business, and when the personality stumbles or acts in a way viewed as untrustworthy, the runaway story can quickly morph into a meltdown story, where the ingredients curdle."

It's not that Juul didn't have an underlying business. In nicotine, Bowen and Monsees saw a glittering opportunity that appeared to embody the platonic Silicon Valley ideal. The global nicotine market is valued at a massive $820 billion a year—a market that includes not just cigarettes and other traditional tobacco products but an array of e-cigarettes and gums and patches and lozenges and sprays. Also, its customers are ideal; they'll buy your product before almost anything else, because, as lab rats have proved, its most ardent users need it just like they need food and water. And for the most part they won't grow bored or tired of buying your product. There's even a decent chance that they'll use it for life, making them incredibly lucrative customers to capture.

When Bowen and Monsees first stumbled upon their idea, they were amazed to learn that the cigarette, of all things, hadn't been touched by Silicon Valley's magic. They assumed that nobody had done it before simply because nobody had been smart enough to do it. But what they failed to account for early on, and what investors glossed over, was that there was a reason the opportunity hadn't been snapped up before with such gusto: At its heart the product for sale was one that had a cursed history, and that had left such a searing bruise on society, that there was no room for error.

Nevertheless, they took their shiny Stanford degrees, and without initially the modicum of care inherently demanded by the product, tackled the opportunity just like one might in any other industry in need of a fresh coat of paint. What they didn't realize, as they built their Silicon Valley story, was they were building it on the foundation of America's very own tortured epic. And for that, there would inevitably be a heavy price to pay.

Steve Parrish, in the end, rightly zeroed in on the fact that tobacco is one of those products that is sold at the mercy of a society that has granted it permission to exist. "We don't make widgets," he famously said, as Philip Morris underwent its transformation. Unfortunately, Bowen and Monsees made a product that they at first treated like a widget.

By marketing Juul like a smartphone or a fashion accessory or a pair of powder-blue curved-waistband chinos, they ignored that there might be consequences for unleashing their highly addictive nicotine creation on the world. They packaged their story about harm reduction and wrapped it in a big red bow, presenting it to anyone who would listen, and ultimately selling their creation to anyone with a credit card. And investors without the requisite institutional memory or appreciation of history, some indifferent to casualty, egged them on. Together they put into motion a well-oiled symbiosis that delivered what they both wanted—what everybody in Silicon Valley wanted— a lavish return.

They did not fully consider the consequences of designing a bauble flashy and small enough to be stashed in backpacks and underneath hoodies, one that delivered gluttonous amounts of a high-concentration nicotine potion laced with the taste of fruit smoothies. By infusing each single pod with a pack's worth of nicotine, Juul found a way to shoot more nicotine into the human body than anyone had ever thought possible. Only the rarest of smokers suck down a pack of cigarettes a day, but with Juul, teenagers were inhaling that much or more on a daily basis. Not even the big bad tobacco companies ever conceived their product to deliver *that much* nicotine.

As a society, after all these years, we haven't quite come to terms with nicotine. There aren't a tremendous number of addictive products sold legally in America. And most that are, like prescription drugs, are strictly regulated and sold as a controlled substance. Nicotine isn't. Yet unlike some highly addictive drugs, nicotine isn't incapacitating or overwhelmingly deadly. It doesn't cause people to get into car crashes. It doesn't result in overdose or suicide. And while nicotine isn't a completely harmless substance (especially in youth), in the end it is a product that's simply very addictive. Setting aside the youth issue for a moment, are we okay with having millions of Americans hooked on a mostly benign drug in perpetuity? What does it matter if adults derive moments of joy and satisfaction from it in an often dull and dreary life?

While nicotine-containing e-cigarettes might have been tied to the nationwide lung disease outbreak, it's also true that most (not all) of those injuries were linked to THC products, many likely bootlegged. And while a massive youth addiction epidemic might have initially sprung out of Juul, what if regulators and retailers and manufacturers could solve for that problem by doubly ensuring that sales were restricted to adults and letting the product live for another day? That's certainly Juul's argument, and others' in the pro-vaping movement. Undeniably, plenty of research has shown that migrating adult smokers away from combustible cigarettes to alternative nicotine products could save millions of lives. Isn't that a goal worthy in itself?

The problem is it's hard to give the tobacco (now nicotine) industry the benefit of the doubt. There have been too many moments of deceit and too many bad actors in the industry for far too long. It leaves a public to wonder, "What is the industry *not* telling us about its product?" Do they know today about e-cigarettes the equivalent of what they knew five decades ago when they spoke only in hushed tones about cancer as "you know what"? Or are they shrouding their science under the guise of Twinkies, like one of the tobacco CEOs did in the Waxman hearing when denying that cigarettes were addictive, only to have Waxman retort, "Yes, but the difference between cigarettes and Twinkies is death."

There are simply not enough answers when it comes to inhaling atomized nicotine into the human lungs over long periods of time. Back in the 1950s, an outspoken anti-smoking physician named Alton Ochsner rankled the tobacco industry when he began publicizing his belief that there was a correlation between smoking cigarettes and the cancerous tumors he was starting to see in disturbing numbers on the lungs of cadavers. He recalled that when he was a medical student in 1919, lung cancer had been so rare that two senior classes were summoned "to witness the autopsy of a man having died of carcinoma of the lung because Dr. George Dock, Professor of Medicine, thought we might never see another such case as long as we lived," he wrote in a later editorial in the journal *Chest*.

Of course, when Ochsner became a practicing surgeon, he began seeing more and more such cases. "In the last 15 years I have seen thousands," he told a reporter in a January 1950 *Reader's Digest* article titled "How Harmful Are Cigarettes?," which sent shock waves through the tobacco industry. "I am convinced that there is a definite relationship between smoking and cancer of the lung," he said. In particular, Ochsner believed that the sudden appearance of lung cancer wasn't sudden at all—it was just only now starting to show up, decades after a generation of young men had taken up smoking in droves (aided by war rations issued with cigarettes) while deployed during World War I. Not only had the soldiers come home with war injuries and trauma, but they'd come home addicted to cigarettes and burdened by lung disease later in life. The cancers took nearly a generation to grow and metastasize before the medical community began witnessing them with their own two eyes.

Might the same prove true for e-cigarettes? Could it be that we won't know about any long-term damage done to the lungs of today's teenage Juul users until they have children of their own? The FDA certainly wondered. Toward the end of Gottlieb's tenure, the agency began doing animal toxicology studies after seeing data that indicated there could be potential health risks from vaping. "We're looking at the potential for direct effects of harm from e-cigarettes on the lungs as well as other health factors that these products could negatively impact," the FDA reported in a little-noticed April 2019 press release. "In particular, we have concerns about the direct effects of e-cigarettes on the airways. This includes the potential for the use of such products to cause changes to airways that could be a precursor to cancer." As Alan Louis Shihadeh, an aerosol scientist at the American University of Beirut, said about e-cigarettes: *"We're conducting a big, uncontrolled and poorly documented set of chemistry experiments inside people's lungs."* E-cigarettes simply haven't been around long enough for anybody to endow them with a clean bill of health.

On the other hand, perhaps we owe it to the smoking generation—

largely now our parents and grandparents—to send them a lifeline today. Given all we know about cigarettes' deadliness, shouldn't it be a national imperative to provide smokers with something safer, even if that option isn't perfect? Many people believe that it's worth hedging their bets. And perhaps it is.

That's not even addressing the most pernicious problem of them all: youth. There is too much evidence showing that those in the tobacco industry who knew better predicated the future of their business on generations to come as much as on their current users. That's why Kessler so brilliantly noted two decades ago that nicotine use is a pediatric disease: Almost all nicotine use starts before high school graduation. Without a next generation of users, the industry's future is a lot less bright. After all, what is a company without customers?

As I reported this book, I had a fascinating conversation with Mike Moore, the former Mississippi attorney general who helped take down Big Tobacco in the '90s and who knows more than most about the tobacco story. When I asked him about tobacco and nicotine, and its seemingly interminable power over us, he gave as succinct and eloquent a response that only a trial lawyer can: "Companies have made billions and billions and billions of dollars getting people to suck something into their lungs," he said. "I mean, I hate to say it so clear, but how could you possibly sell that? There's only one answer. And the answer is nicotine. It's never been about anything else but nicotine. Without it there's nothing. There's no cigarettes. There's no Juul. There's none of it."

This is at the heart of why regulators have struggled so mightily with e-cigarettes. Should they be regulated like drugs, which are typically given a higher level of scrutiny—clinical testing, long-term studies—before blasting them onto store shelves? Or should they be as freely available as a pack of M&M's? Now, under the FDA's Center for Tobacco Products, the agency is trying to thread the needle, and so they are neither. They are tobacco, America's own storied and fraught commodity. Zeller and others in the agency were focused on saving adult smokers' lives, but agency didn't fully implement the nicotine-reduction plan in combustible cigarettes, which was supposed to have been the key trade-off designed to see adults move off deadly, addictive cigarettes and onto other ostensibly safer nicotine products. Even more vexing, the products Juul made were simply too attractive to youth. And so, in 2021, as the agency weighs whether to allow Juul and other e-cigarettes to remain on the market, it is left with that Gordian knot.

The irony and, frankly, the unfortunate truth, is that Bowen and Monsees were onto something when they first grasped the inanity of the cigarette habit and dreamed up the promise of making a major public-health contribution. They hitched their wagon to the harm reductionists like Mitch Zeller and the worthy quest to deliver a product to the one billion smokers that wouldn't kill them. Is it deeply unfortunate that society now has demonized a product more than the one whose universal dangers are fully understood? Yes, but that's what happens when Silicon Valley and Big Tobacco collide.

In America, especially in Silicon Valley, it is not enough to be successful. The unique brand of American start-up has a bottomless, voracious, untethered appetite for one thing and one thing only: profit. It's the epitome of our brute capitalist system that rewards investors for putting every single thing—personal data, storied institutions, even teenage brains—on the altar of profit.

Bowen and Monsees created an amazingly effective technology that indeed did as promised—gave smokers perhaps the first real alternative to tobacco-burning cigarettes. It's just that in their passion, they opted for monster growth over a diligent, plodding path that might have earned them a long-term, viable strategy with buy-in from regulators and permission from society.

The truth is, no Silicon Valley investor would have put their money behind a company that had such a plan for slow, incremental growth. That's simply not what most venture capitalists do. They bet their chips on companies that are poised to launch like a rocket not five years from now, but *now* now.

And so the Juul rocket launched, and it exploded just as it was leaving the atmosphere. Now, as the debris tumbles to the ground, the tobacco industry is facing a reckoning again. Silicon Valley is suffering another fall from grace. And America is left to clean up the wreckage.

ACKNOWLEDGMENTS

Every person contains within them a story, and for some it comes easier than for others to tell theirs. This particular story was not always easy for people to tell, and that's because the topic was and remains a hypercharged live wire. Juul and Altria are both embroiled in litigation, the outcome of which could affect, to varying degrees, the companies' survival and profitability. Also, tobacco industry executives have long been preternaturally opposed to speaking with the media, due in no small part to the historical role journalists played in bringing the industry to the brink. The same goes for the scores of employees and executives who work or worked at Juul, a company that has routinely implored its people to not speak to journalists, in part by cajoling them into signing non-disclosure agreements that are tied to sums of money as they walk out the door, casting a chill over those who were often closest to the heart of the story. For those reasons, and so many others, this story was not as straightforward as dialing up a source and asking them the color of the sky. Many, many people in the tobacco industry, from the lowest ranks to the highest, decided it was worth coming out of their shell to help me tell the most accurate story as possible about a company and an industry that they believed had long been mischaracterized, and that had found itself in a particularly consequential moment in time. Likewise, countless sources from Juul nonetheless decided that they wanted to tell their story, often because they'd felt the company had been mischaracterized and the good intentions of the people behind it clouded by the fallout. For all of those sources, many of which by necessity needed to maintain anonymity, I am grateful that they took a leap of faith in speaking to me, oftentimes at great risk to their personal lives and professional careers. I could not have told this story without them.

I interviewed more than one hundred individuals for this book, many of them multiple times. Importantly, the reader should not assume that just because I name an individual as being in the center of a meeting or a scene, that the information came directly from that individual. In many instances I spoke to people present or to people who were briefed afterward. While some individuals refused to speak to me, I offered them a fair opportunity to respond to allegations concerning them.

There are a few places throughout the book where I pull directly from various legal proceedings involving Juul and Altria, which I cite either in the text or in the endnotes. While these records are public, they reference material that is currently under seal and therefore the implications they convey will likely be contested by Juul and Altria as the cases proceed.

There are so many people I need to thank for making this book possible. The first is my agent, Kirby Kim, who happened to see in my coverage of Juul for Bloomberg News and *Businessweek* magazine kernels of a larger story. His belief in me, and the story, from the beginning and throughout was the wind beneath my wings.

As every journalist knows, your work is only as good as your editor.

And also, as every journalist knows, the good ones don't come along every day, and the great ones even rarer. I am humbled and grateful that my book proposal landed on the desk of one of the great ones, executive editor Kevin Doughten at Crown. Kevin not only believed in my project early on, but he brought to bear a vision of great magnitude and scope that simply could not have been articulated, I believe, by anyone else. Aside from that, Kevin is a brilliant thinker and editor who made my writing immeasurably better and my book the best it could be. A special thanks also to Lydia Morgan, assistant editor at Crown, who helped backstop Kevin's tireless efforts and provided a sense of continuity for a new author. Finally, thanks to the amazing team at Crown for their support and efforts on behalf of the book, including David Drake, Gillian Blake, Annsley Rosner, Dyana Messina, Gwyneth Stansfield, Julie Cepler, and last but most definitely not least, Ted Allen. Thank you to the talented Christopher Brand who created the smoldering-hot book cover.

I am deeply indebted to a whole cast of stellar colleagues at Bloomberg News for helping make this book happen. Among those first in line is Bob Blau, executive editor of Investigations at Bloomberg News. I guess I have been lucky in my career, because Bob is also one of those don't-come-along-too-often editors. His incisive vision and knack for knowing how to zero in on the beating heart of any story has constantly formed the bedrock of my work and has helped me become the writer and journalist that I am today. Beyond that, he generously granted me the time and the space to complete this book, even as the world at times seemed to be coming apart at the seams, and for that I am especially thankful. Thank you to the very talented John Voskuhl, senior editor of Investigations at Bloomberg, who has always encouraged me to follow my gut, chase tips, and pursue stories that aren't low-hanging fruit. And thank you to the talented *Businessweek* editors Joel Weber, Jim Aley and Daniel Ferrara; to Flynn McRoberts, managing editor for U.S. bureaus at *Bloomberg,* for always being a supportive sounding board; and to Steve Merelman, the sharp-witted *Bloomberg* editor who helped launch my career there. I wouldn't have had this opportunity were it not for the enthusiastic institutional backing from many others at *Bloomberg,* including John Micklethwait, Reto Gregori, Laura Zelenko, and Kristin Powers.

A deep heartfelt thanks to Susan Berfield, senior investigative reporter at *Bloomberg* and fellow author, for commiserating with me about the insane personal and professional challenges involved in seeing a book through. I would be remiss to not name several other colleagues across our fantastic newsroom who checked in on me, rooted me on, and so generously shared ideas and sometimes sources with me, including Michael Riley, Ben Elgin, Shelly Banjo, Angelica LaVito, Michael Smith, and Esmé Deprez. A special shout-out to Robert Langreth, the talented Bloomberg News health reporter who did some early and important reporting with me on the health consequences of vaping.

A special thanks to Bryan Gruley, the eminently talented editor, reporter, and mystery-book author who long ago gave me a piece of wisdom about writing that has proved the test of time: Ass. In. Chair. Bryan plucked me out of a news assistant job when I was a young reporter at *The Wall Street Journal* many years ago and has continued to be a source of guidance and encouragement and humor, including throughout the writing of this book.

Thank you to the many expert scientists and researchers who so graciously reviewed some of the more technical portions of my manuscript so that I could maintain the integrity of the surprisingly complicated science behind tobacco smoke, including Neal Benowitz, a physician and professor of medicine at the University of California, San Francisco, and one of the world's foremost experts on the pharmacology of nicotine; and David Peyton, professor of chemistry at Portland State University, and one of the most learned (and patient) researchers on tobacco smoke chemistry.

One person in particular, my sister Kristin Etter, deserves more than a simple thanks in these notes, which I hope to one day be able to offer. She encouraged me in moments when my wellspring of creativity or inspiration flagged during the long, dark Covid months as I hammered out this book, and reminded me that I hadn't come this far to give up.

A special, star-studded thank-you to Jenny Hoff, my dearest friend and fellow journalist, who over the years has been a sounding board, a writing partner, a clear-eyed thinker, a cheerleader, and a source of endless laughs and inspiration.

Also, a special thank-you to Devra for providing me access to her magical garden abode, in which I spent many long hours writing this book. For no reason other than out of the kindness of her heart, she left me sprigs of fragrant lemon verbena and fresh-cut rose stems that she snipped off a vine in her yard. Those little offerings gave me rays of hope and joy while I was in the trenches. I continue to believe that the lizard was good luck.

A deep and heartfelt thanks to my mom and dad, the two people who have believed in me always and stood behind me in every way. It is difficult to convey just how meaningful their support has been in my life. When the pandemic landed me and my family at their home in Montana for months on end, in the middle of my writing this book, my mom ensured that I had a printer, freshly brewed coffee, and the best writing desk in the house overlooking the sun-dappled pine forests. When I needed uninterrupted writing time, my dad spruced up a refurbished barn, and built me crackling, wood-burning fires before I was even up, to ensure the space was warm when I arrived on cold, snowy mornings. It is those gestures, but so much more, that fueled me.

But it is my husband, David, to whom I owe everything. This book in the most literal sense could not have been possible without him. As the pandemic upended our lives, just like the lives of so many, he worked every day to ensure that I had the time and space needed to focus on this project, even as our house at times descended into chaos amid the lockdown that transformed our living room into a Zoom classroom and a puppy preschool. Despite it all, he miraculously managed to maintain his admirable calm, strength, and love for me and for our three little daughters who have the energy of tiny comets. For that I am eternally grateful. And for those reasons, and so many more—
"Count the stars in the sky. Measure the waters of the oceans with a teaspoon. Number the grains of sand on the sea shore."—I have dedicated this book to you, and to our daughters.

NOTES

PROLOGUE

ix **Steven Parrish's airplane touched down** Throughout the prologue, the 1999 Corporate Affairs Worldwide Conference in San Juan has been re-created largely from documents found in the tobacco archive, which were made public by the company as part of the Master Settlement Agreement. The descriptions of the weather reports come from contemporaneous news articles by The Associated Press that were printed in various newspapers, including the *Miami Herald* and the *Orlando Sentinel*. For other items in the prologue drawn from the tobacco archives, as well as such documents throughout the book, I have noted the corresponding document numbers that can be searched in the online tobacco archives.

ix **Parrish was the senior vice president** Information on Steve Parrish was based on interviews, and also books and news clippings. Among those are: Roger Rosenblatt, "How Do They Live with Themselves?," *The New York Times Magazine,* March 20, 1994; Joe Nocera, "If It's Good for Philip Morris, Can It Also Be Good for Public Health?," *The New York Times Magazine,* June 18, 2006; Joe Nocera, "Unlikely Partners in a Cause," *The New York Times,* June 19, 2009; Malcolm Gladwell, "Who Will Be the Next Rose Cipollone?," *The Washington Post,* June 19, 1988; Richard Kluger, *Ashes to Ashes: America's Hundred-Year Cigarette War, the Public Health, and the Unabashed Triumph of Philip Morris* (New York: Alfred A. Knopf, 1996); and David Kessler, *A Question of Intent: A Great American Battle with a Deadly Industry* (New York: PublicAffairs, 2001).

xi **The entire pantheon of Philip Morris brands** For extensive background on

Hamish Maxwell see Kluger, *Ashes to Ashes,* and also Joseph F. Cullman III, *I'm a Lucky Guy* (New York: [s.n.], 1998) (Cullman is a former Philip Morris CEO); also see Maxwell remarks at Yale, October 16, 1989, document number 2501452970.

xi   **The advertising wizardry unleashed** See the rough outline for an unpublished manuscript on the history of Philip Morris by Jerome E. Brooks titled "The Philip Morris Century," document number 2075275523; to read Leo Burnett's letter to a Philip Morris advertising director explaining the new Marlboro ad campaign, dated January 7, 1955, see document number 2040320959.

xi   **a manly ad campaign** For examples of early Marlboro Man ads, see document numbers 2061190195, 2061190403, 2061004622, 2061190419, 1002761175.

xi   **Philip Morris had not only created** For history on the Marlboro campaign see "Cigarette Marketing Today, an Address by Joseph F. Cullman, 3rd," October 20, 1955, document number 2023387914; interview notes from Cullman, George Weissman, and Hans Storr, document number 2073841883; obituary for Ross. R. Millhiser in *The New York Times,* dated December 12, 2003; a talk by a Philip Morris executive on November 12, 1958, titled "Where There's Smoke, There's Fire," document number 1002353218; the *Roper Report* dated February 26, 1957, document number 1001753346; and Kluger, *Ashes to Ashes,* and Allan M. Brandt, *The Cigarette Century: The Rise, Fall, and Deadly Persistence of the Product That Defined America* (New York: Basic Books, 2007).

xi   **Parrish carried out his work** Details about Geoffrey Bible came from tobacco industry documents and news clippings, especially Crocodile Dundee and punching bag references, from Patricia Sellers, "Geoff Bible Won't Quit," *Fortune,* July 21, 1997; also see Suein L. Hwang, "Smokers' Game: Philip Morris's Passion to Market Cigarettes Helps It Outsell RJR," *The Wall Street Journal,* October 30, 1995; also from Bible speech in Bermuda, May 8, 1995, document number 2073767482. Other details from Patricia Sellers, "Rising from the Smoke," *Fortune,* April 16, 2001; the Gyrfalcon painting gift, document number 2076383572; also see personal letter from Bible to shareholder, dated April 4, 1995, document number 2046042448; Bible speech to employees, dated April 9, 1996, document number 2048334053; Bible remarks at annual shareholder meeting, April 25, 1996, document number 2073760382.

xii   **Ernst Wynder and Evarts Graham published** Wynder and Graham study from Ernest L. Wynder, Evarts A. Graham, and Adele B. Croninger, "Experimental Production of Carcinoma with Cigarette Tar," *Cancer Research* 13, no. 12 (December 1953): 855–64.

xii   **The findings made national news** To read the magazine stories about Wynder and Graham and see the accompanying photos, see "Smoke Gets in the News," *Life* magazine, December 21, 1953; and "Beyond Any Doubt," *Time* magazine, November 30, 1953.

xii   **"Salesmen in the industry are frantically alarmed"** See Hill & Knowlton, "Background Material on the Cigarette Industry Client," December 15, 1953, document number 2023335285.

xii   **They decided to smear the scientists** For the "you-know-what" reference, see the August 17, 2006, court opinion in the U.S. government's case against the tobacco industry, page 20; for a link to the final opinion and also relevant trial materials, see U.S. Department of Justice, "Litigation Against Tobacco Companies Home," https://www.justice.gov/civil/case-4.

xii   **When a 1970s British documentary** See, for example, Adam Hochschild, "Shoot-Out in Marlboro Country," *Mother Jones,* January 1979, https://www.motherjones.com/politics/1996/03/shoot-out-marlboro-country/.

xiii   **Philip Morris built a network** See DOJ's August 17, 2006, court opinion, for example, page 1286; also see company correspondence about the "white-coats" in document number 2023542534 dated November 16, 1987; and further correspondence regarding the company's use of whitecoats, from November 25, 1987, at document number 2501254715; also see Naomi Oreskes and Erik M. Conway, *Merchants of Doubt: How a Handful of Scientists Obscured the Truth on Issues from Tobacco Smoke to Climate Change* (New York: Bloomsbury Press, 2011).

xiii   **When Victor DeNoble learned** DeNoble material is extensively documented through author interviews and also through the 2011 film *Addiction Incorporated;* along with multiple books, i.e., Kluger, *Ashes to Ashes,* and Philip J. Hilts, *Smokescreen: The Truth Behind the Tobacco Industry Cover-Up* (Reading, MA: Addison-Wesley, 1996); articles, including Philip J. Hilts, "Scientists Say Cigarette Company Suppressed Findings on Nicotine," *The New York Times,* April 29, 1994.

xiii   **"Please don't ever forget"** Can be found in the prepared remarks of Fuller, dated March 6, 1992, at document number 2073706153v.

xiv   **They said smoking was, after all, just as fundamental** There are documents showing that Philip Morris funded the Alexis de Tocqueville Institution.

xiv   **After the doctor and lawyer David Kessler** For a comprehensive and thrilling history of Kessler's efforts as FDA commissioner to regulate tobacco, see his book *A Question of Intent.*

xiv   **The company launched a "ferocious defense"** See an "absolutely confidential" email dated March 7, 1994, from a company executive with the subject "Ferocious Defense" at document number 2023002837; also see March 11, 1994, memo about meeting at the Willard Hotel to discuss the ferocious defense at document number 2048917940.

xiv   **The company made buttons and ball caps** See merchandise descriptions for the anti-FDA ball caps and buttons at document numbers 2047577218 and 2047577217; and Marlboro Grand Prix "racing day" events where anti-FDA merchandise was to be distributed, at document number 2070134408.

xiv   **The company distributed them** For example, see document number 2046039282.

xiv   **One executive boasted how** See document number 2047029607A.

xv   **In 1994 Mississippi attorney general** For details see Carrick Mollenkamp, Adam Levy, Joseph Menn, and Jeffrey Rothfeder, *The People vs. Big Tobacco: How the States Took On the Cigarette Giants* (Princeton, NJ: Bloomberg Press, 1998).

xv   **DeNoble testified before Congress** See the Waxman hearings on April 28, 1994, https://www.c-span.org/video/?56436-1/tobacco-research-disclosure.

xv   **The *Wall Street Journal* reporter** See Alix M. Freedman and Laurie
        P. Cohen, "Smoke and Mirrors: How Cigarette Makers Keep Health Ques-
        tion 'Open' Year After Year," *The Wall Street Journal,* February 11, 1993.

xv   **If it's possible to identify** CEOs of seven major tobacco firms testify before
        Congress; widely covered, see, for example, Philip J. Hilts, "Tobacco Chiefs
        Say Cigarettes Aren't Addictive," *The New York Times,* April 15, 1994; for the
        live Waxman hearing where CEOs testify, see https://www.c-span.org
        /video/?56038-1/oversight-tobacco-products-part-1.

xv   **The then CEO of Philip Morris USA** For a written transcript of William
        Campbell's delivered testimony before the subcommittee on Health and the
        Environment of the House Energy and Commerce Committee, see docu-
        ment number 2055543062; and here for the live coverage: https://www
        .c-span.org/video/?56038-1/oversight-tobacco-products-part-1.

xvi   **"I know of Spaniards who imitate this custom"** The de Las Casas refer-
        ence pointing to the Columbus encounter comes from the seminal book on
        tobacco and nicotine from 1924, Louis Lewin, *Phantastica, Narcotic and Stim-
        ulating Drugs; Their Use and Abuse* (New York: Dutton, 1931); also more gen-
        erally see Jerome E. Brooks, *The Mighty Leaf: Tobacco Through the Centuries*
        (Boston: Little, Brown, 1952); *Phantastica* represented one of the earliest
        works explaining that nicotine was the reason why people smoked ciga-
        rettes.

xvi   **Researchers knew of the physiological effects** See Jack E. Henningfield
        and Mitch Zeller, "Nicotine Psychopharmacology: Policy and Regulatory,"
        Handbook of Experimental Pharmacology 192 (2009): 511–34; and Jack E. Hen-
        ningfield, Christine A. Rose, and Mitch Zeller, "Tobacco Industry Litigation
        Position on Addiction: Continued Dependence on Past Views," *Tobacco Con-
        trol* 15, Suppl 4 (December 2006): iv27–iv36.

xvii   **Philip Morris has long been one of the best-performing** Philip Morris
        stock is one of the best performing stocks of all time; see Wharton professor
        Jeremy Siegel's 2005 research paper, titled "The Long-term Returns on the
        Original S&P 500 Firms," which found: "The single best performing firm of
        the original S&P 500 Index is Philip Morris, recently renamed the Altria
        Group. Philip Morris yielded an annual return of 19.75% and beat the S&P
        500 Index by almost 9% per year since the index's inception. $1,000 placed in
        an S&P 500 Index fund on February 28, 1957 would have grown, with
        reinvested dividends, to almost $125,000 by December 31, 2003. But $1,000
        put in Phillip Morris would have grown to almost $4.6 million."

xvii   **But by the mid-'90s it was becoming** Tomkins, "Bible Spreads the Gospel
        About Philip Morris"; in addition, see 1999 interview notes from various
        tobacco executives in document number 2082444241 in which executives la-
        ment how litigation has depressed the stock.

xvii   **By 1997 just under a quarter of Americans** In 1965, 42 percent of Ameri-
        can adults smoked cigarettes; for historical smoking data see the November
        1999 publication from the Centers for Disease Control and Prevention
        titled *Achievements in Public Health, 1900–1999: Tobacco Use—United States,
        1900–1999,* https://www.cdc.gov/mmwr/preview/mmwrhtml/mm4843a2
        .htm.

xviii   **"We've got more money than God"** This comes from Kessler, *A Question of Intent.*

xviii   **the PM board of directors took the corporate jet** The April 1995 Sea Island board retreat meeting was reconstructed through author interviews with executives present and also through meeting notes and documents, including document numbers 2046656184 and 2044046538.

xx   **the theme of the San Juan event was PM21** See "PM21 Internal Toolkit" document number 2072446701.

xxiii   **While he expected some criticisms** For Stockholm syndrome and "good-guy stuff" see Nocera's "If It's Good for Philip Morris, Can It Also Be Good for Public Health?"

xxv   **"fortress Philip Morris"** See Sellers's *Fortune* article "Rising from the Smoke."

CHAPTER 1

3   **head of Philip Morris's Youth Smoking Prevention** See Howard Willard written direct testimony in Civil Action No. 99-CV-2496 in the U.S. District Court for the District of Columbia.

6   **In April 1995, an internal** See the career planning memo, document number 2042765535.

6   **In his Midwest VP sales position** For examples of Willard's political letters to clients and business contacts, see a letter dated October 25, 1995, at document number 2047593589 or a letter on behalf of the Philip Morris Political Action Committee, at document number 2040968829.

6   **Michael Szymanczyk, chief executive of Philip Morris** For the Christmas reference see Byrne, "Philip Morris: Inside America's Most Reviled Company"; and for Szymanczyk biography see document number 2069700157.

7   **In October 1999 the company launched** For correspondence re the launching of the Philip Morris corporate website, see document numbers 2072597591 and 2071711096.

7   **Back then the headquarters of Philip Morris** For ashtrays in elevator banks and urinals see Byrne, "Philip Morris: Inside America's Most Reviled Company."

8   **Themes like "healing and reconciliation"** For material from the Harvard sessions, see "Corporate Social Responsibility Meeting" from August 14, 2000, document number 2080985186.

8   **At one event, the company hired** For the Shackleton play, author interviews as well as The Associated Press, "Acting Like a Leader: Consultancy Uses Role-Playing to Drive Home Business Savvy to Employees," July 21, 2002; and document number 2067169444.

8   **In 1999, the U.S. Department of Justice sued** U.S. v. Philip Morris: 1,683 Page Final Opinion, Civil Action No. 99-2496, U.S. District Court for the District of Columbia, August 17, 2006.

9   **"Our goal is to be seen"** Parrish remarks at board meeting; see document titled "Capricorn Board Presentation" dated August 29, 2001, document number 2085241497.

9   **The company anticipated critics** "Putting on a new dress" phrase from "Altria External Communications Plan" dated January 17, 2002, document number 2085247109.

9   **They hired a branding firm** For more on the name change, see email between executives dated October 17, 2001, with the subject "Clarification of name" in document number 2085246804 and internal communications dated December 17, 2001, in document number 2085781485; and proposed names at document number 2085241616; and Gordon Fairclough, "Philip Morris Seeks to Change Name; Critics Claim Move Is a Smokescreen," *The Wall Street Journal,* November 16, 2001.

9   **About a year later, the tobacco arm** Philip Morris USA corporate relocation to Richmond was announced in Philip Morris USA, "Philip Morris USA Will Relocate Corporate Headquarters and Employees to Virginia; Move Will Help Streamline Operations and Result in Long-Term Cost Savings," press release, March 4, 2003.

10   **the parent company, Altria, would remain** For history on tobacco as an important cash crop, see Kluger, *Ashes to Ashes,* and Brooks, *The Mighty Leaf,* among many others. For the move to the Reynolds building, see especially Terry Pristin, "Philip Morris USA Starts Its Move to a Historic Building," *The New York Times,* November 26, 2003.

10   **"This taboo is for you"** For the "taboo" poem, see handwritten notes of Carolyn Levy, document number 2062145828.

11   **In the 1940s Philip Morris paid college students** See "More Cigarets?" in *Time* magazine, March 26, 1945; for "Marlboro, campus favorite in all 50 states" and a "top seller at colleges" see document number 2061001258; and for more generally about Marlboro on college campuses, see a report titled *Exploratory Work on Marlboro's Dominance Among College Smokers* dated June 17, 1969, at document number 2042789212.

11   **Philip Morris executives were nervous** For a discussion on "the beginning smoker" and smokers as young as twelve, see the internal Philip Morris report *Market Potential of a Health Cigarette* from June 1966 at document number 1001913853.

11   **In 1974 the company proposed conducting** For details on the proposed third-grader study, see "Behavioral Research," dated August 2, 1974, at document number 2048370180, and "Plans and Objectives for 1976," dated November 21, 1975, at document number 2021615312; also see John Schwartz, "Tobacco Firm's Nicotine Studies Assailed on Hill," *The New York Times,* July 25, 1995.

11   **In 1981, an internal Philip Morris** For "Young Smokers" reference see "Young Smokers Prevalence, Trends, Implications and Related Demographic Trends" from March 31, 1981, at document number 2077864711.

11   **in 1988, Philip Morris's director** The 1988 correspondence between Dangoor and Levy has the subject "Critical Consumer Research Issues" and is at document number 2080009511.

11   **determine the American archetype of smoking** For discussion of the archetypes, see "Purpose of the Archetype Project" at document number 2062146874; for the "Archetype Project Summary," dated September 1991, see document number 2062146863.

11   **conducted with the help of Clotaire** For more on Rapaille, see Danielle
      Sacks, "Crack This Code," *Fast Company*, April 1, 2006.

12   **By 1994, CEO Geoffrey Bible boasted** For Bible speech, dated February 24,
      1994, see document number 2041225018.

12   **The following year, the FDA's David Kessler** For Kessler's speech at Co-
      lumbia Law, dated March 8, 1995, see document number 2073667629; see
      also, generally, *Preventing Tobacco Use Among Young People: A Report of the Sur-
      geon General,* 1994; and see David Kessler, "Nicotine Addiction in Young Peo-
      ple," *New England Journal of Medicine* 333 (July 20, 1995): 186–89.

12   **second-most heavily advertised commodity** See Kessler's Columbia speech.

12   **Between 1991 and 1997 the number of high school** See data from the
      CDC's Youth Risk Behavior Surveillance System, and also see Centers for
      Disease Control and Prevention, *Cigarette Use Among High School Students—
      United States, 1991–2005, Morbidity and Mortality Weekly Report* (MMWR) 55,
      no. 26 (July 7, 2006): 724–26.

12   **A year later, in August 1996, President Bill Clinton** For Clinton's Rose
      Garden tobacco speech, see a transcript of his "Remarks Announcing the
      Final Rule to Protect Youth from Tobacco" on August 23, 1996.

13   **That victory was short-lived** For the U.S. Supreme Court ruling, see
      FDA v. Brown & Williamson Tobacco Corp., March 21, 2000.

13   **Meanwhile, Philip Morris launched** For basics on the YSP and budget, see
      Philip Morris internal messaging in document number 2071718509.

13   **Part of the funds went to create** For info on the "tween" survey, see inter-
      nal correspondence, including document numbers 2085698132, 2085073173,
      and 2080139189.

13   **One of the company's first major ads** See the company's press release
      about the Super Bowl ad, titled "Philip Morris U.S.A. Introduces Newest
      Youth Smoking Prevention Ad During Super Bowl XXXIV" on January 31,
      2000, at document number 2071375659.

14   **During the 2000 Summer Olympics** See Chris Reidy, "Controversial TV
      Ads to Run During Olympics," *The Boston Globe*, September 19, 2000, and
      document number 2085043877; also more generally see Wendy Melillo,
      "Anti-Tobacco Ads Stir Protest," *Adweek*, March 6, 2000; and Gordon Fair-
      clough, "Antismoking Ads Directed at Teens Begin Airing on TV," *The Wall
      Street Journal*, February 8, 2000.

14   **When Philip Morris distributed millions** For details on the "Don't Wipe
      Out" book covers, see CBSNews.com staff, "Cigarette Maker Under Fire,"
      January 4, 2001; also see transcript from the *Today* show, on January 5, 2001,
      at document number 2081043020; for the company's internal correspon-
      dence re the book covers, including executives' messages to school princi-
      pals, at document number 2072833555.

15   **In damage control mode** See an email from Levy to a school principal at
      document number 2080002449; also see "Groups Request Investigation of
      Philip Morris Schoolbook Covers," press release, January 3, 2001, which de-
      tails a request that the National Association of Attorneys General investigate
      the matter.

15   **In October 2001, the National Association of Attorneys General** See the
      NAAG agenda for that conference, at document number 2085190418.

15   **The "Think. Don't Smoke" ads are** For the notes, see "Notes from Triennial Conference on Youth Smoking Prevention," dated November 2, 2001, at document number 2085190421.

15   **Haviland's comments touched off a bomb** See the letter from Levy to Haviland, dated November 8, 2001, at document number 2085317364.

15   **Four months later, Haviland sent** See response from Haviland to Levy, dated March 14, 2002, at document number 2085317428.

16   **a new head for the YSP** For Levy speaking about Willard, see "Written Direct Examination of Carolyn Levy" in Civil Action No. 99-CV-02496, at document number 5000943653.

16   **"We believe that the data you collected"** See email from Willard to Haviland, dated March 25, 2002, at document number 2085317426, and then the reply from Haviland, dated March 28, 2002, at document number 2085317361.

16   **A few months later** Matthew C. Farrelly, Cheryl G. Healton, Kevin C. Davis, et al., "Getting to the Truth: Evaluating National Tobacco Countermarketing Campaigns," *American Journal of Public Health* 92, no. 6 (June 2002): 901–7; for more information on the fate of the "Think. Don't Smoke" campaign, see Jennifer K. Ibrahim and Stanton A. Glantz, "The Rise and Fall of Tobacco Control Media Campaigns, 1967–2006," *American Journal of Public Health* 97, no. 8 (August 2007): 1383–96.

17   **every perceived slight** For Willard letter to the editor, see "Philip Morris on 'Truth,'" *Orlando Sentinel,* March 11, 2004; for his response to the Movie Guy see "Butts Out in the Movies," *Alameda Times-Star,* April 19, 2004; for letters to the editor in response to "Big Tobacco's Poison," see *Florida Today,* July 23, 2004; finally, for "Philip Morris Is Doing Its Part to Discourage Kids from Smoking," see the *Tallahassee Democrat,* September 26, 2005.

17   **By 2007, the number of high school students** For youth smoking rates, see data from the CDC's Youth Risk Behavior Surveillance System.

18   **Philip Morris was losing** For adult smoking rates, see CDC data.

CHAPTER 2

19   *The Rational Future of Smoking* See the presentation on YouTube, https://youtu.be/ZBDLqWCjsMM.

20   **The Stanford campus had maintained** For the Stanford smoking ban, see a university news release titled "Tough New Smoking Policy Takes Effect at Stanford Oct. 15," October 5, 1993.

21   **Even though a cigarette is a simple product** For a deeper understanding of the carcinogens found in tobacco smoke, see U.S. Department of Health and Human Services, National Toxicology Program, *14th Report on Carcinogens,* November 3, 2016; also see Centers for Disease Control and Prevention, National Center for Chronic Disease Prevention and Health Promotion, Office on Smoking and Health, *How Tobacco Smoke Causes Disease: The Biology and Behavioral Basis for Smoking-Attributable Disease: A Report of the Surgeon General,* 2010.

21   **Which went a long way to explain** For the "up to half of all its users" refer-

ence, see the World Health Organization website on tobacco, https://www
.who.int/news-room/fact-sheets/detail/tobacco; also see the expert on cigarettes and smoking Robert N. Proctor in his epic book *Golden Holocaust: Origins of the Cigarette Catastrophe and the Case for Abolition* (Berkeley: University
of California Press, 2011); and his paper, "Why Ban the Sale of Cigarettes?
The Case for Abolition," *Tobacco Control* 22, Suppl 1 (2013): i27–i30; see also
National Center for Chronic Disease and Health Promotion, Office on
Smoking and Health, *The Health Consequences of Smoking—50 Years of Progress: A Report of the Surgeon General* (Atlanta: Centers for Disease Control and
Prevention, 2014).

21   **Nicotine is extremely addictive** For nicotine as addictive as heroin, see Centers for Disease Control and Prevention et al., *How Tobacco Smoke Causes
Disease.*

22   **While nicotine has been linked** Neal L. Benowitz, "The Role of Nicotine in
Smoking-Related Cardiovascular Disease," *Preventive Medicine* 26, no. 4
(July–August 1997): 412–17; for murder reference, see Dan Good, "Paul
Curry Convicted in 1994 Nicotine-Poisoning Death of His Wife; Closure
into Linda Curry's Death Eluded Investigators for Years," ABC News, September 30, 2014; for nicotine and Parkinson's, see Maryka Quik, Kathryn
O'Leary, and Caroline M. Tanner, "Nicotine and Parkinson's Disease; Implications for Therapy," *Movement Disorders* 23, no. 12 (September 15, 2008):
1641–52.

22   **Yet, the cigarette hadn't been redesigned** For extensive histories on the
Bonsack machine and its role in the modern cigarette epidemic, see Kluger,
Ashes to Ashes, and Proctor, *Golden Holocaust.*

24   **As they started doing research for their thesis** To see the documents, go to
the Truth Tobacco Industry Documents internet archive, which is hosted by
the University of California, San Francisco, at https://www
.industrydocuments.ucsf.edu/tobacco/; also note that some of the individual tobacco companies maintain their own searchable public document archives, including Philip Morris, which can be found at www.pmdocs.com.

26   **Stanford's School of Engineering** "Stanford University Launches Hasso
Plattner Institute of Design with $35 Million Gift," press release, October 3,
2005; also see Anne Strehlow, "Institute Launched to Bring 'Design Thinking' to Product Creation," *Stanford Report,* October 12, 2005.

26   **The d.school was the brainchild** There is a lot written about Kelley, his design thinking principles, and the Apple mouse, including on IDEO's website
(https://www.ideo.com/case-study/creating-the-first-usable-mouse); Betsy
Mikel, "How the Guy Who Designed 1 of Apple's Most Iconic Products Or-
ganizes His Office," Inc.com, January 24, 2018; Kyle Vanhemert, "The Engineer of the Original Apple Mouse Talks About His Remarkable Career,"
Wired, August 18, 2014; and Josh Hyatt, "David Kelley of IDEO: Reinventing
Innovation," *Newsweek,* May 20, 2010; for a more in-depth understanding of
his design thinking, see the book he co-authored with his brother: Tom Kelley and David Kelley, *Creative Confidence: Unleashing the Creative Potential
Within Us All* (New York: Crown, 2013).

27   **It's not uncommon to be swept up** For designing your life, see Steven Ku-

rutz, "Want to Find Fulfillment at Last? Think Like a Designer," *The New York Times,* September 17, 2016; and Ainsley Harris, "Stanford's Most Popular Class Isn't Computer Science—It's Something Much More Important," *Fast Company,* March 26, 2015.

28   **Calling Silicon Valley, and the** For major influences on Silicon Valley, see Adam Fisher, *Valley of Genius: The Uncensored History of Silicon Valley, as Told by the Hackers, Founders, and Freaks Who Made It Boom* (New York: Twelve, 2018); also see Walter Isaacson, *The Innovators: How a Group of Hackers, Geniuses, and Geeks Created the Digital Revolution* (New York: Simon & Schuster, 2014).

28   **Starting in the 1960s and over** For an extensive history of California's antitobacco battles, see Stanton A. Glantz and Edith D. Balbach, *Tobacco War: Inside the California Battles* (Berkeley: University of California Press, 2000); also see Sarah Milov, *The Cigarette: A Political History* (Cambridge, MA: Harvard University Press, 2019). There was widespread coverage of Berkeley's smoking ban, including "No-Smoking Ordinance Approved," *Berkeley Gazette,* April 27, 1977, and "Tough Anti-Smoking Ordinance," *Napa Valley Register,* April 28, 1977.

28   **At one point, one of the most prominent** The film *Death in the West* can be viewed in its entirety at the UCSF Industry Documents Library, at https://www.industrydocuments.ucsf.edu/tobacco/docs/#id=kgcd0111; for the 1983 NBC television piece about the documentary, see https://industrydocuments.tumblr.com/post/156048184716/anything-can-be-considered-harmful-applesauce-is; for a comprehensive description of the documentary, see Hochschild, "Shoot-Out in Marlboro Country"; for further details by the filmmaker of *Death in the West* see Peter Taylor, *Smoke Ring: The Politics of Tobacco*; Kluger, *Ashes to Ashes*; along with several documents in the tobacco archive, including document numbers 2501188108, 2501188095, 2501188122, 2501007620, 2024978801, and 2501007949.

29   **on May 12, 1994, Glantz received** For a comprehensive history of the Brown & Williamson documents, see Stanton A. Glantz, John Slade, Lisa A. Bero, et al., *The Cigarette Papers* (Berkeley: University of California Press, 1996).

30   **"They are the equivalent of"** The "human genome" quote comes from Stephanie Irvine, "Tobacco Documents to Be Placed on the Web," *Nature Medicine* 7, no. 4 (April 2001): 391; and "American Legacy Foundation's $15 Million Gift Creates Permanent Home for Tobacco Industry Documents at UCSF," University of California, San Francisco, press release, January 30, 2001.

32   **When Ralph Eschenbach heard** For Eschenbach's early research on GPS, see Kai P. Yiu, Richard Crawford, and Ralph Eschenbach, "A Low Cost GPS Receiver for Land Navigation," *Navigation, Journal of the Institute of Navigation* 29, no. 3 (Fall 1982): 204–20.

35   **Valani started his career in the scrappy world** See "Gruntal Agrees to Fraud Fine as U.S. Indicts Former Official," by David J. Morrow, *The New York Times,* April 10, 1996.

35   **"Gruntal was an oasis for people"** See "The Shabby Side Of The Street:

The collapse of a 122-year-old brokerage firm opens a window on Wall Street's unseemly ways," by Richard Behar, *Fortune* magazine, March 3, 2003.

35 **As part of the small asset securitization** See "Smart Bonds: David Bowie's brokers set their sights on Silicon Valley's intellectual property," by Anastasia Hendrix, *The San Francisco Examiner*, March 25, 1997; also see "Rock Royalties," by Debora Vrana, *Los Angeles Times*, June 3, 1997.

35 **Before the deal was completed** See "Monsters of Rock Bonds Clashing Over Who Dreamed Up Bowie Deal," by Aaron Elstein, *The American Banker*, August 6, 1997.

35 **The following year he became general partner** See the press release, "GEC Strikes Gold in Heavy Metal: $30MM Securitization of Record Masters and Copyrights for Sanctuary Group's Iron Maiden," February 9, 1999.

35 **Then he broadened his sights** See "Hooked on Sonique: How two college dropouts from Montana made the world's coolest MP3 player," by Eric Hellweg, *Spin* magazine, November 1999.

36 **In 2003 his firm battled for** See the press release, "Global Asset Capital Finalizes Agreement To Take Over Viventures Partners," July 16, 2003.

36 **He invested in GoFish Corporation** See the press release, "GoFish Names New President," February 26, 2007; also see, "Online Reality Show Comes to Life with America's Dream Date," July 3, 2006; and "GoFish and Icebox to Launch Made-for-Internet Program Featuring New and Exclusive Episodes of Hidden Celebrity Webcam," May 14, 2007.

37 **Monsees quipped early on** See "Pax Labs: Origins with James Monsees," by Gabriel Montoya, Social Underground.

CHAPTER 3

39 **Ruyan, which translated into** For material on Hon Lik, author interview, and also various news articles, including by Sarah Boseley, see "Hon Lik Invented the E-Cigarette to Quit Smoking—But Now He's a Dual User," *The Guardian*, June 9, 2015; and Kaleigh Rogers, "We Asked the Inventor of the E-Cigarette What He Thinks About Vape Regulations," *Vice*, July 18, 2016.

40 **when Lik's device hit the market** For "Love of Angel" et al., see document numbers 3005249798 and 3005249791.

40 **Philip Morris's research and development team** For Philip Morris in Beijing procuring the device, see email titled "Simulated Smoke Atomization Electronic Cigarette/Ruyan Atomizing Nicotine Inhaler," dated June 2, 2004, document number 3012410731; and email titled "FW: Fax Regarding Electronic Cigarette-Like Device," dated June 7, 2004; and email titled "Cigarette-like Electronic Device," dated June 9, 2004, document number 3005249776; for an internal Philip Morris analysis titled "Operational Analysis of SBT Ruyan Atomizing Nicotine Inhaler" see document number 3014801382; and also see "New Product Focus Team Test Plan & Status Report for Beijing Saybolt Ruyan Technologies Product," document number 3116215720, and "FTIR Analysis of Electronic Cigarette-Like Device from China," document number 3005250988.

41   **Philip Morris, like nearly every other** For early research and Wakeham presentation to the board describing "weapons system" and "dry ice" tobacco, see document number 1000276219; the examples of code names come from Brown & Williamson executive, document number 2046817009; also see a memo to Wakeham dated 1960, document number 1001801050; for "cat lungs" see document numbers 1003115883 and 1003115691; for "smoking baboons" see 1000151979, 1002646842-A, 1000020934, and 1000268489; for "tracheostomized beagles" see 1003120238; also see Proctor, *Golden Holocaust.*

41   **By the early 1980s, Philip Morris scientists** For Polaroid camera and flashbulb devices see, for example, "New Cigarette Technology," dated 1984, document number 2001115502, and 2022210511; for "Ambrosia" see document titled "Ambrosia: Abstract," dated September 1990 at document 2021557414; for "supercritical extraction," see document 2024272906; also see a deposition by a company analytical chemist who explains the different technologies at document number 3990077745; for drawings and information of "Case" see "Design and Performance Evaluation of GIZMO1 Smoking Device," dated March 14, 1995, at document number 2050811248; also see "Beta Update," dated September 17, 1993, at document number 2051805420.

41   **In 1987, R. J. Reynolds announced** There is extensive documentation of the Premier cigarette, including the well-known monograph prepared by Reynolds titled "New Cigarette Prototypes That Heat Instead of Burn Tobacco," dated 1988; for the fascinating inside story of Premier see Bryan Burrough and John Helyar, *Barbarians at the Gate: The Fall of RJR Nabisco* (New York: Harper & Row, 1990); for an extensive analysis of harm-reduction tobacco products see Institute of Medicine Committee to Assess the Science Base for Tobacco Harm Reduction, *Clearing the Smoke: Assessing the Science Base for Tobacco Harm Reduction,* ed. K. Stratton, P. Shetty, R. Wallace, and S. Bondurant (Washington, DC: National Academies Press, 2001).

42   **An internal Philip Morris white paper** For the paper "Products of the Future," dated 1992, see document number 2046741012; also see this document for the $1 billion market estimate.

42   **"could evolve into replacements for cigarettes"** See an internal 1992 report titled *Situational Analysis* at document number 2050890432.

42   **Almost immediately after Premier was announced** For an internal discussion of "the Greeks," see document numbers 2020156856 and 2020135802; and for a more comprehensive report see *Delta/Sigma/Beta Status,* dated February 15, 1990, at document number 2020129040; also see a board presentation titled "Beta Board Speech," dated June 27, 1990, at document number 2026229350; for a high-level overview of the various technologies, see a 1996 report titled *Alternative Smoking Devices and New Products* at document number 2079071197; also see "Five Year R&D Plan Programs" from 1992, document number 2057718975, which details how "smokers who quit are the major cause of loss of sales of our products."

43   **They accelerated work on** For "Ideal Smoke," see an internal memo titled "1994 CASE Activity Annual Report, Summary Version," dated May 9, 1995, at document number 2051989653; also see "Problem: How Do We Get to

Ideal Smoke?" dated 1993, document number 2021507610; more information on the "capillary aerosol generator" can be found at document number 2078755855, and for how this technology will be a "paradigm shift," see document number 2079072086.

43   **They dropped nicotine on human tongues** See an internal report titled *Psychophysical and Electrophysiological Studies of Nicotine and Related Trigeminal Stimulants* at document number 3102906523; for the electrodes attached to the scalp, for example, see document number 2025988646.

44   **"The kinds of things we have heard today"** For the internal discussion at the research conference, see document number 2023148612.

44   **Around 1995, the company formed** For the report *Table*, see document number 2021113522; also see the breaking coverage of the report in Alix Freedman, "Philip Morris Memo Likens Nicotine to Cocaine," *The Wall Street Journal*, December 8, 1995.

44   **Parrish's group delved deeply** Richard Klein, *Cigarettes Are Sublime* (Durham, NC: Duke University Press, 1993).

45   **In 1997, Philip Morris quietly released** For Accord, see, for example, Judann Pollack, "Philip Morris Tries Smokeless Accord: Tobacco Marketer, Cautious About Brand, Doing 'Consumer Research,'" *Ad Age*, October 27, 1997; and Glenn Collins, "Analysts Mixed on Philip Morris's Smoking System," *The New York Times*, October 24, 1997.

46   **The day the decision came down** For the company's response, including the Prohibition comment to the Supreme Court decision, see "Philip Morris Responds to FDA Decision by Supreme Court," press release, March 21, 2000.

47   **The former surgeon general, Koop** See Koop's op-ed, "Don't Forget the Smokers," *The Washington Post*, March 8, 1998.

47   **Then, in 2001, the Institute of Medicine** The report that touches on clean nicotine: Institute of Medicine, *Ending the Tobacco Problem: A Blueprint for the Nation*, ed. Richard J. Bonnie, Kathleen Stratton, and Robert B. Wallace (Washington, DC: The National Academies Press, 2007).

48   **Health experts, including top officials** See, for example, a fascinating talk given in India by Mitch Zeller titled "Regulation of Tobacco Products" at a conference called "Global Tobacco Control Law: Towards a WHO Framework Convention on Tobacco Control" in January 2000, New Delhi, India, document number 2081371694.

49   **In April 2005, John R. "Jack" Nelson** For biographical information on Jack Nelson, see a court deposition at document number 3990014745.

50   **"Innovation will carry us into the future"** See John Reid Blackwell, "A Step Toward Better Products? Philip Morris Facility Part of Effort to Develop Less-Harmful Tobacco," *Richmond Times-Dispatch*, April 6, 2005; also see The Associated Press, "Center to Focus on Reducing Harm Caused by Cigarettes," April 6, 2005; Anna Wilde Mathews and Vanessa O'Connell, "Philip Morris Gears Up for FDA Regulation," *The Wall Street Journal*, June 21, 2007; and Matthew Philips, "The $300 Million Lab," *Richmond Times-Dispatch*, April 6, 2005.

50   **By 2005 the number of cigarettes sold** See the annual *Federal Trade Commis-*

sion Cigarette Report that contains total domestic cigarette unit sales dating back to 1963.

50   **Philip Morris envisioned the center** For "Innovation Alley" see document number 3034259161.

51   **"Need to be an ENGINE for Creativity"** See the "Research and Technology Planning Meeting," dated June 16, 2004, document number 3009165388.

51   **a colleague outlined a series** See the report titled *Health Sciences Research (HSR): Role, Structure, Direction,* dated October 15, 2004, at document number 3008375432; and also a report, *Research and Technology, Proposed Plan,* from July 14, 2004, at document number 3009737276.

51   **Some of the ideas that emerged** For the Willy Wonka ideas, see an internal spreadsheet with many of these ideas at document numbers 3008372872, 3116015004, and 3009578596.

52   **In 2005, Philip Morris executives were sent** See "Wharton's 'Strategic Innovation' Program Custom Course for PM USA," dated September 2005, document number 3016543922.

52   **In 2004, Willard had overseen the introduction** The study on the QuitAssist program can be found at Patricia A. McDaniel, E. Anne Lown, and Ruth E. Malone, " 'It Doesn't Seem to Make Sense for a Company That Sells Cigarettes to Help Smokers Stop Using Them': A Case Study of Philip Morris's Involvement in Smoking Cessation," *PLoS One* 12, no. 8 (August 28, 2017): e0183961.

53   **The same year, Willard struck a deal** For an example of the agreement between Philip Morris and Duke establishing the center for nicotine, see document number 3007220650; for more on the Philip Morris–backed nicotine research center at Duke, see "Smoke-Out," *Duke Magazine,* September–October 2004; also see Marsha A. Green, "Department Spotlight: Duke Center for Smoking Cessation," *Duke Today,* September 12, 2012; for background on Jed Rose, see Thomas H. Maugh II, "UCLA Pharmacologist Invented Nicotine Patch," *Los Angeles Times,* May 14, 2008.

53   **Meanwhile, Philip Morris struggled with knowing** For more on the attempted commercialization of the capillary aerosol generator, see Vanessa O'Connell, "Rx from Marlboro Man: Device That Delivers Drugs, Not Smoke," *The Wall Street Journal,* October 27, 2005; and Myron Levin, "Philip Morris in Inhaler Deal," *Los Angeles Times,* December 13, 2005.

54   **The company had recently announced** See Ken Elkins, "Philip Morris to Close Concord Cigarette Plant," *Charlotte Business Journal,* June 26, 2007; and Stella M. Hopkins, "Philip Morris Plant Closing May Signal Spin-Off," *The [Rock Hill, SC] Herald,* June 27, 2007.

55   **The center, known as** For the Cube, see PMI's 2009 annual report.

59   **In September 2008, just about six months** See "Costs Tangle Bid by Altria Buying UST Would Require Cleaning Out Expense Line to Justify Premium, Price," *The Wall Street Journal,* September 6, 2008; and Mike Barris, "Lenders Advise Altria to Put Off UST Deal," *The Wall Street Journal,* October 3, 2008.

CHAPTER 4

62   **They'd been diligently pouring** For early coverage of Ploom, see, for example, Daniel Terdiman, "Stanford Grads Hope to Change Smoking Forever: Ploom Aims to Make Smoking More Efficient And Greener. The Company Has a Patent Pending on Their Model One Vaporizer," c|net, May 13, 2010; and "Ploom: A Smarter Way to Smoke?," SmartPlanetCBS, November 5, 2010.

65   **Rose had been conducting groundbreaking** For Rose's salt technology, see "New Smoking Cessation Therapy Proves Promising," Duke University Medical Center, February 27, 2010; and "New Smoking-Cessation Therapy Uses Novel Technology for Delivering Nicotine to the Lungs," *Oncology Times* 32, no. 5 (March 10, 2010): 25.

67   **They enlisted Bradley Ingebrethsen** See Ingebrethsen's patent, titled "Aerosol Delivery Article," patent number US5388574A.

73   **In the fall of 2009 Bowen and Monsees** For Ploom's funding and valuation information, see data from PitchBook.

74   **He was named "Most Influential Industrial Designer in the World"** See Peter High, "Yves Béhar Is The Most Influential Industrial Designer in the World," *Forbes*, August 25, 2014.

74   **He'd had a few dicey design moments** For Juicero, see Ellen Huet and Olivia Zaleski, "Silicon Valley's $400 Juicer May Be Feeling the Squeeze; Two Investors in Juicero Were Surprised to Learn the Startup's Juice Packs Could Be Squeezed by Hand Without Using Its High-Tech Machine," Bloomberg .com, April 19, 2017.

74   **And then his firm's early work** For Theranos reference, see John Carreyrou, *Bad Blood: Secrets and Lies in a Silicon Valley Startup* (New York: Alfred A. Knopf, 2018).

75   **Nick was a cousin of the late Jay Pritzker** For more background on the Pritzker family, see Jay McCormick, "Financial Wizards Pritzkers Maintain Low Profile," Gannett News Service, February 5, 1989; and Sandra M. Jones, Wailin Wong, and Kristin Samuelson, "Industrialist Robert Pritzker Dies," *Chicago Tribune*, October 29, 2011.

76   **In 1988 when RJR Nabisco's then CEO, F. Ross Johnson** For details of the Pritzker bid for RJR Nabisco, see Burrough and Helyar, *Barbarians at the Gate*.

75   **In 2006, the Pritzkers sold their chewing tobacco** See "Pritzkers to Buy Conwood," *Chicago Tribune*, June 24, 1985; and Sharon C. Forster, "Local Snuff Plant Sale Won't Affect Operations," *Leaf Chronicle* [Clarksville, TN], June 26, 1985.

76   **Although the Pritzker family was well-known** For Pritzker family's influence in California politics, see Seema Mehta, Ryan Menezes, and Maloy Moore, "How Eight Elite San Francisco Families Funded Gavin Newsom's Political Ascent," *Los Angeles Times*, September 7, 2018.

76   **Nick, through his San Francisco family office** Tao Capital Partners investment info comes from PitchBook.

77   **The Tokyo-based company that was partly** For "irreplaceable delight," see, for example, Japan Tobacco's 2006 annual report.

78   **Ultimately, in December 2011, Ploom and Japan Tobacco** See "Innovative
      Partnership for Ploom and Japan Tobacco International JTI to Take Minority
      Share in Ploom," press release, JTI, December 8, 2011.

79   **And in June 2012, the new vaporizer** For coverage of the Pax launch, see
      Andrew Tarantola, "Ploom Pax Vaporizer Lightning Review: Whoa Baby,
      Where You Been All My Life?," Gizmodo, June 8, 2012; and Andrew Taran-
      tola, "This Workshop of Wonders Makes Vibrators and Vaporizers," Giz-
      modo, October 18, 2012; also see John Biggs, "Smoke Up: An Interview with
      the Creator of the Ultracool Pax Vaporizer," *TechCrunch,* June 17, 2012; and
      see David H. Freedman, "How Do You Sell a Product When You Can't
      Really Say What It Does?," *Inc.,* May 2014.

80   **In 2013 the company landed a coveted** For the Sundance festival and the
      Pax Cabin, see "Singha Brings You into the Ultra-Secret Pax Cabin at Sun-
      dance," singhabeerusa.com, January 24, 2013; and Jean Song, "Shall We
      Sundance?" *Variety,* January 22, 2013.

81   **By the beginning of 2013 the finishing touches** For coverage of Model
      Two, see Damon Lavrinc, "Review: Ploom Model Two; Unlike the Cheap,
      Chinese-Made E-Cigarettes at 7-11 or the Martian Sex Toys Coveted and
      Customized by 'Vapers,' Ploom Is Doing Something Different," *Wired,*
      July 1, 2013; and Samara Lynn, "Ploom ModelTwo Review," PCMag,
      June 23, 2014.

81   **One of them was a young New Yorker** For Liam McMullan, see Drew
      Grant, "Purple Prince Promotes Ploom," *Observer,* May 15, 2013.

81   **In August 2013, the Model Two was officially** For coverage of the Ploom
      Model Two launch, see "Ploom SF Launch Party," *San Francisco,* August 21,
      2013.

81   **In September, Ploom hit Fashion Week** For the New York events, see Jacob
      Bernstein, "No Sleep for the Wicked," *The New York Times,* September 6,
      2013; and "The Start Up's Cool Brother—Ploom," *Social,* May 30, 2014.

CHAPTER 5

84   **The agency declared them to be** For background on the FDA's early posi-
      tion on e-cigarettes as combination drug device products, see FDA report
      number DPATR-FY-09-23, titled "Evaluation of E-Cigarettes" from May 4,
      2009; also see the agency's "E-Cigarettes: Questions and Answers"; and
      "FDA Acts Against 5 Electronic Cigarette Distributors," press release, Sep-
      tember 9, 2010; and an agency letter to Matt Salmon at the "Electronic
      Cigarette Association" dated September 8, 2010; a transcript of an FDA
      media call on the topic can be found under the title "Transcript for FDA's
      Media Briefing on Electronic Cigarettes" on July 22, 2009.

84   **As the craze took off, it took on** Information on nicotine poisonings and
      exploding vapes comes from public records obtained under a Freedom of
      Information Act request.

85   **The FDA's own laboratory had sampled** For the FDA's lab analyses of the
      products, see an agency report titled "FDA Warns of Health Risks Posed by
      E-Cigarettes," dated July 2009.

85   **But that legal position became clouded** For an excellent overview of the
      2009 Tobacco Control Act, see the website of the Public Health Law Center,
      https://www.publichealthlawcenter.org/topics/special-collections/tobacco
      -control-act-2009.

86   **Being lawyers, and inhabiting a particularly** The court case brought by
      NJOY is Sottera Inc. v. U.S. Food and Drug Administration.

87   **Recognizing this loophole, and sensing** See the April 25, 2011, "Dear
      Stakeholder" letter by the FDA titled "Regulation of E-Cigarettes and Other
      Tobacco Products" in which the agency states that it "intends to propose a
      regulation that would extend the Agency's 'tobacco product' authorities in
      Chapter IX of the FD&C Act."

88   **The last time a tobacco ad aired** See The Associated Press, "Cigarette
      Commercials Off Television for Good," January 2, 1971.

89   **As part of that, in 2011 Altria scientists** To read the beagle study, see Mi-
      chael S. Werley, Paddy McDonald, Patrick Lilly, et al., "Non-Clinical Safety
      and Pharmacokinetic Evaluations of Propylene Glycol Aerosol in Sprague-
      Dawley Rats and Beagle Dogs," *Toxicology* 287, no. 1–3 (September 5, 2011):
      76–90.

90   **Meanwhile, the Richmond group started** For tobacco sticks see, for exam-
      ple, Linda Abu-Shalback Zid, "Altria Smokeless Tobacco Sticks; Skoal and
      Marlboro Products in Test Markets in Kansas," CSP, April 5, 2011; and John
      Reid Blackwell, "Altria Companies to Test New Smokeless Tobacco Stick,"
      Richmond Times-Dispatch, February 24, 2011; for the NXT product, see "Altria
      Expands Marlboro NXT, Preps for E-Cigarette Entry," *Convenience Store
      News,* July 23, 2013; for Tju, see transcript from the company's June 11, 2013,
      Investor presentation.

91   **An analyst at the investment bank UBS** See Nik Modi, "Clearing the Smoke
      on E-Cigarettes," UBS Investment Research, US Tobacco, May 14, 2012.

91   **A well-known Wells Fargo tobacco industry analyst** See Dan Mangan,
      "E-cigarette Sales Are Smoking Hot, Set to Hit $1.7 Billion," CNBA, August
      28, 2013; Chris Burritt, "E-Cigarette Pioneers Holding Breath as Big Firms
      Invade," *Bloomberg,* June 21, 2013; and Melissa Vonder Haar, "Are E-Cigs the
      Wave of the Future? Herzog to Big Tobacco: Electronic Cigarettes Are
      'More Than Just a Fad,'" CSP, August 13, 2012.

91   **NJOY took out a Super Bowl ad** See NJOY Super Bowl ad and more, and
      see Matt Richtel, "The E-Cigarette Industry, Waiting to Exhale," *The New
      York Times,* October 26, 2013; for e-cigarette ads also see more generally a re-
      port written by congressional Democrats titled *Gateway to Addiction? A Sur-
      vey of Popular Electronic Cigarette Manufacturers and Targeted Marketing to
      Youth,* April 14, 2014; and see Michael Felberbaum, "Firms Dust Off Tobacco
      Marketing Playbook amid Pending Regulation of Electronic Cigarettes,"
      The Associated Press, September 10, 2013; also see Stuart Elliott,
      "E-Cigarette Makers' Ads Echo Tobacco's Heyday," *The New York Times,*
      August 29, 2013.

91   **The company also distributed samples** For Fashion Week reference, see
      Carly Cardellino, "Electronic Cigarettes Available for Free at Fashion Week,"
      Cosmopolitan, September 5, 2013.

91   **Between 2012 and 2013, spending** For e-cig television ad spending, see
      Mike Esterl, "Holy Smokes: E-Cigarette Ads Debut on TV," *The Wall Street
      Journal,* December 26, 2013.

91   **In January 2012, Szymanczyk announced** See John Reid Blackwell, "Altria
      Group CEO to Retire in May; Szymanczyk Being Succeeded by Longtime
      Richmond Executive," *Richmond Times-Dispatch,* updated September 18,
      2019.

93   **Then in April 2012, Lorillard** See "blu ecigs the Leading Electronic Ciga-
      rette Company Acquired by Lorillard," press release, blu, April 25, 2012; and
      Mike Esterl, "Got a Light—er Charger? Big Tobacco's Latest Buzz," *The Wall
      Street Journal,* April 25, 2012.

94   **Upon taking the new job** For Murillo's "relentless innovation" sign, see
      Mitch Morrison, "What Altria's Nu Mark Says About Vaping: President Joe
      Murillo on The Past, Present & Future of a New Category," CSP, Novem-
      ber 3, 2014.

96   **Nevertheless, in May 2012, Nu Mark** See "Altria Subsidiary Nu Mark Intro-
      duces Unique New Tobacco Product; Verve Discs Created to Appeal to
      Adult Cigarette Smokers," press release, May 23, 2012.

96   **If that was Altria's idea of innovation** For mussel shells see IARC Working
      Group on the Evaluation of Carcinogenic Risks to Humans, *Smokeless To-
      bacco and Some Tobacco-specific N-Nitrosamines,* International Agency for Re-
      search on Cancer, 2007; for other types of native types of tobacco chewing,
      see Lewin, *Phantastica, Narcotic and Stimulating Drugs; Their Use and Abuse.*

96   **"I don't think anyone's found the magic smoke-free product"** See Mike
      Esterl, "New from Altria: A Nicotine Lozenge," *The Wall Street Journal,*
      May 21, 2012.

97   **In April that year the start-up** "NJOY Electronic Cigarettes Receives
      $20 Million Investment from Leading Consumer-Focused Private Equity
      Firm Catterton," press release, April 9, 2012.

98   **In June, NJOY raised** For Sean Parker et al., see Kelly Faircloth, "Sean
      Parker Has Invested in E-Cigarette Maker NJOY, Because Disruption," *Ob-
      server,* June 11, 2013; and Teresa Novellino, "Sean Parker and Peter Thiel Fol-
      low NJOY's Vapor Trail in Scottsdale," Phoenix Business Journal, June 10,
      2013; and Mike Esterl, "E-Cigarettes Fire Up Investors, Regulators," *The Wall
      Street Journal,* June 9, 2013; also see Alexandra Stevenson, "NJOY, E-Cigarette
      Maker, Receives Funding Valuing It at $1 Billion," *The New York Times,* Feb-
      ruary 28, 2014; also see PitchBook for details about size of funding rounds
      and valuations.

100   **Altria ended up doing business** For details, see Kimree's preliminary pro-
      spectus from 2014, which is available through the website of the U.S. Securi-
      ties and Exchange Commission.

100   **And on June 11, 2013, Altria** For MarkTen unveiled in test market, see
      Sonya Chudgar, "Altria to Launch MarkTen E-Cigarette in Indiana," *Ad Age,*
      June 11, 2013.

CHAPTER 6

103   **John Patton wasn't anyone's idea** For background on Patton, see "He and His CEO Inhaled," *Wired,* March 28, 2006; also see "John Patton: A Lifetime of Adventure," PharmaVoice, December 2003; and John S. Patton, "Interview with John Patton," *Therapeutic Delivery,* 2010.

104   **The lungs are by far** For information on the lungs and absorption, see Proctor, *Golden Holocaust*; also see Neal L. Benowitz, "Clinical Pharmacology of Inhaled Drugs of Abuse: Implications in Understanding Nicotine Dependence," in the monograph published by the National Institute on Drug Abuse research monograph series called "Research Findings on Smoking of Abused Substances" and published in 1990.

104   **In 2006 the drug was approved** For coverage of Exubera, "Pfizer Receives FDA Approval for Exubera, the First Inhaleable Form of Insulin for Controlling Type 1 and Type 2 Diabetes in Adults," press release, Nektar Therapeutics, January 27, 2006; then see Matthew Herper, "Pfizer Kills Exubera," *Forbes,* October 18, 2007; and Alex Berenson, "Weak Sales Prompt Pfizer to Cancel Diabetes Drug," *The New York Times,* October 19, 2007.

106   **It then passes through the blood-brain** For the basics of nicotine and neurotransmitters, see Neal L. Benowitz, "Nicotine Addiction," *The New England Journal of Medicine* 362 (2010): 2295–2303. For the basics on nicotine salts, see the seminal Reynolds study: Thomas A. Perfetti, "Structural Study of Nicotine Salts," *Beiträge zur Tabakforschung International/Contributions to Tobacco Research* 12, no. 2 (February 1983): 43–54; for how acids can make cigarettes smoother and more appealing to youth, see internal Reynolds documents, including one dated December 4, 1973, titled "Cigarette Concept to Assure RJR a Larger Segment of the Youth Market"; and "Research Planning Memorandum on Some Thoughts About New Brands of Cigarettes for the Youth Market" from 1973.

107   **Cigars and other types of old-world** For science on pH of smoke chemistry and free-base nicotine, see especially Proctor, *Golden Holocaust*; also see Anna K. Duell, James F. Pankow, and David H. Peyton, "Free-Base Nicotine Determination in Electronic Cigarette Liquids by H NMR Spectroscopy," *Chemical Research in Toxicology* 31, no. 6 (June 2018): 431–34; also see Centers for Disease Control and Prevention, National Center for Chronic Disease Prevention and Health Promotion, and Office on Smoking and Health, *How Tobacco Smoke Causes Disease*; and see Jack Henningfield, James Pankow, and Bridgette Garrett, "Ammonia and Other Chemical Base Tobacco Additives and Cigarette Nicotine Delivery: Issues and Research Needs," *Nicotine and Tobacco Research* 6, no. 2 (April 2004): 199–205.

108   **Finding that perfect "Goldilocks" blend** See Anna K. Duell, James F. Pankow, and David H. Peyton, "Nicotine in Tobacco Product Aerosols: 'It's Déjà Vu All Over Again,'" *Tobacco Control* 29, no. 6 (October 17, 2019): 656–62.

108   **This new ammoniated tobacco recipe** For background on the "soul" of Marlboro and ammoniated tobacco, see Terrell Stevenson and Robert N. Proctor, "The Secret and Soul of Marlboro; Phillip Morris and the Origins, Spread, and Denial of Nicotine Freebasing," *American Journal of Public Health* 98, no. 7 (July 2008): 1184–94; also see Proctor, *Golden Holocaust*.

108   **One prominent expert witness testified** For the crack-cocaine testimony, see "Expert Report of Channing Robertson" in the state of Minnesota's case against the tobacco industry, 1997.

111   **More specifically, the founders were searching** For an explanation of Ploom's interest in "buzz" and "throat hit" and the related graphs showing heart rates, see the Amended Consolidated Class Action Complaint against Juul, in the case In Re: Juul Labs, Inc., Case No. 19-md-02913-WHO.

114   **It's about a thirty-hour flight** There are few publicly known details about the early Juul trials in New Zealand, but the information I derived came from interviews, and also from information contained in an online database maintained by the Australian New Zealand Clinical Trials Registry; also there is information about their trial in the patent Bowen and Xing filed.

117   **A study later described the formulation** For the "e-cigarette analog of Marlboro" see Duell, Pankow, and Peyton, "Nicotine in Tobacco Product Aerosols: 'It's Déjà Vu All Over Again.'"

CHAPTER 7

120   **Even though MarkTen had been announced** For nationwide expansion of MarkTen, see Mike Esterl, "Altria to Launch MarkTen E-Cigarette Nationally; The Maker of Marlboros Is Playing Catch-Up in the E-Cigarette Field," *The Wall Street Journal,* February 19, 2014; also see Melissa Vonder Haar, "Altria Takes MarkTen National; Lorillard Also Planning to Expand blu Globally," CSP, February 19, 2014.

121   **Just a few months later, MarkTen began** For the increase to 2.5 percent nicotine and introduction of the XL, see Altria's presentation at the Consumer Analyst Group of New York Conference, on February 18, 2015.

121   **By the end of 2014, Altria was spending** For the company's spending on ads for MarkTen, the $35 million figure, and examples of publications in which MarkTen was advertised, see Jennifer Cantrell, Brittany Emelle, Ollie Ganz, et al., "Rapid Increase in E-Cigarette Advertising Spending as Altria's MarkTen Enters the Marketplace," *Tobacco Control* 25 (2016): e16–e18; for many of the MarkTen ads, as well as more than fifty thousand modern and historical ads for all tobacco companies, see Stanford University's Research into the Impact of Tobacco Advertising, which was created by the Stanford professor Robert Jackler and parts of which have been exhibited in the Smithsonian's National Museum of American History.

122   **In September 2013, the Centers for Disease Control** See Centers for Disease Control and Prevention, *Notes from the Field: Electronic Cigarette Use Among Middle and High School Students—United States, 2011–2012, Morbidity and Mortality Weekly Report* (MMWR) 62, no. 35 (September 6, 2013): 729–30; also see Centers for Disease Control and Prevention, "E-Cigarette Use More Than Doubles Among U.S. Middle and High School Students from 2011–2012," press release, September 5, 2013.

122   **Ten days later, a group of lawmakers** The September 16, 2013, letter to Commissioner Hamburg was co-authored by the lawmakers Henry A. Waxman, Diana DeGette, Frank Pallone, Jr., and John D. Dingell.

122   **At the same time, a group** The AG letter was from the National Association of Attorneys General to Commissioner Hamburg, dated September 24, 2013.

123   **By November 2013, the Office** For the meetings with the Office of Management and Budget, I relied on archived meeting records at https://www .whitehouse.gov/omb/oira_0910_meetings/.

123   **Under the proposed rule, the FDA would** For the proposed deeming rule, see "Deeming Tobacco Products to Be Subject to the Federal Food, Drug, and Cosmetic Act, as Amended by the Family Smoking Prevention and Tobacco Control Act; Regulations on the Sale and Distribution of Tobacco Products and Required Warning Statements for Tobacco Products, a Proposed Rule by the Food and Drug Administration on 04/25/2014" at the website of the Federal Register, at the document citation 79 FR 23141, Pages: 23141–23207 (66 pages), and the Docket No. FDA-2014-N-0189.

123   **By January 2014 there were nearly** For the number of brands and flavors by January 2014 see the study by Shu-Hong Zhu, Jessica Y. Sun, Erika Bonnevie, et al., "Four Hundred and Sixty Brands of E-Cigarettes and Counting: Implications for Product Regulation," *Tobacco Control* 23, Suppl 3 (July 2014): iii3–iii9.

123   **The same year the surgeon general released** See National Center for Chronic Disease and Health Promotion, Office on Smoking and Health, *The Health Consequences of Smoking—50 Years of Progress*.

123   **Between 2013 and 2014 as Altria** For the tripling of e-cig use, see the CDC press release about the 2014 National Youth Tobacco Survey: Centers for Disease Control and Prevention, "E-Cigarette Use Triples Among Middle and High School Students in Just One Year," press release, April 15, 2015.

132   **When the Ploom board of directors met** See the Amended Consolidated Class Action Complaint against Juul, in the case In Re: Juul Labs, Inc.

134   **Mumby and Baillie arranged** For the Odin launch, see PAX Labs, Inc., "PAX Labs, Inc. Announces First Fashion Retail Partnership with Odin New York; Leading Vaporizer Innovator Exclusively Launches PAX 2 at Pioneering Menswear Boutique," press release, March 26, 2015.

134   **They recruited the elite fashion designer** For the Richard Chai reference, see Tahirah Hairston and Véronique Hyland, "Vape Life Hits New York Men's Fashion Week," *New York*, The Cut, July 15, 2015; for the Hamptons event, see PAX Labs, Inc., "PAX Labs, Inc. Announces Fashion Retail Partnership with Tenet Southampton; Leading Vaporizer Innovator Partners with Upscale Hamptons Boutique and Lifestyle Brand," press release, September 3, 2015.

134   **Pax even launched a limited-edition** See Evan Minsker, "The Weeknd's Custom Vaporizer Plays 'The Hills,'" Pitchfork, November 3, 2015.

134   **"Chic gadget alert!"** See Tangie Silva, "Chic Gadget Alert! Richard Mumby on the Allure of the Pax 2," *The Daily Front Row,* September 18, 2015; see Nicola Fumo, "Pax Has Brilliantly Positioned Itself as Fashion's Vaporizer," *Racked*, October 13, 2015.

134   *The New York Observer* **quoted Mumby** See Dena Silver, "Vapes Are the Next High-End Fashion Accessory; Pax Is Collaborating with Designer Richard

Chai to Introduce Their Smoking Product to the Fashion Industry," *Observer*, July 21, 2015.

134   **Meanwhile, Baillie was finalizing details** For an invitation to the June 4 launch, see Robert K. Jackler, Cindy Chau, Brook D. Getachew, et al., "JUUL Advertising over Its First Three Years on the Market," Stanford Research into the Impact of Tobacco Advertising, Stanford University School of Medicine, January 31, 2019.

134   **To help ensure that the affair would** For the information in the paragraph containing Grit Creative Group, see a cache of documents produced by the congressional hearing "Examining JUUL's Role in the Youth Nicotine Epidemic: Part I" conducted by the Subcommittee on Economic and Consumer Policy of the House Committee on Oversight and Reform, which can be obtained by going to the U.S. House of Representatives Committee Repository document search; also see Jackler, Chau, Getachew, et al., "JUUL Advertising over Its First Three Years on the Market."

CHAPTER 8

138   **Which was why eleven days** See PAX Labs, Inc. v. Philip Morris USA Inc., August 17, 2015, in the U.S. District Court California Northern District (San Francisco), docket number 3:15-cv-03766-WHA.

138   **Every one of the billions of packs** For background on the "Red Roof" design, see Kluger, *Ashes to Ashes;* also see various internal Philip Morris documents in the archives, for example, "Marlboro—The Pack People Picked" at document number 2045214257; also see Alfred E. Clark, "Louis Cheskin, 72, Studied Motivation and Effects of Color," *The New York Times,* October 10, 1981.

139   **Marlboro had been consistently recognized** See the annual list by *Forbes* called "The World's Most Valuable Brands."

139   **Philip Morris threatened or sued** For the Atari/squirt guns/candy cigarettes reference, see internal tobacco document numbers, 2062097994, 2078020867, and 2062101645.

140   **In January 2016, CEO Marty Barrington** For Altria's fourth quarter 2015 earnings, see the company's financial results in Altria, "Altria Reports 2015 Fourth-Quarter and Full-Year Results; Delivers Full-Year Adjusted Diluted EPS Growth of 8.9%," press release, January 28, 2016; also see a transcript of the earnings call; for coverage of the layoffs, see Tripp Mickle and Chelsey Dulaney, "Altria Group to Lay Off Workers to Cut Costs; Tobacco Company's Earnings and Revenue Increase Slightly," *The Wall Street Journal,* January 28, 2016; and John Reid Blackwell, "Altria Planning 490 Job Cuts, with 200 to 250 in Its Richmond-Area Operations," *Richmond Times-Dispatch,* January 28, 2016.

142   **investments made by Altria Ventures** See Sharklet Technologies, "Sharklet Technologies Closes $2 Million in Series B Financing," press release, December 11, 2012.

143   **Altria received a patent** See "Disposable Beverage Pod and Apparatus for Making a Beverage," patent number US20200138232A1.

143   **That industry had become hot** For the Coca-Cola/Monster deal, see Mike Esterl, "Coca-Cola Buys Stake in Monster Beverage; Coke to Pay $2.15 Billion for 16.7% Stake in Deal That Merges Energy Drinks," *The Wall Street Journal,* August 14, 2014; for Hiball deal, see Jennifer Maloney, "AB InBev to Buy Energy-Drinks Maker Hiball for Undisclosed Terms," *The Wall Street Journal,* July 20, 2017.

146   **In 2014, when he was still CFO** See The Associated Press, "Altria Acquires E-Cig Maker Green Smoke for $110M," February 3, 2014; and Altria, "Altria Announces Agreement to Acquire E-Vapor Business of Green Smoke, Inc.," press release, February 3, 2014.

146   **In a call in June 2015, just days** Willard's remarks in June 2015 were made at an Investor Day presentation on June 23, 2015.

147   **Now the same two guys** David Pierce, "This Might Just Be the First Great E-Cig," *Wired,* April 21, 2015.

148   **Just like they did with the Ruyan** For some details about Altria's internal testing of Juul, see a court deposition of Jason Flora, an Altria employee, dated October 2, 2019, in one of the Engle Progeny cases, number 07-036719, in the Circuit Court of the Seventeenth Judicial Circuit in and for Broward County, Florida.

CHAPTER 9

149   **It "feels too young"** See the Juul class action complaint, In Re: Juul Labs, Inc., Case No. 19-md-02913.

149   **In 1941, Camel erected a legendary** See Brandt, *The Cigarette Century.*

150   **The company had launched a "Vaporized" spread** For the Vice ads, see Stanford's Research Into the Impact of Tobacco Advertising.

150   **Juul's edgy ad campaign had** See Declan Harty, "Juul Hopes to Reinvent E-Cigarette Ads with 'Vaporized' Campaign," *Ad Age,* June 23, 2015.

150   **In early July, Asseily wrote an email** These emails/conversations are taken from the Juul class action complaint, In Re: Juul Labs, Inc., Case No. 19-md-02913.

151   **One of the main conclusions** The December 2014 internal assessment seen by author.

151   **As the sampling tour descended** See, for example, Jackler, Chau, Getachew, et al., "JUUL Advertising over its First Three Years on the Market."

153   **Juul "could be a multi-billion [dollar] opportunity"** For some details of the Stifel presentation, see the Juul class action complaint, In Re: Juul Labs, Inc., Case No. 19-md-02913-WHO.

160   **"Given the current climate with addictions to OxyContin"** See class action complaint against Juul.

161   **The system wasn't built** For details on the warranty system and age verification, see the Juul class action complaint, In Re: Juul Labs, Inc.

161   **People were buying Juul** For the name "Beer Can" et al., see the state of California's lawsuit against Juul.

CHAPTER 10

163   **The Food and Drug Administration's Center for Tobacco Products** Zeller
features prominently in Kessler, *A Question of Intent*; you can see his TED
Talk, "The Past, Present and Future of Nicotine Addiction."

164   **Then he spent a decade with Pinney Associates** For more on Pinney and
the "three-pack-a-day smoker" reference, see Arlene Levinson, "Research
Unit Focuses on What It Takes to Quit: Institute Seeks to Snuff Out Smok-
ing," *Los Angeles Times*, September 25, 1988; and Elyse Tanouye, "FDA Clears
Glaxo's Zyban as a Smoking-Cessation Aid," *The Wall Street Journal*, May 16,
1997; Suein L. Hwang, "Drug Makers Use Slick TV Ads to Get People to
Quit Smoking," *The Wall Street Journal*, May 21, 1996; Suzanne PETREN
Moritz, "Smoking Report Released; Kennedy School Study Aims at Helping
Smokers Quit," *The Harvard Crimson*, April 5, 1990; and Jane Gross, "Death
Forms in 2 States Ask About Tobacco Use," *The New York Times*, January 27,
1989.

164   **He adopted as his patron saint** For background on Michael Russell, see, for
example, his seminal paper, "The Future of Nicotine Replacement" in the
British Journal of Addiction, 1991; and for the quote about smoking being a
"finely adjusted drug-taking activity" see *The Smoking Cessation Newsletter* 1,
no. 1 (1981), which can be found in the tobacco archives, document number
2021539714.

164   **While still at Pinney, he served** For the Strategic Dialogue and "continuum
of risk," see Mitchell Zeller, Dorothy Hatsukami, and the Strategic Dialogue
on Tobacco Harm Reduction Group, "The Strategic Dialogue on Tobacco
Harm Reduction: A Vision and Blueprint for Action in the US," *Tobacco Control* 18, no. 4 (August 2009): 324–32.

165   **Zeller advocated for implementing mandatory** See Mitch Zeller, "Reflections on the 'Endgame' for Tobacco Control," *Tobacco Control* 22 (2013):
i40–i41.

166   **On March 5, 2014, the agency approved** Many but not all of the documents pertaining to the FDA's primate nicotine studies came from a nonprofit organization called the White Coat Waste Project, which opposes
spending federal tax dollars on animal research. The group filed a lawsuit
against the FDA after learning about the nicotine studies and successfully
obtained hundreds of pages of internal FDA documents detailing the monkey experiments. See the company's website for many of the documents.
Also see Amy K. Goodwin, Takato Hiranita, and Merle G. Paule, "The Reinforcing Effects of Nicotine in Humans and Nonhuman Primates: A Review
of Intravenous Self-Administration Evidence and Future Directions for Research," *Nicotine and Tobacco Research* 17, no. 11 (February 2015): 1297–310.

167   **Ironically, almost no long-term research** See Tushar Singh, René A. Arra-
zola, Catherine G. Corey, et al., *Tobacco Use Among Middle and High School
Students—United States, 2011–2015, Morbidity and Mortality Weekly Report*
(*MMWR*) 65, no. 14 (April 15, 2016): 361–67.

169   **The retroactive review requirement was so controversial** See Eric Lipton,
"A Lobbyist Wrote the Bill. Will the Tobacco Industry Win Its E-Cigarette

Fight?," *The New York Times,* September 2, 2016 (be sure not to miss the extensive cache of documents that the reporter obtained and links to, under the subheading "Tobacco War Lobbying Documents").

170   **"The new rule moves us away from a largely unregulated"** See Mitch Zeller, "The Deeming Rule: Keeping Pace with the Modern Tobacco Marketplace," *American Journal of Respiratory and Critical Care Medicine* 194, no. 5 (September 2016): 538–40; For more on Zeller's thinking about e-cigarettes, also see Lipton, "A Lobbyist Wrote the Bill. Will the Tobacco Industry Win Its E-Cigarette Fight?"; and Melissa Vonder Haar, "Blog: Did Mitch Zeller Just Show His True Colors?; Instead of Building a Bridge, the CTP Director Has Blown Up the Nascent Electronic-Cigarette Industry," CSP, May 10, 2016.

CHAPTER 11

172   **Between December 2015 and August 2016** See an internal Juul document in the cache of House documents, titled "Churn: New Pods, Strengths, and Colors in Place."

173   **In one email in mid-2016, Gal Cohen** For the Cohen-Bowen correspondence, see state of Colorado's lawsuit against Juul.

174   **In press interviews he'd plug Pax** See Rob Hill, "Corner Office: Pax Labs Inc. CEO Tyler Goldman Is Disrupting the Vape Industry," *mg Magazine,* November 9, 2016.

174   **Bodegas and gas stations were hoarding** See James Covert, "E-Cig Boss Scrambles to End Price Gouging on Vaping 'Pods,'" *New York Post,* October 13, 2016; for other details about Goldman and the industry under his tenure, see "Pax Focusing on Scale and Supply," *Tobacco Journal International,* February 23, 2017; and also Renée Covino, "From the PAX Perch," Tobacco Business International, November 27, 2016.

178   **The liquid inside the little plastic pods** See Lauren Etter, Ben Elgin, and Ellen Huet, "Juul Is the New Big Tobacco," *Bloomberg Businessweek,* October 10, 2019.

178   **While individually there was nothing alarming** See Robert Langreth and Lauren Etter, "Early Signs of Vaping Health Risks Were Missed or Ignored; Doctors and Researchers Scattered Around the Globe Saw Problems, but 'Nobody Put Two and Two Together,'" *Bloomberg,* September 25, 2019; and Robert Langreth and Lauren Etter, "How Vaping-Related Deaths Put Cloud over E-Cigarettes," *Bloomberg,* QuickTake, October 10, 2019.

179   **At a 2015 presentation** For the presentation to the FDA titled "Toxicology of Inhaled Diacetyl and 2,3-Pentanedione," by the CDC researcher, Ann Hubbs, see "Electronic Cigarettes and the Public Health; Public Workshop," March 9, 2015.

179   **In the 1990s, diacetyl had been** See, for example, Joseph G. Allen, Skye S. Flanigan, Mallory LeBlanc, et al., "Flavoring Chemicals in E-Cigarettes: Diacetyl, 2,3-Pentanedione, and Acetoin in a Sample of 51 Products, Including Fruit-, Candy-, and Cocktail-Flavored E-Cigarettes," *Environmental Health Perspectives* 124, no. 6 (June 2016): 733–79; and Carrie Arnold, "On the Vapor

Trail: Examining the Chemical Content of E-Cigarette Flavorings," *Environmental Health Perspectives* 124, no. 6 (June 2016): A115.

179   **For example, a company memo from** For the April 2018 Popcorn Lung memo, and more generally for the lack of understanding of its flavorings and ingredients, see the state of Colorado's legal complaint against Juul.

179   **An internal database of customer complaints** See Lauren Etter, "FDA's Juul Inquiry Found Consumers Had 2,600 Health Complaints," *Bloomberg,* January 13, 2020.

181   **Eventually, Juul traced the problem** For the off-spec ingredient incident, see, for example, Etter, Elgin, and Huet, "Juul Is the New Big Tobacco."

183   **Juul was "one of the most impressive e-consumer companies"** See Alfred Lee and Cory Weinberg, "Juul Soars Despite Investor Discomfort with E-Cigarettes," *The Information,* June 18, 2018.

184   **His theory of rapid growth** Check out Reid Hoffman's theory in Reid Hoffman and Chris Yeh, *Blitzscaling: The Lightning-Fast Path to Building Massively Valuable Companies* (New York: Crown, 2018).

185   **That's the idea popularized by Marc Andreessen** See Andreessen's original blog post, "The PMARCA Guide to Startups—Part 4: The Only Thing That Matters," June 25, 2007, at https://pmarchive.com/guide_to_startups_part4.html.

185   **Stanford professor Steve Blank** For more on Steve Blank's lean start-up theories, see "Why the Lean Start-Up Changes Everything," *Harvard Business Review,* May 2013.

185   **When the e-liquid trickled into** For details of the problem with the leaky pods and the sensor, see Lauren Etter, "Juul Quietly Revamped Its E-Cigarette, Risking the FDA's Rebuke," *Bloomberg Businessweek,* July 23, 2020.

187   **By the summer of 2017, even though** Juul/Altria/Reynolds, et al. e-cigarette market data comes from data provided by the CDC.

188   **A week later, the company raised** For the $111.5 million fundraising round, see data from PitchBook; also see Ari Levy, "E-Cigarette Maker Juul Is Raising $150 Million After Spinning Out of Vaping Company," CNBC, December 19, 2017.

CHAPTER 12

190   **On May 11, 2017, Scott Gottlieb** See photographs of the swearing in put out by @SecPriceMD on Twitter; also see Health and Human Services, "Secretary Price Congratulates Dr. Gottlieb on His Confirmation as FDA Commissioner," press release, May 10, 2017.

191   **Trump had recently signed an executive order** For Trump's relevant policies, see Katie Thomas, "Trump Vows to Ease Rules for Drug Makers, but Again Zeros In on Prices," *The New York Times,* January 31, 2017; also see "Presidential Executive Order on Reducing Regulation and Controlling Regulatory Costs," issued on January 30, 2017.

191   **At his confirmation hearing just a few** For Gottlieb's confirmation hearing, see the video and a full transcript at U.S. Senate Committee on Health, Edu-

cation, Labor & Pensions, "Nomination of Scott Gottlieb, MD, to Serve as Commissioner of Food and Drugs," April 5, 2017.

193   **In the year since the deeming rule** An important lawsuit against the FDA's deeming rule was Cigar Association of America et al. v. U.S. Food and Drug Administration, July 15, 2016, the District Court of the District of Columbia.

193   **In early May, just a week before** For the Justice Department's motion in the Cigar Association's case, see the Joint Motion to Amend Scheduling Order, dated May 1, 2017; also, Juliet Eilperin, "FDA Delays Enforcement of Stricter Standards for E-Cigarette, Cigar Industry," *The Washington Post,* May 2, 2017.

195   **Nevertheless, in June 2017 the** See Ahmed Jamal, Andrea Gentzke, S. Sean Hu, et al., *Tobacco Use Among Middle and High School Students—United States, 2011–2016, Morbidity and Mortality Weekly Report (MMWR)* 66, no. 23 (June 16, 2017): 597–603; also see Laurie McGinley, "Teenagers' Tobacco Use Hits a Record Low, with Sharp Drop in E-Cigarettes," *The Washington Post,* June 15, 2017.

195   **Given the explosion of interest** For an analysis of why the NYTS numbers might not have reflected the reality on the ground, see Jidong Huang, Zogshuan Duan, Julian Kwok, et al., "Vaping versus JUULing: How the Extraordinary Growth and Marketing of JUUL Transformed the US Retail E-Cigarette Market," *Tobacco Control* 28, no. 2 (February 2019): 146–51.

196   **On the morning of Friday, July 28** Gottlieb's June 28, 2017, speech on nicotine was titled "Protecting American Families: Comprehensive Approach to Nicotine and Tobacco."

197   **On the day of the announcement** For Altria's stock in response, see Matt Egan, "Tobacco Stocks Crushed as FDA Targets Nicotine in Cigarettes," CNN, July 28, 2017.

199   **On September 15, 2017, Gottlieb ordered** See an email dated September 15, 2017, with the subject "E07537.01 Suspension" that states, "No further studies should be performed and catheters are to be removed from all animals."

199   **Gottlieb terminated the monkey experiments** For coverage of Gottlieb's monkey crisis, see "FDA Chief Visits NCTR," *The Pine Bluff Commercial,* February 9, 2018; and also Sheila Kaplan, "Citing Deaths of Lab Monkeys, F.D.A. Ends an Addiction Study," *The New York Times,* January 26, 2018; and Bill Bowden, "FDA Axes Study at Arkansas Lab; Nicotine Addiction Research Led to Deaths of 4 Monkeys," *Arkansas Democrat-Gazette,* January 30, 2018.

CHAPTER 13

202   **Just after ten A.M., after Altria's guests** See a transcript of the event titled "Remarks by Marty Barrington, Altria Group, Inc.'s (Altria) Chairman, CEO and President, and Other Members of Altria's Senior Management Team; 2017 Altria Investor Day Richmond, Virginia," November 2, 2017; a recorded webcast of the event is also available.

208   **When a Goldman Sachs analyst asked** See the transcript of Altria's Q1 2018 earnings call from April 26, 2018.

209   **"There is a dangerous new trend"** See Kristen Smith, "Parents Clueless About Dangerous New Trend Sweeping Through Area Schools," WRIC-TV, February 19, 2018.

209   **Another read: "Several greater Richmond area school"** See Karina Bolster, "School Systems Aware of Juul Vaping Device Being Used by Students," WWBT, April 9, 2018.

211   **Practically the entire reason** Enjoy this excellent story on the Marlboro Ranch, Sarah Yager, "Welcome to Marlboro Country: Philip Morris Stakes a Last Claim in the West," *The Atlantic*, March 15, 2013.

215   **On February 1, Barrington announced** See John Reid Blackwell, "Altria Group's Top Executive Retiring in May; Company's Chief Operating Officer to Become Chairman and CEO," *Richmond Times-Dispatch*, February 1, 2018.

216   **But as Barrington sat on the sidelines** See "The New World of Tobacco—JUUL Starting to Disrupt U.S. Cigarette Industry," Citi Research, April 18, 2018.

216   **Back in April 2011, after** See the blog post, Ben Horowitz, "Peacetime CEO/Wartime CEO," April 14, 2011, on the website of the venture capital firm Andreessen Horowitz.

217   **Just before nine A.M. on May 17** For Barrington's remarks at the annual meeting, see them on the Altria website, "Remarks by Marty Barrington, Altria Group, Inc.'s (Altria) Chairman, Chief Executive Officer (CEO) and President, at Altria's 2018 Annual Meeting of Shareholders."

CHAPTER 14

219   **Atherton, California, was a quiet old** Atherton, "wealthiest city in America": see Shelly Hagan, Wei Lu, and Sophie Alexander, "In America's Richest Town, $500k a Year Is Now Below Average," Bloomberg News, February 20, 2020.

220   **He was brought in from the private equity** See JoNel Aleccia, "Chobani Officially Recalls Moldy Yogurt After Complaints," NBC News, September 5, 2013; and for the TPG investment, see William Alden, "Seeking to Grow, Chobani Secures $750 Million Loan," *The New York Times*, April 23, 2014.

220   **The feat solidified his reputation** See Josh Kosman and James Covert, "Chobani CEO Being Replaced, May Be Stripped of Chairman Role," *The New York Post*, January 5, 2015.

220   **In classic consultant fashion** For the Burns kitchen table incident, see Jia Tolentino, "The Promise of Vaping and the Rise of Juul," *The New Yorker*, May 7, 2018.

220   **That fall, the Paly student newspaper** See an article in the school newspaper called *The Campanile:* Johnny Loftus, "Juuling and Schooling," *The Campanile*, September 27, 2017.

221   **"We could not be more pleased to announce"** See JUUL Labs, Inc., "JUUL Labs, Inc. Appoints Kevin Burns, Previously President & Chief Operating Officer of Chobani, as Its Chief Executive Officer," December 11, 2017.

223   **A finance executive later filed** See Breja v. JUUL Labs, Inc, U.S. District Court, California Northern District (San Francisco), 3:19-cv-07148.

225   **the number of Juul-related** See Yoonsang Kim, Sherry L. Emery, Lisa Vera, et al., "At the Speed of Juul: Measuring the Twitter Conversation Related to ENDS and Juul Across Space and Time (2017–2018)," *Tobacco Control*, March 2020; also see Jon-Patrick Allem, Likhit Charmapuri, Jennifer B. Unger, and Tess Boley Cruz, "Characterizing JUUL-Related Posts on Twitter," *Drug and Alcohol Dependence* 190 (September 2018): 1–5; for the Reddit material, see Ramakanth Kavuluru, Sifei Han, and Ellen J. Hahn, "On the Popularity of the USB Flash Drive-Shaped Electronic Cigarette Juul," research letter, *Tobacco Control* 28, no. 1 (2019): 110–12.

225   **Even before Burns came on** For the Sard reference, see the class action complaint in San Francisco; for the Tower Data reference, see the lawsuit filed by the Commonwealth of Massachusetts against Juul.

227   **Adolescence is defined loosely as** For basics on the teenage brain, see the Surgeon General website, which describes how "until about age 25, the brain is still growing. Each time a new memory is created or a new skill is learned, stronger connections—or synapses—are built between brain cells. Young people's brains build synapses faster than adult brains. Because addiction is a form of learning, adolescents can get addicted more easily than adults."

227   **As the brain undergoes a process of** For "pruning" see, Linda Patia Spear, "Adolescent Neurodevelopment," *Journal of Adolescent Health*, 2013 Feb; For the regions of the brain that govern cognitive functioning, see B. J. Casey, Rebecca M. Jones, and Todd A. Hare, "The Adolescent Brain," *Annals of the New York Academy of Sciences* 1124 (March 2008): 111–26; also see David M. Lydon, Stephen J. Wilson, Amanda Childa, and Charles F. Geier, "Adolescent Brain Maturation and Smoking: What We Know and Where We're Headed," *Neuroscience and Biobehavioral Reviews* 45 (September 2014): 323–42.

227   **Also, nicotine has been shown** See Theodore A. Slotkin, "Nicotine and the Adolescent Brain: Insights from an Animal Model," *Neurotoxicology and Teratology* 24, no. 3 (May–June 2002): 369–84.

227   **"Even brief exposure to a low dose of nicotine"** See Menglu Yuan, Sarah J. Cross, Sandra E. Loughlin, and Frances M. Leslie, "Nicotine and the Adolescent Brain," *The Journal of Physiology* 593, no. 16 (August 2015): 3397–412.

228   **In 2009 Halpern-Felsher got funding** For Halpern-Felsher's The Tobacco Prevention Toolkit, visit the website of Stanford Medicine at https://med.stanford.edu/tobaccopreventiontoolkit.html.

232   **Around the beginning of 2018** Juul's "Education and Youth Prevention Department" is drawn from interviews and documents obtained through a Freedom of Information Act request, as well as documents provided by Juul to Congress.

234   **Meredith Berkman lived on Manhattan's** Some material is drawn from Berkman's congressional testimony that she gave on July 24, 2019, before the House Committee on Oversight and Reform, Subcommittee on Economic and Consumer Policy.

237   **There was growing concern that the array** See Food and Drug Administration, "Statement from FDA Commissioner Scott Gottlieb, M.D., on Efforts to Reduce Tobacco Use, Especially Among Youth, by Exploring

Options to Address the Role of Flavors—Including Menthol—in Tobacco Products," press release, March 19, 2018.

237   **A group of pediatricians and a network** See American Academy of Pediatrics et al v. Food and Drug Administration et al., in the U.S. District Court in the District of Maryland, 8:18-cv-00883.

237   **About two weeks later, on April 18** See Kate Zernike, "'I Can't Stop': Schools Struggle with Vaping Explosion," *The New York Times,* April 2, 2018.

237   **Five days later, Gottlieb revealed** For the "blitz" see the Food and Drug Administration, "Statement from FDA Commissioner Scott Gottlieb, M.D., on New Enforcement Actions and a Youth Tobacco Prevention Plan to Stop Youth Use of, and Access to, JUUL and Other E-Cigarettes," April 23, 2018; and Maggie Fox, "FDA Cracks Down in 'Blitz' on E-Cigarette Sales to Kids," NBC News, April 24, 2018.

CHAPTER 15

240   **One could cite Michael Miles** For details on Miles's tenure at Philip Morris, see Kluger, *Ashes to Ashes.*

240   **As he prepared to take on the CEO role** See Jim Collins, *Good to Great: Why Some Companies Make the Leap and Others Don't* (New York: HarperBusiness, 2001); and also see Klaus Schwab, *The Fourth Industrial Revolution* (New York: Crown Business, 2017); and John P. Kotter, *A Sense of Urgency* (Boston: Harvard Business Press, 2008).

242   **As part of the new structure** See Altria, "Altria Group, Inc. Announces New Structure to Accelerate Its Innovation Aspiration," May 22, 2018; and also John Reid Blackwell, "Altria Changes Its Organizational Structure and Names New Leaders as It Aims to Develop New Products," *Richmond Times-Dispatch,* May 22, 2018.

243   **Press releases and corporate restructurings** For "musical chairs" reference, see "Altria Restructures, Forms Two Separate Divisions to Focus on Core Tobacco & Innovative Tobacco Products," *Convenience Store News,* May 23, 2018.

244   **Charles Payson "Chase" Coleman III** See "Billionaire Partied as Guests Vandalized His $52M Co-op," *Page Six,* April 26, 2018; and also Hema Parmar, Melissa Karsh, and Sophie Alexander, "The Charmed Life of a Young Tiger Cub with a $4.6 Billion Fortune," *Bloomberg,* June 27, 2019.

244   **The company fit neatly into an investment thesis** For details of Tiger investments, see PitchBook.

244   **with the start-up mushrooming** See, for example, Olivia Zaleski, "E-Cigarette Maker Juul Labs Is Raising $1.2 Billion," Bloomberg News, June 29, 2018; also, Jennifer Maloney, "Juul Raises $650 Million in Funding That Values E-Cig Startup at $15 Billion," *The Wall Street Journal,* July 10, 2018; and Alfred Lee, "Tiger to Invest $600 Million in Juul as Valuation Climbs," *The Information,* July 2, 2018.

245   **Now it was a *decacorn*** See Alex Wilhelm, "Juul Makes Being a Unicorn Look (Really) Good," Crunchbase, July 5, 2018; and Zack Guzman, "Juul Surpasses Facebook as Fastest Startup to Reach Decacorn Status," Yahoo! Finance, October 9, 2018.

245 **On Thursday, July 26, when** For Altria's 2Q 2018 results from July 26, 2018, see a transcript of Willard's earnings call that day; also see Jennifer Maloney and Austen Hufford, "Marlboro Sales Drop Sharply in a Shrinking Market; Altria CEO Plays Down Threat from Popular E-Cigarette Rivals like Juul," *The Wall Street Journal,* July 26, 2018.

246 **By August 1, the cherry blossoms** For the August 1 meeting at the Park Hyatt, see the administrative complaint by the Federal Trade Commission, In the Matter of Altria Group, Inc., a corporation; and JUUL Labs, Inc., a corporation, Docket No. 9393.

246 **just a few blocks from the White House** See Sarah Wheaton, "The Obamas' Anniversary Dinner," *The New York Times,* October 3, 2009.

249 **Quigley helped grow its brands** For "Men of Copenhagen," see a public filing from Altria from its Investor Day Conference, June 11, 2013.

249 **In the winter of 2017, consumers started** For the Copenhagen recall, see Jennifer Maloney, "Altria Investigating Whether Recalled Tobacco Products Were Tampered With; Executive Says 'Deliberate, Malicious Act' Done by People Familiar with Quality and Safety Procedures," *The Wall Street Journal,* February 3, 2017.

249 **By now Juul had more than 50 percent** Market share figures come from data provided by the CDC.

CHAPTER 16

256 **Ultimately, Woodring helped land DDB** See Patrick Coffee, "DDB Wins Creative Review for E-Cigarette Company JUUL," Agency Spy, October 17, 2018.

258 **Israel didn't yet have any restrictions** For coverage of Juul in Israel, see Ronny Linder, "Juul, the Hit E-cigarette, Debuts in Israel with No Restrictions on Sales," *Haaretz,* May 14, 2018.

258 **Next Juul announced** For the Russia launch, and the rush to market before government regulations, see "Juul добавит пара, Американцы выходят в Россию," Kommersant; and an interview with Monsees by Kommersant on October 31, 2018 at https://www.kommersant.ru/doc/3786934.

258 **Within weeks of setting up shop** See Reuters, "Israel Bans Juul E-Cigarettes Citing 'Grave' Public Health Risk," August 21, 2018.

260 **San Francisco's Dogpatch neighborhood** See Carl Nolte, "The Quest to Save Dogpatch; Dot-coms and Developers Arrive in Tiny, Funky, S.F. Neighborhood," *San Francisco Gate,* March 29, 2000; also see Jacob Bourne, "Balancing Growth and Livability as Neighborhoods Change," *The Potrero View,* July 2016.

261 **Ever since 2008 when the city** See Alison Heath, "The Eastern Neighborhoods Plan Has Failed Us," *The Potrero View,* July 2016; and the city's Planning Commission site on "Eastern Neighborhoods."

262 **Doumani immediately called up her neighbor** Herrera background comes in part from Julie Lasky, "Dogpatch, San Francisco: A Hub for the Creative," *The New York Times,* December 3, 2016.

262 **He'd succeeded Louise Renne** For more on Renne, see Lee Romney, "Activism Defines S.F. City Attorney's Office," *Los Angeles Times,* March 23, 2004;

and Henry Weinstein and Maura Dolan, "San Francisco Sues 6 Tobacco Firms," *Los Angeles Times,* June 7, 1996.

266   **Many people knew Steyer** For coverage of Steyer, see Natasha Singer, "Turning a Children's Rating System into an Advocacy Army," *The New York Times,* April 26, 2015; also see Andrew Anthony, "Jim Steyer: The Man Who Took on Mark Zuckerberg," *The Guardian,* July 5, 2020; Stephanie Simon and Caitlin Emma, "The Steyer Brothers: 'We're Fearless,'" *Politico,* February 24, 2014; and Stephanie Strom, "Hedge Fund Chief Takes Major Role in Philanthropy," *The New York Times,* September 15, 2011; also see James P. Steyer, *Talking Back to Facebook: The Common Sense Guide to Raising Kids in the Digital Age* (New York: Scribner, 2012).

CHAPTER 17

269   **Gottlieb and Zeller co-authored** See Scott Gottlieb and Mitch Zeller, "Advancing Tobacco Regulation to Protect Children and Families: Updates and New Initiatives from the FDA on the Anniversary of the Tobacco Control Act and FDA's Comprehensive Plan for Nicotine," U.S. Food and Drug Administration, August 2, 2018.

270   **By the beginning of August, Juul had taken part** Information on Gottlieb's at least half a dozen meetings with Juul, and the submissions pressing the agency on flavors, was in documents obtained by the author under a Freedom of Information Act request.

271   **Over the past year, Juul tripled** See Maya Kosoff, "Josh Raffel, Javanka's Former Battering Ram, Takes His Talent to the E-Cig Game," *Vanity Fair,* October 4, 2018.

273   **As Pritzker sent his July 30 opening term sheet** For Pritzker telling Willard about "continued competition" being off the table, see the FTC's administrative complaint.

273   **Juul's annual revenue for 2018** For Juul's $1 billion revenue figure, and 450 million pod "refill" kits, see Willard speaking during the Q4 2018 earnings call, January 31, 2019; also see Dan Primack, "Scoop: The Numbers Behind Juul's Investor Appeal," Axios, July 2, 2018.

274   **That was partly because the most recent** See Teresa W. Wang, Andrea Gentzke, Saida Sharapova, et al., *Tobacco Product Use Among Middle and High School Students—United States, 2011–2017, Morbidity and Mortality Weekly Report* (MMWR) 67, no. 22 (June 8, 2018): 629–33; for Gottlieb's statement, see "Statement from FDA Commissioner Scott Gottlieb, M.D., on 2017 National Youth Tobacco Survey Results and Ongoing FDA Efforts to Protect Youth from the Dangers of Nicotine and Tobacco Products" from the same day; also see Salynn Boyles, "CDC Report Says Tobacco Use Declining in Teens—but Survey Data May Be Missing Increase in E-Cig Use," MedPage Today, June 7, 2018.

274   **On July 17, *PBS NewsHour*** See Kavitha Cardoza, "Educators Worry Students Don't Know Vaping Health Risks," *PBS NewsHour,* July 17, 2018.

275   **He'd seen the models showing** See Benjamin J. Apelberg, Shari Feirman, Esther Salazar, et al., "Potential Public Health Effects of Reducing Nicotine

Levels in Cigarettes in the United States," *The New England Journal of Medicine* 378 (May 3, 2018): 1725–33.

276   **On September 11, Gottlieb put out a statement** See FDA Statement, "Statement from FDA Commissioner Scott Gottlieb, M.D., on New Steps to Address Epidemic of Youth E-Cigarette Use," September 11, 2018; also see Laurie McGinley, "FDA Chief Calls Youth E-Cigarettes an 'Epidemic,'" *The Washington Post*, September 12, 2018.

277   **Over the next forty-eight hours Gottlieb appeared** For Gottlieb on Squawk Box, see Berkeley Lovelace, Jr., "FDA Chief Scott Gottlieb Blames Vaping Giant Juul for 'Epidemic' of Teens Using E-Cigarettes," CNBC, September 13, 2018.

277   **Desperate to share the CDC's not-yet-finalized** See "We Cannot Let E-Cigarettes Become an On-Ramp for teenage addiction," *The Washington Post*, October 11, 2018.

278   **There were now more than one thousand employees** See Catherine Ho, "Juul Hiring Aggressively amid FDA Probe, but Troubled Image a Turnoff for Some," *San Francisco Chronicle*, October 19, 2018.

280   **Several Juul employees and executives were schooled** See Lauren Etter, "Juul Quietly Revamped Its E-Cigarette, Risking the FDA's Rebuke," *Bloomberg Businessweek*, July 23, 2020.

283   **On October 18, 2018, Willard set out** Some details of the Willard-Gottlieb meeting came from the commissioner's notes obtained via a Freedom of Information Act request.

285   **On November 13, the two women** Minutes of San Francisco Port Commission meeting can be found at the Port's website.

285   **After the meeting, which appeared to foreclose** For Herrera's Pier 70 inquiry, see Catherine Ho, "SF Officials Seek Proof Vaping Firm Juul Is Following State, City Rules," *San Francisco Chronicle*, November 28, 2018.

286   **On November 13, Burns announced** See Juul Labs, "Juul Labs Action Plan, Underage Use Prevention, Message from Kevin Burns, CEO, Juul Labs," November 13, 2018.

287   **Two days later, Gottlieb finally** See the Food and Drug Administration, "Statement from FDA Commissioner Scott Gottlieb, M.D., on Proposed New Steps to Protect Youth by Preventing Access to Flavored Tobacco Products and Banning Menthol in Cigarettes," November 15, 2018.

287   **On December 7, Altria announced** For the Cronos announcement, see Altria, "Altria to Make Growth Investment in Cronos Group," press release, December 7, 2018; and for the announcement re Nu Mark products, see Altria Group, Inc., "Altria Refocuses Innovative Product Efforts," November 7, 2018.

288   **Just a few days earlier** *The Wall Street Journal* See Dana Mattioli and Jennifer Maloney, "Altria in Talks to Take Significant Minority Stake in Juul Labs; A Tie-Up Would Represent a Major Reordering of the Cigarette Industry," *The Wall Street Journal*, November 28, 2018.

289   **It was the largest sum ever** Originated from data compiled by PitchBook.

289   **So, as part of the deal, Burns** See Olivia Zaleski, "Juul Employees to Get $2 Billion Bonus in Altria Deal," Bloomberg News, December 20, 2018; also,

Jennifer Maloney, "Juul's Instant Millionaires: How $2 Billion from Altria Is Being Divvied Up; Part of Marlboro Maker's $12.8 Billion Investment Is Earmarked for Cash Awards, Retention Bonuses," *The Wall Street Journal,* December 21, 2018; and Angelica LaVito and David Faber, "Juul Employees Get a Special $2 Billion Bonus from Tobacco Giant Altria—to Be Split Among Its 1,500 Employees," CNBC, December 20, 2018.

292   **Willard announced the top-line news** See Altria Group, Inc., "Altria Makes $12.8 Billion Minority Investment in JUUL to Accelerate Harm Reduction and Drive Growth," December 20, 2018.

293   **To achieve those savings, the company was planning** See John Reid Blackwell, "Altria Group Cuts 900 Salaried Jobs from Nationwide Operations as Part of Cost-Cutting Plan," *Richmond Times-Dispatch,* January 25, 2019.

CHAPTER 18

295   **The Four Seasons Silicon Valley** The Four Seasons scene comes from Sheila Kaplan, Andrew Jacobs, and Choe Sang-Hun, "The World Pushes Back Against E-Cigarettes and Juul," *The New York Times,* March 30, 2020.

296   **On the day the deal was announced** For a transcript of the update, see "Altria Group Inc. Conference Call to Discuss Investment in JUUL Labs Inc.," December 20, 2018.

297   *The Wall Street Journal* **published a column** See Jennifer Maloney, "Marlboro Maker Is Paying a Desperate Price for Juul," *The Wall Street Journal,* December 20, 2018.

297   **Two credit ratings agencies** See Amanda Jean Dalugdug, "S&P, Fitch Downgrade Altria on $12.8B Juul Investment," S&P Global Market Intelligence, December 21, 2018.

298   **On Thursday evening, January 10, 2019** See Brad Stone, "Bill Campbell, Silicon Valley Coach and Mentor, Dies at 75; Apple's Steve Jobs and Google's Larry Page Were Among Those Who Had Looked to Campbell for Advice," *Bloomberg,* April 18, 2016; Jena McGregor, "Silicon Valley Mourns Its 'Coach,' Former Intuit CEO Bill Campbell," *The Washington Post,* April 18, 2016; and Miguel Helft, "Silicon Valley Takes a Break to Remember 'Coach' Bill Campbell," *Forbes,* April 26, 2016.

301   **"It's clear that we're focused on the mission"** See Angelica LaVito, "Juul Combats Criticism with New TV Ad Campaign Featuring Adult Smokers Who Quit After Switching to E-Cigarettes," CNBC, January 8, 2019.

304   **the audience in the FDA's Great Room** See the transcript of U.S. Food and Drug Administration, "Eliminating Youth Electronic Cigarette and Other Tobacco Product Use: The Role for Drug Therapies," public hearing, January 18, 2019.

305   **Juul's federal lobbying expenditures** See data from the Center for Responsive Politics; also see Chris Hudgins and Sean Longoria, "Juul's Lobbying Boost in 2018 Helps Drive Increase in Total Tobacco Spending," S&P Global Market Intelligence, February 19, 2019.

305   **And throughout 2019, the company continued to bring** See Davis Richardson, "Juul Labs Brings on Top Trumpworld Talent as Federal Investigators Circle," *Observer,* June 20, 2019.

306   **On March 5, Gottlieb gave a speech** See U.S. Food and Drug Administration, "Remarks by Scott Gottlieb to the National Association of State Attorneys General," speech, March 5, 2019.

307   **Gottlieb had abruptly resigned** See Laurie McGinley, Lenny Bernstein, and Josh Dawsey, "FDA Commissioner Gottlieb, Who Raised Alarms About Teen Vaping, Resigns," *The Washington Post*, March 5, 2019; also, Sheila Kaplan and Jan Hoffman, "F.D.A. Commissioner Scott Gottlieb, Who Fought Teenage Vaping, Resigns," *The New York Times*, March 5, 2019.

307   **On March 13, with only a few weeks left** See U.S. Food and Drug Administration, "Statement from FDA Commissioner Scott Gottlieb, M.D., on Advancing New Policies Aimed at Preventing Youth Access to, and Appeal of, Flavored Tobacco Products, Including E-Cigarettes and Cigars," FDS statement, March 13, 2019; and Laurie McGinley, "FDA Rolls Out Vaping Policy to Make It Harder for Minors to Buy Flavored Products," *The Washington Post*, March 13, 2019.

309   **Herrera and Supervisor Shamann Walton** See "Herrera, Walton Introduce Package of Legislation to Protect Youth from E-Cigarettes," on the San Francisco City Attorney's website, March 19, 2019.

314   **The day before the annual meeting** See North Carolina Department of Justice, "Attorney General Josh Stein Takes E-Cigarette Maker JUUL to Court," May 15, 2019.

314   **As Willard entered the convention center** See, for example, Edward L. Sweda, Jr., senior attorney at The Public Health Advocacy Institute, at phaionline.org, "These Youth Will Not Be Fuuled: An Overview of the 2019 Altria Group Annual Shareholders Meeting," July 1, 2019; for a transcript of the meeting itself, see "Altria Group Inc Annual Shareholders Meeting" from May 16, 2019.

315   **At an investor conference in Boca Raton** See "Consumer Analyst Group of New York Conference," February 20, 2019.

315   **on June 3, Willard announced that** For the on! transaction, see Altria Group, Inc., "Altria Enters Growing Oral Nicotine Products Category with on! Pouch Product," press release, June 3, 2019; and also John Reid Blackwell, "Altria to Pay $372 Million for Stake in Switzerland-Based Maker of Oral Nicotine Products," *Richmond Times-Dispatch*, June 3, 2019.

315   **Two months later, he announced** For Lord Jones transaction, see Ed Hammond and Kristine Owram, "Cronos Near $300 Million Deal for Owner of Lord Jones," Bloomberg News, August 2, 2019.

317   **On May 15, Juul had filed a notice** See Joe Fitzgerald Rodriguez, "Juul Files Ballot Measure to Block Vape Ban; Backed by Tobacco Giant Phillip Morris, Company Pushing Initiative to Protect E-Cigarette Sales," *San Francisco Examiner*, May 15, 2019.

317   **A few days before the final vote** See Catherine Ho, "Juul to S.F.: We're Staying," *San Francisco Chronicle*, June 7, 2019.

318   **had just spent $400 million** See Jay Barmann, "Juul Just Bought a 28-Story Office Tower on Mission Street Worth an Estimated $400 Million," SFist, June 18, 2019.

CHAPTER 19

320   **It was featured in *Time* magazine** For Children's Wisconsin hospital article, see Jeffrey Kluger, "Saving Preemies," *Time*, May 22, 2014.

320   **In February 2018 Amos gave an interview** See Adrienne Pedersen, "Growing Number of Middle, High School Students Take Up Vaping," WISN, February 20, 2018.

324   **Tyler, a serial entrepreneur** See Melinda Tichelaar, "Who Wants to Be a Millionaire? Busy Westosha Student Already on His Way," *Kenosha News*, April 26, 2018.

324   **A swift-moving and profitable black market** Many of the details taken from records in the criminal case, State of Wisconsin vs. Tyler T Huffhines, Jacob D Huffhines, #2019CF001170.

325   **Data from Wells Fargo showed** Figures from a February 11, 2019, slide deck prepared by Wells Fargo, titled "JUUL Bringing in New Users Driving Growth of Nic Pool."

325   **On July 15, CNBC aired** See *Vaporized: America's E-Cigarette Addiction*, reported by Carl Quintanilla, the hour-long documentary, originally aired July 15, 2019.

327   **On July 25, Gutzeit and Amos stood** See "Teens Hospitalized with Lung Damage After Reportedly Vaping," Children's Wisconsin hospital, July 26, 2019.

328   **The same day, the Wisconsin health department** See "Severe Pulmonary Disease Among Adolescents Who Reported Vaping," Wisconsin Department of Health Service, July 25, 2019; and then for Children's hospital press conference, see "Teens Hospitalized with Lung Damage After Reportedly Vaping"; and then the wider warning, CDC Clinician Outreach and Communication Activity, "CDC Urges Clinicians to Report Possible Cases of Unexplained Vaping-Associated Pulmonary Illness to Their State/Local Health Department," Clinical Action, August 14, 2019.

CHAPTER 20

329   **When a San Francisco nonprofit announced** See Dawn Kawamoto, "Juul-Supported Coalition Submits Petitions for Ballot Measure to Overturn S.F. Vaping Ban," *San Francisco Business Times*, July 2, 2019; and Catherine Ho, "Juul-Backed Initiative to Overturn SF E-Cigarette Ban One Step Closer to Ballot," *San Francisco Chronicle*, July 2, 2019.

330   **Juul began spending money "like a drunken sailor"** See Joe Kukura, "Juul Spending Money Like a Drunken Sailor to Overturn E-Cigarette Ban," *SF Weekly*, August 19, 2019; also see that for "See's Candy" reference.

330   **The company hired Tony Fabrizio** See Dominic Fracassa, "Juul Hires Top Trump Operative as It Shells Out Money for SF Ballot Fight," *San Francisco Chronicle*, May 21, 2019.

332   **On July 25, 2019, Monsees was** See an archived video of the event, "Examining JUUL's Role in the Youth Nicotine Epidemic: Part II," hearings, House Committee on Oversight and Reform, July 25, 2019, at https://oversight

.house.gov/legislation/hearings/examining-juul-s-role-in-the-youth-nicotine
-epidemic-part-ii.

332   **He acknowledged on *CBS This Morning*** See Tony Dokoupil, "Juul CEO
Tells CBS News: 'I Don't Want My Kids Using the Product,'" *CBS This Morning,* August 28, 2019.

334   **It didn't take long for funding to start rolling in** See an online database
maintained by the City & County of San Francisco Ethics Commission,
called "Campaign Finance Dashboards."

335   **The firm was run by David Ho** See Lauren Etter, "Juul Sued for Use of
Contractors in Test for Political Campaigns," Bloomberg News, March 4,
2020.

335   **"I wonder if it ever crosses Kevin Burns' mind"** See Office of the City Attorney of San Francisco, "City Attorney Dennis Herrera's Statement on
Juul's Attempt to Rewrite Election Language," September 6, 2019.

335   **New York City under Mayor Bloomberg, who served** See Michael Cooper,
"Mayor Signs Law to Ban Smoking Soon at Most Bars," *The New York Times,*
December 31, 2002; also see Verena Dobnik, "NYC Smoking Ban Expands to
Parks, Times Square," NBC News, February 2, 2011; Jonathan Allen, "New
York City Marks 10th Anniversary of Smoking Ban," Reuters, March 28,
2013; and Mara Gay, Joe Jackson, and Mike Esterl, "New York City Extends
Smoking Ban to E-Cigarettes; Mayor Bloomberg Expected to Sign into Law
in Regulatory Blow," *The Wall Street Journal,* December 19, 2013.

338   **He was sitting in front of the fireplace next** For Melania Trump's tweet
about vaping, see "Melania Trump Takes On Issue of E-Cigarettes," ABC
News, September 10, 2019; for Trump's Oval Office announcement, see a
transcript of the event, "Remarks by President Trump in Meeting on
E-Cigarettes," on the White House website, September 11, 2019; and
CSPAN's coverage of it here: https://www.c-span.org/video/?464219 1
/president-trump-meets-advisers-vaping-products; and see Kaitlan Collins,
"'Don't Vape,' Trump Says," CNN, September 12, 2019.

339   **There were now more than 5.4 million** For 2019 National Youth Tobacco
Survey figures, see Teresa W. Wang, Andrea S. Gentzke, MeLisa R. Creamer,
et al., *Tobacco Product Use and Associated Factors Among Middle and High School
Students—United States, 2019, Morbidity and Mortality Weekly Report (MMWR)
Surveillance Summaries* 68, no. SS-12 (December 6, 2019): 1–22.

343   **After the bust, *The New York Times* asked** See Julie Bosman and Matt Rich-
tel, "Vaping Bad: Were 2 Wisconsin Brothers the Walter Whites of THC
Oils?," *The New York Times,* September 15, 2019.

343   **On the sixteenth, the CDC activated** See the agency's release, "Investigation of Lung Injury Associated with E-cigarette Product Use, or Vaping;
CDC Activates Emergency Operations Center," CDC Newsroom, September 16, 2019.

343   **By then there were more than five hundred** See a transcript of a CDC call
with reporters, "Transcript of CDC Telebriefing: Update on Lung Injury
Associated with E-cigarette Product Use, or Vaping," CDC Newsroom, September 19, 2019.

344   **At the time, the CDC had already activated** See "CDC Activates Emer-

gency Operations Center for Ebola Outbreak in Eastern DRC," press release, CDC Newsroom, June 12, 2019.

345   **In early September, the New York State Department** See "New York State Department of Health Announces Update on Investigation into Vaping-Associated Pulmonary Illnesses; Department Warns Against Use of Black Market Vaping Products," press release, September 5, 2019; for a broader analysis of the role of vitamin E in the outbreak, see Benjamin C. Blount, Mateusz P. Karwowski, Peter G. Shields, et al., "Vitamin E Acetate in Bronchoalveolar-Lavage Fluid Associated with EVALI," *The New England Journal of Medicine* 382 (February 20, 2020): 697–705.

346   **"Good morning," he said, his frail voice** See Stephanie Fryer, "'I Came Very Close to Dying': Fort Atkinson Teen Urges Others to Stop Vaping," Channel 3000, October 4, 2019.

348   **The same day, Viacom announced** See David Yaffe-Bellany, "TV Networks Take Down Juul and Other E-Cigarette Ads," *The New York Times*, September 18, 2019.

348   **In the United States, Walmart announced** See for example, Erika Edwards, "Walmart to Stop Selling E-Cigarettes amid National Outbreak of Vaping Illnesses," NBC News, September 20, 2019; and Russell Redman, "Kroger, Walgreens to End Sales of E-Cigarette Products," *Supermarket News,* October 7, 2019.

348   **China had recently pulled Juul** See Jennifer Maloney, "Juul's Sales Halted in China, Days After Launch," *The Wall Street Journal,* September 17, 2019; and Ari Altstedter and Bibhudatta Pradhan, "Tide Turns Against Vaping as India Bans Sales, China Sites Pull Juul," Bloomberg News, September 18, 2019.

349   **Burns called an all-hands** See, for example, Timothy Annett, "Juul Labs CEO to Step Down After Vaping Backlash," Bloomberg News, September 25, 2019.

350   **That same day, Crosthwaite announced** See Juul Labs, "Juul Labs Names New Leadership, Outlines Changes to Policy and Marketing Efforts," company news, September 25, 2019.

CHAPTER 21

352   **On October 1, just a month before** See Juul Labs, "Statement Regarding San Francisco Ballot Initiative," company news, September 30, 2019; and also see "Juul Withdraws Support for Ballot Measure Aimed at Overturning Anti-Vaping Law in San Francisco," CBS News, October 1, 2019.

354   **As Norquist himself explained** See Grover Norquist, "My First Burning Man: Confessions of a Conservative from Washington," *The Guardian,* September 2, 2014.

354   **Burning Man had long been a spiritual** See Gregory Ferenstein, "Why Silicon Valley Billionaires Are Obsessed with Burning Man," *Vox,* August 22, 2014; Tess Townsend, "What Elon Musk and Other Tech Executives Say About Burning Man," *Inc.,* August 28, 2015; and Sarah Buhr, "Elon Musk Is Right, Burning Man Is Silicon Valley," *TechCrunch,* September 4, 2014.

355   **Norquist was enlisted by Philip Morris** For one of his proposals to the cigarette company in the tobacco archives, see document number 2079041606.

355   **Whether or not Burning Man had anything** To listen to Norquist on vaping, see "The Grover Norquist Show: Leave Vapers Alone!" from January 7, 2015, https://www.atr.org/grover-norquist-show-leave-vapers-alone.

356   **One vape shop owner in Caledonia, Michigan** See Rachel Bluth and Lauren Weber, "'We Vape, We Vote': How Vaping Crackdowns Are Politicizing Vapers," KHN, October 10, 2019.

356   **Among them was the Libertarian National Committee** See Bernard Condon, "Vaping Group Plotted Lobbying at Trump's DC Hotel," The Associated Press, September 12, 2019.

356   **Big voices backed the movement** See Brian Stelter, "Hannity Has Said to Me More Than Once, 'He's Crazy': Fox News Staffers Feel Trapped in the Trump Cult," *Vanity Fair,* August 20, 2020.

357   **"Our 2019 plans remain on track"** See Altria's Q2 2019 Earnings Call from July 30, 2019; also Altria disclosed the Civil Investigative Demand in filings with the Securities and Exchange Commission; also see the FTC's administrative complaint.

358   **The tobacco giant had gifted Crosthwaite** For the special recognition payment see SEC filings.

360   **Crosthwaite decided to preempt the administration** See Juul Labs, "Juul Labs Stops the Sale of Mint Juul Pods in the United States," November 7, 2019; and for the study, see Adam M. Leventhal, Richard Miech, Jessica Barrington-Trimis, et al., "Flavors of E-Cigarettes Used by Youths in the United States," *Journal of the American Medical Association,* November 5, 2019.

361   **Altria's third-quarter earnings were released** See transcript of the company's Q3 earnings call on October 31, 2019; also see Jennifer Maloney, "Altria Cuts Value of Juul Stake by $4.5 Billion," *The Wall Street Journal,* October 31, 2019; and Juliet Chung, "Hedge Fund Darsana Slashes Juul's Valuation by More Than a Third," *The Wall Street Journal,* October 4, 2019; and Miles Weiss, Sophie Alexander, and Donald Moore, "Fidelity Fund Slashes Value of Its Juul Stake by Almost 50%," Bloomberg News, October 30, 2019.

362   **The spate of lung injuries had become so worrying** See Megan Thielking, "Vaping-Related Illness Has a New Name: EVALI," Stat News, October 11, 2019; and the CDC's report, David A. Siefel, Tara C. Jatlaouis, Emily H. Koumans, et al., *Update: Interim Guidance for Health Care Providers Evaluating and Caring for Patients with Suspected E-cigarette, or Vaping, Product Use Associated Lung Injury—United States, October 2019, Morbidity and Mortality Weekly Report (MMWR)* 68, no. 41 (October 18, 2019): 919–27.

362   **The House Committee on Oversight and Reform** See "Don't Vape: Examining the Outbreak of Lung Disease and CDC's Urgent Warning Not to Use E-Cigarettes," hearing, September 24, 2019, which was announced here: "Oversight Subcommittee Hearing Examined Outbreak of E-Cigarette-Related Lung Disease," press release, Subcommittee on Economic and Consumer Policy of the House Committee on Oversight and Reform, September 25, 2019.

363   **It didn't help that as the lung injuries added** For an in-depth story generally about Juul hiring scientists, see Sheila Kaplan, "Scientists Wanted: Recruited by Juul, Many Researchers Say No," *The New York Times,* May 27, 2019.

365   **By the end, 82 percent** Final figures from the "No on Prop C" campaign;
also see generally "San Francisco Voters Overwhelmingly Defeat Prop C in
Early Election Results," KPIX, November 5, 2019.

365   **When the CDC's** *Morbidity and Mortality* See Benjamin C. Bount, Mateusz
P. Karwowski, Maria Morel-Espinosa, et al., *Evaluation of Bronchoalveolar Lavage Fluid from Patients in an Outbreak of E-cigarette, or Vaping, Product Use–
Associated Lung Injury—10 States, August–October 2019, Morbidity and Mortality
Weekly Report (MMWR)* 68, no. 45 (November 15, 2019): 1040–41 (November 8, 2019, the report was posted online as an *MMWR* Early Release); also
see Jennifer E. Layden, Isaac Ghinai, Ian Pray, et al., "Pulmonary Illness Related to E-Cigarette Use in Illinois and Wisconsin—Final Report," *The New
England Journal of Medicine* 382 (March 5, 2020): 903–16.

366   **And so the agency continued to urge caution** For CDC on don't vape, see
"Initial State Findings Point to Clinical Similarities in Illnesses Among People
Who Use E-cigarettes or 'Vape'; No Single Product Linked to All Cases of
Lung Disease," press release, CDC Newsroom, September 6, 2019, in which
the agency said, "While this investigation is ongoing, people should consider
not using e-cigarette products."

366   **"The CDC is weaponizing a health crisis"** See "CDC Obfuscates on Vaping Illnesses, While FDA Warns 'Don't Vape THC,'" press release, American
Vaping Association, September 9, 2019.

367   **"A flavor ban will cost Trump"** See Paul Blair, "A Trump Ban on Flavored
E-Cigarettes Will Cost Him the 2020 Election: Data on 12 Important Swing
States," Americans for Tax Reform, September 18, 2019.

367   **The Vapor Technology Association hosted a lobbying day** See "VAPE &
THE FDA 4, Defending Your Right to Vape," an event organized by the
Vapor Technology Association, for September 18, 2019 "Day on Capitol
Hill"; for political actions by pro-vape groups, see Rachel Bluth and Lauren
Weber, "'We Vape, We Vote': How Vaping Crackdowns Are Politicizing Va-
pers," California Healthline, October 10, 2019; for Fox News ads, see Orion
Rummler, "Vape Lobby Again Targets Trump," Axios, December 29, 2019.

367   **His then campaign director, Brad Parscale** See Michael Scherer, Josh
Dawsey, Laurie McGinley, and Neena Satija, "Trump Campaign Urges White
House to Soften Proposed Flavored Vape Ban," *The Washington Post,* Octo-
ber 25, 2019.

367   **Norquist's call to stop taxes** See Grover Norquist, Phil Kerpen, Daniel
Schneider, et al., "Coalition Urges President Trump to Protect Adult Vapers
by Keeping Flavored Products Legally Available," R Street, October 3, 2019.

368   **On November 22, more than a dozen people** See White House, "Remarks
by President Trump in a Listening Session on Youth Vaping and the Electronic Cigarette Epidemic," press release, November 22, 2019; and see
CSPAN for an archived video of the event; also see Sarah Owermohle,
"Trump Hosts Vaping Shoutfest at the White House," *Politico,* November 22,
2019.

375   **on January 2, President Trump announced** See Stephanie Ebbs, "Trump
Administration Restricts Most Flavored Vaping Cartridges but Not Menthol;
The Limits Would Not Apply to Flavored Liquids Sold in Adult-Only Vape

Shops," CBS News, January 2, 2020; and Laurie McGinley and Josh Dawsey, "Trump Administration's Compromise Vape Ban Provokes Public Health Outcry," *The Washington Post*, January 1, 2020.

CHAPTER 22

377   **"I'm highly disappointed"** See a transcript of Altria's Q4 2019 Earnings Call, which was held on January 30, 2020.

377   **Shareholders had started filing lawsuits** For the number of Altria's smoking/vaping cases, see filings from the respective years with the Securities and Exchange Commission; and for the impairment/litigation quote, see Altria's financial results from January 30, 2020.

378   **It was a blustery morning in Washington, D.C.** The "Vaping in America" hearing was held by the Subcommittee on Oversight and Investigations of the Committee on Energy and Commerce, on February 5, 2020, at 10:30 A.M.

382   **The board had just recently denied** For Willard's bonus, see the 8-K filing with the Securities and Exchange Commission dated February 26, 2020; also see Reuters, "Altria Says CEO Will Not Get Annual Incentive Due to Juul Investment," February 28, 2020. For Willard's resignation, see Reuters, "Altria CEO Howard Willard Steps Down, Finance Head to Succeed," April 17, 2020.

386   **Juul had landed in South Korea** See Song Kyoung-son, "Juul E-Cigarettes to Hit Korean Stores Tomorrow," *Korea JoonAng Daily*, May 22, 2019; Steven Borowiec, "Vaping Giant Targets Lucrative Asian Market with South Korean Launch," *Nikkei Asia*, June 14, 2019; Song Kyoung-son, "Juul Opens First Offline Store in Korea, in Gangnam Area," *Korea JoonAng Daily*, July 15, 2019; Sangmi Cha, "South Korea Warns of 'Serious Risk' from Vaping, Considers Sales Ban," Reuters, October 22, 2019; Sangmi Cha, "South Korean Retailer Drops Flavored Liquid E-Cigarettes," Reuters, October 23, 2019; and Lee Ho-Seung and Lee Ha-yeon, "Juul Labs CEO to Visit Korea After Vaping Sales Suspension over Health Concerns," *Pulse*, November 4, 2019.

387   **The Philippines president, Rodrigo Duterte** See Jason Gutierrez, "Rodrigo Duterte Calls for Ban on Public Vaping in the Philippines," *The New York Times*, November 21, 2019.

391   **Meanwhile, the fancy San Francisco office tower** See Catherine Ho and Roland Li, "Juul, Shrinking and Under Fire, May Sell SF Office Tower It Just Bought," *San Francisco Chronicle*, November 21, 2019; and Laura Waxmann, "No Deal: Juul's Second Attempt at Offloading SoMa High-Rise Falls Through," *San Francisco Business Times*, September 18, 2020.

AFTERWORD

397   **I find it somewhat fitting that** See, Louis Lewin, *Phantastica, Narcotic and Stimulating Drugs; Their Use and Abuse* (New York: Dutton, 1931).

397   **Enslaved people were brought in chains** Generally see Jerome E. Brooks, *The Mighty Leaf: Tobacco Through the Centuries* (Boston: Little, Brown, 1952).

398   **Aswath Damodaran, a professor of finance** For his blog post, see "Runaway Story or Meltdown in Motion? The Unraveling of the WeWork IPO," September 9, 2019, Musings on Markets, at: http://aswathdamodaran.blogspot.com/2019/09/runaway-story-or-meltdown-in-motion.html.

399   **The global nicotine market is valued at** Market data provided by Euromonitor International, a market research provider.

400   **"We don't make widgets"** See Joe Nocera, "If It's Good for Philip Morris, Can It Also Be Good for Public Health?," *The New York Times Magazine,* June 18, 2006.

401   **He recalled that when he was a medical student** To read Ochsner's article, see Alton Ochsner, "Bronchogenic Carcinoma, A Largely Preventable Lesion Assuming Epidemic Proportions," *Chest,* Volume 59, Issue 4, April 1, 1971.

402   **"We're looking at the potential for direct effects"** See "Statement from FDA Commissioner Scott Gottlieb, M.D., and Principal Deputy Commissioner Amy Abernethy, M.D., Ph.D., on FDA's ongoing scientific investigation of potential safety issue related to seizures reported following e-cigarette use, particularly in youth and young adults," April 03, 2019.

402   ***"We're conducting a big, uncontrolled"*** See Robert Langreth and Lauren Etter, "Early Signs of Vaping Health Risks Were Missed or Ignored; Doctors and Researchers Scattered Around the Globe Saw Problems, but 'Nobody Put Two and Two Together,'" *Bloomberg,* September 25, 2019.

INDEX

ABOUT THE AUTHOR

LAUREN ETTER is an award-winning investigative reporter at Bloomberg News, where she writes in-depth corporate features and investigative stories for *Bloomberg Businessweek*. Previously she was a staff reporter at *The Wall Street Journal,* and she has written for *Vanity Fair* and *The New Yorker.* She holds master's degrees in journalism and in law from Northwestern University. Etter lives in Los Angeles with her husband and their three children.

@lauren_etter